# The Roy Bedichek Family Letters

# The Roy Bedichek Family Letters

Selected by

## Jane Gracy Bedichek

University of North Texas Press
Denton, Texas

Permissions
University of North Texas Press
PO Box 311336
Denton, Texas 76203-1336
940-565-2142

The paper used in this book meets the minimum requirements of the
American National Standard for Permanence of Paper for Printed Library
materials, Z39.48.1984.

Library of Congress Cataloging-in-Publication Data

Bedichek, Roy, 1878–1959.
The Roy Bedichek family letters / selected by Jane Gracy
Bedichek.
p.     cm.
Includes index.
ISBN 1-57441-032-6 (cloth : alk. paper)
1. Bedichek, Roy, 1878–1959—Correspondence. 2. Naturalists—
United States—Correspondence. I. Bedichek, Jane Gracy, 1918–            .
II. Title.
QH31.B38A4  1998              [B] 97-29539
508' .092—dc21                CIP

Cover design by Accent Design and Communications

# ❦ Contents

# ❦ Dedication

This collection of the Roy Bedichek family letters is dedicated to all those who help others to see the diversity and feel the rhythms of nature. May outdoor education thrive! May grandparents and grandchildren garden together and on clear nights watch the mighty procession of the constellations cross the sky!

# ❧ Acknowledgments

I am grateful to Fran Vick, Director of the University of North Texas Press. Her vision brought this book into being and her enthusiasm strengthened it.

Thanks also to Alan Pipkin, Jane Derrick, and other grandchildren of Roy and Lillian Bedichek who saved family photographs, and to the Barker Library, a part of the University of Texas American History Center, which preserves Roy Bedichek's letters and notebooks for all to read.

Jane Gracy Bedichek

# 🌿 Foreword

I have just finished reading this delightful collection of letters circulated among the Roy Bedichek clan. What a family of writers! Everybody in that circle was an educated and sophisticated writer, who had much to say about everything going on about him or her. This included the scope of the social, political, and natural world as the Bedicheks saw it from the 1920s through the 1950s. The Bedichek family letters represent the best of epistolary literature, an art form that seems to have gone under in the face of telephones and e-mail. Or maybe the e-mail boom will revive it.

The Roy Bedicheks were a close-knit family who felt the need to communicate regularly, and this was probably the result of Dad's being a man of words. Bedichek letters have already been recognized as literary treasures with the 1985 University of Texas Press publication of *Letters of Roy Bedichek,* written to his friends and colleagues, especially Frank Dobie and Walter Webb. But these present letters have the added depth and dimension of being the personal expressions of a man within his confines and intimacy of his family. And this was a family going through the Depression, World War II, and W. Lee O'Daniels and Joe McCarthy, and ready to talk about everything with decided opinions. These were episodes and personalities that drew fire during their times, and the Bedicheks were quick to respond. These very personal letters from Roy give the reader an insight into an important man's life during an important time and place.

Bedichek talks intimately with his family about topics that he did not discuss to such an extent elsewhere. His anger over Britain and France's inactivity when Hitler marched into Czechoslovakia, his heartache when his son became so occupied by his duties in WWII that he could not write home, his disgust with O'Daniel and McCarthy and Richard Nixon, his love for Adlai Stevenson, and his distrust of the post-war imperialism of Winston Churchill: all of these national and world problems became a part of family discussion and provide valuable sociological insight into American/Texan feelings of the time.

In spite of aggravations that were perceived by this Texas intellectual autocrat around his epistolary family dinner table, behind it all lay a sense of humor and irony that colored all of his writing. Preachers saying little to the point and the Catholic Church's inane protests against birth control were good targets and close enough to home to be shared by the whole family. Roy's son becoming the legal representative for a large company allowed Roy to eat some of his own words about the evils of big companies, and joke about it.

Throughout his writing we always come back to his adventures as a Texas naturalist, and for those who are not interested in Homer Rainey, state athletics, and the University of Texas, Roy writes about his life with wildlife. He had several adventures with domestic cats and dogs, but more with the wrens and martins and ants and squirrels that he encountered and favored with close observation of their ways and habits. Roy Bedichek is always the naturalist and conservationist, and he is at his best when he writes about his observations of nature.

The letters of Roy Bedichek and his family reflect thoughtful viewpoints by an educated group of people during a particularly significant period of twentieth century history. Some years from now sociologists and historians will still be interested in how one man and his family thought about their lives in Texas and America at mid-twentieth century.

Francis Edward Abernethy
Secretary/Editor, Texas Folklore Society

# ❦ Introduction

"Did you ever notice what a bore a person is who sees only in straight lines, never in curves? Always in one angle, never able to see from your angle, say, or from any other angle but his own?" These words addressed to a creative writing class in 1955 reveal Roy Bedichek's attitude towards life. Never a bore, he was an amiable companion sought out for walks and talks by a wide variety of friends, also for newspaper and magazine articles by editors. His rigorous honesty and many-angled vision may stimulate, in the readers of these family letters, a new way of seeing life around them.

Writing to Little Brown publishers about his first book, *Adventures with a Texas Naturalist*, he confided his aim in writing: "The serious purpose which I cherish and conceal is to inspire more experimentation with nature as a pastime. I hope by telling my readers (if any) what I see, to move them to look in the same direction; and by retailing some of my not unprofitable experiences, to encourage others to undertake similar adventures."

Roy Bedichek was born June 27, 1878. Writing on his birthday in 1920, his mother remembered, "Forty-two years ago at 4:10 A.M. a husky boy first opened his eyes on the light of a coal-oil lamp"— "coal-oil lamp"—another age! His mother had been born Lucretia Ellen Craven on the Monocacy River in Maryland, where the Cravens had a mill and the grandparents in Leesburg, Virginia, had a mansion and large land-holdings. She felt that with such a strange last name as "Bedichek," her children would be better off with short first names; accordingly she chose three-letter names for her three daughters and one son. Ena was born 1872; Ina, 1876; Roy, 1878; Una, 1880.

Roy's father, James Madison Bedichek, had been born in the western part of Virginia. His grandfather, Frederick Augustus Bedichek, was a cabinet-maker born in Berne, Switzerland, who emigrated to New York City in 1837 and later moved south and started a furniture factory in Virginia. When that burned to the ground, he moved to the new territory—Missouri. J. M. enlisted in the Confederate Army as a young man of seventeen in 1861. He took part in five battles before being wounded and taken prisoner by Union forces.

Both of Roy's parents were teachers, and they met in a teacher-training school in Illinois. They taught in a variety of places before moving to the open prairie of central Texas. His father made the rules for the school. Students were grouped by ability, not by age. Corporal punishment was never used. The aim of education, he emphasized, was not acquiring facts but learning how to think. "Your only enemies are hate, jealousy, envy, and malice," he told the pupils. "They harm you only when you admit them into consciousness." He designed blocks for teaching geometry. Greek myths and theatricals were incorporated in the closing exercises. J. M. was so proud of the school that he sent a description of its methods to the educational authorities in his father's native Switzerland.

In addition to his teaching, J. M. Bedichek, like his neighbors, ran a farm. Roy grew up with farm chores. "I learned to milk, chop weeds and pick cotton, take care of a garden, feed stock and handle them, yoke oxen, harness horses, plow, gather corn, shuck it, store it." The same father who gave him farm jobs also gave him *Plutarch's Lives* and Chapman's translation of Homer. Roy grew up a down-to-earth man of the soil and a lover of philosophy and literature.

At sixteen, having graduated from his parents' school, Roy went to work as a secretary, taking dictation in a law office in Waco. A friend, Edgar Witt, encouraged him to enter the University of Texas at Austin and found him a job in the registrar's office there. At the University he studied anthropology, literature, and history, among other subjects; made the track team; joined a fraternity; and edited the yearbook, graduating in 1903. Next to his picture in *The Cactus* is his choice of a motto, "He hath taken his stand in the world."

After graduation and roving—teaching, working on newspapers, homesteading in New Mexico—he returned to Austin in 1913 and a series of jobs at the University of Texas. At the University he found challenges and opportunities, friends to argue with and learn from, experts to consult on natural history or Greek philosophy, an audience and a supportive network of colleagues who took stands on university and public policy.

Roy Bedichek combined what in our day are often considered opposites. He was a country man of the soil and an academic educational pathfinder. He valued social connections and solitude. He kept up an extensive network of correspondence and associations, serving on academic committees and chairing an Austin Land Use committee, yet felt time alone, unscheduled, was essential. Revealing, and to me a surprise, was a letter he wrote his wife on May 11, 1957, while he was my house guest in New York after what I thought of as an interesting variety of visits to museums, gardens, friends.

> Dear Honey, In spite of all the gracious efforts of Jane, Bach and Johnny and Bill, I begin to yearn for the fleshpots of freedom. I can't abide having my hours apportioned and provided for, designated for this and for that. . . . Too many impressions impinge upon consciousness in too brief a time. There's no chance for the digestive process to do its work. I can scarcely recall even in outline what I did day before yesterday.

He valued the alternation of quiet and social interaction. He said, "Out of solitude I get a sort of stability that is firm ground to stand on while dealing mentally with the natural trials and tribulations which come to us all."

He also valued the process of analyzing experience by putting whatever happened into words. He urged his children to write up the challenges they met while the impressions were fresh and sharp. Writing often led to clearer understanding of one's self and the problem at hand.

Before he died he gave all his correspondence and private papers to the archives at the University of Texas. The boxes containing them now stretch fifty-five feet in the American History Center of the University. He kept a carbon of almost every letter he wrote after 1908. He cross-referenced topics in a card file so that if he later wrote on the same subject, he could retrieve his earlier formulation.

The books he wrote—*Adventures with a Texas Naturalist, Karankaway Country, Sense of Smell*—were in a sense a sideline. His life's work was heading the University Interscholastic League of Texas, which used rivalry as a motivating force in the education of the young and set up rules and procedures to make the contests fair and to ensure a wide variety of skills were tested—from typing to extemporaneous speaking.

Roy Bedichek might be thought of as a mentor. The letters in this book show his observations on life, its possibilities and problems as he saw them. Here we watch a wise father guiding his children and grandchildren while paying attention to their interests and enjoying friends, old and new.

The notes are supplied by one of those who learned from him, his daughter-in-law—

Jane Gracy Bedichek

# ❦ Editorial Notes

The following letters were selected from the Roy Bedichek Collection at the Center for American History at the University of Texas, Austin, Texas. The letters have been divided into decades to give an idea of the world situation in which these letters were written, particularly since the family often exchanged views on world events. The majority of the letters are by Roy Bedichek and were selected to show his great interest in literature and writing, in the natural world, in education and in his children and grandchildren.

"Editor's Notes" refer to Jane Bedichek's editorial comments and identifications in the letters. After Roy Bedichek's death and before his papers were transported to the Barker Library at the University of Texas, his wife Lillian appears to have read his family letters and added her comments on a few. Occasional marginal notes were also made by Roy Bedichek. These have been identified when this occurs.

The letters have been corrected in punctuation and some spelling (many of the misspellings appear purposeful and reveal Bedichek's playful sense of humor), but nothing else has been changed. The majority of the letters have not been cut. Footnotes were kept to a minimum, except to identify people, places and events that would help the reader better understand the particulars of the letters. Roy Bedichek sprinkled his letters with quotations from literature, which are identified when possible. People are identified when possible. All of the identifications are made when the quotation or person is first mentioned and not thereafter.

# ❦ The Jumping-off Place

*The following piece was compiled from material re-corded during taped interviews with Lillian Greer Bedichek (Roy Bedichek's wife), in the spring of 1966, from written material given Toni Lynn Cooney (Una Bedichek Beard's great-granddaughter), and from a paper written by Lillian Bedichek over a period of years beginning in 1947. It is a previously unpublished account of Roy and Lillian's homesteading experience in the New Mexico Territory and of the beginning of the Bedichek family.*

Bedi and I and Bo—a man, a woman, and a dog—homesteaded land together in southwestern New Mexico when that state was still a terri-tory, and today, sixty years later, much of the joy and wonder of those days remains. He set out alone on Operation Bootstrap. Two years later I followed him and we were married out there.

In the summer of 1908, he rode out of the little central Texas vil-lage of Eddy, twenty miles south of Waco, on the bicycle that was to take him to El Paso eight hundred miles away. Pedaling happily along vast fields of cotton, rank and smelling powerfully of army worms, he sensed a blessed relief. For once he was free from walls and roofs that shut out the sky, from the strait-jacket of obligations and decisions. He had only to keep traveling westward to where land was to be had for the asking.

He followed the railroad because the trail paralleled the track. Automobiles and automobile roads with their friendly signs were then and there nonexistent. City streets disappeared a short distance out of town. Rough, rutted country roads turned to a sea of mud under tor-rential rains. That happened before he was sixty miles from home, and he had to hole up in a country hotel at Bartlett for four days and wait for a break in the weather. Rain bothered him less after he had passed through San Antonio, although he did have one big downpour at Sanderson on the way to Alpine. From there on he struggled with rocks or deep sand. When the going got too rough, he shoved his bicycle along the track, keeping an ear ever alert for the distant rumble of a train.

Time made little difference; he was in no particular hurry. A good camping place, plenty of water and shade, a good fishing hole might delay him for a day or two. Once in awhile, he stopped to work for a farmer in exchange for a square meal. Still, he felt a strange elation as he led his bicycle over the spidery network of steel spanning the Pecos River canyon, at that time one of the world's highest railroad bridges; and experienced a real triumph as he wheeled into El Paso some six weeks after his start.

He sold his bicycle in El Paso and rode the Southern Pacific another hundred miles into the New Mexican desert to Deming, a little brown town with many windmills fluttering overhead. Dark blue mountains decorated the horizon; golden sunshine poured down from a bright blue sky. Cowboys rode up the wide dusty main street and tied their horses in front of the Palace Saloon. Land agents, health-seekers, homesteaders, well diggers, old-timers, newcomers, everybody and his dog congregated on the corner near the post office at mail time to exchange opinions on this and that and the world in general.

"This is the last frontier," Bedi reflected as he stood among them, "and these are the only free people left."

I entered the University of Texas in September of 1902, when I was seventeen years old. I went to the Registrar's Office to ask some questions and a young man came to the little window to wait on me. He was Bedi; that was my first introduction to him. He worked for Mr. John Avery Lomax, who was registrar at that time. I knew Mr. Lomax. Three years before, Baylor and the University had had a big interschool debate and I had come down to Austin on a special train with the Baylor rooters. It was almost like a football game. The University entertained the Baylor rooters and professors out at the dam; there were several hundred people there. Mr. Lomax took charge of me and my friend, Kate Carroll, saw that we had something to eat, and took us for a ride on the riverboat.

Mr. Lomax said that when Bedi turned away from the window, he said to Mr. Lomax, "That's the girl I'm going to marry."

2

"Well," said Mr. Lomax, "I know her, I know her well. I spent a whole afternoon with her when she was younger."

That year Bedi was a senior and I was a senior. He was twenty-four and had never gone to any school except his father's and mother's, the Bedichek Scientific and Literary Institute at Eddy. He dated me a number of times that year. I don't remember any of the other boys I went with very much except John Lang Sinclair, the man who wrote "The Eyes of Texas."

Bedi and I graduated that following June, in 1903. I went back to Waco and he went up to Oklahoma and worked with his brother-in-law selling land. Afterwards, he got a job teaching in a high school in Houston. We corresponded; sometimes we would be very fond of each other and then the fire would die down. In 1907, Bedi located eight sections of land in the Guadalupe Mountains of Culbertson County, Texas, with the idea of raising cattle or sheep. But the loan promised him by a San Angelo banker vanished in the financial crisis of that year. It was hard for him to give up the dream of independence, impossible to go back into the schoolroom. Instead, he came home to Eddy to build fences and milk cows on his father's farm while he plotted and contrived another attempt to escape from the web of circumstance.

Once a week he walked the twenty miles to Waco—there were no automobiles at that time, not in Waco and not in Eddy—changed his clothes at a friend's house, and came to see me. He was on fire with the teachings of Henry George and the music of George Meredith and of William Morris.

Far-away places beckoned invitingly to him, like New Zealand, whose inhabitants enjoyed the inestimable benefits accruing to them from the operation of an attenuated version of the Single Tax. The appeal of Tristan Da Acunha, a tiny volcanic island in the South Atlantic, was almost irresistible. He could be free there from civilization, not cribbed, cabined, or confined in any teller's cage, law office, or schoolroom on a clock-operated schedule. He could work undisturbed: it was a thousand miles from either Africa or South America, and ships of the British navy called there only once every three years. He could do what his soul yearned, honed, and pined to do: write. What else could he do there? Like Napoleon on St. Helena or Cervantes in jail. He had always wanted to write. I found an old diary of his that began, "Today I was nineteen, I smoked my first cigar and I met a man who writes for a newspaper, and that's what I want to do."

We kept those blue-bound *Reports of the British Navy on the Island of Tristan Da Acunha* in an old trunk in a tent until they were caked with dirt and stained by mountain irrigations.[1] But luckily I was a timid soul, so we never set sail for that remote and lonely shore. We still have the *Complete Works of Henry George*, which I dust regularly and affectionately, for Henry George brought us to New Mexico in search of free land and each other. Sometimes I smile as I ply my dustcloth and think of Bedi, so dauntless and determined, riding off to find freedom and heading straight into matrimony.

Home, safe and predictable, had its own peculiar attractions: Mother had just built a new house with hot water in the bathroom. On the other hand, Bedi was insistent: he had a well dug and a cabin built. As an added precaution, he had a job waiting for me in case I might want to change my mind about marrying him after I got out there. But I must hurry. He added many more potent reasons for haste, but I needed no more convincing. After all, what are creature comforts where love is concerned?

It was not easy to tell mother good-bye the morning I left.

"Oh, Lillian," she quavered, "who will scratch my head for me now?"

I laughed and, throwing my arms around her, kissed her dear face as if departing for a brief visit—one that was to last, however, for four years and two children, although I little dreamed it then.

She must have kissed her own mother just as happily when she left her Louisiana home to go to Texas with her husband. She always smiled when she told how Grandmother Lee had said, "Virginia is going clear to the jumping-off place." Texas was the end of her world, the jumping-off place for the next.

Two days and nine-hundred miles later, I stood on the rear platform of the Golden State Limited in Deming looking down on Bedi's yellow thatch.

As the great transcontinental train slid away from the station, we stood outside the Harvey House together surveying the valley, blinking in the dazzling sunshine, filling our lungs to capacity with the cool, dry air. Deming, some 4300 feet above sea level, seems closer to the sun than that because of its rarefied atmosphere and the absence of

4

clouds. On almost any day, the rocky pipes of the Organ Mountains can be seen seventy-five miles to the east; forty miles to the south, across the border in Old Mexico, the Casa Grande chain rests like a blue cloud on the horizon. Cook's Peak stands a dour and lonely sentinel twenty miles to the north, and at about the same distance due south, the three perfect cones of the Tres Hermanas keep company.

The Floridas (Floreedas), ten miles southeast of town, are the glory of the valley. Rising in places 7,200 feet above sea level, they stretch in a rocky crescent fifteen miles long and ten wide at their widest, like the fossilized bones of some mighty prehistoric monster.

This then, is the valley of the Mimbres, a tiny river that rises some forty or fifty miles northwest of Deming in the lofty Black Range. It waters rich "pocket" farms and orchards as it flows southeast past Indian-haunted ruins, then leaves the hills and disappears into its own sands, percolating as underflow beneath thousands of desert acres, whose soil is richly impregnated with volcanic ash. And wherever a pump brings these buried waters up, little artificial oases appear. The expense of clearing the wild land and bringing water in sufficient quantity to it, however, proved to be the obstacle upon which the hopes of homesteaders went to pieces in countless dismal tragedies. The lure was that magic phrase "free land," which in the last century had peopled the wide, rich valley of the Mississippi, where water was also free.

Homeseekers in this western land had the heartbreaking experience of learning that free land which can only be supplied with the necessary water at twenty, fifty, or even a hundred dollars per acre initial investment is not exactly free, to say nothing of that steady drain on income from the cost of the power that it takes to raise the water to the surface.

Bedi and I came by our delusion honestly. His forbears and mine had trekked across the continent a generation-jump at a time, from South Carolina, Virginia, and Maryland to Kentucky, Louisiana, Missouri, Illinois, and finally to Texas. The momentum of three generations shoved us on.

He had a rig waiting to take me out to see his claim nine miles southeast of town, but first we had to leave my luggage at my boardinghouse, a weather-beaten adobe with a long front porch. On one end of it hung a large olla, or water jar, of porous clay wrapped in a gunny sack continually moistened by the sweating vessel. A little old lady,

5

mistress of the house and self-cooling olla, accepted my trunk and bags, and Bedi and I quickly headed out of town in the direction of Capitol Dome, in the center of the western arc of the Floridas.

Overhead the sun blazed down. West of us the dancing heat devils met a layer of cool air, creating a huge sky mirror, which reflected strange distorted images upon its surface: long strings of freight cars floating upside down high above the trees, roof, and windmill of a distant ranch house. My body, too, felt buoyant; my bones like a bird's, full of air pockets. My heart hurried and my head swam as I floated head-over-heels and body-free in the bright mirage of my emotions.

A narrow, sandy trail led us through mesquite that rose higher than our heads and thrust out thorny hands to snatch at us and beat rhythmically on our buggy wheels. Eight miles from town we broke out into a bare plain littered with the dismembered skeletons of cattle— whitened ribs, huge leg bones, and eyeless skulls. A windmill with one broken vane creaked and whined in the center of this desolation as it forced up a trickle of water into a dirt reservoir.

"A drought hit the country and the owner let them starve rather than buy feed for them," Bedi commented. "They were Gus Baker's cattle, his brother Ben would have bought feed for them at a loss, but not Gus."

He broke off: "Look yonder. There's the roof of my cabin."

The north one hundred and sixty acres of Bedi's claim were covered with big mesquite, a sign of good soil and the promise of water underneath it. On the south end toward the mountains, an immense stand of greasewood began that stretched for miles, covering the gravelly earth with a dainty filagree of lacquered green. Tiny cabins were mere specks upon its surface. With strange, mad optimism, land-hungry settlers had staked out their claims up the slopes of the mountain, where they could never get water—not in a thousand years.

"Nobody but Indians could make a living out there," Bedi said. "The Apaches roamed these mountains as if they were their own back yard. They knew every spring and rocky cistern as well as the wild goats did. Away from water, they could cut off the top of a barrel cactus and squeeze out enough from its pulpy insides to keep a man alive. They ate bread made of soaked, pounded mesquite beans; and for dessert, the dates of the Spanish bayonet or the fruit of the prickly pear.

But their standby was mescal, the century plant. Its roots were roasted over hot rocks in a pit. After two or three days the squaws uncovered a sweet mess that looked and tasted like molasses full of tough, thread-like fibers. But it was food and medicine too, and would keep for months. When game was scarce, they ate dried horse meat and pack rats, even rattlesnakes. But they would not touch fish or bear meat. The bear was the Apache's brother."

"But white people couldn't stay alive long on that sort of food," I remonstrated.

"White men have," he countered, "some of them right here in the valley. Geronimo's captives. His last raid was staged only a few miles from my claim, up in the Little Floridas. When he surrendered to General Crook, those present saw a white boy about ten years old romping happily with the Indian boys. He was as slim, straight, and sinewy as any of them. He had been carried off two years before after a raid on Old-Town-on-the-Mimbres. The general sent him back to his folks. But, come on, you won't have to cook mescal or rattlesnakes, let's drive up the road and see some of our neighbors."

We came after a bit to a cabin among the bunch grass and sotols where a Deming school teacher, Miss Imogene Kaiser, and her mother lived. The latter, a gentle soul who quoted from *The Lady of the Lake* whenever it seemed to her appropriate, which was most of the time, took us to see the pottery fragments that she had picked up in her corn patch. The designs were intricate and pleasing. She wondered who these artists of the yucca leaf brush could have been and why they had left the valley. Was it because of warlike neighbors? A great drought?

Dr. Fewkes, of the Smithsonian Institute, sought an answer to her question some ten years later when he came to Deming to inspect several pit dwellings uncovered by ranchers digging for water. The Indian dead were buried under the floors of their subterranean dwellings, their skulls protected by funeral bowls of unusual beauty, which were photographed and described in a bulletin of the Smithsonian. One enthusiastic critic declared that, in abstract design, even the Greeks were inferior to these Indian artists.

A heated argument was coming out of the tar-paper shack that we stopped at next. Two brothers were homesteading the land around it.

"I wouldn't mind your tryin' to fix that engine, Harve," we heard

Ferd say, "if you would just take off that old stetson and those Spanish spurs. You're getting your rowels all mixed up in the machinery. What are you tryin' to do anyhow, ride the critter?"

Harve turned to us after greetings and introductions were over.

"I keep tellin' Ferd that this engine is too big and complicated for us. He *would* buy it. Thinks he's another John Hund and wants to irrigate on a big scale."

"But John Hund is an old hand at irrigation; learned it out in California," Bedi advised. "Of course, his alfalfa and red pigs are a sight to see, but you'd better go slow until you get the hang of this new kind of farming. By the way, Ferd, I hear a mountain lion as big as a calf walked out of your corn patch last week."

"The brute was big alright," Ferd agreed, "but peaceable, and naturally I wasn't the one to stir him up, not with nothing but a hoe in my hand. I lit out for the shack to get my gun, but he didn't wait for me."

Harve had found gold in the sand brought up by their well. An El Paso man had seen it and wanted to buy their relinquishment. What did Bedi think?

"That looks like gold alright," Bedi said, "but somebody is always finding gold in the valley sand. Sure, there's gold up in the Black Range and the Mogollones, and the ancient river washed it down, but not in paying quantities. I wouldn't sell my relinquishment now. Your land will bring a lot more after you have proved up on it."

The after-glow of the sun dropping behind Red Mountain filled the sky with rosy light as we turned homeward. The old sphinx of the Floridas sat shrouded in a deeper purple.

Back at the boardinghouse I heard voices outside my room, late arrivals from Chicago, a lady and her daughter. They were sitting on the sunny end of the porch when I left for school the next morning, Mrs. Ketchum and her fifteen-year-old daughter, Helen, deep-eyed, thin. She coughed.

The job Bedi had waiting for me was teaching in the Deming high school. Swarms of noisy, running children from the lower grades were playing tag as I entered the school yard, most of them "anglos." Off to one side dark-eyed "natives" had clasped hands in a ring and were singing in shrill Spanish the ballad of Maria Blanca and the Fat Old Man who had to "break a Pillar" in order to capture her. Upstairs my high school pupils waited, alert to size me up, but friendly, like every-body else in Deming.

The Ketchums were on the porch when I returned from school that afternoon. Mr. Laughran, the real estate man, had found them a house, a rambling nine-room adobe. But they did not like to be alone in such a large house.

Helen spoke up frankly, "Mama means, Miss Greer, that if you are not afraid of my 'bugs,' you could live in one end of our house and we'd live in the other." So I moved in that afternoon.

During sunny autumn afternoons, Helen lay on her cot on the front porch always ready to talk to me on my return from school about her cat Towser and her white-footed terrier Sox, left behind in Chicago.

Helen told how her illness began. "There were three of us at first, now only me. They thought that we had whooping cough, but it wasn't. But I'm going to get well. I'm stronger than the others and, besides, the Virgin will heal me."

"Of course," I said, "why, I have scars on my right lung from an old attack—the school doctor told me so. And I didn't know it. You saw Centri*few*gal John this morning, the red-faced man who sells veg-etables. He came out here four years ago on a stretcher. Couldn't lift his head."

"That's a funny name, Centri*few*gal," she remarked.

"That's the way he pronounces it, with the accent on the 'few,' and that's what everybody calls him. He says he has invented a cen-trifugal pump and would be rich if he could get it patented."

"He's a funny old man."

"When he first came out here," I went on, "he did everything he could to get well, even went down to where they were butchering steers and drank the warm blood."

"That's horrid. I don't see how he could do it."

"It probably wasn't at all necessary, but he thought it helped. And," I laughed, "he used to peel off all of his clothes and roll in the hot sand."

Helen smiled. "Didn't it burn him?" she asked.

"Perhaps," I said, "but he got used to it. He said that the sun's rays killed the germs. They also turn glass blue, you know, if you leave it out in the sun long enough."

"I don't have to do anything to get well," she declared. "I don't like milk or eggs and I don't have to eat them to get well. I don't have to do anything I don't want to. The Virgin will heal me."

So she demanded a miracle, and one drawn to her own specifications. As if every defeat of the "dread destroyer" were not a great miracle!

"Perhaps Helen would be better off in a sanitarium," I suggested one day to her mother. "There are some good ones around here, and nurses know clever ways of handling stubborn patients." Mrs. Ketchum had thought of it more than once, but the child was so homesick as it was that she was afraid to think what might happen if they were separated.

School traveled its inevitable course until providentially interrupted by the Christmas holidays. On Christmas Eve Bedi called at the house around noon.

"Bill Hughes, the county clerk, is coming by in a few moments," he said. "I didn't think you'd like to go to the courthouse and all the publicity. In this territory the woman has to be present also when a license is issued."

"License?" my eyes must have inquired.

"Yes. We're getting married in the morning. It's the only way that we can go away and spend the holidays together," he laughed. "The Edwards Act, you know, is a federal law devised to encourage marriage. In the early days the sand was so deep, the waterholes so far apart, and the preachers so scarce that many of the best-intentioned folks in the world just dispensed with the formality of getting married. After this act was passed, they had to marry, and it was sort of embarrassing for some of them with a lot of half-grown children standing around."

"But I thought we were going to wait until June. You said—" I protested.

"Now, honey, you're not going to make me homestead that land all by myself, are you? We're getting married tomorrow morning. Wear your warmest clothes: we're going up in the mountains to Faywood Springs."

We were married on Christmas morning in 1910, by an elderly justice of the peace in failing health. Although it was not quite seven o'clock, he was clean-shaven and neat in his Sunday clothes; but, as the train left at seven-thirty, we could not wait for him to put on his shoes, so he married us in his sock feet. His wife called in two of the boarders to act as witnesses and herself wept as if Bedi had been an only son. She had never seen us before, never saw us again. Perhaps she was remembering her own wedding.

While waiting at the station for the train to Faywood Springs, John Corbett, president of the Bank of Deming, came up. I was alone, Bedi had gone to buy the tickets.

John inquired, "What are you doing down here at the station this time of day, Miss Greer, and on Christmas morning?"

"Well," I said, "Bedi and I are going up to Faywood to spend the week."

"Well, that's fine," he said. "I hope you have a good time."

I forgot to tell him we were married. But he didn't bat an eye and he didn't tell a soul when he got back to town.

The train stopped some twenty miles north of Deming at Faywood Station, just a name on a sign post where a hack waited for passengers and mail. The hot springs, famous since Indian times, were three miles from the railroad. The hotel, a two-story U-shaped adobe structure with a frontage of over a hundred feet, stood a short distance from the largest spring, whose abundant flow of hot water kept the hotel radiators warm in winter. Our room was on the first floor with windows opening on the long front veranda—a great convenience for our dog, for we had brought Bo with us.

A pack of keen-nosed hounds who made their headquarters under the far end of the veranda immediately picked up Bo's scent, so that whenever he slipped out to go scouting around, the whole pack chased after him in full cry as he turned and ran the length of the porch to our room. We soon learned to open the window for him.

Although the mornings were nipping and the mercury near freezing, we spent our days in the open. To escape the full force of the wind, we sought shelter in Trujillo Canyon or camped in the lee of a massive boulder of the City of Rocks, a notable example of wind erosion. These huge stones, shaped like strange animals, aboriginal gods, giant chairs, some forty feet high and big as a church, presented from a distance the illusion of a city.

While Bedi drove, I got out and ran along the flinty ground behind the buggy until my hands and feet thawed out. Meanwhile Bo

ranged far and wide routing out chilly rabbits, investigating tantaliz-
ing smells, then returning to see how we were faring. He was glad
enough, though, to lie down with us by a fragrant cedar fire until the
sun was high and the wind had died down. In mid-afternoon we returned to the empty old hotel. Not that we minded the lack of company.

From Bedi's earliest days in Deming the dog had been his constant companion. I don't need to look at the picture on my desk to
remember Bo, a big terrier, Airedale or Dandy Dinmont with a strain
of English Bull. A hefty forty-pounder at three years of age, all bone
and muscle, his wiry black coat and white underparts, muzzle and legs
fairly glistened. The white tip of his tail waved proudly like a warrior's
plume.

Bo had been a resident of Deming longer than Bedi or I. Folks
said a rancher up on the Mimbres found him in an old stump with the
rest of his litter and took him home. From the time he was whelped he
was boss of the rest. Grown older, he tried to follow the rancher into
town, but was always brought back and tied up until one day he ran
away for good.

Soon after he arrived in Deming, the Albuquerque Boosters came
to town with their mascot, a half-grown cinnamon bear. When they
heard about it, the owners of fighting dogs brought their dogs down to
the railway station to meet the bear, who stood chained to a post on the
depot platform, waiting at the end of his tether to slap down any dog
who came close enough. But all dogs held back; none wanted to fight.

Suddenly a big black-and-white terrier bounded into the circle of
men and dogs and nipped the bear, who slapped back viciously. But
Bo had already danced out of his reach and was nipping the bear from
another direction.

"A bear dog!" someone cried. "Who does he belong to?"

"Nobody. He's a stray, a tramp."

"Well, hobo or not . . ." the rest was lost.

Several men tried to adopt Bo. But all made the mistake of tying
him or shutting him up, so he would have none of them. Finally, because he had to have someone to love, he took up with a drunken
paperhanger, who never confined him and even let the dog sleep with
him. But he didn't always feed Bo, so the dog would hang around
back doors at the eminent risk of a scalding. To his last day, he would

dodge even a spoonful of water thrown at him. Mange and sores afflicted him. He left the paperhanger and began to haunt the doors of eating houses.

Bedi saw Bo one night in front of the Chinaman's and noticed his eager eye, his prominent ribs. When Bedi had finished his meal, he gave the Chinaman a dime and asked him to wrap him up some bones for his dog. Bo caught the big bone Bedi threw to him before it hit the ground. As Bedi walked on, he heard bystanders laughing as he passed them.

"Looks like you've got yourself a dog," one called after him, and, in effect, Bo was following Bedi, the bone gripped tightly in his jaws. When Bedi stopped, Bo stopped and gave his bone a working-over. When Bedi moved on, the dog followed suit. That night and for several nights Bo slept on the sidewalk by Bedi's door. When other dogs began dying from eating poisoned meat, Bedi called Bo inside. A new day had dawned for the hobo dog.

Our honeymoon week over, we settled down to the serious business of making a living and homesteading our land; which meant spending as many nights as possible on the claim, driving out late in the afternoon and back again early in the morning. Bedi had, besides, the hard work and excitement of running his own newspaper. For he had borrowed money and bought an interest in *The Deming Headlight*, official organ of the Democrats of Luna County, from its owner, Mr. George L. Shakespere.

I always hurried to the *Headlight* office as soon as I could get out of school, to make myself useful until Bedi could drive us out to the claim. On Thursdays we all pitched in and got the paper out on time, provided Walt stayed sober. He was one of a series of tramp printers hired to help the regular printer. But he was usually snoring off his drunk in the storeroom when we needed him most.

On the nights that we stayed in town, I sometimes lay awake listening to poor little Helen cough; silently counting, against my will, each spasm that racked her: sixty-one, sixty-two. Would it never stop? After a brief pause it began all over again. "If they live through March, they will live another year," folks said.

Every Friday we drove out to spend the weekend on the claim, a two-hour trip for our short-legged pony, Billy, and tried to cook supper before we were too sleepy to eat it. Then stumbling around in the dark outside (there wasn't room inside), we spread a tarp on the sand and placed pillows and quilts upon it. Our heads toward the cabin and feet toward the wind, we folded the other half of the tarp back over us. Billy crowded close, his swishing tail nearly brushing our faces. Bo occupied a pair of Bedi's old pants not far from us, when he was not charging real or imaginary prowlers in the mesquite.

In late February, nights were stinging cold. As the sun rose over the Floridas, the pearl of dawn grew into pink, crimson, scarlet, orange. The succession of seasons brings no great change to the face of the desert. Sage, greasewood, yucca, and cactus are green in summer and winter alike. It is the sun, drenching the swift-moving earth with light, that shifts the color and shapes of things and, departing, leaves not so much another day as another world.

That winter we added an eight-foot screened porch to our cabin and another room as large as the original one, with an adobe fireplace wide and deep enough to accommodate sizable mesquite roots. Out there you dug for fuel. The mesquite trees would grow only two or three feet above the sand, but they had roots thirty feet long, which made very good fuel. It was all finished by March and high time, too, for dust storms were increasing. We had moved into a tent with the first of them, but found sleep, even with a wet towel over one's face, almost impossible. Now, with our cabin doubled, living was made much easier and we moved out to the claim for good.

Months may go by without a sandstorm, then the dun monster would rage for days on end. A vicious one overtook us one afternoon late in May, blotting out the mountains and reducing the sun to a dull glow. Cattle stood with their heads down and their tails to the wind. Bedi tied a handkerchief over the lower part of his face and pulled his hat low over his eyes. I covered my whole head. The sand and gravel beat against us; our throats were stiff with dust. We could see, feel, taste, and smell nothing but the suffocating cloud. In the heart of the wind, I seemed to hear moans and wild shrieks. Suddenly, after ages, our cabin loomed up only a few feet away.

Southwestern New Mexico is an arid land with a perpendicular climate: most of the rain and snow falls on the mountains. March is the driest month in the whole dry year, in which normally less than ten inches of precipitation occurs. But drought does not hold back the spring. The tough desert plants have already stored up under their leathery hides and in huge root systems the moisture of all the months before. And now they burst into bloom, spilling prodigally their hoarded wealth in order to achieve a sort of immortality. Wine-red roses nestle among the cruel spines of the cane cactus. The truculent prickly pear displays sulphur yellow blooms; the hedgehog [cacti] and the nipple cacti boast dahlias larger than the parent plant. The fierce cholla wears imperial purple.

Out on the western slopes of the Flowery Mountains, the fierce barrel cactus wears a yellow crown, and the defiant ocotillo marches uphill waving long wandlike arms tipped with gaudy scarlet plumes. A succession of flowering plants keeps step with the cavalcade of days. Then some night in June, when the moon floats up from behind the Little Floridas and the mockingbird and Crissal Thrasher sing all night long, La Reina de la Noche, the night-blooming cereus, will put on her corsage of desert lilies, perfuming the night for a hundred feet around. By day she resembles nothing so much as a bundle of dead sticks hiding at the base of a clump of desert shrubs.

The rainy season usually begins about the fourth of July and lasts through August and into September. It was raining hard outside our cabin one July night; the water gods on the Floridas were emptying their ollas on our roof. Bedi was petting Bo.

"Honey," he said in a lull in the storm, "the old dog loves you better than he does me."

"Nonsense," I retorted, "he was your dog long before I came. And you have to tie him up every morning to keep him from following you into town, and you know how he hates that."

"All the same, he likes you best and I can prove it. Woman!" he shouted, "Get down on your knees and beg for your life!" picking up a stick of wood, he brandished it over my head. I fell to the floor screaming. Bo ran around us whining and growling by turns. Suddenly he leaped straight for Bedi's throat and it was all Bedi could do to fend Bo off with the stick. We stopped play-acting at once and did our best to reassure our dog. Finally Bedi put his arm around me and we both petted Bo and talked to him.

"Poor fellow," Bedi said, "he thought I'd gone crazy."

Then suddenly Bedi dashed for the door, throwing off his clothes as he ran.

"Got to bank my well," he shouted back. "Looks like a mountain irrigation, the way the water is moving in. It's a foot deep at the door."

Water covered 200 acres of our land the next morning and stayed on the ground for days. Sometimes these irrigations creep silently down to the plain where not a drop of rain has fallen. It is never safe to make camp in a dry wash.

One morning after the weather had cleared, I had a visitor, an event so unusual that Bedi customarily took his bath out by the well, often at midday, without fear of interruption. I had filled my tubs and had gone into the house for the soiled clothes when I saw a big white-faced bull entering our pasture. When I came out again, the benign, curly-haired old fellow was shaking the last drops of my hard-won water from his whiskers and preparing to depart.

My heart sank, but I resolutely drew water until I had filled my tubs again, and armed with a bar of Fels-Naptha soap, manufactured by that great and good Single Taxer, Mr. Joseph Fels, second only to the High Priest Henry George himself, I rubbed with a will, removing more skin from knuckles than dirt from my clothes in the process.

Miss Maggie White drove up in her burro cart while I was in the midst of my labors.

"I see where Baker's cattle have broken down your north fence again," she began. "You poor child, your knuckles are plumb raw. Look here," and she hopped down and took hold of my rub board, "this is the way to do it. See? But I think you'd do better to cut up a bar of that soap and melt it in warm water and soak your clothes overnight. I'll come over tomorrow and help you get them out."

Miss Maggie lived several miles north of us on a piece of land that Gus Baker had used so long that he thought he owned it. He had even dug a well and put a windmill on it for his cattle. Gus was always persuading someone to homestead land, hoping to buy it for a song in some drought-ridden year. Sometimes he was successful. He had offered to buy Miss Maggie's relinquishment for one of his cowboys, but it wasn't for sale. Then, his cattle began breaking in and trampling her garden so often that it could hardly have been accidental.

One afternoon while she was in town, Baker's men came and carried off the old windmill. One night they tried to put wheels under her cabin and roll it off, thinking that she was away from home. This time, however, they had guessed wrong; she was inside.

She was tiny little woman, but had a man-sized tongue, such a lashing she gave them as she came boiling out. They protested that it was all a mistake; they were terribly sorry. Must have got hold of the wrong cabin in the dark.

"And the wrong woman too," cried Miss Maggie, not afraid of the devil himself. "I'll have the law on you, Gus Baker, as sure as God made little apples!"

I learned about washing from Miss Maggie and about cooking from Marian Harland's *White House Cook Book*, four inches thick and bound in white oilcloth. Our presidents either had large families or many guests, judging by the amount they cooked at one time; and many of the ingredients of their recipes were not to be found in any of the grocery stores of Deming.

Unlike the White House stoves, mine had only two eyes and, instead of an oven, a cylinder called a drum, fitted into the pipe about three feet above the eyes. You could bake a small pan of biscuits in it. It was a rickety rudimentary sort of cooking apparatus, but it served. The stove rested on three legs and a brick, which was eternally falling down and emptying out hot ashes and often burning coals that had to be shoveled up in a hurry.

Bedi would call the stove names, long and loud, in most picturesque language. One afternoon as he approached the cabin, he heard someone inside talking to the stove very much as he was accustomed to speaking to it.

When he got to the door, he said, "Honey, who was that with you in the cabin? Who was talking to you?"

I said, "Nobody."

"Well, who was that talking?"

"That was me," I said, "talking to the stove."

"Well, honey, you mustn't talk like that," Bedi said. "You're a woman."

"Well, that's the way you talk to the stove," I replied, "and you're a man."

Imagine my loud and heart-felt rejoicing when Bedi drove in one afternoon perched up on a kitchen range that filled his old buckboard from stem to stern. It was second-hand, of course, but clean, and boasted of six eyes and a capacious oven. Unfortunately, we needed one more length of stovepipe in order to reach the flue. So Bedi carefully measured the distance from pipe to flue, then held the tape against one after another of several large pine boxes lying in our yard. One proved to be exactly the right height, so he placed it under the flue, then inched the heavy range up a strong plank until it rested squarely on top of the box and presto! The pipe reached. Now we could have real meals. It was a bit inconvenient, though. With my stove so high in the air, I had to balance myself on the edge of the box in order to stir the contents of a skillet. On the other hand, it was comfortable not to have to bend down in order to look into the oven.

"Never mind," Bedi consoled me, "come Monday I'll get that extra length of stovepipe." And he did.

One morning Bo got tired of being tied up until Bedi was long gone. Instead, he got up before sunup and went into town alone. Later I was awakened by the noise of chickens squawking and I saw several of my beautiful white leghorn pullets fly past my window. Something was chasing them, coyotes, I thought. I woke Bedi and he grabbed his gun and ran out. But the coyotes were gone and so were our beautiful pullets. The only thing left was blood splashed all over the packing cases in which they had slept, and a few white feathers.

"Hobo! Where's the dog?" Bedi raged. "He wouldn't let coyotes do this!" He got his answer when he arrived in Deming a few hours later and found Bo waiting for him.

Bo's rage and grief were a sight to see when Bedi showed him the bloody chicken feathers at the end of the day. When the coyotes returned a few days later, he chased them away. But then there were no more pullets to defend.

It was so lonely out on the claim. While Bedi was in town, I often sewed on tiny baby clothes, went shopping in the Montgomery Ward's catalogue, and read all of our books twice. I used to shiver when I would hear a road runner on the roof; his voice was so like a human's. When he would run up and down the ridge-pole of the roof and holler down my chimney, I felt like it was a panther or some human being up there. So I would strap on my shoulder holster or pick up my rifle and call Bo, and we would walk over the claim. Sometimes I would shoot a rabbit for Bo, for he had to have something to eat.

Bo was a great comfort to me when it got dark. Sometimes Bedi was late getting home, and before it got too dark, I would go out and climb up on the cover of the well. When I did, Bo would stay near and guard me, especially when the coyotes sang too loud. They were in the bushes not twenty feet from the cabin, and Bo would charge into the bushes, rout them out, and chase them off. But they always came back and I was happy to hear the limbs of the mesquite bushes knocking against the spokes of Bedi's buggy wheels. He would shout from the gate and I'd shout back.

One afternoon he came home early with great news. I heard him whooping and cheering long before he reached the house. I had won a fifty-dollar prize from *Collier's* for a letter written months before on "The Newspaper in My Town," *The Headlight*, of course. Now I could order the softest of creamy-white flannel, the sheerest of nainsook and dimity, some shirts for the new baby-to-be.

In December we moved into town for the birth of our first child, Mary. She arrived one chilly afternoon in December. From our window, Cook's Peak up on the Butterfield Trail wore an uncommonly wintry look. Bedi and Bo had to sleep out on the porch that night, leaving our one bedroom for the baby and me and the doctor's wife. He slept cold, he reported while he mended our fire the next morning, but later on felt warm and comfortable, although snow had drifted in on his bed.

"Next morning," he said, "I felt a movement at the foot of my bed, and something rose up and jumped to the floor, shaking itself vigorously so that the snow flew away in every direction. Old Bo had slept with me."

We visited the Ketchums more often, now that we were in town again. Helen was almost transparent, wraithlike, smiling faintly in recognition, asking with her eyes for her miracle. When our baby was three months old, we moved back to the claim. That afternoon, before leaving, we went by the old adobe to tell the Ketchums goodbye, as they were leaving for home the next day. A few days after their arrival in Chicago, Helen went to her long home. It was mid-March.

It was close to noon one day, judging by the blinding sun directly overhead and the small darkly contracting shadows of the sage. I pulled an old felt hat down to shade my eyes and stepped out into the silent glare. No scream of hunting hawk, no rustle of scudding rabbit or cotton-topped quail reached my ears. The hot air rippled like the waters of a clear stream, confusing the outline of Ben Franklin's profile at the south end of the Floridas.

I picked up the ax on my way to the woodpile, thinking to break up a little kindling for a quick fire. Before I could strike a blow my hands were empty. My eyes stared at them unbelievingly, and my mouth flew open in amazement tinged with fear as I caught sight of a pair of dark, horny feet, toes protruding from crude rawhide huaraches, faded pants, the ends of an old wool poncho, my ax resting in rough brown hands. My eyes traveled swiftly up to his head, stuck through a hole in the center of his poncho, coarse hairs scattered over his chin, gimlet eyes peering from beneath his sombrero.

He had the ax. He was between me and the house. Perhaps he was an outlaw, maybe a Villista, one of those who had captured Ciudad Juárez in May, two weeks before Porfirio Díaz, the aged dictator, had left Mexico forever. His country was in a turmoil: the El Paso papers screaming for intervention; armed peons and ranchers playing hide-and-seek with U. S. troops deployed up and down the border. Columbus down on the line was less than forty miles away.

"I must not get frightened, for my baby's sake, for my own sake," I thought. "These wild Mexicans are not afraid of the longest knife in the world, but they are mortally afraid of firearms." But my pistol was in town for repairs; my rifle in the house not even loaded. "Don't talk Spanish to them. Keep the screen door fastened," Bedi had warned. It was too late for that now.

Bo came up to the man cautiously sniffing, growling softly; but the Mexican stood his ground, made no move until Bo wagged his tail. Then he patted the ax and pointed at the woodpile, touching his lips afterward as if asking for food. I nodded and he went to work, while I went boldly into the cabin and began laying out food. Bo stayed with him, watching him narrowly.

I brought him his meal when he had a good pile of wood cut. He ate as if famished; then nodding and smiling his thanks, he slipped off toward the mountains and I thought that he was gone. But no, he came back shortly leading a string of burros and began drawing water for them from our well. They drank long and eagerly. With a friendly wave of his hand, he drove off. His hat bobbed above the bushes for a little while, then he was gone.

The Mexican filled my thoughts for days. He might come back; well, I had my pistol now. I strained my ears for all sorts of noises: the distant lowing of disturbed cattle, the creak of an unoiled windmill, the jingle of harness, the rattle of wheels, hoofbeats up on the road. A roadrunner's curiously human notes as he sat on my low roof brought me up in alarm.

A week later as I was bathing, stripped to the waist before a small tub in a chair, a shadow fell upon me. I looked up instantly to see the Mexican staring at me through the window a few feet away. Outraged, I jerked my dress up over my bare body and stormed across the porch and into the kitchen where my revolver hung in a shoulder holster. I strapped it on. He had moved with me and now faced me at the open kitchen door, his face blank, eyes bright with interrogation.

I drew my gun and threw it heavily upon the table, pointing his way. Then I demanded in Spanish what he wanted. The *patrón*, meaning Bedi, would be very angry if he found him here, and I was expecting the *patrón*.

He held out his hands in apology: he wanted only a little rice and beans, some matches. I gave him all and more, but did not hide my cold anger at his spying. He left and I never saw him again.

Bedi once served on a jury that was trying a man for cattle rustling. When the jurymen retired to consider their verdict, the foreman asked him how he was voting.

Bedi replied, "I don't believe that Mexican stole that calf."

"Well, all the rest of us think he did," replied the foreman. "What's the matter with you anyhow, Bedi, ain't you from Texas? Remember the Alamo, remember Goliad!"

"I do," Bedi answered. "I studied Mrs. Pennybacker's history at a country school, but I still don't think that Mexican stole that calf."

By now Bedi had been a hard-working editor for over a year, and the once pitiful sheet had begun to assume the appearance of a real newspaper. Then, an unexpected complication arose, the prohibition election of 1911.

Luna County, of which Deming was the county seat, was mainly Democratic and English-speaking; in contrast with the rest of the territory, which, except for a few of the eastern counties, was overwhelmingly Republican and Spanish-speaking; so much so that Spanish was the language of the territorial legislature and the courts.

In the Spanish counties, the story went, the voters did as their bosses told them. Didn't Don Salomón, boss of Valencia County, hold back the election returns until he had heard from the Republican boss in Santa Fe just how many votes were needed to give his party a safe majority? And wasn't that number often more than there were men, women, children, and sheep in the county?

Luna County residents resented dictation. Many had their roots in the Deep South. Some had known the loss of freedom or their parents had. Others had come out even before the Civil War, when the Butterfield Stage was still running and Fort Cummings was full of soldiers who guarded Cook's Spring, where the stage stopped for water and the Apaches laid their ambushes.

Still other lovers of personal liberty had come in with the railroad to run the twenty-four-hours-a-day gambling parlors of the early eighties; complete with liquor and faro, dealt by painted ladies in pink tights who danced upon the tables for the further delectation of the cowboys, prospectors, gentlemen of fortune, and charming remittance men, many now grown respectable with the years.

Oldtimers were furious at the proposed interference with their right to consume or sell liquor and, most of all, at the Methodists, who had been active in sponsoring the election and who owned a majority of the stock in the *Headlight*. Bedi, who was no Methodist and no prohibitionist, soon found himself writing an editorial beginning, "Why does Deming with a population of only 3,000 need sixteen saloons?"

For this question his opponents had a ready answer: if Deming's saloons were closed, the thirsty would have to ride forty-five miles to Silver City, sixty to Lordsburg, or forty to the cantinas of sleepy little Palomas across the border from Columbus. As for the exact number of saloons, they were all full and running over on Saturday night, weren't they?

The pinch came when two of the *Headlight*'s biggest advertisers warned that they would withdraw their patronage unless the paper "quit siding with the drys." To close the saloons, they argued, would ruin business, theirs and everybody else's, including the *Headlight*'s.

In general, the electorate of Luna County were opposed to change, any change. They loved their land just as it was, with all its faults, like a beloved wife. Not even the President of the United States could criticize it with impunity. In the fall of 1912, the train of William Howard Taft had pulled on to a siding in Luna County for an advertised station-stop. A cluster of men on horseback had gathered about the rear of the train and waited respectfully for their Chief Executive to appear.

Friendly Taft wanted to say something to them before beginning his prepared speech, but, thrown off his guard by this queer equestrian audience and the wild desolation of the landscape, he could only blurt out, "How in the world does anybody make a living out here?"

Touched to the quick by the aspersion cast by a fat easterner upon the beloved sand flat, a young cowman in the rear of the group rose in his stirrups and demanded in a voice of terrifying resonance, "What the hell is that to you, you great big stiff?"

The famous Taft smile soon made amends, however. The President made his speech, and as the train pulled away, the desert-dwellers agreed that he was a pretty good sort after all; a judgment later confirmed when Mr. Taft signed the bill that gave New Mexico statehood.

Bedi's "dry" editorials were costing the *Headlight* more patronage every day, costing him more friends. Old Tony, bartender at the Palace, now bristled visibly when Bedi and his compadre, John McTeer, called for more beans with their buttermilk. To such a pass had the brave establishments of pioneer days come that they now sold not only whiskey and beer but buttermilk!

"One buttermilk, one bean," Tony sternly laid down the law to Bedi and Mac. "You damned prohibitionists are eating up all the free lunch from my regular customers."

Navajo Bill, porter at the Palace and once Bedi's unconditional admirer, now looked the other way. Navajo had been one of General Crook's scouts during the last Apache campaign. Bedi used to visit the old man in his tent in the Chinese graveyard, burial place of the coolies who died while working on the railroad. Navajo lived there all alone except for his pet bull snake. He enjoyed talking about his fights with the Apaches. He had once received one of their arrows in his backside while escaping on horseback and still had the arrow to prove his story. He would show you the scar too, if you encouraged him.

When hungry or in trouble, the old scout could always count on Lola Denison for help. An oldtimer herself, Lola was still in business, the oldest in the world. Occasionally, on a bright Sunday afternoon, one might see Lola taking an airing in a handsome carriage driven by a woman of about her own age, a pink-tights associate of other years, now grown wealthy and respectable. But so deep was the love of the older and more influential members of the community for the auld lang syne, and so profound the reverence for the friendship that endured through fair weather and foul, that there was never a slurring whisper, nor an eyebrow lifted as the carriage passed along the main residential streets of the town.

The prohibition election was soon history. The "wets" won, a foregone conclusion. Deming had its saloons and the *Headlight*, grave financial problems. If Bedi could get his note extended at the bank, he might be able to continue in business a little longer. But the bank president, like the big advertisers, was not interested in keeping Bedi in business. He called that note. Bedi hated to give up his paper. When he talked to me about it, he even cried.

Eventually Bedi got a contract to write publicity material for some big developers of the valley, land agents who dealt in town sites and farms complete with well, pump, and electricity furnished. His news stories appeared for some months in the *El Paso Times and Herald*. Meanwhile a retired minister was trying to keep *The Headlight* alive. Perhaps he should have let it die and be decently buried.

Long after I had spent my prize money and forgotten all about it, *Collier's* published my letter about "The Newspaper in My Town." Soon letters began arriving at the *Headlight* office asking for copies of that remarkable paper. At that time, the editor and printer were feuding. As a result, the paper was spotted with pied type and smeared with printer's ink and dirt from the floor. Nevertheless, the editor printed each letter as received and duly sent a copy of the paper, of the current issue, in response to each request. They must have been somewhat bewildered when they compared the finished product with the lyrical description that won the prize.

Bedi came home one afternoon, after an all-day trip with land agents and prospective buyers, carrying Bo in his arms. I was alarmed. Had he been in a fight?

"No, he's only dog-tired," Bedi reassured me.

Bo had refused to ride in the automobile when they started out that morning. It was the first vehicle of its kind in Deming, a crude, bicycle-chain affair, with wooden wheels and hard rubber tires, and Bo, on principle, never rode in anything with wheels. When Bedi pulled him in by the collar, he jumped out again. So, they let him follow, thinking he would give up after awhile and go home. But he didn't. The car was far ahead of him most of the time, but he managed to catch up with it when it stopped, which it did frequently, for the old machines seldom made over twenty-five miles per hour on those sandy trails.

Bo was so utterly worn out that he lay on his pallet for a week, barely able to raise his head. I fed him raw eggs and milk and brought water. The next time he was invited to jump into a car, he needed no urging.

Poor Bo was bedridden after another trip he took with Bedi. Man and dog would take pony and buckboard, tent and camping equipment, and explore the land from mesquite to greasewood and yucca flats and the knees of the mountain. Once Bo bounded ahead to seize a coiled rattlesnake and received in his lower lip the stored venom intended for his master. Bo's head swelled up as big as a bucket, but in two weeks he was as good as new.

Nearly three years later Bedi and I, with Mary and tiny Sarah in our arms, stood by the track of the Southern Pacific, listening to the Golden State Limited out of Los Angeles whistling for Deming. We were strangely sad for a pair going home to Texas after a long absence.

"It's tough to leave the old dog behind, but I've scoured the whole town without seeing hide nor hair of him. You'd think he didn't want to go with us!"

"Bo wouldn't be happy in heaven without you, Bedi," I said, "he just doesn't understand what's going on."

"Oh, but he does!" Bedi said. "Why he has been nearly crazy since he saw the furniture carted off. He would have bitten the boys who hauled off the stove if I hadn't grabbed him by the collar."

Just then our dog ran up in time to board the train when we did.

In Austin, Bo no longer enjoyed the fine freedom that was his as a desert dog. Street cars and automobiles made life dangerous for him. He became more my dog than ever, since he could no longer follow Bedi everywhere. Two years after leaving Deming, he was run over by a car one night while trying to follow Bedi and me.

We finally proved up on our claim and still own the land. So near and dear it seemed that we could not bring ourselves to sell it, even after we returned to Texas. Twenty years afterward, we revisited Deming and camped out on our claim in the shadow of the Floridas, spent a day at Old-Town-on-the-Mimbres, and another at Faywood and the City of Rocks.

Up on the Mescalero Indian Reservation in Northern New Mexico,

Kate Cross-eyes, wife of Geronimo, last great Apache chieftain, passed on in the summer of 1957 at the ripe old age of ninety-four. Her husband had died a prisoner at Fort Sill, Oklahoma, in 1909, a year before I arrived in Deming. Today his name is only a paratrooper's jump word, a meaningless measure of time, mere syllable to fill a man's throat and help ward off a devastating gasp as he leaves the plane.

Sixty years! A long time, yet the memory of our homesteading is still sweet, but not so sticky that I cannot enjoy a good guffaw at a recent sally of John McTeer, Bedi's friend and ally in selling land, in politics, and in everything else that made life out there interesting.

John wrote: "I am very much interested in the report you give that the wells of the Mimbres Valley are belching out a red fluid which the engineers in Santa Fe claim is due to rusted pipe. My own theory is that it is the blood of homesteaders like you and me, who tried to stick it out."

[1]These copies of *Reports of the British Navy on the Island of Tristan Da Acunha* are now in the Archives of the University of Texas along with the rest of the Bedichek material.

*October 29, 1908 to June 10, 1927*

*Editor's Note: In his early letters, Roy Bedichek wrote in the flowery style of a would-be poet. He and his literary friends at the University of Texas modeled their writing on Byron, Browning, et al, and engaged in elaborate word play.*

Eddy, Texas
October 29, 1908

Dear Lillian:

To those people who have not seen me for several months, I begin my letters thus: "You will have to excuse me for writing on the machine. I have a terrible bone-felon on my pen-finger which makes it impossible for me to use that weapon which Hugo eulogized as having the 'lightness of the wind and the power of the thunder-bolt.'" And then if I want to spin out my song a little longer and give further evidence of erudition, I ring in something about Byron's famous apostrophe—"O Nature's noblest gift, my grey goose-quill," etc. But to you who have so lately pressed my tender digits (fingers), this story would hardly seem credible, and since it is so much trouble to make up another lie, why I'll just tell you that I'm too blooming lazy to use a pen.

I enjoyed the two or three times we were together very much, especially our drive up the river and around. It seems to me that you are made especially for fresh air, and that you harmonize with rural landscapes much better than with street and lawns and parlors. This may be only another of my unreasonable fancies, however. I have the same feeling about many flowers. For instance, I feel that carnations are made for parlors and ball-rooms, roses for gardens, violets for mossy banks of woodlands, and daisies for the eternal hills. If these flowers—at this juncture, I was interrupted by a caller this morning. When he left, I set about getting my dinner. After washing up the things, I intended finishing this, but just then the train came, and I went down town to get a paper. I have just finished reading *The News*, and now I shall try to pick up the thread of my discourse. "If these flowers"—

what in the Dickens was I starting to say? Something like this, I guess; If, in the beginning, the rose had been put in the woodland, the violet on the hill and the daisy in the hot-house, we should feel that there was something essentially wrong with the universe. We might not be able to tell what the matter was, but we would know that there was something wrong. Just so, while we are climbing around the rock above Barton Springs, or looking across the Brazos to a stretch of farms skirted by woods, with green hills further in the background, I feel that "God's in his heaven, All's right with the world,"[1] but when we play whist, things are not just right, even if we win. So there—I must say, critically, that in this instance, I have spun out the thread of my verbosity longer than the staple of my argument.[2]

Speaking of verses, what do you think of these:

> If up the sky in burning flight
> > Some mad star scorched his way:
> And if the mark, blood-red by night
> > Turned black as night by day;

> My love I'd liken to that star
> > Which did so wildly start
> The mark I'd liken to the scar
> > Which burns across my heart.

It occurs to me that I am the author of those passionate speaking lines. Maybe Lula Taylor overheard me declaiming them in secret and rolling my eyes in a fine frenzy (I don't mean that she could overhear me rolling my eyes—I mean that she *saw* that—oh, dear, dear, you school-teachers are such terrible precisionists) and that is why she conceived the idea that my youth had been blighted. Really this is the first time that I ever saw them on paper. But plague it, can't quit talking about them. My mind is smeared over with gummy stuff today and it sticks unmercifully to everything it touches.

My heart, my heart! it has led me into so many foolish scrapes. Which had you rather be cursed with, a weak brain or a sentimental heart? But I here resolve never to be mushy again. I actually go along the public road sometime grinding my teeth in rage at the foolish situations I have made for myself. If I ever have a son, my parting advice to him will be to avoid sentiment. I shall tell him to go forth, swindle, rob, embezzle, swat old women in the head with his pogamoggan, to commit every crime in the Penal Code, but for God's sake and mine, to never get sentimental.

Bedi

[1]Robert Browning, from "Pippa Passes."
[2]Paraphrase of William Shakespeare, *Love's Labour's Lost*, V, i, 18.

❦

Eddy, Tex
Nov. 9, 1908

Dear Lillian:

When, the moment one has read a letter, he hops warmly on to his machine, glowing meantime with some strange, inward ardor for expression and commences answering the said letter, it is safe to say that such an one has derived some little entertainment from the same.

*Pupil*: What is pleonasm?

*Teacher*: A "pleonasm" is the use of more words than are needed for the full expression of a thought.

*Pupil*: What is redundancy?

*Teacher*: It is excess, superabundance.

*Pupil*: What is verbosity?

*Teacher*: "Verbosity" is the use of more words than are necessary.

*Pupil*: What is circumlocution?

*Teacher*: It is a round-a-bout way of saying something. My dear child, you must have in mind the opening sentence of this letter. Yes, all the words you have mentioned may be applied to it, as well as others, such as, "tautology," "periphrasis," "paraphrase," "prolixity," and the like.

My dear, this letter you send me this morning is bright, bright, bright. Considered either in its ensemble or in detail, it is bright—anyway you turn it, from whatever standpoint you wish to view it, it is—bright.

I sometimes think that you are a very bright girl anyway. At any rate, I have seen duller creatures, and that's no lie, as the boys say down here. I shall proceed to educate the lingering sentiment out of you, and then you'll pass.

So, to my task. I shall ask you to kindly cast aside the dictionary definitions of sentiment, such as, "Noble, tender, or artistic feeling, or susceptibility to such feeling," etc. The word sentiment, as used between young people, usually means merely that attraction which exists between two members of the opposite sex when they are along about the marriageable age. A more exact term would be the "Romantic Ideal," although it includes considerably more than is indicated above. I cannot give a better definition of "The Romantic Ideal" than to quote the following lines, entitled, "Fate":

> Two shall be born the whole wide world apart,
> And speak in different tongues, and have no thought
> Each of the other's being, and no heed;
> And these o'er unknown seas to unknown lands
> Shall cross, escaping wreck, defying death;
> And, all unconsciously, shape every act
> And bend each wandering step to this one end—
> That one day, out of darkness, they shall meet
> And read life's meaning in each other's eyes.
>
> And two shall walk one narrow way of life
> So nearly side by side that, should one turn
> Even so little space to right or left,
> They needs must stand acknowledged face to face;
> And yet, with wistful eyes that never meet,
> With groping hands that never clasp, and lips
> Calling in vain to ears that never hear,
> They seek each other all their weary days
> And die unsatisfied—and that is Fate!

It's nothing of the sort—it's a lie.
Or again,

> The night has a thousand eyes,
> The day but one, etc., etc.,[1]

you know that one.
Or again, take Adelaide Proctor's[2] a woman's question, or something like that;

32

Does there within thy dimmest dreams
   A possible future shine
Wherein thy life could henceforth breathe
   Untouched, unshared by mine?
If so at any pain or cost,
Oh, tell me before all is lost.

Look deeper still. If thou canst feel
   Within thy inmost soul
That thou hast kept a portion back,
   While I have staked the whole;
Let no false pity spare the blow,
But in true mercy tell me so.

Is there within thy heart a need
   That mine cannot fulfil?
One chord that any other hand
   Could better wake or still?
Speak now, lest at some future day
My whole life wither and decay.

And so on.

The Romantic ideal may be summarized further as follows: The young man is born into the world with one affinity. He meanders through life, and Fate, if she is kind, leads him to this affinity, they recognized each other immediately as such, they love, marry, and die in the faith.

The Romantic Ideal is the life and soul of much of our fiction, and the inspiration of nine-tenths of our lyric poetry. We are taught it from the time we can talk, taught it always by precept, never by example, and those people who never put their precepts to the test of experiences, never compare them with the facts that are rubbed in their faces every day, go on blithely (blindly, I should say) through life believing this nonsense, yet feeling, for some reason which they can't quite explain, out of kelter with the universe. The man or the woman who fixes his or her eyes on this ideal, and follows it in hope is mistaking a candle light on the horizon for a star, and will find in good time their lives bounded in shallows and in miseries.

Such a person sees life in a most distorted perspective. Marriage, to his mind, instead of being a mere incident, attains a factitious sanctity; its importance is exaggerated out of all proportion. Marriage is to life what eating your breakfast is to the day's work—an incident. You can get along very well without breakfast, as I have found out by experience. So can one get along very well without marrying, as I have also found out by experience.

Marriage should not be the end and aim of life, pace ambitious mamas, and anyone who looks at it that way is doomed to disastrous disillusionment. No man is great enough to satisfy any woman, in the way in which the Romantic Ideal contemplates; nor is any woman, in and of herself great enough to satisfy the humblest man.

To take a startling example, suppose you marry. All right. I mean that the example is all right. Notice how the trammels of convention tighten about you. Suppose some good gentleman friend of yours comes to town, a man with whom you can spend an hour very pleasantly, would you dare go driving to Lover's Leap with him? Not on your life. Why not? Simply because Convention, speaking through your husband, says you sha'n't. This may have nothing to do with your husband's individual feelings in the matter. If you remonstrated, his answer would be, "Why, dearest, think what people would say!"

No, you must eat with your husband, drive with him, walk with him, receive company with him, go calling with him—and, oh, how tiresome his jokes get, and oh, the dreary, weary channels in which his thoughts run, and oh, his everlasting hobbies! There is no man so infinitely fertile in fancy as not to become tiresome when you have to be with him all the time, and with no other man.

And believe me, a girl with your insight will soon see through the man she marries, and then he will become totally uninteresting. I really think that it would be better, granting that you just must marry, to marry some exceedingly stupid person, for it is quite possible to be charmed for at least a year or two with amiable stupidity. And, moreover, you would find a stupid man who thought you a goddess, infinitely preferable to a brilliant man who showed occasionally, though even the faintest, signs of disillusionment.

The woman who hasn't been there says, "Well, I wouldn't be estopped by marriage from having gentlemen friends." But she is all the same. No Friendship can thrive, nor begin even, unless the two between whom it is possible can be alone together frequently, and, of course, this for a married woman under our present system is impossible. Oh, it smells of the Orient all right, but it is an accomplished fact. For confirmation, just look about you.

When you marry, you are naturally thrown with your husband's friends more frequently than with any other men. What if you detest them, as you would, most likely? You would surely be cut off from associating with men whom your husband disliked, and there you are. And the man's case is equally hopeless.

Given those conditions, you soon commence hating each other, each holding the other responsible for the dwarfed life he is living. It is neither's fault—it is the fault of the system, of the conventions which bind us.

A man, however, is in a better position to stand it than is a woman. His business takes him out into the world where he meets other men and women, too, in a business way (conventions don't forbid that), and so his life is larger than is that of his wife. To say the brutal truth, woman upon her marriage passes into a sort of benevolent slavery. Married women are denied legal life, they are denied a business life, they are denied political life, they are denied intimate association with men with whom they are congenial, and all these denials cannot fail to narrow and dwarf them. Brave is the woman, and all honor to her, who conscious of what she is going into, marries nevertheless; but if I were a woman I should never so martyr myself.

Yes, honestly, I enjoyed the latter part of your letter more than I enjoyed the first part, although the parodic nature of the first part appealed to me. I have read some several hundred themes, as no doubt have you, entitled "Why I was Tardy," or, "How I Escaped Being Tardy," in all which some fortuitous circumstance, such as you related, saved the author at the last minute. Yours is told in the manner of a Munsey[3] storiette; it hath beginning, middle and end, ergo, unity; it is well conceived, artistically executed, spiced here and there with original turns of expression; it is final, conclusive, and—there is nothing in it. You can't fool me. Back of this simple sketch, lie a hundred, all modeled after the magazine fiction of the day, Edith Wharton, and the like, polished off, posted, and let us hope, only occasionally, returned.

If you really want to know marriage as she is, read Johann Heinrich Daniel Zschokke's short story, "The Leg." You will find it in *Little Masterpieces of Fiction* edited by Hamilton Wright Mabie and Lionel Strachey, Volume III, p. 117. This set of books is widely circulated, being given by Doubleday, Page and Co. as an inducement to sub-scribe for the *Review of Reviews*, so I am sure you can find some one in Waco who has it. I have Edgar Witt's[4] set.

By the way, you haven't translated any of Heine's lyrics literally for me yet. Can't you do some?

Yours, as ever,

Bedi

---

[1] *From Among the Flowers*, Francis William Bourdillon. "The Night Has a Thousand Eyes."

[2] Adelaide Proctor, 1825–1864, wrote *Legends and Lyrics: A Book of Verses*, and her poems were collected in *Poems of Adelaide Proctor*, published in 1880, with an introduction by Charles Dickens.

[3] Roy Bedichek is possibly referring to Frank A. Munsey, journalist and fiction writer, 1854–1925.

[4] Edgar Witt, also from the vicinity of Eddy, remained a close friend through their days as students at the University of Texas and throughout his life.

Eddy, Texas
February 6, 1909

Dear Lillian—

I am sending you by mail a little book of essays by Tolstoy which you may read until you're tired and then return to me. I recommend that you read at once—before your conference with Brother Barton—"An Appeal to the Clergy" p. 343, and then his answer to the Synod's letter of excommunication. Some of the more abstruse essays are "Religion and Morality," "What is Religion" and the like. But the appeal to the clergy is enough to confound Brother Barton. Ask him to read it and just give you one sensible answer to any argument that Tolstoy propounds. I wish I had a chance to talk to the old hypocrite—if he comes to you, you have a golden opportunity.

This little book of essays contains some of Tolstoy's deepest thought. I tell you frankly that I know of no other girl to whom I would recommend the book. He gives also an interesting afterword to the *Kreutzer Sonata.*

You are not very angry. Of course, it would be pleasant for me to think that you are—that you just boiled over when you found out that I had been to Waco without seeing you—but pleasant as it would be to think so, I can't quite. You women are such adroit flatterers—you seem to know instinctively just what to say and do, just what pose to assume to please simple man. It would be some compliment to a man for a girl to take the trouble to assume anything just to please him, but it's her nature to want to please—"simply the nature o' the critter." So, after all, he can argue nothing from her evident desire to please him.

If there's one thing about you which is supremely beautiful and expressive when you are animated, it is your eyes. They glow like coals of fire. And it is a beauty of which you are unaware, I am sure, because they are only at their best when you are too much absorbed to think of looking into a mirror, and even if you did and rushed to the glass when some one told you to, I am sure that light from heaven would fade out as you commenced to vainly contemplate yourself. I don't know why I am moved to thus suddenly communicate this bit of knowledge. As a rule your eyes are not exactly lustreless, but I should say simply not extraordinarily brilliant. If I still sonnetized, I don't know but what I should attempt a sonnet to them—octave to deal with them as they are ordinarily, and the sextette to rhapsodize appropriately concerning that access of light.

I've often wondered concerning the phenomenon above described. There must be some sort of chemical action which takes place in the ball of the eye which causes this scintillation or irradiation, as one may say. Perhaps your medical friend can tell you—she has doubtless dissected eyeballs.

But I have bidden a long farewell to such sillinesses as sonnetizing. As you say, I love cats and calves and things. I respond readily to those lines of the Frenchman, Louis Bouilhet:

> I hate the poet who with tearful eye
> Murmurs some name while gazing tow'rds a star
> Who sees no magic in the earth or sky,
> Unless Lizette or Ninon be not far.
> The bard who in all Nature nothing sees
> Divine, unless a petticoat he ties
> Amorously to the branches of the trees,
> Or nightcap to the grass, is scarcely wise.
> He has not heard the eternal's thunderstone,
> The voice of nature in his various moods,

He cannot tread the dim ravines alone,
　　And of no woman dream 'mid whispering woods.

Doughty[1] is to be married in a few weeks to Miss Annie Blakeney of San Saba. The announcement of it struck me dumb yesterday. I enclose his letter—also Harry's[2] which I found this morning.

I think that the fool will marry. He is the last of my friends except Harry, and he is no good as game—got to running with Booth Tarkington and cattle of that sort. No, just for spite, I'm going to show up some day with a big, double-jointed apple-cheeked country girl for a wife whom I shall take a fiendish delight in rubbing in the faces of my friends. "There," I shall say, "you all married and drove me to it and you see what I've got—treat her with the utmost respect, pray,—she is my wife." Here I swell up. And my wife, going home, says rather disconsolately, "Hunny, yer friends seems sorter stuck up." And I biff her on her jolly, fat shoulder and say, "Shucks, cheer up, old gal, them crazies simply don't know no better—they got no manners."

I'll show 'em. Not a one of 'em should have married, and down in his dishonest heart he knows he shouldn't—and then it's "dear old Bedi"—the hypocrites.

If I ever wound up a sonnet with the line you quote "God knows, I never loved a girl as I love you" why I'[d have] been a worse sonnetier than Embry, and so bad that I should never try to write another line of poetry. (Understand I'm not discussing the fact stated, merely its expression.) As it stands it is flat—flat as a large pan-cake lying on a greasy goodsbox. Please, for my sake, look up that sonnet and see if the line stands thus. I can't imagine that I should write such a line except a sort of desperate earnestness has throttled me, and I was merely gurgling out anything that would gurgle.

Well, well, here I've written on into the morning. It was twelve when I started. Be good.

　　Bedi

[1]Leonard Doughty, a lawyer who wrote poetry published in a University of Texas magazine, lived in Goldthwaite, Texas. Doughty became a friend and often helped Bedichek with his poetry.
[2]Editor's Note: Harry Steger and Bedichek were close friends at the University of Texas. Steger was editor of the *Cactus*, the annual, the year before Bedichek was its editor. Their friendship was so close that Steger called Bedi his Siamese twin. From 1904 on they had planned to tramp around Germany for two or three months and

write articles about their experience for publication. They made the trip at the end of Steger's year as a Rhodes Scholar at Oxford. In August, 1907, they sailed together from Glasgow to Quebec. There Bedi took the train to Texas. Steger went to New York and landed jobs with publishing firms, first Walter Page then Doubleday Page. He edited short stories, rediscovered and published O'Henry, met and mingled with cultural elite, and played tennis with the likes of Booth Tarkington. Bedi may have felt his boon companion had sold out to the eastern literary establishment.

❦

*From Deming, New Mexico*[1]

If you could see the stub of a pencil I am writing with you wouldn't wonder at the peculiarity of the characters. I am backed up against a primeval oak, feet drawn up close to where I am sitting down, knees thus elevated to about the level of my manly chin, pad against right leg, held there with left hand. My poor dog after following me over a perfectly hellish road fifty miles yesterday is sore and stiff and is stretched out with his head resting on my left foot. I was unable to get him anything but a few chicken bones last night. The cook failed me this morning again, and I intimated that unless he had something for Hobo today that he himself might make a fair meal for a hungry dog.

It is so strange to be in this "new" country which has been settled for thousands of years. There are ruins here which have stood for ages— there is one at my elbow—a hut which was once inhabited by a member of some prehistoric race. The wind thru the oak and piñon coughs reminiscently—the mockingbird sings—another strange bird calls— occasionally the whirr of doves' wings—

Well this is the setting. All artistic efforts have settings—why not a letter? and all this letter lacks of being an artistic effort is that it is not artistic and not an effort.

You can tell from the handwriting at the beginning that started to scribble idly—I believe I have developed more interest in it now, and may even finish it and send it to you. Darn it, I wish I had a[n eraser], so that I wouldn't let you in to the fact that the polished pieces of literature you have seen from my hand didn't come hot off of the reel, but were changed and changed, finally, only finally, after many erasures and superstitions and interlineations, reaching that perfection of form and grace of utterance for which I am so much admired. But

39

without a[n eraser], I must erase out my false start, thus putting you wise to my literary methods.

Oh, well, you threaten unless I get personal you will not take the trouble to finish reading this. Women are such personal creatures—I mean are creatures with such a passion for personal discourse—that to keep them interested one must leave the mountains of generalities and abstract statements and descend to the valleys of the intimate, the specific and the personal. Even this statement is too general to please you. You would rather I would say what Lillian Greer is like, or what I think she is like. But in my perverse mood, I don't think that I am going to tell you—further than that she has made me quite contented with the world recently. You know I started it, Lillian, and you stopped it, so it was but fair that you start it again. If you had just shown some disposition to melt the last time I saw you in Waco, we would now be living happily ever after.

Do you know, you have always appealed to my better nature. That is a very commonplace thing to say, but I am compelled to set it down because of its literal truth. Passion after passion has flamed up in me and died, sympathies have drawn me this way and that, and some wild impulses at one time or another, have moved me to do senseless things, but since that glimpse of you through the grating I have known in my heart that there was one land-locked haven of repose if I could ever find the way into it. When I thought it unattainable, I naturally busied myself arguing it out of existence. The glimpse I had of it was a mirage. It was one of the pack of illusions that attack a person in his youth. It was one of those pleasant fancies devised by some malignant deity to tease youth on into manhood—it was, oh well, it was anything but what it really was: the sight of a girl who would grow into a woman who would possess every quality which my torn lonesome soul longs for and loves. Our inner natures are very sensitive to essentials and very blind to very obvious things which are of no importance. I saw you through the grating and I knew all this and the knowledge elated me, and when you didn't respond to my moods and seemed not to understand anything except Greek and English poetry and jokes—then I commenced to argue, and I covered up this thing which my heart knew from the start with trash of theories and wretched false reasoning of every kind.

It reminds me of a spring which I drank from just now. Last fall I was up here deer hunting and I came across this spring in the bottom of a ravine. I drank from it and then my woodsman's instinct moved me to fill it up with sand and cover it over with brush. This keeps the cattle out of it. When I came on this place a moment ago, I found the brush still there. Moss and ferns had grown over it . . . I pulled the brush away and dug there with my hands in the sand until I uncovered the spring. After a few minutes it got clear and I drank my fill—then I covered it again.

Since, I have written it out, I can see that the allegory is weak in points but 'twill serve.

I came off up here to think about you. The distractions of work didn't allow me to really go into that semi-trance state when things that were dark become clear. With stupendous effort, I visualized your face a few moments ago and I saw your high forehead slightly bulging, the eyes wide apart, the nose a trifle irregular, the high color of your cheeks and lips, and mouth with a delightful way of staying open just a little—but your eyes—

> Your eyes are dreams—
> I meet your glance and I behold
> The blue sea reaching to the sky:
> And Aphrodite in the gold
> Of her blown hair is wafted by—
> Your eyes are dreams!

It is only my knowledge of your keen sense of humor that checks this rhapsodic strain. In many respects a sense of humor is not desirable. The absence of it has made many men great. Imagine Luther with a sense of humor—no reformer can have much humor about him. I think it's all that keeps me from being a great reformer and a very great lover—I mean a lover in the class with Browning and Heloise and the Portugese lady who wrote that wretched French soldier those immortal letters and the Duke of Buckingham et al. If it weren't for the ridiculousness of it.

Take this situation, for instance—neglecting business, fifty miles up in the mountains with my dog, painfully pencilling this pad full of stuff—it is ridiculous, now isn't it?

Have missed my dinner and it's 3 o'clock and the sun has gotten onto my nice place and I'm going to trek right now.

And this is the morning of the second day. Up the hillside is a lone pine tree. I suppose he is dreaming of a palm tree "in a far fair southern land" etc. That's the poetic way to look at it, under the circumstances—and I hope you catch the suggestion.

I have held myself in a receptive attitude now for ten minutes willing and ready to entertain thoughts, and none have come. Thoughts have quite independent ways. You've heard of people commanding great thoughts, haven't you? Well, I'm here to tell you it's just the other way. Great thoughts command people. You're helpless as a baby when in the clutch of a great thought. They are the most royal things in the world. The greatest men have been slaves to them.

The great thought that is clutching me right now is that you and I can have an ideal life together if we will. We have a long way the start of most people. We were born with a good start for that matter, and we have been gaining all the time. I think most people allow life to become too wretchedly commonplace for any use. And it becomes so through laziness chiefly—because they are content with the satisfaction of their senses as a hog is, and they gradually descend to the brute level and drivel along and eat and sleep and work and die. But when I think of you I know that life is something else—

> Your eyes are dreams of sea and soul
> For sea and soul are like akin
> Abroad the sea's strong billows roll,
> The soul's unseen surge up within
> Tho wide and vast from pole to pole
> Old ocean gleams, to me he seems
> Of lesser compass than the soul
> Your eyes are dreams!

Your tutor in the gentle art of poesy. You have caught, God knows how, the trick of the masters. The excellence of some of the lines makes me doubt my own judgment regarding one or two faults—the person who can write the best lines would not or could not make an error which my dull ear could detect. Ergo—it is perfect.

Dearest, dearest heart, I will read every line of this precious letter a

*42*

thousand times before morning. I hate the cringing cowardice of my soul—(a euphonius name: "good judgment") which keeps me away from you longer than the next train could get me there.

Yours

Bedi

I have known since the aforesaid grating episode that with you life would not drivel down to the mean and commonplace—there's just that spiritual fire about you that elevates and ennobles—and I have in me the stuff that takes fire from it.

And there is between us also an intellectual companionship—and we have youth and health and education, physical and mental strength— why we are favored with everything except money, and it is possible to make that.

[1]Roy Bedichek's pencil note reads "about 1909 or 1910."

❦

Dearest heart—[1]

Thought I would wait outside until the fire went out and the shack got cooler before starting this, but I have more to say than I can say before bedtime, so I am in here sweating and at it.

Walking out here this afternoon I kept thinking over the letter which I had just received, and I stopped under the shade of mesquite bushes along the way and reread it several times.

So you have a mother! By Jove! I had forgotten that fact. Not once since this strange correspondence sprang up between us have I thought of your mother. But there she is—I remember her now.

When you come to realize how deep and astute I am you will be able to account further for her antipathy to me. I shall let it pass thus mysteriously. Ask me no questions.

When she asked you if I had anything, why didn't you tell her that I had a homestead and a tent and a typewriter and a buoyant disposition? And that I've got a dog that I wouldn't take $10,000 for in cold cash. When I have time, I must tell you about this wonderful dog of mine.

Dearest love, such questions as she asked you are indicative of the conventional opinion of matrimony. I who if it suited me wouldn't hesitate to adopt the "free bone" doctrine, am not half so crass as those good conventional souls who hold to their "kept woman" notion of marriage.

For instance—ambitious mamma wants her girl to marry a man who is getting on in the world, and support her without work. She asks no questions about compatibility of temperament, agreement of tastes, etc., etc. I know women who hold themselves ready to make that sort of a bargain with a man, for a month, a year or ten years or for life, and such a woman is taken in polite society. Pray isn't her position less hypocritical than the one who sells herself under cover of a marriage license and some pious nonsense muttered by a priest? The red woman makes a straight bargain open and above board. The other, stultifies herself first with an avowal of love which she does not feel and then solemnly swears to her lies at the altar, and then lives with the man in consideration for her food and clothes and spending money, etc., and all their rant and cant and licenses and priestly mutterings can't change the essential nature of a bargain like that.

If I had to choose between two such women, it wouldn't take me half a minute.

I sometimes think that love would be purer and union between man and woman put upon a higher plane, if there were no dependence of one upon the other for anything—but it seems that is impossible.

I have been having chills in my back bone ever since reading your letter. Marriage—marriage—all the excruciating details of it—ugh—meeting the family—procuring a license—the badinage of our friends and acquaintances, the smiles and smirks, the *double entendre*—the time set—the interval—the damn preacher—and all the rest. Oh for the wings of a buzzard—oh to fly off to the woods with you and in the primeval bush forget this stupid, stupid world and its bunglesome crass ways of doing delicate things. Dearest how it will kill me—if it does not kill, it will break my spirit so that I'll never be fit for anything again. When the time comes, let's run off. I'm not marrying your family and you're not marrying mine. You don't care a whoop about my family—(I really don't think you would like them much), and I don't care a whoop about yours. I did rather like those kid brothers of yours, but—

If it's possible, let's go to New Zealand or some place where we won't be visited and bothered. This may seem heartless, but it's not—

it's in line with nature. The old bird doesn't try to domineer or direct when the young one can catch the butterfly by himself, and the old one has done no more for the young one than the old one's parent did for him. When a man marries, his obligation lies forward, not back. This has no reference, of course, to cases where the old ones really need help.

I have just been outside. There is a perfect half moon and the mountains are misty and blue in the moon light. A strange bird is making a strange fuss off somewhere and now and then a cow bawls. My tent is white, so white—did you ever notice how white a tent is in moonlight?

If you were here tonight—I enclose some verses I wrote last winter when the same thought occurred to me.

But love, pioneering is terrible on women. You can hardly find a woman out here that likes it. All the gentle influences which women love and old associations are absent. One of my earliest recollections is of my mother breaking into tears as soon as my father left the house every morning for his work. It was then a frontier country.

I can imagine you here while it is cool and the moon shines, but I can't conceive of your being here those long but dusty desert days—no, it's impossible.

Have you still that infantine fresh look? how I long to see you!

> You were a child and liked me yesterday
> Today you are a woman and perhaps
> Those softer eyes betoken the sweet lapse
> of liking into loving; who shall say?
> Only I know that there shall be for us
> No liking more nor any kisses now
> But they shall wake sweet shame upon your brow
> Sweetly, as in a rose calamitous.
> Trembling upon the verge of some new dawn
> You stand as if awakened out of sleep
> And it is I who called to you arise—
> I who fain would call back the child that's gone
> And what you lost for one world how you keep,
> Fearing to meet the woman in your eyes.

I do fear to meet thee again, oh gentle creature, I do fear thee. But I am

45

not coming soon—things are in a critical shape out here—don't know how they will turn out. But however they turn or whatever happens, I love thee, angel. I love thee!

RB

Notice the rubbed place. I had signed with a flourish which looked frivolous under such a solemn asseveration.

[1]Roy Bedichek's note reads: "in pencil, early in 1910."

Deming, N.M.
April 1, 1910

Dear Lillian:

I singled your letter out of a dozen I got from the office this morning, and broke it open first. That was an hour ago and I haven't broken the others open yet.

Let me see, how old are you? Barton Springs, centuries ago, you were let me see, seventeen. That was in 1902 wasn't it? So you must now be—how impossible twenty-five—in the perfect summer of young womanhood.

"If I were a woman" etc. I have no imagination or instinct, or intuition or anything that will tell me what I would do. I have tried to think it out but can't. But I will tell you of a little experience I have been having, which may throw some light upon what I would do, being a man.

I have been a stranger in a strange land now for a year. A family here, and a good-blooded, good intelligent family took me right to its heart. The mother of the family is heavenly; the father a southern gentleman of the old school; the son a reprobate; the daughter—let me see what to say of the daughter. First, points easily settled: she's at least twenty-seven, fine form, good, I might say elegant bearing, perfect breeding, conventional ideas, brunette—for the rest a gentle, homey, repressed creature who would never think of trying to dominate a man. In the solitude of my shack I have determined a dozen times to propose to her simply because she was available material near at hand, and I have decided vaguely that it is best, all things considered, to

*46*

marry. I am scarcely ever alone with her. The last few times I have been alone with her I have cold-bloodedly set about proposing. I have worked the thing up to the proper point, never making love, I will not be a liar, but telling her pretty things about herself, which most women like, but in the pause which comes before anything important is said, my mind becomes clear as glass and I see the thing in a hundred new phases, and instead of saying what I had it in mind to say a minute before, I say "The stars are bright tonight," or "The wind has gone down," or "Hobo (my dog) is a loving creature" or what not. At the last moment, on the edge of the precipice of decision, I shrink back. It is no abashment. I am perfectly cold blooded—she is the one that flutters. I could state my position with precision and argue her into it with logic, not with love.

Now to account for this as nearly as I can. There is a brutal familiarity about marriage. That is stating it baldly, but it is the truth. A person does not have to be sentimental to shrink from it—he merely has to be decent. And this thing of romantic love is Nature's trick, or concession, or device for overcoming this feeling in us. It is Nature's business to see us paired off or mated—it is so ordered for the world's increase. She don't care a damn about the individual, or the individual's feelings or sentiments—what she wants is—results. She is like the soulless corporation in this regard.

Now then the reason I can't propose to the young lady in question is because I do not have a glimmer of romantic affection for her: and that is why you cannot marry that good, decent man who proposes to you.

My dear child, let me, at the risk of being a little more brutal, tell you why you cannot afford to marry this man—no, I cannot tell you, but perhaps these words of introduction will suggest it to you.

I think I once advised you to marry a stupid man, one that you could always make think things otherwise than as they are, rather than a man who got occasionally a glimpse through and beyond you. I must have been instinctively true to my sex instead of to you. It would be happier for him, but not for you. You must have a man who, if he cannot give you the affection for which your heart longs, at least is able to throw some sort of romantic glamour over the brutal truths of life. From your description, I hardly think this business man can do it.

But your intuition is worth ten times more than all my advice—simply be true to your intuition, do not try to reason it out. There, that is the best advice I have given you.

And I had better stop before I spoil it.

As ever,

Bedi

P. S. Guess I'll be home this summer—if so, we can talk it over.

❧

April 27, 1910

Dear Lillian:

Yours came this morning. I feel relieved to know you turned the wretch down. I think I should feel uncomfortable if I knew you were going to be married upon such terms, or perhaps, upon any terms. How much of this feeling is personal and how much merely a general shrinking from the institution of matrimony, I am unable to say.

You can see by this stationery that I am no longer dreaming in the still dusks and dawns out near the mountains.[1] I go out nearly every night, but I am so hurried that I have little time to enjoy the coming of spring. I am working for that leisure which you speak of. If things turn out here as I am endeavoring to make them turn out, I will be in pretty easy circumstances inside of five years. Otherwise, I shall start hoboin' it again. I don't know which I want to happen:

> Give me a long white road and the gray wide path of the sea
> And the wind's will and the bird's will, and the heartache
> still in me, etc.

appeals to me yet—I'm just that crazy.

Damn it, I can almost imagine the smell of blue-bonnets on this spring air that is breathing so balmily into my window—I'd best stop—or—non-sense.

Yours

[1]Editor's Note: Bedichek was appointed secretary of the Chamber of Commerce in Deming and had to walk the eight miles into Deming and back to the claim nearly every night. He spent some nights in town, then and later.

❧

Deming, N.M.
May 27, 1910

Dear Lillian—

This letter of yours is not like you in the flesh at all, but I believe I like you in the letter better than you in the flesh. I really don't like that humility which you assume, however—when you realize so poignantly what a tiny flicker of inspiration you have been, etc. why, damn it—

But let me tell you that outside your letters I have never seen that I meant anything particularly to you. You were always content, you know, with your side of the parlor; and I have been at loss to explain the occasional cropping up in your letters of expressions which were never borne out when we were together. I have explained it to myself in this way: When we are away from people we frequently idealize them, especially if they have been associated in our minds with blue-bonnets and college days and the golden olden glory of the days gone by. This is especially true of young unmarried people of about the same age and opposite sex, and still more especially true if one or the other or both have that fatal gift of writing letters which go to the spot—that longing, hungry spot in the heart. Feeling no pride and affecting no humility, your humble servant when in good form and not too much preoccupied with beans, can write a fairly effective letter. Perhaps you've noticed it—no?

Now then—in this idealizing mood you write me and you feel that I mean oceans to you and you are the tiny flicker aforesaid: but just let my ungainly form loom up on the horizon and "all your visions you resign."

Frankly, dear child, isn't this about the way of it? Don't tell me it isn't—I'm rather proud of this bit of psychologizing.

Now I would go about ten times as far to see you as I would to see Edgar and Gwynne[1] and about five times as far as I would go to see Edgar. If I could come to Waco and see you for a week I would start on the next train, but if I go to that part of the state I would have to stay a month. I haven't a month—I just haven't a month and can't get it. It's impossible. The homefolks, you know, would demand three weeks anyway—I simply couldn't get away under three weeks. Now, if you were visiting in San Antonio, for instance, I could make a surreptitious trip to that point without anyone up the state knowing about it. I would make this trip for the purpose of preserving my illusions and breaking yours and for the dear joy of seeing you once again.

Lillian, let me tell you something about my situation. You accuse me of being secretive. Do so no more.

I left home you know along in March a year ago. I bummed through the country on a bicycle, laying out o'nights and getting along the best I could. My cyclometer read 983 miles when I sold the bicycle to a barber who was shaving me. I then took the train, the freight train, and bummed some more. I finally hit here.

This country is an absolute desert. You would faint if you saw it. Sage brush, a disreputable looking weed and scrub-mesquite cover the face of the earth. Barren mountains surround the valley, not so picturesque as you imagine, except about nightfall and in the early morning and in moonlight.

There is a tremendous underflow of water here which can be pumped profitably. In time land will be worth money—in time—now it is not. I went out eight miles into the aforesaid sage brush and mesquite and filed a homestead and desert claim (320 acres). I had six months in which to get on this land. During this time I plied my trade as a stenographer—think of it, the proud scion of an old family—a stenographer. Well, when my time was getting about up, I borrowed what money I could, got a camping outfit and a man, went out to my place and dug a well and built a shack 12 x 14 and stretched up a tent. During the winter months, I lived in the tent, cooked and ate, slept and read and wrote in it. It is 9 1/2 x 12. I had no success in selling stuff I wrote. I lived on frijole beans and rabbits which I caught in traps—I lived to myself like a lone wolf in a cañon.

Meantime they organized this Chamber of Commerce and offered me the job of being its secretary at salary of seventy-five dollars per month. I make about fifty dollars on the outside writing irrigation and farming dope and corresponding for newspapers. I couldn't afford to keep a pony in town so I sold him, and I walk eight miles night and morning to my shack and am thus homesteading it.

There are cracks in my shack that you can throw a cat through. My tent is getting a little ragged.

You can see how far the "bunch of bluebonnets" which the Editor

*50*

handed me is from representing the situation as it is. God, but I get lonely at times, and yearn for sympathy or any human feeling or companionship, but still prefer this life to the life of a city or of the older communities.

> Lo, if a man magnanimous and tender
>> Lo, if a woman desperate and true—
> Make the irrevocable sweet surrender
>> Show to each other what the Lord can do—
>
> Each as I knows a helping and a healing,
>> Each to the other strangely a surprise,
> Heart to the heart its mystery revealing
>> Soul to the soul in melancholy eyes.
>
> Where wilt thou find a riving or a rending
>> Able to sever them intwain again?
> God hath begun and God's shall be the ending
>> Safe in his bosom and aloof from men.
>
> Her thou mayest separate but shalt not sunder
>> Though thou distress her for a little while
> Wrapt in a worship ravisht in a wonder,
>> Stayed on the steadfast promise of a smile.
>
> Scarcely she knoweth if his arms have found her
>> Waves of his breath make tremulous the air—
> Or if the thrill within her and around her
>> Be but the distant echo of his prayer.
>
> Nay, and much more; for love in his demanding
>> Still not be bound in limits of our breath,
> Calls her to follow where she sees him standing
>> Fairer and stronger for the plunge of death.[2]
> etc.

Do you think this particularly appropriate? I did when I started quoting it.

But supposing such love—what in God's name do I have to offer.

Haven't I made a perfect waste of my life? It is of so poor and pale a stuff, it were not fitly done, etc.

Write to me at once.

Bedi

[1]Edgar E. Witt and his wife Gwynne.
[2]On the letter is the following note: "George Meredith's 'Married Love,'" written in Lillian Bedichek's hand. Mrs. Conkle says "she [Lillian] found this packet of letters after his death and they made her feel surrounded by his love." Virginia (Mrs. Ellsworth P.) Conkle was a close friend of the Bedicheks.

Deming, N. M.,
June 4, 1910

Dear Lillian:

A letter which I wrote you under pressure has just been mailed. A dust-storm is raging without end, there is no one in the office or likely to be, so I have more time for thinking what I want to say. So be on your guard, I'm calculating.

You very generously deny that I have made a waste of my life. I will not embarrass you by asking you to tell me what the devil I have ever done worthwhile. In very truth, I have made a sad mess of things. I have side-stepped all responsibility. I have reveled in freedom and taken a delight in blowing opportunities to the wind. I have been oppressed with a sense of my capacities, because in some way I have felt that capacity means work and responsibility—means a check upon my ungovernable desire for freedom. I have shied around love and suppressed it in my heart and cursed it for the same reason. True love is an unselfish emotion—you give, give, give and neither exact nor expect anything in return. In the selfishness of my heart I have always feared it. Recall my last letters from Eddy and you will realize how I fought it, and how determined I have been to smother and forget that old feeling for you. But when you call, as you have in your last three letters, why . . .

It was easy enough when I was with you in Waco. You made it easy—but now, it's different. You have stirred that young, old giant in my heart and I'm having trouble with him. Whatever suggested the idea to you? How the thunder did you know that such a letter as you wrote me and such intimations would not disgust and drive me away as it would have done 999 out of every 1000 men? How the thunder did you know it, I say? The intuition that prompted you to it is uncanny.

At this juncture, in comes the gassers. We pass hours in frivolous discourse, and now it is morning—another day—and how many more hours of gab and nights of wind and fresh clear mornings until I see you again!

Yours,
Bedi

Deming, N.M.
June 17, 1910

There is a desert plant in New Mexico called the Sotol. It is a very strange thing—it is neither weed nor bush nor tree. It has the same power of storing water for future use that the camel has. It is a very slow growth and it is a very shabby, prickly, rough, uncouth looking affair. But after years spent in attaining six or seven feet, behold a slender, white, tender shoot starts out of the top of the plant and grows with amazing rapidity. I watched one for a while measuring it every morning and it averaged 18 inches growth every twenty-four hours. When this slender stalk has shot up straight twenty feet into the air, the end of it bursts into a spray of beautiful white blossoms. In the spray there are sometimes as many as 100 individual blossoms, and each blossom is as large as a hen's egg. They are beautiful—they are so defiant of the desert—the white banner of blossoms is flaunted so exultantly—it is a veritable "hurrah—at last" of vegetation.

Now, beloved, this sotol reminds me of our acquaintance-ship—it has grown in the desert—it has had little chance—it was but a scrubby, sunburnt affair, until lo! with some strength which it gathered mysteriously in the past—from some occult germ which has been nourished in its heart—it suddenly throws up into the golden sunshine that banner of blossoms which we call *love*. Such an unlikely plant to have such heavenly fruit!

I thank you a thousand times for the picture—it is you, natural as life—only the light was a little strong and I cannot see your dear features as plainly as I long to. It is a dandy snap-shot of the baby.

Dearest love, tell me if you detect in my letters one single note of insincerity. It is so lovely that I think I must be deluding myself. It is not possible that I love you and you love me. Fate has made a mistake. He will wake up pretty soon and show us that we are mistaken.

It is true that love has been told so often that there is no new way under the sun of telling it. Flaubert in his *Madame Bovary* does make this so pathetic—read it? It's where Madame Bovary tells her lover how she loves him, but uses just the conventional world-old phrases. Her lover thinks of it afterward and is disgusted, little knowing that deepest feeling often finds conventional expression—indeed must of necessity do so.

But your words are not common-place to me. I seem never to have seen those phrases before—"I do" is a very common phrase, but I can imagine certain conditions and circumstances where your saying it would fill me with unutterable happiness. So stand not back on phrases—tell me you love me in any old way—it sounds good—and I shall tell you, angel, in every way that a very happy man, who is therefore content with a few ecstatic grunts now and then, can think of.

You ask about my business—well—it's hell, that's all. What do you think of grinding out rot about beans and wells and irrigation and rise in land values and new industries all the time? What do you think of writing letters all day telling Mr. Snickerfritz of Dayton, Ohio, that you received his request for information concerning this portion of New Mexico and that you take pleasure in mailing him under separate cover descriptive booklet, etc., and that you will be pleased to furnish him further information, etc.? and what do you think of collecting money from 125 gracherinas every month? and so on. But I never had a job I liked except bumming. I'm a natural born hobo—my heaven is the open road—my symbol a staff cut from the woods—hello! Walt, when did you bob up? But my manifest destiny is truck-gardening with you, dear, and hoboing it with you in our dreams—and maybe if things turn out right, in reality.

You ask me what Joe and Ed and Harry[1] and the rest of that heathen crew will think—Being a man of few words, I say I care not a damn what they think. There—don't show that ugly word to your mother.

Yours
Bedi

---

[1]Joe Hatchett, Edgar Witt, Harry Steger, all friends from the University of Texas.

Deming, N.M.
July 17, 1910

Dear Lillian—

I proceed to tear up the very sentimental sheet I have been two hours writing and start again. I can't be sentimental or write sentimentally when I don't feel it.

Your very sweet and lovely letter came this morning, but I am not in the mood to answer it. I enjoy reading this letter over and over, but nothing appropriate comes into my head to say in reply.

I'm very glad you feel as you do about leaving me if you decide you don't love me. Them's my sentiments. There is no use in the world in filling the days with agony and the nights with pain trying to coax a dead love into life again. If the time ever comes (Heaven forbid it!) that either one of us ceases to love the other we will just quit and that will be an end of it. There may be complications but the best way out would be to kick out.

There is little use, however, of discussing such a remote possibility only to have an understanding. I think I know you pretty thoroughly as well as I ever knew any woman, and you know me as well as any woman ever did know me: and upon such knowledge, I think it safe to marry.

I think we had better agree, however, not to speak to each other before breakfast: a man is usually grouchy and a woman's hair is usually frowzy—and grouchiness and frowziness do not get along well together. Of course, after we become wealthy enough to have a hairdresser dress your hair while you are yet in bed, and a servant to bring me a cup of coffee when I first wake up, it may be that by carefully choosing our subjects, we can talk a little. Or if we live in the country and I do hard physical labor during the day, this precaution will be unnecessary for then I wake up in a heavenly humor.

Well, well—we can settle all these details as it becomes necessary.

The only thing that keeps me away from you is the fact that I should have to go into debt in order to come and get you and I'm

55

powerful afraid of debt. It makes a slave and a cur of a man and you could never love a slave and cur.

Yours

Bedi

❦

Deming, N.M.
August 5, 1910

Dear Lillian:

Your letter from Mansfield came yesterday. Lomax[1] is here with me now and I have been having so much to do that it has been not quite impossible, but very nearly, to write to anyone. Gee Whizzer that's a cold sentence. Let me start again. Dear Lillian, I have been neglectful about writing but there is some little excuse for it. Lomax has been here and I have been very busy with other things so that I have not had the time to sit down and write letters any way representative of my feelings. Lomax and I have talked a good deal about you. He is a great admirer of yours, and I myself think quite well of you so our comments have been mainly laudatory. Lomax thinks I'm about half crazy to be out here living as I am, and I in turn think he is crazy to live as he does, but each in descanting on the other's craziness forgets the unhappiness incident to his own, so our stay with each other is good for us both.

Really this is simply to tell you that I am going to write.

Yours,

Bedi

[1]Editor's Note: John Avery Lomax, registrar at the University of Texas, gave Bedichek a job in his office when he first arrived as a freshman, and looked out for him at other critical junctures. They became lifelong friends. Lomax was collecting folksongs during this stay. The Foreword to his *Cowboy Songs and Other Frontier Ballads* is dated "Bedichek's Ranch, Deming, New Mexico, August 8, 1910." Lomax collected and published *Songs of the Cattle Trail and Cow Camp* and edited other collections with his son. He was one of the founders of the Texas Folklore Society.

❦

[Written on Deming Chamber of Commerce stationery]
Deming, New Mexico
August 18, 1910

Dearest Love—

Your letter is just here. It is foolishness to suppose that we can't get along as well together as we can separately. Look at the idiots who are getting along. Your health is the deciding factor. It is insane for you to stay there any longer. Money—money—the devil—what is money in comparison with your dear throat or nose or lungs or any other dear part about you. I can cut out my cigars and that will be almost enough to feed us. Come on, dearest love and let's have done with all this waiting and planning and hoping. Let's do as we want to and arrange things afterward. I've never denied myself anything yet that I couldn't just as well have had, and if you'll look back you will see the same is true of your life. Read Browning, "The Statue and the Bust" and come on. I'll meet you half way any old place that you wire me to meet you. This method economizes time and money, and I haven't much of either. I have just taken on additional work here which is very exacting and I have to be on the spot every day.

Now for the facts.

Shack—already described. We shall have to have rooms in town and go out and homestead as we get a chance two or three times a week—or we can get a pony and buggy and come in every day (8 miles) and back at night. I believe that's better. How the devil for you to amuse yourself here in town is the problem that vexes me. We could fix up a room in which you could read and write, and do whatever your tastes incline you to, while I did my work— Sometimes I should have to stay in town at nights, so we would have to have a room here anyway. It takes an hour and a quarter to drive in from the shack. I ought to be here by eight o'clock, so we should have to start from the homestead at 6:30—we would have to get up at 5:30 (Jesus!). We could start from town usually by 5 o'clock—get out there 6:15—get supper over by 7:30—get to bed about 9—that would give us enough sleep, wouldn't it? And this program can be changed in February for at that time I can get deed to my homestead and we can go where we please. Sorry I mentioned that—now you'll want to wait until February. Please tell the doctors to go to, and forget everything they ever told you.

I am to the best of my recollection $500 in debt. My assets are 320 acres of land which will in time be valuable—now not worth much. Also a dog and a job that will feed us—Slim start ain't it?

If you were in perfect health it might be well to wait, but as it is—waiting is impossible. You'll develop tuberculosis or some other horrible something. Del Rio would be a very happy place to meet. No one knows us there and marriage would be relieved of many embarrassing factors. Scenery is good. Not a bad place—Del Rio—pretty name, too. To go there from Mansfield direct would save complications at home.

Dearest love, I do not know how wise you are in ways of the bad world. If you are wise, you may want some such statement as I mean to write. If you aren't, the statement will not hurt.

It is this! My blood is as absolutely pure and free from taint of any sort as it was the day I was born. I have never been affected with any of the bad maladies that are common to young men of my class.

There, I'm done with that embarrassing subject for all time. I "end with hit as I begin"—it is silly to suppose that we will have any harder time to get along than we are now learning—in fact, we can get along cheaper from a pure money standpoint—and then we will be just that much to the good—oh the devil. I can't say what I want. —I mean that we will lose forever the time that we put off our marriage. We have each decided upon it and what's the use of losing time—time is the stuff that life is made of. Life is short and time is fleeting. Another year is probably a high per cent of the rest of our lives—1/40th anyway—why throw it away?

If I didn't know you for the sensible creature that you are, I wouldn't want to hasten matters, but I know that we can get along better together than we can apart.

Wire me, if you decide to come and pick out any place on the map except Waco or Eddy and I will meet you. But don't go to *preparing*; and don't allow yourself to worry a moment, as to fear, once you do decide to come. Just say "Here's for a fling at it—nothing very bad can happen" and it will all be much simpler than you suppose. All the old women's stories about the wonderfulness or terror or whatnot of marriage is all hash—you are just on your way to join a loving friend—and love you, my dear, I do with my soul.

Yours,

Bedi

[Written on Deming Chamber of Commerce stationery]
August 25, 1910

Dear Lillian:

I am very much disappointed. I really thought that you would meet me, vain man that I am.

I wish I had the throat of the world to hiss my scorn at the word "business" and everything that hateful word stands for. You were willing until you found out I was in debt and happened to think of some debts of your own!—and sentimentalists still talk of Love being Lord— Lord! He sits like a sycophant in the corner near a cuspidore until my Lord Business bids him rise. It was not thus when "men for love's sake trod Death's barren ways."

But in this day and time it is the part of wisdom for you to marry the business man you asked me about. The advice was wrong and given in a moment when I was dreaming of a different world—go ahead and marry him, it will solve the debt- and estate-problem. I'm in my right mind now. There's a widow with a few thousand here whom perhaps I can stomach when all the fumes of Romance die out of my brain and I am entirely sober, but By God, not yet!

A successful business man is a man who is intelligently and perpetually selfish. That definition is as sound as any in the dictionary.

Before this reaches you, I shall be up in the mountains toward the Colorado line out of reach, thank goodness, of U. S. mails or other evil devices for sending bad news; and I shall stay a month or two and come back feeling better, I hope.

Bedi

*Editor's note: This letter with its threat that she can marry her "business man" and he can focus on a "wealthy widow" evidently converted a hesitant Lillian. The next missile in their correspondence is a telegram of September 17, 1910, with news of a job for her and arrangements for meeting her when she arrives on the Southern Pacific.*

Night Letter
The Western Union Telegraph Company
Deming NM
September 7, 1910

Miss Lillian L. Greer
1410 South 5th Street
Waco

Board elected you assistant principal to teach beginners Latin Caesar
Cicero Rhetoric orthography and elementary physics or geometry salary eighty five per month school is in session now come immediately
wire acceptance
DR P M Steed
8:24 PM

Deming NM
September 7, 1910

Miss Lillian L. Greer
South 5th Street
Waco

Board wired you this afternoon wire me from San Antonio name of
number of S.P. Train you take if you come by Ft Worth wire when you
leave there San Antonio best route.
    R. Bedichek

*Editor's note: She came to Deming. What courage and self-confidence
she must have had to travel alone to a strange new place where she
had no friends or family to look out for her if plans with her bold
young suitor did not work out well! Years later, at the time their son and
I married, they wrote each other that our happiness reminded them of
their time and looked back on that period as blissful.*

✿

1910
[Deming Chamber of Commerce stationery]
My dear love—

You were so pale and lovely tonight that I'm afraid I shall dream of you as a ghost holding out beseeching hands to me that I cannot reach—and what unutterable anguish that would be for me.

The wonder grows in me that I have been able to exist so long without you—seven years since I first saw you—Jacob or one of those duffers waited seven years; but he was where he could see Rachel every day, and I have hardly averaged seeing you once a month. I shall never be able to live without you again—

But what's the use of writing I love you, love you, love you—it all comes to that at last

Bedi

✿

1910
Shack

Dearest—

I could hardly bring myself to stay out here tonight 8 miles away from you until I thought of the expedient of writing to you. This shack was never lonesome before—it has always been a struggle to tear myself away from it; now I can scarcely keep out here. I want you here so bad that I am sick—you in this cramped and dirty little shack with a dingy, flickering lantern for a light! I'm glad I'm not rich—then I would suspect you. Do you get the transition between the above two sentences? I mean that being so poor, and this shack being so dingy and mean a calculating girl would think twice and you don't seem to have thought at all: thus it has the appearance of love—the real thing. And then your face and eyes do beam so affectionately when you look at me sometimes, that I must think you love me. Now I have argued it out so much to my satisfaction that I will quit. I will not think of the repugnance you have for school teaching or anything else. I will stop with the blessed, beautiful thought that you love me.

Angel heart, if you knew how beautiful you looked to me this afternoon leaning back against that adobe wall, you would commend my heroic restraint in not literally sweeping you up and making off with you, running over the dear little doctor and scaring our sweet old friend into a fit. Really the temptation was almost overpowering. I hope you appreciate the strength of character thus evidenced by the man whom you have chosen for a mate. I'm nothing if not strong.

Dearest, do cultivate some bad traits and don't be as overpoweringly sweet, or there'll be hell to pay and you will be to blame.

Dear heart, I love you—must love you—You are the fairest and best woman in the world and it is sweet to be able to acknowledge this truth to you, my lovely mate—

There—goodnight

Bedi

❦

1910

[Deming Chamber of Commerce stationery]

Dearest—

If I had not gotten this note at noon I should have blown up—and such a dear sweet tender note it is. I could kiss the dear hand that wrote it eternally.

I disgraced myself last night by breaking up the dinner-party at eight o'clock—very shortly after we had finished eating and rushed down to Mrs. Ketchum's[1] only to see the cots occupied on the porch. I went on by and back by another street to my office where I worked until eleven o'clock. Then I went to bed but could not sleep. Then I wrote the driveling verses which I enclose. I wrote them in bed with a book for rest. Then I thought of you another hour or two and recalled all the lovely things about you—your beautiful, spiritual face and your voice and your heavenly smile and your soft white hands—oh, dearest, dearest you are the loveliest being alive—and I shall hold you tonight in my arms and we shall go off into another one of those ecstatic trances which Mrs. K's voice broke so rudely the other night.

I shall go to Mrs. Merrill's[2] tonight and you will likely not get this until after I see you—but I am writing it more for myself than you. I wish I could wipe the long hours of this afternoon out of time.

Bedi

62

1910
*Midnight*

> Alone, and *thou* in this few-streeted town *alone*!
> The air so still, the space between so slight
> I fancy thou must hear a breath or moan,
> Saying, "O Love, how lonely is the night!"

RB

[1]Editor's Note: Lillian lived with Mrs. Ketchum during the fall of 1910. Mrs. Ketchum came from Chicago hoping that the desert air of Deming would cure her daughter's tuberculosis. She offered Lillian a room in their big adobe house to provide young company for their sick daughter. (See pages 8–9 in "The Jumping-off Place.")
[2]Mrs. Merrill may have operated a lunch room.

❧

*Editor's Note: Roy and Lillian married on Christmas Eve, 1910. They lived in Deming for three more years. They had two small children, and Lillian was caring for them in their desert shack without running water; living conditions were primitive. Mary Virginia Bedichek was born December 11, 1911, and Sarah Craven Bedichek ("Sally") was born April 25, 1913.*

*After losing a newspaper he had purchased in Deming, Roy decided to take Lillian and their two daughters back to Austin. There, Roy had friends and at the University there were many writing jobs. Dudley K. Woodward, a friend from school days, helped him get the appointment of secretary to the Young Men's Business Club of Austin, and not long afterward he was writing publicity for the University of Texas and working for the Hogg Foundation. Soon after their return to Texas, Lillian took their two small daughters to Waco for a month's visit with her mother and the rest of her family.*

❧

The Young Mens' Business Club of Austin
Office of Secretary
September 28, 1913

My love,

I never knew before how necessary you are to me. This short separation is a good thing for me, but it has already served its purpose, and for God's sake let's make it as short as possible. I can't go to sleep at night for thinking of you, and every morning is dreary the moment I realize upon waking that you are not near.

I would that every morn you brought me violence, if it were necessarily violence that brought you—just so you came. I'm ashamed to say that it's not Mary or Sarah that I think of once in ten times that I think of you although it would please me immensely to have Mary in my arms again. Dearest love, I want to kiss your dear face a thousand times. But I hesitate to write you loving letters for fear it may delay your coming. I'm afraid to satisfy you with letters. Much like a child, I feel like saying, "If you want my love, come and get it."

There are so many lovely places around here to love in—whatever little dullness, dinginess or film of darkness has gathered over the gold of our love will vanish here, at Barton Springs, or in the luscious sensuous glades towards Mt. Bonnell, and the original fresh lustre will return. Angel mine, finish that dreary visit as soon as you can.

However, if you are resting and feel good and strong, stay your month out—I can stand it if I know this.

Frank was waiting for me in Lomax's office yesterday afternoon when I got out there. We three went for a short walk out to the house and I showed him the room which I thought he would occupy when I rented the place. The little devil had already, however, engaged accommodations for 3 months somewhere or other. I think he wants to be out from under the supervision which he imagines might be exercised over him staying with us; and maybe it's as well not to insist that he stay with us. I left him perfectly free, by telling him that he could get some boy to take the room he has engaged until Christmas, and come out with me if he wanted to. He can't get enough work in the engineering department to keep him busy for 3 months, so I told him I could furnish him employment here in my office. This seemed to interest him and I guess I will put him on to the collection about October 15th. He's a bright-looking dignified young chap and pleases me greatly.

Don't let the sun set on you without having written me. Saw Emily Maverick[1] the other day and she is very anxious to see you. Mrs. Yarrington rang up and wanted me to tell her when you would be here.

With much love,

Bedi

[1]Emily Maverick was a University of Texas friend from San Antonio.

🌿

The Young Mens' Business Club of Austin
Office of Secretary
October 2, 1913

My dear, dear love—

The O in October above was just rounded into its present perfect form when the mail man entered and I expected a letter from you, but instead he delivered a bill from the Tobin Drug Store and a notification from the MK and T Ry Co. that our freight from Deming has arrived.

You know yesterday I filed a complaint against the King of Dreams for not permitting you to appear, and behold last night you put in an appearance. You were a dumpy woman of forty with brown pop-eyes and a very large jaw and terribly evil temper. You bawled me out something awful. It seemed I was in one room and heard myself in another and adjoining room trying to kiss you and you snapped out "Let me alone," "Let me alone, I tell you"—biff, biff—it seemed you were defending yourself militantly from my caresses.

I guess I'll not complain of the King of Dreams anymore. He's a cynical kind of a cuss.

Same place October 5, 1913

When you begin to get tired, Beloved, of the steady stream of letters from me all with more or less the same burden of lonesomeness and love, you can effectually silence the twanging string with the thumb of your disapproval. Out of the heart's fullness, however, I must write, and if not, not at all.

I am worried to death about Mary[1] not that she is ill or ailing particularly; but that she is ailing right in the bosom of a dope-giving family. For the love of heaven and truth and all the beatitudes, do not fill my child with dope, or let your mother do it, or let any superstitious doctor come thumping or prodding around her.

You say nothing of seeing Edgar Witt. Is it possible that he has not called to see you and the babies?

Accept my congratulations upon refraining from the use of coffee. You deserve to be patted approvingly on the head.

I was nearer suicide last night than ever in my life before. It seemed to me that there was a chunk of aching thoughts the size of my fist right in the center of my head. I couldn't speak to any one, I was so choked up with emotion—painful emotion.

I decided, to start out with, that you loved me no longer. I piled all your recent letters on the table before me and went carefully to work to find the needle of love in the haystack of indifferent expressions. I then got out all the old letters of yours I could find and compared them page by page with the recent ones, coming to the terrible conclusion that, like so many of the fair things of other years, your love had gone. I could see in your recent letters only the bare trimmings of a very mild affection. This line of thought went on in me, until I thought my head would burst, and I devoutly wished it would.

I went back over all the quarrels we have ever had, and saw myself much to blame, but you also much to blame. I wanted to get up and blow to the other end of the world where I might never see [sic] a familiar voice, where I might bury every thought I have ever had deep in irretrievable sub-consciousness. For what a poor failure I have been, if living with a woman 3 years, and such a woman, her love dwindles down to, at best, a sort of mild affection.

But I am better this morning. When I finally got to sleep, I slept dreamlessly and like a baby until ten o'clock this morning. But someway I feel about ten years older. It's not years, but just such experiences.

[The rest of the letter is missing.]

[1]Editor's Note: Bedichek is referring to their older daughter Mary Virginia. He mistrusted doctors and medicine.

❦

The Young Mens' Business Club of Austin
Office of Secretary
July 6, 1914

Dearest—

I am at my office bright and early like a new office boy, after eating a sixty-cent breakfast at the Maverick. The ticket read, as follows:

| | |
|---|---|
| 3 eggs | $.20 |
| Hot cakes | .10 |
| 2 coffee | .10 |
| bacon | .20 |
| | $.60 |

Besides three large slugs of butter were consumed with the cakes and I managed to make off also with one roll, and three glasses of water. I'm pining but not starving for you.

I am sending you under separate cover several copies of the *New York Call* which is a very interesting paper. You will find therein a long writeup of Dr. Sun Yat Sen which I read with great interest lying abed last night while the gloaming gloamed outside, and a zephyr zephed gently under my nightshirt.

I am the duly constituted secretary of the Hogg organization this morning with a salary of $2500 per year and whatever perquisites I can lay acquisitive hands upon. That explains partially the sixty-cent breakfast. But, really, this shall be my one last extravagance. I simply will not spend that $2500 before I get ahold of it. Be damned if I do! I want oh so much, and I shall endeavor, oh so earnestly, to chug $140 of that $208 per month into the bank. I am really saving money in my dreams these nights—in my dreams alas!

I enclose herewith Wasson's[1] letter about Keasbey's[2] article. I showed it to Keasbey and he naively copied the first paragraph. Please save the letter, though you needn't return it.

Honey, please don't bawl me out about that breakfast—I'll send you a statement of dinner and supper, and guarantee that the whole shall not total a dollar. I had just walked down town to save carfare and was hungry.

I got a statement from Sanger Bros. which I enclose. If this is all right, and you are dead sure they haven't tackled your mother for it, let me have it back and I will pay it.

Women certainly do hate each other. I heard a most unpleasant controversy between Mrs. L. and her mother yesterday—a real nasty quarrel about the privilege which the one claimed of doing things and going to great trouble for the other! That's the best I could make out of it. And if a quarrel could develop about that, think of the exhibition put on when something really serious comes up. It's curious how women hate each other—oh, the dear, deadly hate of women for each other!

Here's the mail man and my strenuous duties begin. Maybe a letter from you, who knows? He's put a stack about six inches high on my table in the other room. Surely one of them is from you. Honey, you know really sixty cents ain't much for a grown man's breakfast.

The stack of letters contained a dear one from you, a somewhat pitiful one from Una[3] (enclosed), a funny one from that scallywag Doughty (enclosed) which please return, and a bunch of other stuff that I will find courage to look at sometime during the forenoon.

I passed old 3003 yesterday, and Mary's wing-wing[4] almost made me cry with its air of utter dejection. The board was slightly awry and it looked so limp, futile and deserted that I could hardly bear to look at it. I imagine the ha-pa[5] on the sleeping-porch looked even worse.

I spent only eighty cents for meals all day yesterday, so if you average up those three meals with that sixty-cent breakfast, it isn't so bad, is it?

My stenographer has arrived and will put me to work so I had better quit, not, however, without much love and longing.

Affectionately,

Bedi

---

[1]Alonzo Wasson was an employee of the *Dallas Morning News*.
[2]Lindley Miller Keasbey was a professor at the University of Texas.
[3]Editor's Note: Una is Roy's sister who had gone with their parents to Deming, New Mexico. They had closed their school in Eddy and moved to Deming to take over Roy's land claim. His father put up a windmill and other equipment and farmed successfully until his death in November 1916. Una taught at Deming and Roswell.
[4]Baby talk for swing.
[5]Baby talk.

The Young Mens' Business Club of Austin
Office of Secretary
July 8, 1914

My dear, dear wife:

It was a dreary thing, this waking up and getting out of bed this morning, and it lasted from the first peep of day until "the dull dawn dragged itself away" to quote from a sonnet of my immature years. But suddenly a little pink thought was born, and as it grew life became more and more worth while. The thought may be arranged in words as follows:

I am secretary of an organization for promoting higher education in Texas, and have at my disposal some 25 or 30 thousand dollars per year. Naturally, the first thing for me to do is to familiarize myself with institutions of higher education in Texas, and see just what is being done. Baylor University, dear old Baylor U is an institution of higher education in Texas, or purports to be and hence logically comes within the purview of my initial investigations. What more natural then than that the first act of my official existence should be to visit Baylor U (expenses paid). And then, and then, for the first time it occurred to me that just across the street from the said institution is the palatial residence of Mother Greer where the feckless bettumcheckums are temporarily domiciled. And this is the thought that got me out of bed. I'faith, is it not a happy thought?

Poor John Sinclair! indefinitely postponed! He misses this train and that from the depot of non-existence, apparently oblivious to the clarion "all-aboard" of the conductor. Oh wraith, perhaps-never-to-be-embodied, thinner and more subtle than ether that floats between the stars, inchoate spirit, when wilt thou seize upon that microscopic car, distilled in a moment of ecstasy, which is to bear you shivering into this heavy world? Alas and alack! roam on, but I pray that the trains keep up their regular schedule, and that the company (Bedicheks, inc.) provide extras upon occasion, and that missing connection does not become such a habit with thee that the years of lame and halting service shall find thee still wavering and uncertain among those shadows of shadows beyond the thin outposts of existence!

I went up and selected my office this morning. It is a large comfortable place on the first floor of the main building. I have an elegant roller top desk of old oak which makes me look like the president of the New Haven in its palmy days. The thing must have cost $100. I am getting swell and stuck on myself, but I'm not spending any money. Enclosed is money order for five bones. And bank will cash it, or any store, for that matter. My expenses yesterday were as follows:

| | |
|---|---|
| Breakfast | $1.25 |
| Coffee | .05 |
| carfare | .10 |
| Bottle beer | .15 |
| Two collars | .25 |
| Supper | .40 |
| | 1.20 |
| Lunch | .15 |
| | $1.35 |

Hobo is happy. Hoping you are the same;
Affectionately, Bedi.

Dear love—your two enjoyable letters I am devouring—Bless your heart!

❦

Young Men's Business Club of Austin
Office of Secretary
July 9, 1914

My own dearly beloved,
'Tis the witching hour of 8:30 A.M. The fan above my head is in intermediate, and the banked hills of south Austin look very green in the morning light, and from out my eight-story window I catch a most bewitching glimpse of a bend in the river, a loving bend like the crook of a lover's arm about his mistress, a bend which beckons to the burbling rapids beyond, and I can smell the river bank smells, and hear the wind in the tall pecans, and we are hand in hand, what time our hands are not engaged with ticks and chiggers—ah, me!
Would that we were heeling it up the heely[1] in the vasty wilds

alone except for Hobo. Say, that blooming animal stood off the dog-catcher the other day. I met him with his dog-patrol wagon yesterday afternoon, and Hobo was following me. He told me that he cast his rope at Hobo a few days ago near the University campus, and old Hobo lunged at him and drove him back into his wagon. He then saw the ring which fastened his tag to the collar and surmised that Hobo's tax had been paid, and that he had lost the tag. So he let him alone. But what do you know about that vicious streak emerging during the old hound's old age? Or did he know the dog-catcher for the hyman fiend that he is, and fearless in the face of destruction, "dauntless set the slug-horn to his lips"—the old scoundrel gets more of a puzzle every day. The soul of Socrates is in that carcass, I verily believe.

Hobo is the antithesis of the man, George Gay, of the *Spoon River Anthology*. Hobo never shrank from anything. With tail a-curl over his back, head poised to strike or lick, he'll snap a bear or nose lovingly a child. He knows not fear. When a pup of five months he grabbed hold of Destiny and has been twisting Destiny's tail ever since. Conquering he has come, sowing his seed with fine unconcern where they will sprout fice or bull-dogs—what is eugenics to him? "I'll do my part" says he proudly, "let Nature do hers." With glorious gusto he chased the auto sixty miles, and took his three days' helplessness stoically. He followed me among the pointed hot rocks of the Santa Rita mountains until his poor feet swelled twice their normal size, and yet the gleam of triumph never faded from his agate eyes. I remember three tremendous lion-like Saint Bernards jumped on him at the close of a weary day, and he rose to the occasion like Ajax. He smote them hip and thigh until they respected him, and smelt him in a dignified way, and allowed him the same immemorial canine privilege. His fight with the mange and the fleas is also typical. He will actually scratch and bite the flesh off to the bone if I don't relieve him with the mange-cure.

There is deep wisdom in the stanza about George Gay. The same wisdom that is in "Childe Harold to the Dark Tower Came"—a wisdom that Gwynn and Una have never learned. Ena[2] is a success, don't you think, simply because she met Life's issue squarely, if blindly, and Una and Gwynn are not because they haven't. Gwynn has turned vicious, however, while Una has turned too sweet. If you hadn't taken the bits in your teeth you would now be scuttering around the globe maybe trying to forget last year's work and catch up with something you know not what. And yet "your life may end in madness" but you have gotten some meaning into life anyway, and "life without meaning is the torture of restlessness and vague desire."

And right today, if I felt that a fuller life for me lay away from you, I would tear loose irrespective of damage to the roots of my affection; and I believe that you would do the same. There is no lawlessness about this—it is merely the inalienable right of the individual to expand according to the law of his being, just as an oak root bursts up the cement-side-walk. There is a certain lawfulness about decay. But I'm getting deeper than I can make clear—but I believe you will get the idea from what is not said.

I love you, dearest, and think of you at least half of the time. I am overjoyed at Sarah's phenomenal growth. Buttermilk is better than Shipp,[3] whose bill, by the way has suddenly leaped to nine dollars.

Be sweet and write to me, and do not eat too much for I have fears of your form, even as thou hast of mine.

Affectionately,

Bedi

[1]Gila wilderness in New Mexico.
[2]Ena is Roy's oldest sister.
[3]Shipp was a well-known Austin doctor.

❦

Young Men's Business Club of Austin
Office of Secretary
July 10, 1914

Dearest—I had just written that, which is the word which nearliest (Boo-Bouck) comes to expressing you to me and for me—I had just hit the 't', when the telephone rang and a part with a deep bass voice informed me that he would give himself the pleasure of calling on me in a few minutes as he wished to discuss a matter with me. I do not know who it is, but I hope if he gets to the eighth floor before I get through this letter to my love that the elevator cable breaks and lets him suddenly down into the basement, and that the ambulance will arrive and take his jumbled remains to the Seton Infirmary or to Wm. Tears, undertaker, I don't much care which. I dislike people with deep bass voices who wring a man out of his seat at o'clock in the morning just as he is beginning to type-write a letter to the only woman he ever loved or will ever love—they (such people) are among the cardinal nuisances, and if this particular one happens to be a stock-salesman, I shall deliberately kill him—I'll stick him through the goozle with my paper-knife.

But I must be getting on with this letter. Beloved there's nothing really melts you like five bones. I wish I could send you five in every letter and thus insure a real love letter as a receipt. Much genuine sentiment, it seems to me, is spilt among the lines of yours which I received this morning—is it the five bones or the salacious moving-pictures? Which? This question I shall leave right where it is—occupying the third and fourth lines of this page.

Poor Mrs. Lomax has fever every time she moves. If she stays still, flat of her back, neither reading nor speaking, her fever runs down to about one-fifth of a degree, but if she walks across the room it rises. She certainly looks wretched. Poor Old John A. has had a tumor cut out of his side, and he has to walk along hitched over to the left, and old lady Brown, who sets anyone's nerves on edge, is constantly "invading the home," and all in all they are in the devil of a fix.

I don't believe it would be a good plan to take poor little Sarah off of Mother Greer's buttermilk for the sake of a visit to Eddy, at least until she has established herself solidly on the other side of twenty pounds, or showed herself so vigorous that you have no fear of her going back on account of a change of milk.

Are you doing anything with your short-story work? Please don't let those dear sweet little brain-cells of your become immersed in little globules of fat. Keep them exercised and lean and lithe. With Mother Greer's[1] groaning table to minister to your bodily nourishment and white slave moving-pictures as mental pabulum, I have serious fears for you. You'll be joining the church next! Puck offers a weekly prize of $100 for the most humorous contribution of five hundred or a thousand words. Why not try that? Get real killingly funny—or serious either. Cast out—hitch your wagon to a star and perform. Too much to eat and too much sleep and white slave moving-pictures will make Lil a dull darling, in a fat woman's corset.

But never fear, my only sweetheart, my love will encompass you long after my arms are unable to. I was just offering a little advice for

73

your own comfort. And my thoughts in this connection were not suggested by your letters—they are brighter than last summer's—but merely by thinking of what the life you describe would be to me.

I am getting lean as a greyhound with long walks through the woods. My belt is taken up to the limit, and further reduction must bring a shorter belt. I sweat a gallon or so every afternoon, take a cool bath and a light supper and sleep like Mary. My conscience is as light as one of your most successful loaves, and the knowledge of having such a beautiful loving wife insures perfect digestion. Am I not a favored man? Well I guess yes!

Hoping you are the same
Affectionately, Bedi

[1] Editor's note: After her husband's death, Virginia Lee Greer operated a big and successful boarding house in Waco for Baylor students who called her "Mother Greer" and praised her counsel and guidance.

❧

Young Men's Business Club of Austin
Office of Secretary
July 11, 1914

Sweetheart, I open your letter first every morning, and then write you before going into any of the rest of my mail. I don't want anything to intervene between your letter and mine. Do not waste any sympathy on me. I am not working to hurt myself at all. Indeed, I am largely taking mine ease. I make some little effort toward work between the hours of 9 A.M. and 12:30 when I go out to lunch; but after lunch, I read mostly, until four o'clock when I beat it to my room, change clothes, and hike out across the country with Hobo. I get back about 6:30, bathe, and go to dinner. I then return to my room and read until I fall asleep, usually about ten o'clock. There's certainly nothing wildly exciting about this regime, but there are no difficulties about it—it's like a vegetarian dinner, mildly pleasing and harmless. But let me tell thee, Lillian Greer, I miss more kisses than the howdy and good-bye ones, and you can mix that with your chewing-gum and chew it—don't you?

Honey, I shall be driven, I'm afraid to employing a female stenographer. They are so much cheaper and more efficient than males. I have one in mind now that I can get for $65 a month who is fast as lightning (I mean fast on the machine and at dictation), and who is willing to work from 8 A.M. until 5 P.M. or 6 if necessary. This trifling boy of mine, and about the best boy I ever had, is slow as molasses in winter, gets down about nine unless I am always prodding him, and wants $75 per month. This girl, a Miss Armstrong, has been stenoging five years and is really one of the best I have ever seen, and she makes a measly fifty dollars a month now. A male able to do her work could get easily $100 per month.

Regarding the present habits of Hobo, he stays at the Lomax's apparently satisfied all day. Shirley says he occasionally goes off for two or three hours, but always returns before I get back in the afternoon. He follows me, of course, on my walks and to dinner in the evening where he gets a plentiful supply of scraps, having already won over the heart of the landlady.

Am sending a *Harper's* and *The Masses* under separate covers. Have read *Harper's* very scantily, but I think I read every line of *The Masses*.

After all, the feminism of Floyd Dell[1] is a very cold proposition. If children are to be raised by the state, all the sweet affection (a very considerable and essential part of life, it seems to me) of parent for child and child for parent is done away with. Don't you see me, for instance, relinquishing Mary to Mrs. Holden, and Sarah to the fellow who is not dog-catcher, or Miss Katie Daffan. No doubt but what that kind of people would be employed by the state in this work, and in return, you and I would have the blessed privilege of having a room each in a different part of town, visiting theaters, clubs, political meetings, and getting to our respective rooms together or separate just any old time in the morning we wanted to. It seems to me that it is always the Bohemian who is visualizing the horrors of the wedded state, in the radical magazines. To the real Bohemian nothing is more horrible than regularity in the abstract. But under our present system, it seems to me that the Bohemian is provided for. He can have his whore or his childless mistress—nobody seems to care much, until he begins insisting on everybody doing just as he does. Then, of course, there are objections. And looking only at the woman's side of it, instance the women of rich husbands who have as nearly perfect freedom as it is possible to have, servants galore, no children to bother with, no household duties, the ideal you may say of the state Floyd Dell is preaching, and are not these very same women the most unhappy as well as the most despicable of the race?

There is no getting behind Christ's wisdom—the kingdom of God is within you. If anyone feels that the work he or she is doing is worth while, and that it is being done well, that person is, if not happy, satisfied. Economic conditions, however, condemn about nine-tenths of the human race to work that they do not consider worth while, and such conditions should be altered, so as to give human beings the wide choice that essentially belongs to them, but Floyd's idea of forcing Bohemianism upon the world, it seems to me, is utterly futile. And the unhappiness in the home which he points out is due chiefly to the economic conditions in which the home is immersed—he fails to take into account the home-making, child-loving, parent-loving instincts.

I am so afraid Mary will forget me that I've a notion to get on the noon train and go to Waco, but I shan't. However, a month is a long time to stay away from my beloved wife, and my babbling brats.

Affectionately,
Bedi

[1]Floyd Dell was an editor, author, dramatist, who wrote *Love in the Machine Age*, and was editor of *The Masses*; he was a spokesman for the jazz age.

❦

Young Men's Business Club of Austin
Austin, Texas
July 13, 1914

Beloved, if I had written a good letter yesterday morning, I would have beat it to town and mailed it so that you would get it this morning, but the fact that it was a very futile effort disposed me to go off into the woods yesterday afternoon and forget it. I am enclosing it herewith, however, since you are my wife and entitled to know the worst that I do as well as the best. It is just this that gives the lover an unfair advantage over the husband. The lover is always scented up and on dress parade and band-box manners, while the poor old sweaty husband has to pull off his dirty socks right under his wife's nose, and rise and operate and even talk in that bleared-eyed hour between rising and breakfast; and in these things also has the mistress the advantage of the wife. I am speaking, of course, of the middle-class wife and husband. And it seems to me that no better more convincing proof of the omnipotence of love can be found than in the fact that only one couple in twelve get divorced. With all the terrible and depressing handicaps of middle-class marriage, the brutal familiarity of it, eleven out of every twelve couples rise superior to it, and stoically, if not lovingly, and decently, if not virtuously, tolerate each other for a quarter or half a century. And sprinkled among the eleven couples that shall receive each a golden crown in heaven, there are several whose love dominates the trivialities of constant intercourse in a compact dwelling, and you and I, I verily believe, constitute a drop of this divine sprinkle.

Anyway, Love, at the present writing, my love stands regnant and unterrified in the presence of your expanding form[1]; and thy love, I would fain believe, while blenching before my pre-breakfast grouch, bobs up serenely about nine A.M. and holds the fort pretty well until we are both snoring on the sleeping-porch.

Now don't commence to talk about not having any mind, and don't begin assuming that retiring and humble pose, or you will hypnotize yourself into that very condition. The only reason one person is superior to another is because he believes that he is. Belief in superiority does not result from superiority, but vice versa, superiority results from belief of superiority. Do you know that you think that you lack the ideas, the plot-making ability, and so forth and that you possess the facility of expression, but just the opposite is the case. You have the ideas, the point of view, the plot-making ability, and all, but you do not have the facility of expression; and that will come only with practice. The other could not be gotten by practice or study or anything else— that's what God gives; but mere facility in expression comes with hard work. That's all—hard work. Had you ever stopped to think how much more the average writer has written than you before he ever tries to write a story? The average short-story writer, Barry Benefield,[2] for instance, is graduated from a reportorial staff. For ten or fifteen years, perhaps, he has been writing two or three columns a day—four thousand words. The immense quantity of writing that he does, if he is the developing sort, gives him facility in expression, and by facility or expression I do not mean merely turning graceful phrases (you do that by instinct) but I mean giving your whole story proper proportion, throwing just the right emphasis on every detail, in a work, presenting the story as it occurs to you to the man in the street. That's facility of expression, and that's what it has taken Barry Benefield fifteen years of hard writing to get. If you printed all his writing it would make some thirty volumes[3] four hundred pages each, while you have not written a tenth of such a volume. Besides, you do not write consecutively, every day, you take it by fits and starts. The reporter grinds out a certain amount every day, and it is just this constant hammering that so fashions the brain-cells and the connections between them which make possible facile expression.

Well, that is quite a lecture, and you will reply that with the constant interruptions you cannot get down to work. Well, maybe not, and maybe that is the sign that you are not to be a writer of short stories. Who knows?

I didn't start out to lecture, however, I started out to love you after getting that blessed letter from you this morning. When I finished it, I wanted to kiss you one hundred times right upon your lovely talkative mouth.

Does Mary still ub peep-art daddy?

Affectionately,

Bedi

[1]Editor's Note: Lillian, who was pregnant at this time, had had two unsuccessful pregnancies.
[2]Barry Benefield, born at Jefferson, Texas, in 1877, was the historian of the class of 1902 at the University of Texas, winner of the *Cactus* short story prize, editor of the *Cactus* and editor of the University of Texas magazine. Later he was editor of *The Dallas Morning News* and *The New York Times*.
[3]Handwritten in the margin, presumably by Lillian: "Thirty volumes—nothing! He writes a volume a month—12 a year, 144 in 12 years."

Young Men's Business Club of Austin
Austin, Texas
July 16, 1914

My own sweetheart,

Yesterday afternoon about three o'clock, Hobo and I went to the country. We found an appropriate place on the river, and I went in swimming, much to Hobo's discomfiture. I let the current sweep me far out into the stream, and old Hobo stood on the bank and yawped as if I were drowning. I never saw him act so unstoically. Finally he plunged in, and if I had not rescued him, I verily believe he would have drowned. I thought it very curious that a dog should know so little about water, until I happened to think that he came to maturity in a country where an irrigation-ditch is the extent of the water area. I certainly had a lot of fun. I finally got across the river and out on a steep sand bar of the purest whitest sand I ever saw. I climbed to the top and rolled down, buried myself in it, and did a number of other seashore tricks. When I had waded and swam back against that terrific current to my clothes I was utterly worn out, flabbergasted, wilted; but the look of supreme and heavenly joy on Hobo's countenance was worth going miles to see. I wish you could swim—it would be such fun to go swimming together, and play in the sand, and worry Hobo. One of the first things I am going to teach Mary is to swim. It is simply glorious. It is a youth-renewer. It makes you feel prehistoric, almost, to wallow in the sand and slide off into the strong current of the river. In the racial memory, which is submerged in every human being, a wallow in the mud or sand and a whirl in the current brings up amphibious delights experienced away back yonder in the fresh morning of the world. The sun, wind, mud, sand, water—these are the revivifiers of the human body.

I haven't any letter from you this morning. Have you ceased to love me, or is the mail service defective? As a patriot I cannot admit the latter; as a husband, the former is unthinkable. I was never in such a mental dilemma. What shall I think? Nothing. That's easy. I will just think nothing. But I did think one or the other, or each by other, in propounding the query. How shall I make it as though the thought had never occurred to me? How shall I spit on the slate, so to speak, and rub it out? God knows. Let us pray.

Here—I had written "here"—and the Mayor came in with a long line of talk, and I have forgotten what I started to say. What conceivable sentence would begin with "here"—what possible thought could "here" initiate. Alas, it is lost.

I enclose a bill for Frank, opened by mistake. I was so used to opening window envelopes that I tore right into it by reflex action. Ah, I have the thought that I lost. I had started to say "Here is a bill for

Frank." How often the diver brings up pebbles for pearls. I was diving for this thought—you get the idea without my pursuing the figure further.

It's hot and too much trouble. Beloved good-bye. For this time.
Affectionately,
Bedi

❦

*Editor's Note: By 1917 Roy Bedichek had started his life's work with the University Interscholastic League, encouraging competitions in the schools of Texas, and seeing that the rules were fair and fairly administered, enforcing eligibility qualifications. The first contests were all athletic; under his leadership debating, extemporaneous speaking, music memory, and many other non-athletic contests were added. As editor of the League paper, he stimulated discussion about how to set up contests for a wide variety of participants in a way that the rules were understood by all.*

*While working for the Interscholastic League, he often used his vacation to teach either an English course or, in later years, outdoor education. In the following letter he is teaching English composition. He particularly liked Alpine with its altitude and cool climate. Summer heat in Austin drained his energy to accomplish anything.*

❦

[Sul Ross State Normal College, Alpine, Texas
Office of the President stationery]
June 25, 1922

PUSSUNAL
Dear Love:

I came up here to the Normal Building at seven this Sunday morning to make some typewritten outlines for my students to cram by, but before beginning this dreary task, I shall write a word to you.

I do not feel the same isolation from you that I did the first summer I spent here. Our spending the summer here together in the meantime has in some way identified you with the places, scenes and the general landscapes in such a way that I do not feel at any time very far from you. When I go climbing, I remember places where you had some

*80*

difficulty last summer, or where I took a kodak view of you in your rompers, or where we paused to get wind; and when I walk about the streets and come suddenly on the little Tippet house, as I did yesterday afternoon, it seems that I could open the front door and call and be answered. This is one reason, I suppose, why I am not so keen on correspondence as I was during the first summer.

Another reason why I don't write so much is that I seem to have lost a certain pride in expression which I used to have. I used to write just for the sake of writing, and I rarely have the impulse to do that now. I preach it to my composition classes but I do not practice it any more. And this is no sign either, that I am coming into the sere and yellow leaf. I'm choke-full of ambitions of various kinds. I think if I had an opportunity to greet you, for instance, this morning, my ardor might surprise you somewhat. Distance, perhaps, lends enchantment to certain of the rougher aspects of our past lives. The remembrance of the little quarrels we have had, principally, as I remember, concerning literary interpretations and other academic considerations, arouse no bitter feelings, but on the other hand are quite pleasant to dwell upon. One quarrel of last summer makes me chuckle it is so ridiculous, especially when I look upon the wrinkled visage and stiff, mature and abundant form of what might be termed, scientifically, the focal infection of this particular domestic disturbance.

There is not a sound in this big building this morning, except the click of this typewriter and the tick of the big clock out in the corridor. The whole town is attending a Mexican "kermess" among the adobes south of the S.P. tracks. Just what kind of mess this is, I shall leave you in your studies of Spanish philology to determine. I mean to go over a little later as there is a big Mexican dinner to be served about noon. If there is a dish of those soft well-cooked beans with tortilla frida, I shall be satisfied. I shall have to forego Brother Ray's sermon this morning, I'm afraid, as I am now taking time which I had really apportioned to making the outlines above-mentioned.

Is it not about time you were making definite arrangements about coming out here, setting the time? etc. A week or so in this bracing air will do you good and break the hot grind of the summer in Austin. Has Louise[1] visited you yet? If not, when is she coming? Can Ena come up and stay with mama,[2] and can you unload the more mature portion of our offspring upon Mama Jenny?[3] These are all questions to be considered and settled. There are heights to be scaled and the "cool, silver shock in the pool's living water" waits patiently. A little more rain, by the way, would make the pool's water a little more *live*. The prophets promise more rain early in July.

And speaking of dreams! — best not! There are some things one does not confide even to the privacy of a diary, even if he intends to burn it up next week and keep it in a safety-deposit box in the meantime.

If you can read this letter and not see that I have at last attained a sort of artistic restraint in composition, you fail entirely to get the interlinear significance of the same.

Yours, in a certain sense, forever,

Bedi

[1] Lillian's sister, Louise, married to Frank Ramey.
[2] Roy Bedichek's mother, Lucretia Ellen Craven Bedichek. She came to live with Roy and Lillian in 1917 after Roy's father died in 1916.
[3] Lillian's mother was called "Mama Jenny." Bedi was trying to reapportion family responsibilities so Lillian could come enjoy the cool air of Alpine, Texas.

❦

Austin, Texas
May 16, 1927

Dear Ina:

I want to write you frankly about a matter and won't you please write me just as frankly. Since my girls have gotten big, they do not get along with mama.[1] It's no use trying to blame anyone, but the result is that mama is, I'm afraid, not as happy with me as she has been in former years. As you know she is nearly eighty, but wonderfully well-preserved and capable of much enjoyment of life. Bachman[2] is in the hard-headed period in which he is rebellious of all authority, and especially of that of his grandmother, although she is much more tolerant of him than of the girls. Lillian is like a woman and like a mother, and during the past few years, there has been considerable bitterness engendered between her and mama—although most of the time they get along all right.[3]

The girls have gotten to the age when they dress up in finery and take on a few airs,[4] all innocent enough and natural, but mama has gotten the idea that they think themselves better than she is, and this is enough to keep their relations in a constant strain.

82

I have been trying to devise some plan for separating them for at least a year. As soon as Mary enters the University (which will be the fall of 1928) we shall likely place her in a dormitory. Sarah will be a year older, and Bachman not so uncontrollable, I hope.[5]

I have thought of a hundred things, but they all have serious objections. I have thought of getting a room here for mama, because I would like to be near her, but without anything to do, she would be absolutely miserable. Eddy is such a dreary place, I feel that she would not be satisfied there. And I have thought that maybe if I paid for her room and board (say $30 per month) you might like for her to stay with you a year.[6] I, of course, would not want her to know that I was paying you anything, yet at the same time I don't feel that you could afford to have any extra financial burden to those you are already carrying. Since your girls are gone, I think there would not be any danger of the same situation developing [in] your home as has in mine. She is very fond of Casey and Kay[7] and gets along better with boys anyway.

I am making this only as a suggestion, and want you to write me frankly just what you feel about it. If you think it will not suit you, some other arrangement can be made. Please tell me just what you think, no matter what it is, and don't let mama know we have had any correspondence about the matter. Address me "University Station."

Una spent three weeks with us. Her religion[8] seems to make her quite happy, but you know it's easy to be happy when one has assumed no responsibilities—or is it just the other way around?

Affectionately,

Roy

---

[1]Lillian's note at the top of this letter reads: "Grandma (Roy's mother) thought that Bachman was perfect, like his father, he could do no wrong. She was very critical of Mary and Sarah."

[2]Bachman is Lillian's and Roy's youngest child, born January 19, 1918.

[3]Lillian's note: "Without shedding blood."

[4]Mary was sixteen years old and Sarah was fourteen years old at this time.

[5]Lillian's note: "He was a good boy! Grandma said to Bachman when he was quite young (3 to 5 years old) in my presence and more than once, 'Your father does not love you. Your mother does not love you. Nobody loves you but Old Grandma.' I always corrected her, saying, 'Nonsense, Grandma, that is not true and you know it. We both love him very much. He is our only son!'"

[6]Lillian's note: "She stayed 8 years. Made life miserable for Ruth & interfered in Ina's affairs, etc."

[7]Ina's two youngest children.

[8]Una was a Christian Scientist.

May 26, 1927

Dear Ina:

I read your letter with very great interest, and it is just the kind of a letter I expected from you—noble and self-sacrificing. I could not consent, however, for you to take on any financial burden in this matter, and if the arrangement suggested is made I must be allowed to pay the entire expense. How much will it cost to fix up the screen porch and room? If it is not too much, I shall be glad to pay the cost of it, and think I ought to, by all means. And also I shall pay the board, whatever that amounts to. As for your owing me any money, please forget it. I do not consider that you owe me a cent. In any case, it would be an experiment for a year, and she would not want to come before September, I think. I want her to go to New Mexico and also to Kansas City to be with Uncle Ratio[1] a while.

She has put me in a most embarrassing situation by asking me to find out from Lillian whether or not she, (Lillian) wants her to come back. If Lillian says "yes" it will not be true and said only out of regard for my feelings; if she says "no," it will amount to a fracture in their relations that can never be healed. So you see, either way I am in a difficult position.

What makes it particularly hard for me is that Mama thinks that she has to take care of me. Her favoritism for me is one of the main things that has angered Lillian and the girls, but, of course, she cannot see this nor could it be possibly explained to her.

When I think of all that you have gone through with,[2] I can hardly consent at all for you to be bothered with the matter at all; and still as I wrote you in my former letter, mama is unhappy here. I would ten times rather she would consent to live with us and relieve her altogether from any household duties,[3] for it is in these that the conflict comes. We could easily hire a girl to do the work at an insignificant cost. I suggested this to her some time ago, and she would not hear of it. She said she would rather be dead than doing nothing. Of course, I had to put it on the ground that the work was too great a burden, which idea, of course, she scouted.

If we do decide upon the arrangement suggested, and you agree to let me stand the money expense, perhaps you had better write her sometime during the summer suggesting that she stay with you for a year as a change, etc.

There is another matter that is troubling me, and that is that boarders often do not like to eat with elderly people.[4] As you say, we had as well face the facts and look at all possible angles of the matter. It would not do to allow this arrangement to interfere with your business. You are a better judge of this than I am, so please tell me just what you think. Is it your custom to have the family eat with the boarders, or do you all eat before or after?

Now please let me know:

1. How much it will cost to build the room and screen-porch.
2. Will you let me pay for this and for board?

–0–

I wish I had time to write you a long letter about a matter suggested in your letter—viz., suppression of bitter and angry thoughts concerning people who do us injury. I have struggled with this same thing and have found out, as you have, that it is futile from every standpoint to nurse grudges of any kind. Jesus preached and lived forgiveness, and while I sometimes cannot forgive, I can at least ignore and refuse to allow myself the luxury of having bitter thoughts. If I allowed myself to do so, I could easily work myself into a passion about Una's attitude[5] toward mama and toward you. I prefer, however, to excuse her on the ground that I cannot possibly know what she has gone through with, how many bitter experiences she has had which have driven her into what seems to me to be a silly interpretation of a not too wise religion at best.[6]

Mama complained to me that Una would hardly talk to her at all, and actually told mama that she would not think of allowing her (mama) to live with her (Una). I would have thought that mama certainly misunderstood her, but for the fact that Una told me practically the same thing. "Oh," she said, "I would not think of it. We have so much freedom now. We can go where we please and do what we please with nothing to interfere." I thank the Lord that what little religion I have

85

does not allow me to pass upon my actions solely upon the ground of what is pleasant and what is convenient for me. But there I go . . . it's no use even thinking such self-congratulatory thoughts.

Affectionately,

Roy[7]

[1]Horatio Trundle Craven, born 1851, Roy's mother's younger brother.
[2]After their ninth child was born, Ina's husband Mark Cowan left her and provided no child support. She managed by opening a boarding house and later a cafeteria.
[3]Lillian's note: "At 80 years of age she would hardly be expected to do household tasks. She didn't. It all fell on me and I was teaching a full load. Grandma was happy—Lillian was not."
[4]Ina ran a boarding house.
[5]Lillian's note: "Una came to my house, found me in the hospital with an operation. Insisted on Grandma's living with one of her 3 daughters after 11 years with us."
[6]Lillian's note: "Long live Christian Science!"
[7]Lillian's note at the bottom of the letter: "Bedi was ruled entirely by his mother. She favored him above his sisters." Addition: "Una offered to keep her mother near her in a C Science home for the aged but naturally Grandma would not agree."

⁂

June 10, 1927[1]

Dear Ina:

Yours written "Tuesday night," which I take to be June 7, was received this morning. I wired you as follows:

"Write mama today along line suggested yours seventh. She leaves here Tuesday. Glad to furnish money."

Just go ahead and have the room built and I will pay whatever it costs. It will not be necessary for it to be ready before September 1, as she will want to visit around until that time. Perhaps this is the best solution of the matter, although I sorely fear that it is adding too much of a burden to you.

If I could be at home all the time, I could maintain some sort of peace, although at times I have failed. Sarah has an awfully mean tongue and a frightful temper.[2] As a matter of fact, she has a good deal of her grandmother in her, as much as both of them would repudiate this suggestion. Lillian and Mary are in Waco, and will be until Tuesday, when I shall take mama, Bachman and Sarah up to get her, leaving mama with Ena on the way. That is the reason I wired you, as I wish it settled before mama goes, and I did not want to suggest the arrangement to her until she had heard directly from you. As soon as she receives your letter, I shall take the matter up with her as you suggest. I am sure it is best for mama, as the continual nagging[3] here is telling on her nerves. One cannot have good digestion, even, if he is continually in a bad humor, and the outdoor activities you suggest will have a beneficial effect. Then, too, she needs to be thrown a little more with people. You see, during school time, she is left alone in the house all day, and although she says she enjoys this part of the day most, it cannot be wholesome. People need to be taken out of themselves, except those rare individuals, philosophers, who seem to thrive in solitude.

Anyhow, we can try it for a year and if it does not work we can make some other arrangement.

When you write me, always address letters to "University Station."[4]

Affectionately,

Roy[5]

[1]Lillian's note: "I am reading Bedi's letters for the first time. He is often cruelly unfair to me, but I must remember that Grandma read his letters to Ina."
[2]Lillian's note: "Sarah had to take a lot from her grandmother who ruled the whole family with a 'rod of iron'."
[3]Lillian's note: "Grandma did all the nagging and had for eleven years."
[4]Lillian's note: "So that Lillian cannot ask to read them."
[5]Lillian's note at the end of the letter: "Bedi told me when Bachman was born, 'Honey, you will have to look out for the little girls and the dogs. Mama hates girls and can't stand dogs. She will spoil the boy to death, just the way she spoiled me. But she never could get along with her own daughters.'

"Grandma was jealous of everybody. Bedi could never kiss me or the children in her presence. *She* had to get the mail. *She* had to answer the phone and was resentful if Bedi asked for me. She planned the new house, just like the house in Eddy."

❧

James Madison Bedichek, 1911, Eddy, Texas, a schoolteacher who started the Bedichek Academy in Eddy. He was twice elected County Superintendent of Schools for Fall County, Texas. *Courtesy of Jane Derrick.*

Lucretia Ellen Craven Bedichek, who also taught in the Bedichek Academy. *Courtesy of Jane Derrick.*

Lillian Lee Greer, 1903, *Cactus* yearbook graduation picture, the University of Texas. *Courtesy of Jane Derrick.*

Lillian Greer Bedichek and Hobo, Faywood, New Mexico, 1910, on her honeymoon. *Courtesy of Jane Bedichek.*

Roy Bedichek and his sister Una Bedichek at Deming, New Mexico
c. 1913. *Courtesy Jane Bedichek and Alan Pipkin.*

Roy Bedichek, 1912, Deming, New
Mexico, at the door of *The Deming
Headlight.* Photo taken by Lillian
Greer Bedichek. Note the pencil
behind his ear and the reporter's
notebook in his top left pocket.
*Courtesy of Alan and Louise
Pipkin.*

Roy Bedichek as a young
businessman, 1918, Austin, Texas.
*Courtesy of Jane Bedichek.*

Sarah, Bachman and Mary Bedichek, 1920.
*Courtesy of Alan and Louise Pipkin.*

Bachman Bedichek in front of the house on Manor Road in Austin, where the Bedicheks lived from 1918 to 1922, before building the two-story white frame house on the opposite end of the block at 801 East 23rd Street. c. *1922.* *Courtesy of Alan and Louise Pipkin.*

Roy Bedichek with Bachman and Sarah c. 1920. *Courtesy of Alan and Louise Pipkin.*

Front seat, Lillian; back seat, Grandma Bedichek (Lucretia Ellen Craven Bedichek); Sarah and Bachman beside the car, 1923, on a drive out Manor Road, east of Austin, Texas. *Courtesy of Alan and Louise Pipkin.*

Lillian and children at Barton Springs, 1923.
*Courtesy of Alan and Louise Pipkin.*

Lillian Greer Bedichek, c. 1925.
*Courtesy of Jane Derrick.*

*July 23, 1931 to October 30, 1939*

July 23, 1931

Dear Honey[1]:

I was in a beautiful mood to write a letter when I slipped this sheet into the typewriter, but the door opened before I had put finger to keyboard and in walked a damned whining crook with his whinier, less intelligent and more voluble wife, both of them to whine and carp and complain about a penalty which we had imposed upon his school. That was an hour ago and the beautiful mood is gone.

Night owl, do you take any sleep in the daytime? If not, you will return to me a rag and a bone and a hank of hair. Operas, plays and other nocturnal entertainments and diurnal excursions, with Sunday, the day of rest, wiped off the calendar! Peace! Take a day now and then to contemplate and dream and loll about.

Your letters are read avidly—I would say, devoured—but devour connotes destruction, and they are not destroyed, but passed on to Mary, Bachman, Mama, and then by mail to circulating Sarah, who passes them on to the household in which this itinerant zoologist happens to be sojourning. So keep them coming, although I am at a loss to know how you find time to write anything except picture post cards.

I am afraid you will return to this country an anti-revolutionist! Yes, it's too bad to have good men killed as always happens in revolution, but it is too bad, also, to have good men killed and oppressed *before* the revolution. So many good men acquiesce in wrong and outrage as long as their own precious skins are safe and comfortable. I looked over a master's thesis the other day giving the history of a Brazos Bottom county. I saw photographs of five negroes hanging to one tree, their pitiful figures mutilated horribly. I read accounts of the most terrible whippings, of peonage of the worst kind, sufferings and oppression worse than the worst that the Children of Israel ever suffered in Egypt. The law is in league with oppressors and supports them in their most heinous crimes: I am in league with the law. Why do not "good" citizens like me get up and cry to heaven upon these dastardly outrages to which we are all a party? Why, in my own case, because I want to be comfortable, I want to roll and stretch in a clean soft bed when I awaken in the coolth of the morning, and I want to go down stairs and make and sip a cup of strong coffee, and then get out and mow the lawn or in other ways get up an exhilarating sweat; and then I want to go into a nice bath and dress in cool clean clothes and drive a new Ford down to the office; and because at noon I want to loll and slosh about and sunbake in Barton's and, with appetite whetted, eat a good meal after which a nap. And because I like to anticipate the return of a loving wife, and so on—because in short, I want to be comfortable. This league with robbers which I have formed supplies the comforts of life.

But suppose—just suppose—(impossible, of course) a turning of the wheel when these oppressed millions, negroes included, under intelligent though merciless leadership, got the upper hand. And in the course of the turning of the wheel incidents occur, such as pictured so pathetically in the photograph of the "good man" lying murdered with his children in the background—we would all, those who escape, be sitting mournfully around in border towns, soliciting the pity of wandering strangers and tourists with our tales of oppression. So it has ever been with revolutions and so I guess, it will ever be.

You will notice in the papers how the good, patriotic citizens of Germany (that is, the ones who have money or credit) are rapidly converting into foreign exchange their worldly possessions and getting them well-deposited in foreign banks. It's the flight of capital which precedes the flight of the owners. The other capitalistic countries are making a great "humanitarian" effort to *save* Germany, thinking of course, not once about their investments in Germany which will all go to pot if the Hitlerites or the communists get the upper hand. I don't believe they will be able to stem the tide except temporarily. But the point is that the upper classes are now providing themselves with a soft place to light.

I transmitted your message to Bachman about the mineral oil. He snarled and declared that you have a "positively superstitious reverence for that stuff." No, he hasn't taken a swallow, and I have been too nerveless to undertake the struggle necessary to get it down his goozle. But I have accomplished one dietetic masterpiece, experienced one culinary triumph. I have concocted a sandwich that he begs for, and makes an evening meal on. (I tried to stop on "for" but a preposition should not end a sentence, so I went on to "on.") I toast brown bread slowly until it is crumbly all the way through. I smear a piece with mayonnaise, thinly. Upon this, cut to fit, a leaf of crisp lettuce, upon the lettuce, thin slices of tomatoes, and upon this, little chopped pieces of crisp bacon (bait), and upon that another leaf of lettuce, and surmounting the whole, another piece of toast thinly smeared with mayonnaise. Children cry for it, and when supplied with one, proceed to eat lettuce and tomatoes. I shall have to abandon this when Sarah comes, for she will not tolerate the crunching necessary to masticate the same.

I watch mama calmly violate every every law in the dietetic code. For instance, today at the cafeteria, she ate: boiled Irish potatoes covered with greasy gravy, roast meat (beef) and gravy, a piece of strawberry pie, cup of coffee with rich cream and half a cup full of sugar. Quite a problem, I fancy, for an 82-year-old stomach to deal with.

You are like a kid off at school writing home to dad—ten pages of extra-curricular activities and a perfunctory sentence at the end: "My classes get more and more interesting." That, thinks the naive youngster, will satisfy dad.

Mary is buckling down to her studies again. She read her first assignment in logic—thirty pages of "Right Thinking," or something of the sort—the other afternoon and that night I asked her casually what it was all about. She gave me a perfect summary of the thirty pages. I looked it up later on the sly, and she didn't miss one essential point. I think I should have had to bone over it at least a day to have made such a perfect recitation. The younger generation may be going to the bow-wows, as reformers assure us, but there is certainly a small fraction of it that is not.

Well, so much for today. I've got to get to work.

Affectionately,

Bedi

[1]Editor's Note: Lillian was in Mexico City attending summer school at the National University of Mexico from June 30–August 21, 1931. She was head of the Spanish Department of Austin High School and was writing a textbook for the study of Spanish language and culture.

❦

Austin, Texas
April 12, 1932

Dear Crozier[1]:

"Still harping on me daughter!"

I have a girl of twenty this year finishing her B.A. work in the University. Her training lies in French, Latin, Physics, Biology, Chemistry, majoring in the last. She is healthy, really robust, good-looking, despite certain physical characteristics which indicate that she is in all probability genetically mine.

Besides being a Phi Beta Kappa (with a dozen free A's to spare) she is among the five best women tennis players in the University, and was ranked second in the University "form" tournament recently. She knows tennis as a sport and as an art. She could coach women's tennis admirably. She is fair in music (piano), having had a number of years under the best teachers we can find here.

You have suspected that I am looking for her a job, and (shrewd detective that you are) you have divined correctly. You are visualizing the long waiting-list of applicants, all card-catalogued from A to Z, and you are framing a reply to "Dear Bedi" telling him what he already knows, viz., that you are awfully sorry, that any other time, that you will be glad to file her application, that maybe something will turn up later, etc., etc. But spare yourself the trouble of a reply. I know all that. File her between the "bee's" and "bee" for a job in one of the grades. No teacher who has had her but will give her an enthusiastic recommendation.

Yours,

Bedi

P.S. Besides her bolsheviki cognomen with which you are familiar, she is called Mary Virginia.

R.B.

[1]Editor's Note: This letter to Crozier, a school superintendent, and the next letter to Felix Smith, San Angelo superintendent, are Bedichek's attempts to get a job for Mary Virginia in the depth of the Depression. Both attempts failed. After the rejections, the family decided that medical school was the answer.

April 17, 1932

Mr. Felix E. Smith
San Angelo, Texas

Dear Felix:

I quite realize the futility of trying to get a job for anyone, but I now have a daughter who has been assured throughout her high school and university years that a job would be forthcoming if only she applied herself and made a sufficiently good record. She has delivered; and now it is up to me. I have to make the effort although with half a heart for I know that there are no jobs.

During her high school period, she made every honor roll for four years. In the University, she has avoided the snap courses and specialized in science and language; and in spite of the difficulty of such courses and the high standards maintained here in them, she is getting her B.S. this year with Phi Beta Kappa honors and a dozen free A's to spare. She has had five years of the best instruction in French, but she has majored in Chemistry, and Schoch tells me that such a science student as she is has no business "wasting herself" teaching, but [should] go in immediately for medicine. She has physics, chemistry and biology well in hand, as her grade-sheet shows, and actually knows something to teach. She was a prize Latin student in high school and represented the Austin High School in the central Texas Latin tournament, winning the Essay event. She has had five years in Latin and did the University part of it with such distinction that Leon, the best Latinist in the South, will give her unreserved recommendation.

Being a daughter of mine I have encouraged her to build up her body and maintain her health. She is not only healthy, but robust. I can't remember when she was ever ill even for half an hour. She is among the three or four best women tennis players in the University— knows the art of tennis—takes high rank in form tournaments competently judged—is President this year of the University Racquet Club. Moreover, she is a superb swimmer and has taught swimming in girls' camps. There is hardly a stroke that she can't demonstrate with excellent form.

As to disposition, she is calm, almost imperturbable, sweet-tempered and can get along with people with a minimum of friction. This I consider her most valuable asset, but I shall not enlarge upon it.

There really ought to be somewhere a job for this girl, now twenty years old. I know that her lack of teaching experience automatically bars her, even in prosperous times, from such high schools as yours. She is willing and anxious to teach in the grades, and it has occurred to me that some far-sighted superintendents may be taking advantage of the depression to fill in the grades, whenever an opportunity offers, with young teachers of training and talent, so that later they may have a body of qualified talent to draw upon for high school and junior college work, when (if ever) the cloud of this damnable depression lifts, and competently trained teachers become harder to get. This is the only hope I have of securing a place for her now, and the only reason I am writing you about her.

I forgot to mention that she plays the piano with fair competence, but I do not consider her competent to teach music.

If there is any use of her filing a formal application with you, send me a blank, and she will fill it out and return it.

With kindest regards, I am

Yours faithfully,

Bedi

※

[Written on stationery from New Nicollet Hotel, Minneapolis, Minnesota]
May 13, 1932

Dear Honey:

Behold a man of character—strong, determined, invincible! 72 hours of discussions, papers, addresses, dinners, luncheons, gab, conversations, lobby lounging,—and still fresh as a daisy, and now retiring early leaving a call for five o'clock so that I may get out and look at a few birds before I leave here. I have controlled my belly with an iron hand—stuck to lettuce, dry toast, buttermilk. Eschewed ham, although tempted at every meal; yielded only once or twice to chicken, and not a single steak. Others taxied from this hotel to the university two miles away—I walked, except last night when encumbered in tuxedo. Am I not a strong character? Am I not master of my fate & captain of my soul?

Am going to Sioux City to the National Forensic meet tomorrow. I hardly think I shall stay through it unless it proves to be more than it promises. I am interested, of course, only in the organization of it, and I think I can get that quickly.

Much love,
Bedi

🌿

December 19, 1933

Dear Una:

The season is around again when we remember more vividly our past lives and past associations, and especially the days of childhood. Hence I am sending along this as the cheapest and perhaps the best memento. I started to write with my hand, as a more familiar and suggestive method, but alas! I have forgotten how to write: that is, to write so that anyone can read it readily. The cold machine has invaded everything, even to interposing its chilling touch between the writer and receiver of a Christmas message. You have the habit of going one step further into the machine-age and simply resorting to the telegraph on Christmas morning, but that does have the compensation of immediacy.

Dear Una, I doubt if you would even recognize your brother now if we met, say, unexpectedly, in Hong-Kong. The years take a steady, steady toll. I note when I shave (the only time I really face myself) that lines are deeper, hair a little grayer around the temples, neck-skin a little looser, eyes a little more owlish, and other little touches that time adds (or subtracts) to (or from) the physiognomy.

When I examine myself internally, however, I believe I am a little kinder, a little more tolerant, less dogmatic, riper, and certainly richer in experience than when I was fresh and blooming physically. Thus I do not feel that I have lost any major engagement, although I have been sadly discomfited in many skirmishes.

In some miraculous way, I find myself surrounded at home with three strange grown people who call me "papa." Bachman is a good inch taller than I am. I don't have to bend perceptibly to kiss either Sarah or Mary on the cheek. They are unbelievably big. Mary is mild and sweet with a curious lack of self-confidence for one of her abilities and accomplishments. Sarah and Bachman have inherited the fiery Craven[1] temper, and they have disciplined me because I have had to exercise my controls to get along with them at all, and every now and then I feel my radius rods loosening and the machine of my disposition shivering towards an embankment. But they are each possessed of fine qualities. Sarah has the keenest sense of responsibility and the most intense, sensitive and alert loyalty that I have ever known in a human being. Bachman, I believe, is as clean as a hound's tooth, but is at that difficult age when everything, even the most sacred and important things, are dismissed as "baloney," "bosh," "bull," or all something else—(whatever the latest comic section jargon is for pish and piffle.)

I wish that these kids might have been associated with you in their growing up. They all admire you and your influence would have helped them immensely.

Financially, I face an increasing budget and decreasing income, especially disquieting to a man of my age. By the way, you seem to have put a spell on that rent-house of mine. I have never had any trouble renting it since I wrote you about it seven or eight years ago. The tenant which Lillian says you supplied stayed with us until just the other day. In response to a 36-word ad, one insertion, I received 23 bona fide applications by noon, and I sat back and took my choice, a lovely family, the father a Professor of Economics in the University. This property, half a block, with my home on one end, has stood the depression better than any other residence property in Austin that I know of. My salary was cut 30 per cent. Lillian lost her job[2]; and the cost of living is rising rapidly.

So the tale is about told. Much love and Christmas cheer for you and Ned.[3]

Affectionately,

Roy

---

[1]Craven was his mother's family name.

[2]Editor's Note: The Austin School Board decided to drop any teacher who had a spouse on the state or city payroll. Lillian bitterly regretted giving up her job as

chairman of the Spanish Department and year book adviser at Austin High School.
[3]Ned Willard, Una's husband.

❧

University Hall[1]
Galveston, Texas
March 25, 1934

Dearest Dad,

I never was so glad to see anyone as I was to see you to-day. I surely wish you could have stayed longer—but business is business, I guess. You certainly made a hit here. Everyone is talking about what a charming person you are. Gee! I suppose it's time for you to make your bow.

Just after you left I went upstairs and tried to study physiology but fell asleep and was dead to the world till six o'clock. I'll have to get to work sure enough now.

Lovingly,
Mary

[1]Mary was studying at the University of Texas Medical School in Galveston.

❧

Austin, Texas,
March 27, 1934

Dear Mary:

I didn't get home until nine o'clock. Much of the trip was in face of a cold, driving rain sometimes so hard that I couldn't see down the road with any certainty above one hundred yards. Pavements were slick nearly the whole way. Bachman, on return from Houston, was in a car that turned over but no one was hurt. I passed many cars in trouble.

Found your mama and Sarah well and in fine spirits. Bachman was grouchy due to several bawlings out concerning his recent trip. He did come to Galveston, but declared he was tied up all the time.

I am instructing the Co-op[1] to send you half a dozen tennis balls. If they don't come holler.

*105*

Your note of March 25 came this morning. Glad you went to sleep. Don't pull on your reserves even to make A's. You'll need reserves for more serious affairs of life later. It would be quite natural for your friends to be polite and give me the benefit of any doubts, especially in talking with you. I hope you follow suit and say nice things about any relatives of your friends who happen to show up. Society tacitly agrees that no such lies are charged up against the person telling them. But of course if one can be sincere in his praise, so much the better.

I composed several fatherly letters to you on my homeward trip but since I couldn't operate a car and use the typewriter, they were not written. They were all along the line of the "Self-made Merchants Letters to his Son" or the more famous Chesterfield letters. Age often arrogates to itself a wisdom which it does not possess in advising the young. There is one thing I would like to rescue, however, from the composed but unwritten letters that went through my head while driving in the rain, or two things:

1. I am delighted with the beauty of your eyes. Does that sound strange from a father to his daughter? As a young man I lied to so many girls about their eyes that I hesitate to try to tell the truth about eyes. Eyes are one thing the mirror lies about. No one knows, therefore, what his eyes look like except while he is in that unnatural state of mind he is always in when he looks in the mirror. The thing about eyes is that they change with every passing emotion or with the entertainment of different thoughts. Changes are so subtle that the mirror does not or could not catch them even if they occurred or could occur while looking in the mirror. The eye is the light of the soul. You may dissect ten thousand eyes and you will never find this light. You might dissect a radio and never find the sound. The only instrument delicate enough to appraise the light of the eye is another eye, and the other eye must be especially trained to do this. So when I see your clear brilliant eyes only so of course under certain conditions of thought or emotion I, as a father, am greatly gratified for I see in them good thoughts and wholesome emotions. Now don't run to the glass and try to see what I see, for you will only find an electric globe with the current off. So much for eyes.

2. You have unfortunately been filled with fears all your young life. Your mother received hers from negro nurses, and your grandmother, Mama Jennie, got hers from the same source. They are afraid

of too many things; and your grandmother Bedichek had some phobias which she transmitted to you in your young and tender years. Of course, all of these three individuals transmitted to you many things that are fine and helped to form your character in most wholesome ways, but in this one thing of "being afraid" their influence in my opinion is wholly bad. The only way to get rid of fears and realize their stupidity and irrationality is to know their source and this is why I am revealing their source to you. "Don't cross the street, you might get run over." "Don't walk down by the stadium, somebody might get you," "don't _____, _____": fill the blanks in with any one of a thousand don'ts and any one of a thousand catastrophes. That is the formula. Begin with a don't and end with a threat. That finally creates a "don't—threat" complex and just here is where it paralyzes effort, paralyzes initiative, paralyzes the adventurous impulses, inhibits thought, and so on. 99 out of 100 people are filled with this stuff from their childhood, and they can remedy it only by realizing how these prohibitions, once very logical in keeping a child from being run over, say, built up a fear-complex.

This is the reason why courage-literature is so popular. It is the antidote which we use against irrational training in early years. Tennyson wrote a long poem one time (I can't remember its name) in which he figured a knight charging terrible looking things which turned out when he struck them to be entirely harmless. If one entertains fears, he will have no time for anything else and no ability to face realities. Nearly all religions preach courage. How often do Christians in the last extremities "place their trust in God," which is just another device for quieting fear. And it works. But a rational person does better, in my opinion, to simply refuse to entertain fears, and trust himself.

These paragraphs and many more I composed during the dreary drive.

Affectionately,
Daddy

---

[1]The student co-operative book store at the University of Texas. Editor's Note: Roy Bedichek wanted the exercise of tennis to balance out her strenuous studying.

❦

304 Fulton Street,
Denton, Texas,[1]
June 5, 1934

Dear Sarah:

Your letter relieved my mind on two points: Bachman and the dogs. Mary and Bachman had gone off to play tennis when I left home, and every now and then an uneasiness would take possession of me which upon analysis proved to be caused by some sort of subliminal fear that one of those old time fusses would develop on the court and Mary return in tears and Bachman swelled up to the bursting point.

My other uneasiness was caused by the vision of Lucy (especially Lucy) and the Pop[2] in a dog-wagon—

>Is there, in human form, that bears a heart,
>    A wretch, a villain! lost to love and truth!
>That can with studied, sly, ensnaring art
>    Betray sweet Jenny's unsuspecting youth?

I fear there is, and I am glad to have the protecting arm of the City Government thrown around her. When I revise Dante's *Inferno*, I shall make an especially disagreeable place for dog-catchers.

Two mornings I have reconnoitered the northward environs of this town to see what birds there may be. I have found two vireos and am not certain about either of them. One is, I think the Bell's, but I have no bird book; the other I keep trying to call the Warbling, but again I am not sure. Robins are nesting all over this town. It is curious, I didn't see a one in Dallas or in Ft. Worth. There are chickadees and titmice in the postoaks, cuckoos, fieldlarks, dickcissels, mockingbirds, red-birds, and the usual horde of non-descript sparrows that we find around Austin. A green heron seems to be nesting down in a swag where there are little dirty pools strewn along with considerable underbrush, reeds and tall weeds.

The most surprising statement in your interesting letter is the intimation that Mary is to teach you tennis. If you go at this game with your usual determination it will do more for you than anything else you have ever undertaken. Like Walt Whitman I like "fierce and athletic girls." You are already fierce enough, but not quite as athletic as I should like you to be. Your arms need developing and your shoulders. Get Mary to give you some exercises for this.

So far I see that I have gone to birds, dogs, and physical exercises. You are expecting me to discourse now on vegetable diet, to cuss out motion picture shows and radios, and wind up with some fatherly advice about taking plenty of sleep. Other matters, however, are pressing upon my attention. I find that I am to be switched from English Literature to American. All my reading of the last few months thus goes for naught so far as preparation for the summer work is concerned. I must now bone up on Cotton and Increase Mather, Jonathan Edwards and other dreary and futile compositions which make up what the selection collectors insist is early American literature. I find that one collector has inserted a selection of Henry George and with this as a basis or an excuse I shall probably give my poor students a headachy course in the Single Tax. After all, one has to teach what he knows, and I probably know Henry George better than I know any other American prose writer.

Tell your mama I think she is doing well to back out of an education course this summer. She can take one as well in the long session if she wants to, and it will be better given and certainly in pleasanter weather.

Hoping that the family is profiting by the advice given in the article "The Organs of Indigestion," I am

Affectionately yours,

Daddy

[1]Bedichek was teaching summer courses at North Texas Normal School (now the University of North Texas).
[2]Lucy was Mary's dog and Pop was Sarah's dog.

❧

July 2, 1934
Denton, Texas,
304 Fulton Street

Dear Honey:

Sparrows, dried bermuda, hackberry trees: this is my summer. A philosopher might make much of these, but I'm not a philosopher. I am anxious to get away and back home. I can't just determine as yet the hour of my departure. My last class is 3–4:30 P.M. Saturday, July 14. Grades must be made out, however, and reported. How long this will take I do not know. It may be the following Monday morning before I can get away and hence Monday afternoon, the 16th, before I arrive in Austin. I shall make every effort, however, to get away on Sunday.

It was a mistake for me to attempt this business, but one never knows anything until he finds out by experience. The time is too short and the duties too numerous to do anything well. One is therefore under the constant uneasiness of neglecting something he ought to be doing. A kind of sub-conscious worry eats on him day and night, especially night.

Worried am I also about Bachman. What chance in the world does he have if he is going to begin his university work on a low C average? I greatly fear that he is too much like his father. But Epictetus advises us not to consider anything that is out of our power to remedy, and this matter belongs in that category. I am also concerned about Sarah and dislike to think of her sweating it out this summer in the physics laboratory. But that also is a matter not in the power of my own will, so, Epictetus, I let that go too. Indeed, most things we worry about lie beyond the province of our wills, and if Epictetus would only tell us how to will these things out of our consciousness I would read that chapter with great interest.

You will note that I bravely started out to write to the whole family, but I was far too ambitious. It just can't be done on this Corona. If I had Miss McCoy[1] here to operate it, I might be able to furnish the dictation, for I do think of things all the time that I want to communicate, not that they are worth communication, but seem at the moment worth a few lines.

There are compensations for the inconveniences of this midsummer's madness of mine. After thirty years divorcement from a student's boarding house, I am in it again, but not of it. Thirty years make a powerful lot of difference, not in the scenes (they are the same as ever) but in your point of view. There is the same ganging up in the dirty lobby before meals, the same banging on the old rattle-trap piano in a room off the lobby, the same pre-prandial impatience, the same old jokes and joshing, the same human types, the same landlady, patient, fat, worried, and the same landlady's daughter with sheep's eyes for some of the likely young fellows: indeed, what is there that is not the same? Except me, and of course, that makes all the difference.

Then here is a class of youngsters reading English classics, or trying to. I run across some thought wonderfully expressed and I feel the thrill of communication, but alas! How many years and how much experience will this class of youngsters have to have before they could possibly get an inkling of what is meant, and my ardor cools. But there is much, also, that they can understand. Some things they understand better than I do. And this experience is worth something.

Then the matter of a rigid routine. I haven't had one for years. Days punctuated by inevitable bells! I am getting to know that and my sympathy reaches you and forty thousand other teachers whose days are paced by periods and whose time is chopped up for them into mathematically even allotments.

And there is the lonesomeness of bachelorhood, which is quite wholesome for a married or family man to experience. One little division of a house to occupy, from which to emerge in any except one direction is to trespass—cabin'd, cribbed, confined. To feel oneself a stranger is also helpful. Walk the streets for an hour and see no one you know, and the next day the same, and the next, the same. It is a sharp corrective for egotism. You begin to feel that the world would likely go on about the same without you. The Roman's or Greek's fear of exile becomes understandable.

But six weeks is enough. I can survive and be well without a longer lesson, and so I'll be see'n you!

Bedi

P.S. Do you need money or can you make out until I get back?
R.B.

---

[1]Editor's Note: His second secretary in the Interscholastic League office. He sometimes had 200 letters in one day's mail to respond to.

❦

Denton, Texas,
304 Fulton Street,
July 8, 1934

Dear Honey:

This is probably my last letter from this address, for the week ahead promises to be taken up completely with examination papers, reports, packing, etc. I intend to bend every effort to get away on a night train Saturday, but I am not sure that I can make it. If not, then the next morning.

I have nibbled the cookies and given some to my landlady who praises them highly. But for the fact that abstemiousness is the better part of appetite, I should have eaten the whole box at one or two sittings. I have made of them linked sweetness long drawn out.[1]

Tell Sarah I took thirty on a bird-hike this morning with one pair of glasses. You may imagine how many birds kindly waited until all thirty got a look through the glasses! Some of them were very accommodating, however. They were all greatly interested, and I gathered them together in a bed of an old creek and talked to them at some length about birds.

Mary's industriousness does not surprise me at all. She usually does what she sets out to do. Congratulate Bachman for me on his B in English and tell him I hourly await that letter.

Hope the drouth has not cut the watermelon crop for I have been looking forward to watermelons. If they are high, though, we shall have to refrain except on rare occasions. I have two dining-out engagements ahead of me, and in one of them there was an intimation in the invitation of watermelon. I don't look forward with any pleasure to paying for old man Patterson's[2] hauling water to his peach orchard. I wonder how the orchard on nineteenth street is faring.

A girl passed out at the close of one of my classes yesterday. The fact that it was unbelievably hot is rebuttal for your immediate accusation that I talked her into insensibility. She was resuscitated in about ten minutes. I fanned her with my hat with much the same vigor as you have seen me use in trying to start a camp fire with wet kindling.

It seems to me that I have been gone from home at least six months. I can hardly visualize the domicile and its environs. The office has completely gone to the devil in spite of Miss Thompson's heroic efforts. More and hotter work, I fear, through latter July and August.

Much love,
Bedi

P.S. Talk at once with Mathews, Registrar,[3] about the house. He often has requests for houses from summer school students coming in the last term of summer school and expecting to spend the year. Its not being furnished will prevent its renting to majority of these, however. Whatever you do, don't rent it to delinquent.

[1]From John Milton's *L'Allegro*.
[2]A man who sold fruit (not to be confused with professor of the same name).
[3]Mathews was the registrar at the University of Texas.

❦

[No date]
304 Fulton Street,
Denton, Texas

Dear Mary:

All of you except Bachman are doing your part in writing me letters. Tell him I am daily expecting a long letter from him. I can't write to each and every one, so this letter will have to serve the whole family until I get a little more leisure.

Had a fine letter from your mama which I enjoyed greatly. Read it several times in order to get all the nuances. Your mama is strong on nuances.

I seem to bore my classes no more than the average prof does. Occasionally I actually see signs of interest—in spots. My social life so far has been entirely solitary. This morning I walked far out into the country with my field-glasses looking for birds. There's no great variety. Orchard orioles, scissor-tails, meadow larks, grackles, crows, mockingbirds, Texas king-birds seem to make up the list. I worked about two hours this morning trying to find a vireo's nest, but the little fellows were too smart for me. I noticed them carrying food to a stretch of hackberries along a creek, and I know the nest is there. But when I seated myself in one part of the thicket, they would come and fuss around me and then when I went to another, they would do the same and as long as I was in the thicket, they did no feeding. I stalked a pair of red-wings for some time trying to locate their nest, but to no avail. As a naturalist, I make a poor showing.

I'm tempted to send you an old shirt for Lucy to smell so that she wont forget my BO. Being a female, I have no confidence whatever in her fidelity. The foregoing sentence is a good example of a dangling participle. Note that it is only because you know the writer that you know whether it is Lucy or me that is female. Don't ever dangle *your* participial phrases.

Please describe to me in detail the first family fuss that develops. Give me, first, the cause, if any. Then show the line of its development. Introduce the characters, showing how each member was drawn into the fray, and the angle from which he or she entered. Finally, indicate the upshot or denouement. This will relieve a certain feeling of nostalgia that I find creeping on me at times.

You and your mama are doubtless making a great team—brains and brawn in proper cooperation can accomplish wonders. In making the above remark, I aint namin' no names.

Before I forget it, I disown any originality in the suggestion for keeping Lucy constant. I get it from the *Confessions of Rousseau*. He kept the undershirt of his mistress handy to take a whiff of every now and then, and the odor, he declares, brought tears of tenderest emotion gushing from his eyes. Now if only Lucy would weep over an old shirt of mine. I would always consider it the pinnacle of my career as a wooer of dogs. I hope that Sarah doesn't feel hurt that all my talk is of Lucy. Assure her that I haven't forgotten Pop—especially in "the first sweet sleep of night."[1]

There is a neighborhood feud raging in the environs of 304 Fulton Street over cats. One family insists on keeping six. The family across the street lost mysteriously twenty-five of their 27 chickens. A cat was caught devouring the 26th. This was 26 too much, and the man of the family forthwith killed the cat. Funeral with much ceremony occurred across the street. Women discussed the tragedy across their respective back-fences. My only landlady, good soul, found one of her goldfish dead by the side of her pool, its side gnawed away by felonious teeth. Suspicion points his skinny and accusing finger at the five remaining cats. I try to be neutral, that is, to one side I praise cats, and to the other side I praise chickens and goldfish. But my oil on the troubled waters instead of quieting ignites spontaneously.

Well, continue your letters, and tell Mama, Sarah and Bachman to write me and by the end of the First Term, we shall have the family

saga duly recorded.
    Much love,
    Daddy

[1]Percy Bysshe Shelley, *The Indian Serenade*. Editor's Note: Roy Bedichek later wrote a book on odors, *The Sense of Smell*, published by Doubleday in 1960.

Denton, Texas,
304 Fulton Street,
July 9, 1934

Dear Bachman:

I am pinning a dollar to this sheet for you to buy tennis balls with. You will note that I am adopting newspaper style in writing to you, that is telling you the most interesting and sensational thing in the first line. You will doubtless experience a falling of interest until the close.

I have no stationery left and am forced to the extremity of using some scratch-paper which I bummed from the mimeograph bureau up at the College. This makes this communication appear sloppier than it is.

You surprise and pain me greatly concerning your attitude towards study. Please read Bacon's Essay entitled "Of Studies." You will find therein that one of the wisest men believes that studies are for delight, ornament and ability; and that crafty men contemn studies, simple men admire them, and wise men use them. I shall have to believe, then, that you are "crafty," since you contemn them so vigorously, whereas I had hoped you were of the wise who would use them. You will find in this essay, also, that some books are to be tasted, some swallowed whole, some merely sampled and others read with diligence and attention. Cellini is to be swallowed, not merely tasted and that in its worst spots. You will find also that reading maketh the full man, conference (or conversation) the ready man, and writing the exact man; and other sage advice.

I am glad you are having a good time socially, barring a little inconvenience now and then with transportation facilities. During your swimming operations, I wish you would learn the Red Cross life saving tests. That will give you a job in some camp sometime or in recreational work. The boy here at this place was being considered for a good job in a camp, but could not be taken because he didn't know the life-saving tests. Learn, also, as many different strokes as you can and qualify as an expert swimmer. Your tennis along with swimming makes a good combination. Bird-study falls in with this kind of thing nicely, and we'll try to get some of that in when I get home.

What of Marlowe are you reading? Do you mean Christopher Marlowe? If so, I very much approve this excursion into the classics. I always like *Tamburlaine* and *Dr. Faustus*, and Ben Jonson used a very happy phrase when he referred to Marlowe's mighty line, for indeed, it is mighty. But there is in Marlowe somewhat of the "gong and cymball's din." It's a little noisy.

Now as to living with women, a great wit has said "you can't live with them and you can't live without them." So just put that in your pipe and smoke it. It becomes increasingly a just remark the longer one lives. Why, if you are so set agin women, do you read de Maupassant. He associates one with women from page 1 to finis.

Don't get the idea that any one needs dissipation. One needs relaxation and recreation, but not dissipation. You are in that golden time of life now, and don't waste or squander it. Build up your physique, nerve power, controls, and increase your information against the time when you will sorely need them all. Buckle down and buck up, "scorn delights and live laborious days."[1] Don't dissipate.

I am fighting this typewriter against the time when I have to don a coat (think of it!) and go out to a dinner, and the fatal time approaches: six o'clock and it's now five. And I have to shave: just thought of that. Well, well, I'm glad to have gotten your good letter, and though you may not enjoy this one, it is sugar-coated with the enclosure.

Much love,
Dad.

[1]John Milton's *Lycidas*.

❦

University Hall
Galveston, Texas
July 9, 1935

Dear Bedi:

The fountain-pen is Bachman's, not mine. I gave it to him when he entered the University. I'll bring it back with me. I'm sorry I couldn't get word to you sooner.

I don't mean to cast any slurs on your cooking, but don't you think that cooking is quite a responsibility? And the weather is hot and you have a lot of other work to do, too.

How is Grandma feeling these days? I am actually feeling much better than I did in Austin. The extra exercise I have been taking has done wonders for me.

I only hope Mary doesn't work herself to death.[1] She is really getting a wonderful experience but a little of it goes a long way with me. I talked about half an hour with a lady from Ft. Worth who nursed a paralytic son thirteen years, buried him on Saturday and went raving mad the following Monday. I felt so depressed afterward that I almost doubted my own sanity. And the thoughts of poor little Mary working all day long and part of the night in that house of nuts nearly made me cry. There must be a baker's dozen of the mentally ill, men and women, in that house. There are three medical students (including Mary), Mrs. Myers, her sister and brother-in-law (and several negro maids and one negro man during the day). Mary went to bed last night at eleven and was wakened at four this morning and has worked *all day long*. I don't see how she stands it. And she is cheerful and happy.

Well, I'll shut up—

Worlds of love,

Lillian

P.S. I seem to be getting my mail at University Hall after all.

[1]Editor's Note: Mary Bedichek was in her second year of medical school at the University of Texas at Galveston.

❦

Austin, Texas[1]
July 10, 1935

Dear Lillian:

I am forwarding in the envelope in which it came a letter which comes, I take it, from your Illinois patient. Perhaps you and Mary have had enough practice now to be able to diagnose this case.

Am through with first term classes today; Examination Saturday; Grades in Monday; Registration second term Tuesday; Classes second term Wednesday. Hope I am as lucky in picking up an assistant in the second term as I was in the first. Mrs. Imle is nothing short of an academic daisy.

Bachman is due today, but at present writing (3 P.M.) he has not put in an appearance.

Don't worry about Mary or Mary's work. Remember you haven't had the preliminary training for this sort of thing. She has been trained to take a detached attitude. They are so much *material* to her on which to practice and this material was made without her knowledge or consent or any responsibility. Her creative ability is employed to make something, if possible, out of what is handed to her. This is an attitude of mind that we can't get, of course; but it's the only attitude possible for a physician. The people whom society sets aside to take care of the afflicted have to be made of sound stuff, and they ought to be awarded at least as many medals as the war people who inflict so many wounds and leave them for this other group to take care of.

If the woman who went crazy after nursing her afflicted child for years had studied with understanding and made a habit of practicing the simple lessons contained in that Bennett volume which I sent you, she would have had no collapse. "All the water of the seven seas can't sink a ship unless some of it gets inside." It's a person's business to keep up his mental defenses shipshape; keep the gaskets of the crankcase tight and dust-proof.

Mama potters about quite contendedly. Nothing from Sarah this week. Meta rang up a while ago and inquired after her. She has apparently written no one in the biology department since she left Austin. So much the better, for it's a sign she is getting a good rest from it all. I think she has written Patterson. At least I told her to in no uncertain terms.

If you get this before Friday night, be sure and watch Antares come out from under the moon at 8:44 P.M. Wish you had a good pair of field glasses. This famous star goes under the moon while it is still light and hence cannot be seen with the naked eye, but if it is a clear night you can see it come out. This happens only once in a great while. Emerson said that if the stars appeared only once in a thousand years, most people would stay up all night looking at them. We attach so much importance to the unusual.

I am getting a lot of good stuff for the declamation bulletin. I make the cuttings and send them to Barker in Colorado for the historical notes. Looks as if we shall go to press about September 1.

Guess I shall have to get to work right away on my lecture course for the second term. I had the good sense to get a fine descriptive bibliography prepared by my last summer's class: more than a hundred citations. So I'll make 'em do a lot of reading. Then there's the eternal spelling list and the Constitution and Rules, and so on.

It has gotten to be really Barton Springs weather, but I haven't a bathing suit. Bachman lost his on his trip to Galveston and he took mine to Port Aransas with him. He'll be back today, however, and if need be I'll buy him another suit.

Did you notice that the Italians are shipping vast quantities of chemicals to Ethiopia to strew in the paths of the barefooted Ethiopians for the purpose of burning off the skin and flesh of their feet? Since this is a sort of religious war, I suppose the souls of the Ethiopians will be in better shape after their soles are burnt off.

Much love for you and Mary. Tell Mary that I am depending on you to keep her advised of my welfare and conduct.

Bedi

[1]Lillian's note: Mary was attending the skin clinic during most of the day and working in Dr. Titus Harris' Convalescent Home for Mental Patients at night. I went down to see how she was faring and ended up working there myself for two weeks.

❦

P. O. Box 1930
University Station
Austin, Texas
August (after 7) 1935

Dear Bachman:

I have read with great interest your letter to your mother, and enjoyed especially some of your wisecracks. A recruit into any established organization, civil or military, is always subjected to certain inconveniences and irritations.[1] I remember well my experience as a cub-reporter on several newspapers. The older reporters had the same unreasonable privileges which you mention. An old reporter could get drunk and not be fired. If a cub-reporter didn't show up exactly on the stroke of the clock, he always found someone else on his job. This was irksome to the cub-reporters, but really there is a rough sort of justice in it, since a group of which one becomes a member naturally wants to try him out by various devices and find whether or not he's a good fellow. They put unusual stress on him instinctively to see whether he bends gracefully or not.

I will leave the auto accident to other members of the family. Suffice it to say that I was driving south on Red River about dusk Saturday afternoon, and a wretch came down the twelfth street hill from the east and struck the rear wheel of my car and turned us over on our side. I fell on Mama Jenny and in the melee she suffered two breaks in her collar bone and bruises on the hip and side. She is in bed and will continue there for at least a month.

Sarah was in the back seat and came out with only one scratch, and outside of getting my neck popped pretty hard, I was not hurt. Neck still a little stiff.

I should like mighty well to have your schedule: what do you do in a single typical day from the time you get out of bed until you go back to bed?

I sent your tennis racquet on August 7, and it should have reached you by this time. I sent you also a University Directory from which you may obtain all the addresses for which you ask your mother. I'll mail you today a telephone directory for out-in-town folk.

Since writing you the other day about your ten-day leave Christmas, you might prefer to go to New York and look that little burg over before rather than spend so much time travelling home and back. The theaters and Grand Opera will be going full blast there at that time. But there's plenty of time to consider that matter.

I trust you will become a real "cosmopolite," which consists mainly in a sympathetic understanding of points of view of people all over the country and all over the world. "There's a reason" for every widely-held human belief or prejudice, and the liberal mind studies prejudices and beliefs with this taken as axiomatic. I recall the time in London when I was invited to take part in a doubles tennis match, mixed, and found to my consternation that "mixed" included not only sex but race.

I was paired with a chocolate quadroon, with whom we had tea later. She was a Mrs. Taylor, the wife of an English army officer, third son of some earl or other. The explanation is that race segregation is not necessary to preserve the "purity" of a given race, when the race to be avoided is numerically insignificant. Fill England with negroes half and half, and very quickly our down-south prejudices would assert themselves, especially if the negro half were far down in the economic scale. The aristocratic prejudice is so strong in England that George Bernard Shaw told a public meeting during the war when the anti-German feeling was at its height (Germans were all fiends incarnate, chopping off hands and feet of little children in conquered territory)—Shaw told this meeting that there was not a single upper-class German-baiter in the audience who would not prefer a German count for his daughter's husband to the English brick-layer. And of course he spoke the truth. So, we all have our prejudices, and curiously enough "there's a reason" back of every popular prejudice. But that's not saying, of course, that there is a present justifiable reason in all cases. Texas was a great ku-klux state.

I am anxious for you to take to the physical part of the training with a good will. You need it. So stay in there and pitch, for a distinguished physique and bearing is a prize that is worth all it costs.

Sarah has returned sunned and strong from her "military" camp, and she is going to work at her flies with great enthusiasm.

Perhaps this is a longer letter than you have time to read.

Much love,

Dad

[1] Editor's Note: After his freshman year at the University of Texas (in which he was part of a dispute over fraternity hazing), Bachman received appointment to the U.S. Naval Academy from Senator Tom Connally who grew up in Eddy near the Bedicheks.

⚜

8 November 1935

Dear Father,

At last I have an instructor who appreciates my writing. My new English instructor likes my themes. Also I received a bouquet from an unexpected source. Each Sunday night, the plebes at my table have to put on a play. Just a short skit, but our hides depend upon it. As I am the only plebe there that has any initiative or imagination, *I* write the plays and teach the dummies their parts. This afternoon a first classman came around and said that he was the director of the annual musical show, and that he had heard of my plays and wanted me to write for the show. He further explained that he could not contact anyone who had any imagination or who could write dialogue. He said that furthermore, when I had some ideas outlined, he would call the heads of the various clubs that assist in the show (orchestra, glee club, etc.) and let me explain the thing to them. This is all very flattering to me, a mere plebe. However, the thing appeals to me very much, as it is the very kind of thing I have longed to do. Write a play. Of course, this won't be a real play, but I will have a fine chance to write some good dialogue. Consequently I am already at work on it, and intend to put some real effort into it. They must be pretty hard up for brains if they have to call on a plebe. The director says that all of last year's writing talent graduated, and that it was a rather thankless job anyway, so consequently it was rather difficult for him to get any help. At any event, I am going to put all I have into making a good job of it. At least it will bring me into a more favorable contact with the upper classes, which will be a big help.

In regard to remarks about Christmas, I favor the New York trip. Stark Robertson[1] says that he will be there, and together we should have a good time. Also I have accepted an invitation from Mother's cousin to spend the first day of leave in Washington. From thence I will go to New York. I can drop up to West Point and see Dick[2] (unfortunately he doesn't get a leave). That will leave me about seven or eight days in New York. In that time I can see an opera, a couple of good plays, a ballet, and a good many of the sights.

At this point I must close, as it is near taps.

Your son,

Bach

[1]Editor's Note: Stark Robertson and Bach were on the Austin High School tennis team and close friends; his uncle Stark Young, novelist, had taught at the University of Texas and was at this time a theater critic in New York.

[2]Editor's Note: Dick Negley was from San Antonio, and a close friend. He and Bach exchanged West Point/Annapolis cuff links the Christmas that Bach spent at West Point. Negley graduated from West Point and was sent as a young officer to the Philippines. He was taken prisoner of war by the Japanese and died on the Death March.

Austin, Texas
P. O. Box 1930, Univ. Sta.
November 12, 1935

Dear Bach:

Your 8 Nov. letter gives me a great excess of parental pride. It seems to me that you are doing famously. Your forty push-ups have me quite pushed off the map. In spite of my well-known weakness for magnifying the achievements of my youth (a failing shared by all the aging) I can't claim to have ever been able to push up more than a dozen or fifteen times, or chin a bar more than nine times. Nor do I remember ever having seen one of my generation able to push up forty times. All fathers try to make out that they were hard to beat at anything in their youth, ladies, athletics, or any other of the glamorous things which youth sets such store by. But I shall have to give up. And fencing! How I wish I might brag about a wrist of steel at 21. But alas, my wrist was mere pine or dogwood at the best.

But boy, I could turn a nice sonnet or a graceful villanelle before I was out of my teens, and now you even threaten my supremacy in this field. I'm not surprised that the dialogue-writers are scarce. It's a genuine gift to be able to turn out good dialogue. Crisp dialogue, where one speaker picks up the thought or a fanciful conceit just at the right point and carries it on just far enough, and then with a sort of triple pass it goes on to another—that is a real art. And speaking in character: that taxes the wit—gives it a thorough workout.

I have noticed this about writing. Ideas come at the most unexpected moments. They come from nowhere. The pollen-laden intellectual breeze happens to direct a particle of its dust against the moist viscous surface of a mental stigma, and behold by magic an idea germinates. Now this idea has to be nourished and worked over. Here's where industry counts. It was from some terrible toil in fashioning an idea that Milton exclaimed

"Alas, what boots it with incessant care," etc. Incessant care, that's the secret when one once has an idea to work on.

Practically, it is well to keep a piece of note-paper about and a short stubby pencil—the stubbier the better. When an idea comes, or a turn of expression, or you hear a picturesque turn given to slang, jot it down. Then at your leisure, copy it into a notebook for future reference. You'll find that when genius refuses to burn, you can turn through your notebook at random and catch onto an expression or description of a situation that will start genius burning again. These promptings, or ticklers, are kept by practically all literary men.

But the finest thing to keep one's mind open to pleasing suggestions is to banish care and worry and ill-feelings of every kind. One must give one's mind a chance to function and it simply won't if it is cluttered up with every kind of useless and heavy lumber.

All this suggests to me that you might submit some of your material to the Annual. I have looked over a couple of issues of the *Academy Log* and must say that it needs lightening up a bit. With your genius for picking up slang, you ought to be able to do some quite clever things with the slang there. It strikes me as a quite workable medium.

As to, regarding, in regard to, or simply *in re* the Christmas vacation, you have outlined a very satisfactory program. You will get a peep at the big world, you damned provincial. Study the offerings in the *N. Y. Times*, which I suppose you are getting, although you have not mentioned it. List them and make out a schedule. But don't be quite like a Texas small town merchant and visit New York for a week without spending some time in the American Museum of Natural History, which is the greatest single educational institution in this country. Keep your head clear by refusing to gorge, or drink, or smoke or do any of those silly and conventional things. Bowels open, mouth closed, feet warm and head cool: that's the secret of a happy outing.

By the way, since you will be with Stark Robertson, most likely you will meet his uncle Stark Young. I shall send you a copy of Stark Young's novel so you may read it. Literary men like to meet people who have read their books. He is one of the editors of the *New Republic*, and writes charming things of the *belles lettres* sort. He's a specialist in Italian literature, and altogether a charming man. I hope you do get to see him.

If you should happen to get into any trouble in New York, which I do not at all anticipate, call Dan Williams,[1] editorial writer on the *World-Telegram* and he will get you out.

Well, I have no time to be writing this long letter to you or to anybody else. I have forty short letters to write that have been waiting for me three days.

Yours,

Dad

[1]Editor's Note: Dan Williams had been a cub reporter on the *San Antonio Express* 1916–17 when Roy Bedichek was city editor there. They exchanged story ideas and critiqued each other's writing in the following decades.

❧

Austin, Texas
November 19, 1935

Dear Bach:

For one with little practice, I think you do it quite casually and in approved one-to-indulgent-dad form. Enclosed is the two bucks.

Each knocking letter I get from you rather disposes me to look with favor upon the educational system there. For instance, herein you mention rowing. I didn't know before that you rowed. You are becoming a real sea-dog, rowing, sailing, swimming. Contrast the amphibian with the land animal, of which I am a pitiable example. Doubtless before you get through with it you will be able to fly an airplane. Then you will be able to live in three dimensions, sure enough. What glorious freedom. What an amplification of what God really intended us to be—a sort of creeping thing, weaker than the big cats, slower than the wolf, a mere longing gazer at the birds. O what a piece of work is man![1] or at least, what a piece of work he is coming to be. I wish you were a good rider, but I guess that's expecting or wishing too much. I don't suppose the Academy has a polo team.

The only hazing I ever underwent is the mild type of the cow camp. They have a way of hazing the tenderfoot there, principally with practical jokes. Of course, certain deadly sins, such as breaking wind during lunch, is punished with a severe strapping. In all settled groups which receive accessions now and then, we have some form of hazing. Most of it seems to me utterly senseless, and some of it really cruel. But man is built that way, and what can't be cured must be endured. From what you tell me of the hazing there, there is at least some method in it. Why don't you keep good systematic notes on hazing for writing up in the future sometime? You have a great opportunity to get really firsthand information. Capitalize your experiences. Set down and sketch articles you mean to write. Capture impressions while they are fresh. That's the secret of many a man's success in literature. I am keeping your letters, and in future years, I daresay you will read them with great interest and you will be able to get many suggestions from them. You may use me as a note-book or note-repository, if you wish. I'll keep 'em in my steel file letter case until you want them. I would give a great deal now for the letters I wrote when I was your age.

Remember, also, that you are getting something out of this experience. Fencing, tennis, rowing, sailing, swimming, shooting: where would you have the opportunity of learning these valuable skills outside some such institution as the Academy, and where else could that wonderful body of yours be really whipped into shape? I don't have any fears about your mind. You have as good judgment, and as good technique for acquiring information as the average man of 25, or better. As soon as you develop the ability to control your emotional balance you'll make a splendid academic record. Stay in there and pitch. You are getting invaluable experience. An unpleasant situation often is rendered less so by adopting an objective attitude towards it. Consider it a sort of laboratory. Study it objectively, as the scientist who starved for forty-two days just to be able to experience firsthand the sensation of starving and to note carefully physical and mental reactions. And it's a short time to Christmas, and then but a short hop to June.

"And this, above all things, to thine own self be true."[2]

I have bought a copy of Stark Young's novel, *So Red the Rose*, but hesitate to send it. Perhaps you would not have time to read it, even hurriedly. It's long—430 pages—and tedious in places. It describes however, the life of some of your ancestors, those of your mother's side of the house, and those of my mother. The antebellum South, also the South during the Civil War.

I note a terrible storm in the east. Have you felt the effects of it in your snug little harbor?

All of us are well. Enclosed are a few more stamped and addressed envelopes.

Dad

[1]*Hamlet*, II, ii.
[2]Paraphrasing of *Hamlet*, I, iii.

Austin, Texas
November (no December) 1, 1935

My dear boy:

The thought that I might have a letter from you disturbed my slumber about 4 A.M. this morning and caused me about 5 A.M. to arise, brew my coffee, squeeze out the juice of four Texas oranges, absorb the same and come on down here from which place I have been absent these last four days. You see, I went to the Teachers convention in San Antonio Wednesday and returned about 11 last night, going straight home without stopping (as usual) at the office to look over my mail. I found that your mother had not had a letter from you when she and Sarah returned from a picture show about 11:15. Then I went to sleep with the thought that a letter might have come to the office in my absence. This thought gestated in my subconsciousness during my slumber and arose to the surface at 5 A.M., as above stated and with the above stated result.

Sure enough, on top of a huge stack of mail, Miss Thompson[1] had placed your letter, knowing that it would be of more interest to me than any other. She is a most thoughtful secretary.

If the impositions of upperclassmen on the plebes are proportioned in severity to the decisiveness with which the Navy is defeated by the Army, then you and your compadres must be catching hell. The account of the game which I read, however, gives the Army little comfort. The ability to come back under a terrific handicap and make it a fight to the everlasting finish arouses my own enthusiasm to a much greater pitch than does any spectacular burst of speed while the game is young. You recall that you declaimed Kipling's "If" when you were a freshman in high school. Can you recall it now? It seems to me that the honors according to Kipling's definition of manhood must go to the Navy. This is especially true if the incident of foul play described in the press accounts attributed to an Army player be true, and if the Navy did not retaliate in kind. Practice of the control of temper under the most provocative situations I consider the prime value of football as we play it. Of course, this does not appeal to the ordinary fan, but you know that I am no ordinary fan, having had to study the smooth as well as the seamy side of football for twenty years, as a professional man must study his subject.

Speaking of the control of temper, I am delighted with what you tell me concerning your own experience. I am really proud of you. If, by the time you are 21, you learn this one art—I call it an art and I think it is—of restraining any exhibition of anger, you will master an enemy that I have been unable to conquer in nearly sixty years.

The fact that you are in the Academy threatens to pervert my morals in this way: Every rotten picture show which comes along with an Annapolis background I feel that I must see in order to catch a photographic glimpse of your environment. I went to see that damned flat-faced crooner Dick Powell in *Shipmates Forever* just to get a close-up of Bancroft Hall. He and his "sucking dove"[2] (I forget her name and it makes no difference for not the woods but the dives are full of them) made me ashamed of being a human being throughout the performance. The navy propaganda in this show is pitched on the plane of the most transparent patent medicine formula: viz., "before and after taking." We see the singing sop at the beginning; then the navy; then the hero saving the ship. The lesson: if the navy can make a man from such material, think what supermen it can make when given cloth with some fiber to it. But that is propaganda for nitwits, for none but a nitwit could see any real transformation take place. He was a sop to start with, and anyone with the ghost of a talent for reading character from the face must see that he was a sop and still a sop at the end. If, now, they could have gradually introduced another actor with some character in his face after the first year at Annapolis, and then another with a little more character at the end of the second year, and so on progressively, using motion-picture sleight-of-hand to do it, until the heroic part was played by even so poor an actor as James Cagney, then this "Before and After" propaganda might have been put over. But of course, having to start with a cabaret singer, the job was impossible. But I did enjoy the scenes around the Academy. I noted the faces of the first-year men particularly (not the ones *acting* first year men) and I saw faces behind which one may easily postulate character without doing any violence to one's common sense. And now I see the blurb of *Annapolis Farewell* which appears to be even worse, but which I shall have to see. Let this be the last! Why don't you write a script burlesquing this foolish propaganda which can only result in recruiting nitwits. The army and the navy both ought to go out after brains and character. They have plenty now but they can't get too much.

I met someone the other day who told me of a visit to Annapolis and he or she (I forget which) said that the easy and gentlemanly politeness of the students there impressed him (or her) beyond anything else. This pleases me very much. The Graves[3] were impressed with this same thing.

I note that you are not heroic enough to undertake a 500-page novel before Christmas. I deduce this from your ignoring of my offer to send you Stark Young's *So Red the Rose*. I see the motion pictures are presenting it. Maybe you will be able to absorb enough of it from seeing the picture to talk intelligently of it if you happen to meet Mr. Young.

In my next letter I will enclose money for your New York trip. Please tell me just when your vacation begins. Also estimate as nearly as you can how much you will need. This will have to be my Christmas present, as funds are low as the holiday season approaches.

Of course, Texas is down and out so far as football is concerned. Yes, they are howling for the coach's scalp, as usual at the end of a disastrous season. Defeated institutions usually solace themselves by claiming superior virtue in the matter of subsidizing players. And so on, but it appears that we are as unvirtuous as funds permit, so even this thread of comfort is torn rudely away.

Mary is here but I have not seen hide or hair of her, as she got in late last night and I got off early this morning. Your mama says she is looking fine and is heading up in the first ten per cent of her class at the medical college.

Please answer this: just when does your summer leave begin and just when does it close? I need this information in order to plan the family's schedule for next summer.

If you can find so revolutionary a writer as Walt Whitman in the library there, get a copy of his poems out and read the one called "Faces." I say this merely for the record, as I do not expect you to accept literary assignments. Nothing would surprise me more than to receive from you an exegesis of this poem.

Cutting a ten-page letter in half, I be and remain

Yours affectionately,

Dad.

[1]Willie Mae Thompson was secretary of the Interscholastic League.
[2]William Shakespeare, *A Midsummer Night's Dream*, I, ii.
[3]Editor's Note: Judge and Mrs. Ireland Graves were long-time friends of Roy's. Roy had put her picture on the Beauty Page, a feature he initiated when in 1903 he was editor of the *Cactus*, the University of Texas yearbook. Ireland Graves was a prominent lawyer and book collector, who gave Roy handsome nature books like Gilbert White's *Natural History and Antiquities of Selborne* in vellum binding. Bachman dated their daughter Mary Ireland Graves, "Miggy."

❦

P. O. Box 1930, Univ. Sta.
Austin, Texas
December 9, 1935

Dear Bach:

Your sketchy treatment of the academic situation, meaning grades, leads me to conclude that it is one of those questions which you think the less said about the better. I have not received from the Academy any report good or bad or indifferent concerning your scholastic achievements. Now just what is the unvarnished cold-figure, perhaps bitter and undeniable truth concerning your scholastic marks to and including the day on which this letter is delivered? The doctors say my heart is fairly sound for a man of my age, and with elaborate preparation you have made in casual (all-too casual) references to this matter, I think I can stand it. Although this question is phrased in about a hundred words, it can be answered in a line. So, be brief and explicit.

In gauging roughly what it would cost a young yokel from the deep Southwest to spend a 9-day vacation in New York, my mind hovers around $75, and so I am enclosing a certified check for $80. My suggestion is that you do not cash this until ready to leave, and just on the eve of departure, to purchase six travelers checks in $10-denominations, taking balance in the depreciated currency of this realm.

The McAlpine Hotel is centrally located and it advertises rooms $2.50 and up. If one waits till he gets there, however, he finds that the cheap rooms are all taken, so I should write for a reservation mentioning price of room and requesting an answer advising whether or not reservation is made. Then be sure and have your letter ready to stick under the nose of the room-clerk when he commences to look gloomy and say that there is nothing left "in that price range." It might be that a weekly rate is somewhat less and so you might save some by taking a room by the week, specifying, of course, the day you expect to arrive.

Cash your travelers checks at the hotel each time, and don't accumulate in your pocket more real money than you need immediately. Keep a list of the numbers of the travelers checks and notify the bank immediately if you lose any, saying just what numbers are lost. Instructions about this are printed in the folder in which these checks are issued.

Conservative fathers of my acquaintance are doubtful of my course in this matter, and I would not so arrange a vacation for any less cool and calculating son than you are. I can't see how one can learn anything unless he is on his own responsibility now and then, even when he is young. The ancient Greeks went on the theory that a man was a man when he was eighteen, and our dear bolshevistic Russia is acting now on the same theory.

One matter about you disturbs me considerably: you never mention any friends, not even your roommate. How about these boys you associate with daily and intimately. Are you ever able to help anybody, or does anyone ever help you? You are now in the friendship-making age. The older one gets the scarcer new friends become.

Your intimation that the Navy played a "bit rough" brings up another seamy side of football. It's nearly all seams, no matter which way you turn it. I can't discuss this adequately now for it has too many angles to it. I am under pressure.

The family is all ok, I sent the book the other day and it should get there before this letter does. The enclosure must stand as Christmas present from mama and me. The exechequer is in usual state of pre-holiday debilitation.

One more piece of advice: Take care of your eating if you want to enjoy your vacation. Remember you will have an exercise appetite and the exercise will be cut off. So cut down on eating and be careful what you eat. You can spoil your whole trip by a little indiscretion in this matter.

Yours affectionately,
Dad

15 December 1935

Dear Father,

I received the cheque. It should be plenty for me to have a fine time on. I intend to go up to West Point for a couple of days to see Dick. Also I will be able to see Stark Robertson in N.Y. I received and read *So Red the Rose*. It is a very good book. Have you read it? If not, I'll send it down.

Mother wrote me that Felix was injured. I hope the poor devil doesn't die. He was such a good cat. What did you do with Keedy's latest offspring?

I get out at 12:20 on the 21st. Say, for God's sake remind me of the name of Mother's cousin in Washington. She always spoke of her by her maiden name.

You know how you hate to put on a tux; you ought to try our full dress uniform. A contrivance of the devil himself. Even so, the foul fiend must have been in a nasty mood when he invented it.

You asked for my grades on a basis of 4.0. Chem. 3.2, English 3.2, Drawing 3.1, Math 3.2, French 3.3 These are the figures as I remember. There are some fractions to each one, which I don't recall. All of these are somewhat of an improvement over last month. Passing mark is 2.5. I am sure I can do better in everything. In fact I am doing much better in math. The grade in chem would have been a good deal higher had it not been for a most unfortunate examination.

My roommate is a fellow from Miss. This is fortunate, because now we both don't have to put up with a "foreign" accent. He is a very likable fellow, and I get along fine with him. I get along pretty well with everyone, but I haven't formed any close friends like I have at home. The upperclassmen like me pretty well, too. In Philadelphia a third-classman who is a friend of mine took me out to his house and introduced me to his father who is a rear admiral. A few contacts like that shouldn't hurt me if I remain in the service. Well, I'll write you before I leave, and when I arrive in N.Y.

Yours,
Bach

❦

27 June 1936

Dear Father,[1]

I could easily have written you from Portsmouth, but I didn't, for the reason I now give. Nothing of importance happened until I went to London, and when I got back it was too late to mail a letter. Really, nothing of importance happened in London, but I feel that you would be interested in knowing everything, unimportant as it is. So I start from the beginning.

At 11:00 5 June I received my first promotion in the Navy. Mid'n 4/c to Mid'n 3/c. I suppose you have found by now that I stood 434, almost exactly in the middle. Above if you count the men who flunked, and below if you don't. You can raise all the hell you want to when I return. I promise you I won't get sore. I have had so much hell raised with me in the past eleven months, that I am utterly indifferent to it. So if it will do your soul any good, I'll take it with (check choice) (1) smile (2) hurt look (3) firm promise to do better (phooey) (4) angry retort (5) sneer (6) blank look.

Life on the ship is pretty tough, but by now I can take it. It (the life) sort of runs off me; it has about the same effect a heavy sea has on the ship. It shakes me up, and occasionally dumps cold water on me, but eventually it ceases and leaves me about the same as ever. And of course there is always the port at the end for the ship and for me. I decided the life on the ship must be tough because I always hear the other fellows kicking about how tough it is. Well, I don't enjoy it myself.

We had quite a rough crossing. This ship weighs 30,000 tons, but it doesn't seem to realize that when the sea starts kicking up. The damn thing seems to think that it is a bloody (picked that horrible piece of profanity up in England) rowboat. I was a trifle pleased to note that I don't get the slightest bit seasick. Some of the boys stationed down in the fire-rooms where it gets 150°F had to be carried out when the weather got rough. They just dump them on deck and let the spray do the rest.

The *Oklahoma* left its Marine Guard at Norfolk, so when we sailed into Portsmouth I found myself among those drafted to render the honors to the dozen or so admirals we passed going in. For a matter of five hours I stood at attention, and presented arms by the way of diversion.

In Portsmouth I bought a second-hand bicycle for $4.25, recovered $1.25 on it, and rode it for two days. It was well worth the investment. I rode through the countryside (about 30 miles each day), stopped in the little villages and had tea in tearooms, saw points of interest, etc. I'll wager I saw more of England for $3.00 than plenty of people see for $1,000. Hell, tombs and churches don't make a country. It is the people themselves. As a conservative estimate, I believe that I have talked to fifty different English people for a period of over fifteen minutes a piece. Of all classes too. You'll see that presently. In Portsmouth I chatted with mechanics, trades people, farmers, beggars, waiters (pretty hard to talk to them), sailors. In London I added hotel men, guides (phooey), chambermaids, and members of Parliament to the list (more about that).

I was forced to change my cute (what a miserable word) little program drastically. The mid'n's executive Lt. Commander Ansel (the skunk) issued an order saying that if we didn't want to take Cook's Tours we could stay on the ship. So I had to get off the ship by paying for a lot of junk I didn't want. Consequently I have to cut down on expenses. On the London trip I stayed inside my new budget by a matter of $1.25. No air trip to Berlin, and no fine camera. But the field glasses.

When I got off the train at London I had a lot of fine ideas about seeing the important things in London. Well, I started out by taking in the Tower, Westminster Abbey, a museum (forgot name) and St. Paul's. Bored me a bit. Most interesting thing I learned was that a small bust of T. E. Lawrence attracted more flowers to St. Paul's than had ever been there since Christopher Wren built it. I came back from the sightseeing trip with a headache induced by the guide's voice and the murky air of vaults. So I decided to let the tours go to the devil. I spent hours every day and half the night wandering about the city of London by myself, talking to people and seeing everything *living* about the town, from the stinking fish-markets to the palaces. The English people I talked to said I was a fool (in a polite way *of course*) to wander about the tough sections at night. I didn't say so, but if a 6 ft. 4 in. American can't handle any eight of these runty little English toughs I saw, then this country is coming to an awful pass. In fact, one of my classmates half my size was attacked by a half dozen thugs after he caught one trying to pick his pocket. He took an awful licking, but he left two as

*134*

cold as ice and he escaped with his money. But I didn't come any closer to that experience than being approached by a fellow one night about 1:00 A.M. who thought I was innocent enough to take a taxi ride with him to "see the sights." He was probably only a pervert any way. I was approached by four of them and a man pimping for his daughter in the course of five blocks. My only regret about the trip is that I slept right through the last morning which I had allotted to the British Museum. This was extremely disappointing.

I had tea with Lady Astor on the terrace of the House of Parliament. This is a very, very high honor over there. She invited about 40 of the boys, and I managed to get my name into the list. Say, nothing you have heard about her has been exaggerated. She is a powerful personality. She had a half dozen members of Parliament showing us about, and at each table she had a positively stunning debutante. One of her chief delights is to fight the Revolution and the Civil War over again. Everything she says has a couple of barbs and a laugh in it, and the members of Parliament are positively afraid of her. When she says "frog," they jump! I chatted with her a while, and in the first sentence she congratulated me on being a Southerner, and the next sentence was a triple edged remark (I'd give a dollar to remember the whole thing) about a state which would be governed by the Fergusons.

I was leaving, having paid my respects, when I was button-holed by an old codger who proved to be a member of Parliament who had an especial liking for Americans. At least, so I surmised, for he took us (four of us) all over the place, and even got us into the distinguished visitors section of the House of Commons (the darned thing is held in private) by representing us as visiting American naval officers! The four of us were deeply grateful to the old boy, and we are going to send him one of the "super super" Christmas cards the regiment uses next Christmas.

An agent of a French perfume house came aboard and took orders to be delivered and paid for in Cherbourg. I know he is genuine, because the store on board approves him, and Uncle Sam makes few mistakes. I am going to get some perfume from him. Your letter was very valuable, for it enabled me to talk the agent's language, and get what I think is a fair bargain. It is $1.50 under what you estimated. And by the way, the Paris price which he quoted was precisely what you said $6.50 an ounce.

We are just leaving the English Channel and heading north into the North Sea as I write this. I may think of something else in the next few days at sea, so I won't seal the letter now.

28 June

I discovered a delightful little thing about Germany. You buy your marks for 40¢ going in and get 23¢ coming out, so Herr Hitler gets you going and coming. Strangers are allowed to get 16 for 23¢ marks going in. So I am getting part of the allowance of a couple of class-mates in order to have enough to get the glasses. There are some glasses by "Otto Schwartz" for $12.60 which are labeled 10 x 30, but I don't believe a word of it. I tried them. They may be 30 cm glasses, but they have a color fringe that does away with 7 or 8 cm. And I'll eat them if they are more than 7X. I am going to get Zeiss, where I'll know what I'm getting.

Oh yes! I forgot to tell you that I have got in on an ingenious little plan that will save me at least $30. Six Texans including me have hired a new Ford V-8 for September for a hundred and twenty dollars, that is, twenty a piece. Gas and oil will come to about $20 a piece. This makes about $40 a piece, as contrasted with the $75 or $80 it would cost on the train. What is more, since five of us are good drivers, we are going to work in shifts, stopping only for gas, oil, and food. This way, by driving at a reasonable rate we can cut ten or twelve hours from the train time. The only disadvantage besides the discomfort will be the fact that while I will be dropped off at the house, I will be picked up in Dallas. But I should be able to get a ticket to Dallas with $30, don't you think? And as for the discomfort, well, three months on board makes it almost a pleasure. But when I come rolling up to the door, I'm going to take an honest to God tub bath, and turn in for a matter of ten hours. Then you and the family can drag me out of bed, and I'll give you an account of the wanderings of Odysseus. I've been a lot of places and seen a lot of things, and I've changed an awful lot. I'm not a reformer any more. If I had that fraternity mess to go through with again, I'd just resign and if they wanted to know why, tell them as painlessly as possible. Then it could have been hushed up more suc-cessfully, and everyone would have been happy.

Here I cease until I think of something else.

1 July 1936

One of my classmates was killed the other day falling out of his hammock. I am on the only ship that has bunks instead of hammocks.

My battle-station has been changed from plugman to left supply. This doesn't mean a darned thing to you, but I'll explain briefly. The plugman opens and closes the breech on a 14 in. gun, while all the left supply man does is toss 60 lb bags of powder. A soft job. The plug man has a wonderful chance to have his leg broken by the locking lever.

2 July 1936

Tomorrow I hit port and head for Berlin. That country seems to welcome visitors like poison ivy. The Germans want to know your date and place of birth. In England our uniform was our passport.

We have been cruising about in the North Sea. Yesterday we were only a couple of hundred miles from the Arctic Circle. We have been coasting about Norway a bit. The great, tall mountains rise right out of the sea, and little villages are sort of daubed on them. There is snow on the tops of the taller mountains. It does not get dark all night. The sun is down for only an hour and a half, and when it is, there is light enough to read newspaper print with ease. I tried it.

I'm in fair health except for loss of sleep. We are up at 5:30 and in bed at 9:05, but about 3 nights out of seven we have a four hour watch in the night. Then any time you want to take a bath, night is the best time to take it to avoid the crowd. I have acquired the habit of lying down on the deck wherever I am when I have 15 min. off, and going straight to sleep. I'll demonstrate some time when I get home.

Well, I'll mail this tomorrow, so I close now.

Yours,

Bach

[1]Editor's Note: Written from Bachman's Plebe cruise.

❧

Jefferson Davis Hospital
Houston, Texas
July 23rd, 1936

Dearest Dad,

I wouldn't take millions for my high powered education and all the advantages I have had. I can almost weep over the poor little children that I am bringing into poverty, half-starvation and ignorance. I feel that my education is the thing which will make my marriage a success. I'm sure that I don't want to be a true professional woman if I must wake up one day a lonesome old maid—and I've never seen any man who I really felt would make as ideal a husband as Gay[1]— and I know that, as much in love with him as I am, I would never marry anyone else; so I'm not going to let him go by the board so that I can be a true professional woman. I'd have a sore spot the rest of my days.

I enjoyed Bach's letter lots. You know, it is quite graphic and colorful, isn't it? He is a good, cute old kid with a real interest in the world, even if he does seem to pose a little. I think the best thing was his getting himself into the distinguished visitor's section by being represented as a visiting American Naval Officer.[2] I think his cockiness is a good sign.

I'll be seeing you in eight more days.

Lovingly,

Mary

[1]Gay Carroll, the man she married August 2, 1936. He later entered medical school and became an orthopedic surgeon.
[2]Editor's Note: Mary misread Bach's letter. It was a friendly member of Parliament who got the midshipmen in the distinguished visitor's section.

P. O. Box 1930
University Station
Austin, Texas
November 22, 1936

Dear Sarah:

Yesterday about two P.M. your letter of the 18th made connection with me in my office, that being the moment of my arrival from wanderings in the East Texas woods, amongst the red hills, the colored leaves, the rooting razor-backs, and the snuff-dippers. I wish you would put Jasper, Texas, down on your list as a place we are to visit sometime in the fall of the year. It has possibilities. It is a saw-mill center, and radiating from it into the deep woods are logging roads on which trains run only once or twice a day, and crossing which are numerous wagon roads and by-paths every so often. Towering above the roads and paths are great trees, pines, beeches, sweet gum, pin oaks, red oaks, and so on. In these trees, there are many twittering little creatures which possess interest and charm. Not the least of Jasper's attractions is the Bell-Jim Hotel, wherein a black culinary goddess presides who knows just how to cook turnips and greens together, fry chicken, prepare celestial biscuits, bake the sugar-oozing yam, and perform other prodigies of kitchen-magic which lift gustation up onto a plane so far above the grosser sensual experiences as to make it of almost spiritual grandeur and to sublimate the satisfaction of a physical need into a ritual or ceremony of high moral significance. Do you get what I mean? Excellent rooms are available for a dollar a day, and a couple of meals which supply all the nutriment one can take with profit during 24 hours may be had for fifty cents each. So keep Jasper on your list.

Your account of your physical exercises delight me. One who neglects physical exercise grows torpid in liver and brains. The body was developed through countless ages of stresses and strains, exhaustion and rest, excitement and repose, and since civilization has removed the conditions which make continuation of this strenuous life obligatory, we have to supply artificial stress. Athletic sports and games are the best things we have yet devised to meet this need. So keep up your tennis with the little "sick" girl, and your dancing, which is for the female perhaps as fine a thing as football is for the more rugged males. One thing that sports do not supply, however, (I mean the more conventional sports) is contact with nature. You should get that at every opportunity. Take a day off in the woods now and then. But this is all old stuff to you. I have talked it to you for many years and I write it now simply to make the record.

Your arrangement for returning to Denton[1] Saturday is o.k. with me. I can run up there Saturday afternoon if you get back in time for a hike in the afternoon, and spend the night there and be ready for another jaunt Sunday. But don't hurry your trip on this account. I can amuse myself Saturday afternoon up the Trinity River in or near Ft. Worth.

I find everything all right at home. Your mother is cheerful, Gay is ever the same, neither exuberant or depressed, running on an even keel. Had a letter from Mary yesterday. She is trying for an internship in St. Mary's at Galveston, but I doubt if she gets one. A letter from the Superintendent of the Naval Academy, in answer to one I wrote him, confirms all Bachman has told us about his eyes.[2] The Superintendent adds that the Medical Examiner does not believe there is much chance for his eyes getting any better. Diagnosis: Myopic Astigmatism. I am writing Mary to tell me all she can find out about this eye ailment.

Your grandma Bedichek is failing, I fear, very rapidly, but I get very brave letters from her. She tells me not to let Ena make me believe that she is in a bad way. She maintains that she is all right, only weak, etc.

If you want to communicate with me any time this week, you should write at once upon receipt of this, for I leave for Ft. Worth early Wednesday morning. If you write as late as Tuesday, address me care of Thomas Fletcher, Superintendent Masonic Home and School, Ft. Worth. I shall stay at the Blackstone Hotel Wednesday night and move out to Tom's home Thursday morning and there be and remain until Saturday.

Yours,
Dad

[1] Editor's Note: Sarah earned her Ph.D. at age twenty-three, with the unusual record of having made an "A" in every single University course she took. She went to Denton as an instructor in anatomy and physiology at Texas State College for Women, now Texas Woman's University.
[2] Editor's Note: Since Bachman's eyes fell below the navy standard at Annapolis, he could not be commissioned a naval officer.

❦

P. O. Box 1930
University Station
Austin, Texas
December 9, 1936

Dear Sarah:

"Desparate" is spelled "desperate" in English. And to get even with me you needn't tell me how hemorrhage is spelt for I have already looked it up.

Alan[1] told your mother about the little flurry you were in and she told me last night. I told her, although I am not sure of my facts, that some other teacher had already been teaching a little weak course in genetics designed for immature minds and that of course the authorities didn't want to take this course away from the other teacher when she had done the best she could with it.[2] I assured her you didn't give a darn about it for you were such a sincere and outright person that if you were much disturbed you couldn't to save your life write such a buoyant letter as the one she (your mother) had just received. This calmed the maternal bosom but I could see from the smoldering fire in her eye that "nobody had better not" tramp on the cub of this she-bear and expect to get away with it. Mama's little cub must be treated very respectfully. So, as a home matter, the incident is closed and she'll never think of it again unless you bring it up either personally or by proxy. So really, honey, you're unduly excited about a matter of administrative routine that takes place every day of the week in any respectable sized institution. Think of the years your mother taught history while linguistic numbskulls were trying to teach the poor high school children Spanish. At this moment, the University is wasting the best English teacher in twenty miles of this spot on a pesky little administrative job that almost anybody could do. *Naming no names.* Think of the years J. Frank Dobie was weighted down under the dead hand until he struggled out from under. Moreover, none of us can have his way [all the time]. Every step in life is a compromise, and rightly so, for if we are going to live together in groups instead of each in his separate lair, like the cat tribe, our differences must be composed in good spirit.

Except that I don't like for my dear little daughter to be disappointed, I'm glad you're not to teach the flimsy little course in genetics, which can't be anything but something so elementary that I could take a book and teach it myself. You're really getting more by keeping up with the courses you have had no special training in. And now I do fear your becoming a narrow specialist. You're at the age when you should broaden, not constrict. Branch out, take all knowledge for your province, as Bacon did at your age.

Please tell me just the hour, if you can, when you received the airplane letter I mailed you yesterday. I sent it at 11:15, and am interested to know when it was delivered. I'm going to try another one of my pretty airplane envelopes on this, but am going to mail it in time to catch the 10 o'clock plane out of here. Please note just when it is received and tell me.

I think you did just right in sending Miss Hamilton a note. Now make up to her; help her, if she calls for help; you've no idea what magic a little kindness of this sort will work. Nobody can resist it.

Much Love. Dad

---

[1]Sarah Bedichek was to marry Alan Pipkin in September, 1938.
[2]Editor's Note: Sarah received a Ph.D. in genetics, summa cum laude, working under Dr. J. T. Patterson and Dr. H. J. Muller in 1937. Dr. Muller won a Nobel Prize for gene mutations he created with x-rays.

❧

University Station
P. O. Box 1930
Austin, Texas
January 5, 1937

Dear Sarah:

Well, the projexin' son has returned, and there was enough fatted turkey left in the refrigidaire to supply his immediate physical needs. He is now ill of a bellyache, a cough, and a slight fever.

My cousin Josephine Chandler,[1] of Washington, D.C., took nice care of him during the holidays. It seems that your grandma had written Josephine about him, so she went over to Annapolis and captured him completely. He stayed or visited in the Chandler home for a week. She showed him the old Sinclair, Craven and Trundell estates scattered over southern Maryland and northern Virginia, the house where (or, rather, in which) your grandma was born, and pumped him full of family pride and snobbery, a la the Deep South. I don't think he realized before that he was a gentleman to the manor born: he had assumed that he had had it thrust upon him. He will write you about it, I hope.

I am enclosing an express company receipt for your valise and box. Trust it reaches you promptly; if not, make the company pay up. I insured each parcel for $25.

Otherwise, things are going on as peacefully as ever. I hope you have by this time recuperated from your vacation.

Affectionately,
Dad

[1] Editor's Note: Josephine Craven Chandler, Roy's cousin, knew where their grandmother Lucretia Ellen Craven had lived as a child. She took Bach to see that and
other family home sites in Maryland and Virginia. Having been abruptly asked to
leave the Naval Academy because his eyesight was no longer up to standard, Bach
was disappointed and dejected. Josephine's hospitality softened the harshness of his
unexpected departure from Annapolis.

❦

801 E. 23
Austin 3, Texas
January 15, 1937

Dear Lillian:

Yours of Saturday (12th) came yesterday. Glad you are finding
situation so congenial. Happy the person who finds the friendship of
childhood still holding firm at 62. Little short of a miracle, I should
say.

I am still feeding on left-overs. Small bits I consolidated in a soup,
if one may speak of soup as "solid,"—any way they were assembled
in a stewpan and merged, as you suggested, with can of ?—can't think
of the name,[1] but whatever it was you left on top of the refrigerator. I
made up enough cornbread stock to last for hoecake for a month, and
chipped up cracklings into fine bits which make the stuff flavorsome.

Am just recovering from my debauch of research incident to the
T&G[2] paper, and for last three days I have been answering that unholy
package of Christmas cards—some get only a few lines, others quite a
letter. It is tedious but I guess worthwhile. One shouldn't let bygones
be bygones so far as friends and friendly acquaintances go. In the bunch
I find some interesting letters scribbled upside down and sideways
around the splendiferous illustrations of the Yuletide. One correspondent got so enthusiastic that he wrote right across the three wise men
and the star, too.

Forwarded letter from Sue[3] yesterday.

Much love
Bedi

*143*

[1] Lillian Bedichek has written in the margin of the letter "clam chowder."

[2] Town and Gown was a local discussion club made up of town and university people.

[3] Editor's Note: Lillian's cousin Sue Nabors, mother of the Broadway playwright and director Josh Logan, of the original Broadway productions of *Annie Get Your Gun*, *Mr. Roberts*, *South Pacific*, *Fanny*. He wrote a play, *Wisteria Trees*, a variation on Chekov, based on the kind of stories of Louisiana plantation life that his mother told so well.

❧

Austin, Texas
P. O. Box 1930
University Station
February 3, 1937

Dear Sarah:

There's not much drive behind this letter as you have announced an intention of descending upon the parental homestead this weekend. But Pop's fortunes and misfortunes demand consideration. In the first place, his old bathrobe was removed from atop the feather comfort in his chair-bed, said bathrobe being required by Keety who immediately delivered three kittens into its ample folds. But this leaves Pop face to face with a feather comfort. He tries to nose it down, and it puffs up in another place. He tries to scratch it down, but it puffs up at each lift of his paw. He rolls over and snuggles, and the baggy fluffy thing bulges out around him, gets in his eyes, tickles his whiskers and otherwise annoys him. He rises, turns around rapidly five times, like a top, and squats. Again the refractory comfort fails to nest-down to receive his body. He really reminds one of a vaudeville performer.

But this is not all. Felix[1] has discovered Pop's weakness, so in the early morning Felix hops on to Pop's bed and lolls over on him, and keeps on lolling and lolling until Pop leaves the bed. If lolling fails to work, Felix surreptitiously sinks his claws into Pop's tender belly, and with a whining complaint Pop vacates.

Apparently aware of your impending visit, he has followed me down to the office to get a bath. I doubt if I have time to give it [to] him. Another thing to his discredit: He made quite as much ado over Mary as he does over you. This argues unfaithfulness—which in the world of dogs is a sin against the Holy Ghost—or he mistakes her smell for yours—which is a physical defect in the dog world compa-

*144*

rable to blindness in the human world. Either way you take it, either horn of the dilemma, he is defective: defective either spiritually or physically. Well, enough of him.

The following message on a postcard came from your grandma this morning:

"Just received your long-looked for letter and am sending you this card lest you get off before I get a letter written. Don't forget that I sit here day after day and hold my hands and can't even see out the windows they are so wet."

Her eighty-eighth birthday is approaching.

Cheerless and wet describes this awful spell of weather—months of it. A bleak and discouraged sun is peeping around in and out of clammy looking clouds right now. Starlings literally darken the heavens. Blue birds have been driven into town by some freak of weather or other cause and hundreds hop around among the trees here on the Little Campus[2] every day. Myrtle warblers abound. No robins in town: the starlings have eaten all the hackberries. A cloud of them descends on a hackberry tree full of berries and when they leave in a few minutes there's not a berry left. This is hard on the waxwings, too.

Your mama has been putting up some fancy grub lately, inspired, no doubt, by Bachman's favorable comment on the "chow." Then Gay and Mary were here for a day or two, and that added to her inspiration. Hope you get here before the inspiration plays out.

But, this letter has spun out the thread of its verbosity longer than the staple of its argument.[3] So let's snip it off right here.

Dad

[1]Felix is one of the family cats.
[2]Historic buildings on the southeast area of the main University of Texas campus where the Interscholastic League and extension bureau had its offices.
[3]Shakespeare, *Love's Labour's Lost*, Act V, Sc. 1.

❦

[Written on Raleigh Hotel stationery, Waco, Texas]
February 13, 1937

Dear Sarah—

Yesterday Shelby[1] and I came here and I had a little piddling busi-

*145*

ness which I attended to this morning, & now am rarin' to go—but no Shelby. So in the interim a few inconsequential words:

1. Your Dad is ill—throat & lungs tight & sore. I went to a doctor with my sore throat & he wanted to pass me around to the other doctors for picking my financial bones. First, to x-ray man & dentist to see about my teeth—$25.00. Next to blood analysis man—$5.00. Next to a general diagnostician—$35.00. His own bill likely about—$10.00. Making total of around—$75.00.

Well, I didn't pass. After blood man I went no further down the line, as I don't have the money. I appreciate the compliment, but $75.00 is too high a value to place on me. So I inaugurated a "sit-down" strike against the Medical Profession which is rapidly becoming a "lay-down" strike. It is a constant temptation to retire and lie down. It's not the "walkin' flu" I have but the "layin' down" flu.

Haven't seen any of the Greer kin here except Bachman[2] whom I met on the street just now. He's looking exceptionally well and prosperous. Reports all the family well except Hazel[3] who fell & fractured bone in base of her spine—an injury, I judge, much like the one Shirley Lomax[4] had, but I hope not as serious.

Your mama enjoyed a couple or three days at Manor teaching, about which I suppose she wrote you.

Well, here's Shelby also rarin' to go.

Dad

[1] Thomas Hall Shelby, director of the Bureau of Extension 1920–24 (then dean of the Division, as the name changed in 1924, until 1951.)
[2] Lillian Bedichek's brother for whom her son is named.
[3] Hazel Iliza Cannon Greer, Bachman's wife.
[4] John Lomax's daughter.

❦

P. O. Box 1930
University Station
Austin, Texas
April 4, 1937

Dear Sarah:

Coming down to the office just now through the sunny air of this lovely April afternoon, I gathered up a flower to identify. I found Alan's

*146*

brother's book in my desk, and proceeded to hit it the first rattle out of the box, although it is no credit to me, for we have identified it before. Nevertheless it was pleasant, and it made me think of you—hence this letter instead of my doing some office work, as I had intended.

Mary sailed in yesterday afternoon fresh and blooming as a rose, and was wafted away just now on her return trip to Galveston. She hopped a ride with Virginia Thompson who happened to be coming this way and wanted someone to come with her. She has gotten rid of her rash and her complexion is soft, silky and blooming, unless my old eyes have gotten so weak as not to detect any artificial complexion. She is in exuberant spirits.

Bachman is in just the contrary state of mind. He goes around scowling like the heavy villain of a Victorian melodrama. My how he scowls! My how he bawls out your mother! The secret is that Mary Ireland has turned him down quite definitely. Just two dates and, though she is to be here several days longer, I heard him bid her a wistful goodbye *over the telephone*. I think the young lady didn't particularly fancy his being off to the coast for three days after her arrival. Beauty will be served, you know. It's awful hard on the beast's family, however. He's off this afternoon to shoot it out,[1] and I hope his score is high, for that will return him to the fold about nightfall in a more cheerful humor. I heard him making a date for tonight with some girl at the Littlefield Dormitory,[2] in a rather rough and ready big he-man tone which he never uses to Mary Ireland. He had threatened to wash the car which he is using tonight, but he evidently thought better of it after making elaborate preparation and posted off to shoot.

Mama finished censussing, cashed her nine dollar check from Manor, and threw the thing off her mind, which of course, was the sensible thing to do. No fit of anger is worth three dollars, and that's all she would have made by collecting what was due her.[3] She prepared a lovely meal for Mary and Gay, so good that even Bachman unbent a little and condescended to be merry. Father was lying on his bed on the sleeping porch and overheard the table chatter. He wasn't participating since he is on a starvation diet trying to rid himself of a cold. Grapefruit is all I have had in the last fifty hours, and it's going on until tomorrow noon, which will make seventy-two hours, and longer if this damned cold doesn't let up. It's broken now, but hanging on by its tendrils.

Got a letter from Oberholser[4] asking me to send him a rain and temperature map of Texas, which I did at once. I took the opportunity to ask him for information about the Texas Pyrrhuloxia. I'll let you know what he writes about this gorgeous creature. Had you been here this morning, I should have insisted on going down there again today, and thought once of going by myself, but didn't feel quite chipper enough. I feel quite sure they are nesting in that pasture. If I can find a nest, I'll pass it on to your museum when the bird has finished with it. However, I have a notion you can't tell one from a redbird's.

Have seen nothing of Alan, but your mama and he went out after the customary bucket of blood the other day, and he took her to a movie the other night. An association built upon blood and the movies seems a rather curious phenomenon in human relationships.

Say, I ran on to a good word for you in some book I was reading the other day. It's "relaxative." It's just what you need, every day, a relaxative. You tension too much. You strain and champ the bits too hard. Let up, loosen down, take a relaxative, as we did that day we discovered the Pyrrhuloxia and ate the steak in the cold and rain. That was the best piece of a dead animal I ever ate. Wasn't it savory, wasn't it juicy, wasn't it flavored deliciously with the scent of mesquite coals? That day is [what] I call taking a relaxative.

How did you make out until train time with mama and Oat[5] and Ena? Hope you have something good to eat. Mama is very pitiful, isn't she. She seems to have gotten smaller and smaller, but her spirit is unbroken and her courage never seems to fail.

> Out of the night which covers me,
>     Black as the pit from pole to pole,
> I thank whatever gods may be
>     For my unconquerable soul.[6]

I wish I had gotten that gene, but I didn't. Maybe it is recessive in me and dominant in you. I hope so.

Well, well, if I chatter on, I won't get any work done at all. And I have so much to do, and so little time to do it in, as Cecil Rhodes said as he died. But this letter has served as a relaxative.

Much love.

Dad

[1]Editor's note: Bachman was at target practice.

[2]Women's dormitory at the University of Texas.

[3]Editor' note: Lillian is taking the school census. For the school census, household-ers are asked the number and ages of children in their homes. Lillian was owed three dollars more but that amount was not worth the struggle to get it.

[4]Harry Church Oberholser, ornithologist, biologist, worked for the U.S. Fish and Wildlife Service and compiled a great study of Texas birdlife. RB tried to raise money so that it could be published. In 1974, after Oberholser and Bedichek had both died, the University of Texas did publish it in two volumes. Edgar Kincaid, a nephew of Frank Dobie, edited the 12,000 pages of manuscript.

[5]Ena's husband, Oatis (I. O.) Beard.

[6]From "Invictus," by William Ernest Henley.

⁂

Austin, Texas
April 19, 1937

Dear Sarah:

Far be it from me to discourage a bird enthusiast, so take her on and her hubby, too. In order to get an early start, shouldn't you come over to Dallas Saturday afternoon? You might find a good show Satur-day night, if my engagement doesn't interfere, and if it does, you might see one by yourself, or with your friend. Go ahead and make any ar-rangements you want to with her, and I shall accommodate myself thereto—except of course, Saturday night, as I don't yet know what will be expected of me by the Conference authorities at whose in-stance I am coming to Dallas.

Your mama and I went to Onion Creek Swamp yesterday. Started about six and got back at 12:30. Your mama had Bach's glasses and really looked at birds. She saw the Hermit Thrush (think of his being here now), and the Brown Thrasher (and he's lingering long, too). She was so excited about this that in telling it later, she said: I saw a Brown thrusher and a Hermit Thrash! She saw also the Maryland Yellow-throat, the Black-throated Green Warbler, the red-bellied woodpecker and a number of other beautiful birds. We also identified some flow-ers. We cooked our breakfast dinner (bacon & eggs & toast) and a good time was had by all.

Bach is loosing interest in field study. He's running to marksman-ship with a pistol.

I hereby acknowledge receipt of Savings Bond Q219808C, Series C, dated Federal Reserve Bank Dallas, April 14, 1937 for $25. It goes into your hoard. By the way, if this is business, you should acknowledge receipt of the warrant I returned to you.

Enclosed is a copy of a letter from Oberholser for your bird file. You never did send me a copy of that list we made at Center Point the rainy day, I think it was March 27, wasn't it?

Glad to know that Lowell Thomas was sufficiently impressive. Really there is a slight resemblance. I had never noticed it, though. Please, please, please, let up your strenuous schedule a bit, or you won't be able to go to England[1] or anywhere else. Take a relaxative.

I met the President of a higher education institution the other day, and he told me he had his eye on you. He said if the legislature gives him the position (and the legislature usually does give this man what he wants) he is going to institute genetics in his institution and offer you $2400 to take charge of it. Now don't spill this to anyone. I oughtn't to tell you. Maybe nothing will come of it. And don't ask me who it was, for I won't tell you. Suffice it to say that there are plenty of men in the institution, faculty and student body. But you have to be healthy. He asked me particularly about your health, and I told him a Duroc Jersey pig with plenty of buttermilk had nothing on you. So get the Duroc Jersey look.

Much love.

Dad

[1] Sarah had received a fellowship to study at University College, London, with John Burdon Sanderson Haldane, British geneticist whose work, with that of Sir Ronald Aylmer Fisher and Sewall Wright, provided a basis for the mathematical study of population genetics.

❧

[Written on The Baker Hotel stationery, Dallas, Texas]
April 26, 1937

Dear Sarah—

The day with the bird-nuts did me a lot of good & I hope it improved your condition somewhat. And what sweet nuts they are! I have never determined whether nature study just selects out of the herd the sweetest people, or whether the selection is random, & nature study sweetens them all alike. No doubt about the sweetness—only doubt in my mind is how it got there. Those two young peacocks are going to give our sweet & patient old hen a lot of grief, I'm afraid, before she gets them well raised. Wasn't the story of why she gave up Camp Fire work pitiful? I rather feel that it's shouting against the hurricane for the sensible parent to try to compete with the motion-picture & radio. Ah me! man's days are few & full of trouble[1] & all is weariness and vexation of spirit,[2] & specially raising youngsters. You can see that the hopes of the family are beginning to be pinned onto the little boy, & your statistical math will tell you that there are chances considerably against hopes being realized. And still this is an unusually happy family—at least in the happiest ten per cent. What must the other 90 percent be like? I draw the curtain & invite your attention to more pleasing prospects.

Don't forget to send me copy of your bird-list, & of dates when we saw T.P. & also copy of the Easter bird-list.

As to turtle & such like incidents: Just go ahead as if nothing had happened. Dismiss it from your mind, remembering that it's not *what happens* that matters, but how we allow what happens *to affect us*. Take your mental tweezers & pull the mental splinters out so that there may be no mental festering. The world is wide and there's much to do & think about & there's no time left for bothering about turtles, museum, or any other kind, especially about *snapping turtles*.

How do you like my speed? I went to the 10th floor of the hotel, got that package & letter & was back before the bus left, & me nearly sixty, & nobody will believe I'm sick.

I'm having to go over to Ft. Worth today unless the long distance call I'm now waiting for necessitates immediate return to Austin. I'm sorely tempted to buy a pair of old shoes & go back out to that swamp & spend the day, but that would be too bad. If I had a day to myself around the edges of that swamp I'd find out a lot, wouldn't you? Someway I can't study very well in a crowd.

Hoping you like the "passport purse" your mama and I got for your birthday remembrance, Sarah, with much love,

Dad

[1]Bedichek is paraphrasing *Job* 14:1.
[2]Bedichek is paraphrasing *Ecclesiastes* 4:6.

Austin, Texas
P. O. Box 1930
University Station
June 8, 1937

Dear Sarah:

How many times have I wished that I had positively instructed you to cable me collect the moment you got yourself settled in London. I want to know that you are there are settled and I don't want to wait for a letter. I have come near cabling you, but 31 cents a word is quite an outlay, and then to pay for every word in the address also. Please let me have the cable address of the university, or better, of the college, or better still, of the Department of Zoology, if it has a cable address. Usually an institution such as that has one word registered with the cable company for the convenience of its cable correspondents.

Nothing startling is happening here. We are drifting into our summer routine. I dig around the yard until about nine, take a bath and go to the office. Return about 12:30 for nourishment, nap about half or three-quarters of an hour; attack office again and stay until five. If there's a motion picture show your mama wants to see and I feel that I can tolerate, we go to that. I ordinarily go to bed early and get up early.

Last night just at deep dusk, your mother and I were sitting out in the east yard when our attention was attracted by a Carolina Wren who kept chirping about us as if he had lost something. We thought first that he was defying the cat. But presently he showed us what he wanted. He entered Bachman's bathing trunks which were hanging on the clothes-line and cuddled up for the night—at least he stayed in there as long as we were out there. We are going to watch for him again tonight.

Bachman and I tried a bird expedition Sunday morning but the rain drove us in about 8:30. It's getting hot and you are to be congratulated on being in the far nawth.

Mary telephoned the other night and your mama said she sounded as if she were down in a well. Her first week of interning had left her rather exhausted, it seems. Gay is over in San Antonio this week. Alan— I don't know where Alan is.

Please do take time to write to us. Remember that you are getting impressions you will never get again. Let those first impressions fade out and they can never be touched up again. So take time to write, either diary, or letters or both, and you will not regret it.

By the way, Gay has enlarged that snap he took of you and me sitting on a log looking up a bird in a bird-book, and it is really very good. Do you have a copy? If not, I shall send you one.

Nothing has come out of the Governor's office yet about the appropriation bill, but there is no rumor that he is going to do anything to it. If he were going to get nasty, it would leak and we'd all be in a furor about it.

I'm going to send this airmail tho it isn't worth it.

Love, Dad

༂

Austin, Texas
University Station
P. O. Box 1930
June 11, 1937

Dear Sarah:

It's an uphill job—this writing note after note to somebody out across the hazy Atlantic who never answers. I've always held that true correspondence is an interchange. This is a monologue. But anyhow, I guess you are getting your letters coming this way. I hope so.

Your mama told you, I suppose, that the Governor signed the educational appropriation bill without scratching a single item, which means that your job came through unscathed. Now, how does it feel to be un-birged?

Just had a note from Mary. Her first case handled alone was a little boy who mistook a beer-bottle filled with gasoline for something good and drank it. She gave us a nice account of how beautifully she handled the case, but left out the point I was most interested in—did the little boy die?

The *National Geographic* has issued its long-advertised book of birds—two volumes—1,000 color drawings by Allan Brooks—life histories of 663 species—all for $5. I'll just have to get this, but I can't afford it. There's an article on London in the current (June) issue of the *Geographic* which might interest you, and a dandy detailed map of England folded into the issue. The map alone is worth the money so I advise you to buy it.

Here's a further report on the bedding habits of the Carolina Wren, mentioned in my letter of June 8: The next night, Bachman had used his trunks and they were wet and hung up in another part of the yard. My trunks happened to be left near where Bachman's were when he bedded down for the preceding night. Just at dusk, he came scolding in from the oak trees, calling Felix more foul names in wren-language than I could write on this page. It took him some time to get all this out of his system, but finally he dashed over to the clothesline and found that Bachman's trunks were not there. This made him angry again and he let loose another volley of oaths. But his attention was attracted to my trunks and he examined them critically. He perched above them a moment, ducked up and down two or three times, like a canyon wren, and then uttered two or three soft low notes like a good night prayer or something of the sort (the little hypocrite) and dived in. However, my trunks didn't suit him. Maybe the smell of age is not as nice to go to sleep by as the odor of youth, or for whatever reason, he kept coming out, and finally made off to the trees.

I decided that my trunks were too flimsy to suit him, so I got out your old bathing suit and folded it over the line near mine in such a way as to provide an attractive entrance. But we were at a picture show the next night at the wren bedtime, so we made no observations. The next night we watched him. About sundown, he sang around in the trees very joyously and we thought surely he would come back to bed. But for about half an hour after sundown, no wren was in sight. At nearly dark your mama, Bachman and I were still watching, and lo and behold here he came positively slipping into bed. Not a sound, not a chirp, and only silent prayer, if any. And he chose my trunks, not yours. That was last night. We'll watch for him again tonight. This little comedy intrigues your mother very much. She can hardly wait for dusk to come, and mentions it a dozen times a day. And perhaps she has written you all about it, and this is to you a twice-told tale.

Oberholser keeps writing me for the dates we saw the Pyrrhuloxia, and I can't give them; and he is also anxious to get the date we saw the yellow-crowned night heron nesting near Dallas. I think I can dig up that date, but I don't think I can get the Pyrrhuloxia dates.

Well, I would end this letter right here as I have nothing else to say, but the thought of sending this much blank paper three thousand miles offends my sense of economy, so I am going to fill it up if I have to write "now is the time for all good men to come to the aid of the party," over and over again. It's about time for me to ring up your mother and inquire about the supply of buttermilk, which I shall do presently. And then I shall propose that we go out to old man Patterson's orchard and get a bucket of beautiful plums which he said would be ripening this Friday afternoon. After that we shall return and eat a snack and then watch our wren go to bed. On the trip for the buttermilk, I shall mail this so as to catch the 7:40 airmail in hopes that it will be delivered to you sometime towards the latter part of next week— Saturday, June 19, Emancipation Day.[1] Please tell me when it is delivered, so I'll get the run of how long it takes. My guess is that it will be Monday, June 21.

We haven't seen hair nor hide of Alan since you left—one exception perhaps. Wonder if he would care to go out in the country on Sunday mornings—maybe I'll suggest it to him.

J. W. Calhoun has been made President, ad interim, of the University while the regents search for a permanent president. Now, I have run out of soap, sure enough, resorting to personals.

Much love, Dad.

---

[1]Texas slaves were belatedly freed on June 19, 1865. The day, called Juneteenth, has been celebrated throughout the state since 1865.

❦

Austin, Texas
University Station
P.O. Box 1930
June 18, 1937

Dear Sarah:

Your scotch cablegram relieved us greatly, and the day after, or rather two days after it, we got your letter of June 8 which gave us substantial and satisfying information. As it happened, your letter came just as Mary and Gay and Alan and Bachman had assembled under the parental roof for one of father's far-famed steaks "with trimmins." It was passed around and read with avidity—the letter, not the steak. I am particularly proud of you for learning to find your way around London by yourself. Shooting oneself around in the tube is great fun. That was one of the first things I mastered when I got to London. I landed at the Waterloo station by myself just about thirty years ago and the last time I was at the Waterloo Station I saw George Bernard Shaw and Mark Twain meet. They met quite by accident, Twain coming in to be doctored by Oxford, and Shaw being there to meet his American literary agent. I wasn't quite close enough to hear what passed between them.

Please refer to our letters by dates, for in these long-distance correspondences one can never keep track of what letters the other has received, except by dates. This letter of yours took ten days, although Alan's letter mailed June 9 reached here on the same mail. So we may count on nine or ten days. I hope you give me a good sketch of Haldane's personality. I have read quite a bit of his writing and am anxious to have your personal impressions of him.

Mary has recovered some of her abounding vigor. She extracted a pair of tonsils all by herself the other night and her patient is doing well. She is, of course, proud to bust of this operation. She is getting daily practice in surgery, cutting right along with the surgeons on major operations. She is here now for a few days boning before taking the state medical exam next Monday. It will be held in the Austin High School, since the Legislature is in session and occupying the chamber where the examination is usually taken. It will be quite a thrill for her to return to the old high school for another examination.

I wish I could give you as good an account of the animal contingent as of the humans. Sad to report, Felix devoured a young mockingbird this morning. Keety retired the other night from the study, where her one kitten is waxing fat, to the front room and used one of the rugs for a purpose which rugs were never intended to be used for. Next morning after much heaving and grunting I got the rug hung over a clothesline in the back yard for cleaning, airing and sunning. Pop is greatly depressed. He walks around meditatively, hanging his head, plunged in deep canine thoughts. His mistress has departed for foreign shores and he is taking it much to heart. His chief solace is a large bone which he gnaws and buries and unearths and gnaws and buries again. The weather is warm and the bone is o'er-ripe and his breath does not smell like a rose by any means.

I told you something of the agarita jelly. Well, it didn't jell, and your mama had to re-cook it with Certo—about twenty jars duly jelled now adorn the shelves in the pantry. Patterson's peaches are getting ripe. That makes summer look better, and watermelons are coming in, so I guess we'll somehow make out. But those temperatures you record in your letter arouse in me a great dissatisfaction with Texas climate. Every day now we have it somewhere between 90 and 100. I am sitting here now, as the shades of night are falling fast (a way they don't fall in your latitude) sweating, with an electric-fan stirring the moist and sticky atmosphere of this office.

Please send me the cable address of the College, if it has one registered, so that I won't have to spend my good money spelling out that terribly long address in case I want to communicate with you by cable. I am sending you under another cover a code and keeping an identical copy, so if we do have to communicate by cable, we may be able to beat the great American Telephone & Telegraph Company out of a little money, or rather, keep it from beating us out of money. Please advise me of receipt of the code when it comes, so that I will know you have it.

One omission in your letter pains me very much. You don't mention having seen a single English bird. Surely you have seen just one. When Neville Chamberlain, the present prime minister, was Chancellor of the Exchequer and there was a big stew over the budget and everyone in England was looking for some important pronouncement on the budget from this functionary, a letter from him appeared in the *Times*. A breathless nation devoured this letter, which ran something as follows: "Walking in the Park this morning I saw a grey wagtail. I mean a grey wagtail, not a spotted one."

Shelby and I are going to the hill country tomorrow to spend Saturday night and Sunday, and I hope to be able to report some birds.

Don't get into the abominable European habit of staying up all night and sleeping in the morning. The morning is the time to be alive in Europe as well as in America, or in Africa or Siam for that matter.

Much love, and write often.

Dad

Austin, Texas
University Station
P. O. Box 1930
July 4, 1937

Well, well, dear Sally, you are coming out of the daze in which the ocean trip and a new country put you. You have actually mentioned a bird, or rather birds, for you have not yet said anything of a special individual. Are there no birds in London? Not even in the parks? You have a grand project of preparing a Texas Daglish. Yes, I'll go in with you and we'll produce something that will make the ornithological world set up and take notice. If old Man Oberholser would just publish that work of his, we could fashion our course so as not to duplicate anything that he has done. But whether he publishes or not, we'll go ahead with ours.

There is going to be a marvelous opportunity here in Austin and vicinity to study the effect of changing environment on bird life. Those great lakes on the Colorado are going to shake bird life to its foundations. Just think of creating nearly a hundred miles of lake in the middle of a semi-arid country. I was up at and above the Buchanan Dam yesterday. The gates are closed and the lake has already begun to fill. Slowly the water will creep out and out over the flats and up the draws, starting the succulent shoots of a thousand different species of plants, bringing grubs and worms to the surface. When the fall migrations begin, it is going to be a bird paradise. I am going to spend a week up there above the dam very soon and then I shall try to visit there again every two weeks or so to check up. Of course, the Buchanan Dam is only a beginning. There is the Inks Dam, the Marshall Ford dam, and the Austin dam, and others and others still, eventually converting the whole length of the Colorado for a couple of hundred miles into a string of lakes, some of them ten or twelve miles wide in places. How the old Canada Goose will stretch his neck and honk his melodious honk when he first sees these lakes, and ducks, and avocets, and long-billed curlews—what a great rejoicing there will be among the shore birds at this thousand or more miles of new shore-line! So this will be a chapter in our book.

By the way, I was with Dr. Patterson all day Sunday. He asked many questions about you, and seemed highly pleased at my account of your activities.

Bachman, I fear, will never get around to telling you of our trip to Port O'Connor. He studies fairly well in the week, and week-ends he socializes. Last night he had a date with Mary Ireland, and this morning at 10:30 he is out with Bill Houston's[1] sister shooting. This afternoon, he will sleep, and tonight, he will see the movie *Captains Courageous*, and so on.

Patterson told me that Dr. Hubbard[2] applied again to him for recommendations to fill the place you left open. Patterson recommended Elsie and Meta. Elsie wouldn't and Hubbard didn't want Meta—confidential, of course. I can tell him that Meta is his best bet. Please repeat none of this to anyone.

We hear nothing from Mary. She's not as ready a writer as you are. I think she takes so much pains she doesn't write at all. After all, one's got to blurt ahead and say something, even if it's wrong, if he ever expects to write. Indecision is a species of paralysis. The Irishman's story of the mule situated between two haystacks starving to death because he couldn't decide which stack to go to illustrates what I mean.

Your mama speaks of going to Galveston now and then, but I think it will be sometime before she brings herself to the point of actually pushing off. I encourage her every time she mentions it.

Much love,
Dad

[1]Editor's Note: They were target practicing. Bill Houston is a friend from Austin High School.
[2]A University of Texas Biology Department faculty member.

❧

Austin, Texas
University Station
P. O. Box 1930
July 8, 1937

Dear Sally:

This perfectly corking letter of yours dated June 28 is the best entertainment I have had this summer, and I have seen some screamingly funny movies. You put a great strain on me when you suggest that I not show it to Lil. If your suggestion were on a separate sheet of paper, I'd show it to her anyway, for the suggestion that I not show it to her is the only part of it I don't want her to see. However, you may be right. Her imagination is active, and by the time she had slept on it a night, she would visualize you backing out of a drunken genetics carousal with an automatic pointed movie-wise at the whole bunch of lusting geneticists holding them at bay while you used your high-kicking ability to touch off the police-signal with your toe. If it becomes necessary, you may suggest to some luster that you have a lover who is an awful "tough guy" and a father and six-foot-four brother who are expert pistol shots, and that this "crew" constantly lusts for trouble, especially since we are having a dull killing season this summer.

And I do not dare show it to Patterson for he is an awful gossip, and I can't think of anyone else that I can show it to who would understand it. Gossip of this kind travels and grows and things said in jest become serious matters, so it is best to hold it in iron-bound limits. So it will go with your memoirs in my steel filing case, and you will enjoy it in later years.

Of course, you are a sort of curiosity to those people and they naturally want to sound you out and get your reactions, perhaps meaning no harm whatever. And you mustn't make the mistake of judging English society by this. There are Tennysonians left in England, large numbers of them. You happen to have been plunged into a genuinely Bohemian crew, much like our psychology crew here at the University, only—and this is a big ONLY—your crew is really distinguished in science. That you wrote under considerable excitement is evidence by your use of "arrived *back*" and misspelling Casteel's name. You are getting some real experience, and "all experience is an arch where through gleams that untravelled world whose margin fades,"[1] etc.

The whole lusting bunch are weaker and more inefficient for their liquor and their lusting. Observe them as you would observe the mating habits of a colony of herons or phalaropes—study them objectively. And by the way, this reminds me that you have not yet mentioned seeing a single English bird. Bachman tells me that he wrote you an account of our two days down on the Texas coast. One sight we had which he tells me he forgot to mention or describe should really be recorded. We took up the west beach at Port O'Connor just at sunup so the light was to our backs. It was still, and the bay didn't have a shimmer on it—it was smooth as glass. About three hundred yards away, and our glasses brought them to one-eighth of that distance, we saw five magnificent white pelicans, scooping with their enormous bills and throwing their heads up now and then, exhibiting their pale yellow pouches. Immediately behind them walking in solemn procession, like Egyptian priests performing some ancient rite, were seven (mystic number) wood ibises, with their bills plunged into the water up to their eyes, treading along without raising their bills for five minutes at a time. Flanking this procession on either side were several (ten, I think) roseate spoonbills, in full mating plumage, the scarlet "drip" showing on two of them, and the rest delicately rosy, also feeding, swaying their huge bills from side to side. For fifteen or twenty minutes this procession went forward in the glow of the rising sun, and it is hard for me to believe that it wasn't some kind of solemn religious pageant. Bachman was delighted, and it is curious that he didn't describe it in his letter.

And another incident that Bachman was too delicate to mention was our encounter with a colony of least tern. These little fellows were nesting on the west beach, but their young had left the nests and were scattered here and there still being fed by the parent birds. When we got into this colony, the old birds, fifty or sixty of them, raised a great hullabaloo, and began diving at us from great heights. They hovered over us as they do when preparing to dive for fish, and darted at us in terrific nose-dives that brought them within a few feet of our heads. I held my field-glasses to my eyes to get a little better view of one as he was diving at me, and just as he dived very close, I felt something very light and soft hit me between the fingers. I looked and sure enough, it was the little fellow's "bomb" un-explosive, but the best he had. This tickled Bachman very much as I wiped the stuff away, and he bragged that none had hit him. He had on a white shirt, and as I looked at his shoulders, I saw that the bombers had scored three hits on him! And of course, I know not how many in his hair, for the colors blended.

I caught old man Felix trying to capture a cardinal this morning while he was feeding on watermelon seed in the back yard. I have no intention of baiting that bird-trap, so I have made a platform in one of the oak trees on which to spread watermelon seed hereafter.

Have a nice long letter from Mary today reporting on more successful tonsil operations. She seems to be gouging and whacking right and left into various portions of the human anatomy without boosting the undertaking business to any considerable extent.

Since reading your last letter, I am glad you are taking England in broken doses. I wouldn't like for you to stay in that atmosphere for a year at a time, just yet. August 28 will bring you back to the good old U.S.A where men are men and women are glad of it. Someway there is something decadent about the society you describe. Maybe Mussolini is right. But, as above noted, one may find Bohemian cults almost anywhere.

Much love, and write often.

Dad

P.S. The 3 scenes of the "drammer" are fine. Now let's have the 2nd act.

RB

[1]Alfred, Lord Tennyson, *Ulysses*.

❦

Austin, Texas
University Station
P. O. Box 1930
August 19, 1937

Dear Sarah:

Patterson phoned us bright and early this morning your cable announcing appointment to Fellowship.[1] This is grand news. It's not only a feather in your professional cap but a diamond in your tiara. The only disappointing thing to us is that you may decide not to make [a] trip home and we will not see our dear little chicken for a whole year. Rather against the grain, I cabled you this morning as follows:

"Patterson glad ship stocks etc mama pack Denton junk all on your instructions congratulations family and zoology department."

I told Patterson on phone you seemed to be worried about your fly stocks[2] and he said he would be glad to ship whatever you want. In making your decision about home trip, I wanted you to have all the information. I trusted your own good sense to supply (without paying tribute to Cable Company) that we are all dying to see you, but are willing for you to make trip home or not as you deem best. You know the situation so much better than I do that I cannot (or could not) offer any sensible advice. I figure the trip could not be made under a month, but if it saves you two months time it would of course be well worth while, to say nothing of the jollification you coming will cause at 801 East 23rd Street. And it might help your spirits, although I don't think your spirits ever sink really to a depression level, as do those of your old and incompetent Dad. You see there are so many things to consider that I give it up.

I am writing this with no distinct notion of when I shall send it or where. I am sure you will notify us by cable if you decide to come home, and in that case, I shall send it to New York; otherwise to your London address. And so this is the first installment.

August 21, 1937

Guess I will send this to the steamship company in New York for delivery to you when the *Normandie* arrives, with instructions to forward to 18 Taviton Street, if not delivered at the boat. Alan told me last night that you had said in one of your letters to tell us that you were coming home whether or not you received the Fellowship. This was news to me, and if I had had it I would not have sent cable or written the foregoing part of this letter. I have scanned your letters for similar information, and find written in margin of yours of August 5th the following: "If I get fellowship I want to come home and then return." So I guess you are coming and all hail! Perhaps it's not the best thing for you but it is certainly the best thing for me, for I feel that I can hardly wait a year to see you. I might decide to come to England and see you, and this would blow up the family finances for all time to come. And then I would have a divorce case to fight through the courts when I return, you mother alleging "unspeakable cruelty" in my chasing off to see you by myself. So all in all, your trip home may be worth the time and money.

Your adventure was quite exciting, and your telling of [it] thrilled us to the marrow. If you are going to continue to pick up chance acquaintances on the street and chase off with them to the slums and the country, I am going to insist on teaching you how to shoot a pistol. Eventually you will get into a situation where such knowledge will come in handy. Unless you are really going in for adventure, it is best to stay within conventional lines. Don't run around with anyone to whom you have not been well and truly introduced by responsible mutual acquaintances. I offered to put you in touch with some folks outside your college routine, but you didn't take me up. I admire your style of narration including all the essentials without bothering with needless detail. You could write stories if you turned your hand to it. But I don't advise you to, because you can do more important work.

So endeth the second installment.

August 22

Yours of the 13th came this morning with the first definite news straight from you to me that you are coming home. I wired you immediately as follows:

"Wire from New York time arrival in Denton meet you there. Overjoyed that you are coming."

You can get the man who sells you ticket, or from any ticket agent or information bureau at the station, the exact time you will arrive in Denton. I think it will be on Texas Special arriving Denton 8:32 A.M. Sept. 1 or 2. Please give me the exact time, so I will know when to start from Austin. I have two business trips pending, one to Dallas and the other to Marshall. The Dallas trip is not tied to a fixed date and I can vary it by a week, but the Marshall date is fixed for 9 A.M. September 4. I had intended to do both on one trip, that is, go to Dallas, thence to Marshall. So the situation permits of several permutations and combinations:

1. Your mama and I can meet you in Denton. You can do up your junk, pack in car and we can come home, provided car will hold you, me, your mama and junk. Then I should have to make a special trip the next day or two to Marshall.

2. If you arrive Denton on 2nd, and it took you a day or so to do your errands there with mama's help, I in meantime could make trip to Marshall, return via Denton and pick you up and come home on afternoon of 4th.

3. If not too crowded, I could load junk you and mama in car at Denton, drive to Marshall (four hours) Saturday morning (the 4th) and come direct home from Marshall that afternoon.

4. I could take your junk in car as soon as gathered and packed, and you and mama could come home on train, leaving me to make Marshall trip.

All of these except No. 1 would perhaps give you and mama a wait of 12 to 24 hours in Denton, provided you arrive there as early as I anticipate. Any of them are ok with me, although No. 1 will cause the State of Texas to burn up a few gallons more of gas, but perhaps save it a hotel bill. You may be mulling over these options on the train and take your choice.

This Fellowship with a year's study abroad is just what you need to establish your professional prestige. If you take care of your health, it will give you a wide choice of jobs, although I think you are committed to stay with Davis at least two years, although I did not give him the promise that you authorized on this score. But at Arlington you will have a fine opportunity to establish yourself as a successful instructor. Then the world is yours, so far as jobs are concerned. I should like for you to keep a long-distance eye on Cornell, for they are strong in ornithology, and you know that's your minor.

I drove out this morning to a home in the hills about seventeen miles West of Austin and showed the whole family how to identify flowers, and you should have seen the joy in that household. They had all been yearning to know the names of the flowers and they actually didn't know how to begin to find out. I made the lady identify a lobelia from the key and she was as tickled as a child with a new toy. I went out there to show them birds, but they were up in those cedar covered hills where no birds are found at this season; so I turned them onto flowers.

Thus endeth the third installment.

August 23

Felix got on the table and ate up a considerable portion of a three pound mutton roast on which the family expected to live for the next week, and messed up the rest. Pop is on a rampage with a female visitor and her escorts, and night is rendered hideous. I go to sleep with a bucket of boulders by my cot in the backyard and hurl these unavailing missiles in the general direction of the canine furors at intervals of about twenty minutes from 1 A.M. on till daylight. I'm going to build a big fire in the furnace and cremate every cat and dog on the place. I've hung up the remains of an adult mockingbird that Felix left lying around to show you when you return. If I forget it, look in the first oak tree to your right as you leave kitchen door about the place where the clothesline is attached. Only the tail, legs, and portion of one wing were considered by his Ornithophagus Majesty unedible, and there they shall remain to keep me in a proper rage against the kindling of the first furnace fire this fall. There shall be a literal biblical hell for this bird-eating cat. I may relent about Pop, but Felix! I am nursing my rage to keep it warm.

I am sorry you are going to miss the harvest moon. It is brilliant these nights, not the dingy, smoked out, timid tentative thing you see in London skies, but a bold, domineering orb, literally Queen of the Night. If my eyes were a little younger, I could read the evening paper by it, lying out on my cot in the coolth of the evening. There is no dawn these mornings—nothing to intimate the approach of the sun until he blazes over the eastern horizon.

And so endeth the fourth installment.

August 24

Well, it is nearing the time when this thing must be mailed if it is to be delivered to you on the boat in New York harbor. With the limitation of foreign postage, I have become discursive and can say whatever comes into my head without thinking of the extra penny that it will cost—instead of a "penny for my/our thoughts" it is now a fourth of a penny for your thoughts, and they're not worth even that.

Time, however, will hang heavy on your hands en route from New York, and if you weren't reading this, you would perhaps be wasting your time with some of *Collier's* or *Liberty's* impossible fiction.

Felix must have read my thoughts, for he came up to my cot this morning about daylight with a huge rat in his mouth. He showed it to me as much as to say, "see here, I catch rats as well as mockingbirds." Then he went to an open space on the lawn and proceeded to play with his catch. He turned it loose pretended to fall asleep, while the rat made away. Then he would come out of his cat-nap and race across the lawn and grab up the fleeing rodent by the skin of his neck and return him to the center of the lawn again. Once he let the rat get half way across Oldham Street before he made a dash after him. Finally, he ate him, beginning with his head and consuming him in the leisurely fashion of the epicure, head, neck, shoulders, guts, hind-quarters and finally the tail. Felix then became frolicsome, and skinned up several oak trees, one after another, frisking here and there. Last he walked straight up to Pop and swatted that unsuspecting cherub full on the jaw. But he needn't be so cute: judgment has already been passed upon him.

Thus endeth the fifth installment.

August 26

This "linked-sweetness-long-drawn-out"[3] of a letter is turning sour, and unless I can get it mailed today, it'll have to go into the garbage-can. Really, I hardly know how to address it. I don't know for damn sure that you are on the *Normandie*. Your mama says so, but you've never told me or her (directly) that you are coming back on the *Normandie*. I look in the *New York Times* and it fails to give the where-abouts of the *Normandie*. Then how do I know that mail sent to it will be delivered anyway. I know it is delivered to passengers on departing boats, but I am not sure about incoming boats. Then you'll be here in a couple of days or so after you land, so I could just keep it and give it to you when you get here. But when you're here, I could tell you every-thing in it in a few moments so why give it to you. Dear Letter, you are getting mighty close to the waste-paper basket. Perhaps that's where you'll land. And I've already run the postage up to six cents besides the air mail, and if not airmailed at this late date, it won't get there in time.

There's one thing I want you to do when you return to England and I may forget to tell you while you are here. In Stratford near Shakespeare's old home, some enterprising Shakespeare Society has planted a bed of flowers, including every flower Shakespeare men-tioned in any of his plays or poems, some three hundred odd different species. I want you to visit this flower garden at different seasons and see all these flowers in bloom and identify them. It would be a nice little project to read Shakespeare's plays and poems and underscore each bird he mentions, identify him if he is still existent and write a little note about each individual you identify, just where, etc., as well as investigate which species he mentions which, according to bird au-thorities, are not now in the island. He wasn't as strong on birds as flowers, however. I'd like to see the particular species of primrose "that comes before the swallow dares and takes the winds of March with beauty"[4]; I'd like to see "the freaks and dartings of the black-winged swallow," I'd like to hear the "nightingale's first undersong";

or see the "humming bird's green diadem," or the king fisher's "plumage bright vieing with fish of brilliant dye below"; but I believe I have mixed up some of Keats' birds with three of Shakespeare. Which reminds me that next to Wordsworth, Keats is the greatest nature poet of the Romanticists; or no, maybe, Shelley; or maybe I don't know. Terrible admission!

So endeth the seventh and last installment.

Dad

[1]Editor's Note: Sarah won an International Rockefeller Fellowship to continue her study for a year.
[2]Editor's Note: Sarah's studies were mainly based on fly ("drosophila") populations since it is possible to experiment with them. She was looking through the microscope at chromosomes, counting individuals with color differences for studies on polymorphism. She carried a basic stock of flies, whose ancestry she knew, whenever she moved.
[3]John Milton, *L'Allegro*, l 135.
[4]William Shakespeare, *The Winter's Tale*, IV, iv.

❦

University Station
P.O. Box 1930
Austin, Texas
September 12, 1937

Dear Sarah:

I am chasing you with this letter for I forgot one of my last injunctions to remind you to be sure and wire Dean E. E. Davis,[1] Arlington, final word, just as soon as you have the information.

Somewhere between here and New York this letter will zoom over you, for I find I have one airmail envelope left. That was pretty good guessing. At the beginning of the summer I bought a supply to use in my correspondence with you, and I find but one left. Good guessing for three months, isn't it?

Well, your dear old mama snuffed a few times and wiped a tear or two away on our return from the train, but she fell to preparing dinner and was soon humming in the good old way. I hope you started humming, too. These pangs of parting are really pretty bad, but we have to get used to them. The longer one lives the more partings, and then, of course, comes the final one when he says goodbye to all at once and has done with it for good. Home is a fine thing, but the time must come when it gets thin, and before that time comes, one must build up other interests. Many a time, I have been torn to pieces with home-sickness, but the torn places heal, and Nature is so wonderful that finally home becomes a sort of congeries of beautiful memories, which birdsongs or the smell of leaves burning in autumn or a flower or something or other recall without pain or even regret. But this is all too philosophical for you now as you are getting straightened around on the boat. Buck up with a heart for any fate. You're really quite a heroic youngster and I'm proud of you.

Old Mary simply had to be dragged away, saying she wished something would happen to make her miss her train. But I guess she's now bumping along on the old H & T.C. somewhere east of Elgin. Frank Ramey[2] was at dinner with us today looking as sweet as ever. I hope you take time to write me while you're on the boat and mail it at Southhampton.

My long-deferred business trip to west Texas must begin Tuesday about four o'clock, and I will be out of writing range for some time, so don't expect many letters immediately following this one. I hope on my return, however, to have one from you. Of course, if I happen to see a real bird, I'll just have to report it—a phainopepla, for instance—doubt if that's the way to spell it. I will get on the edge of his territory.

Be sure and tell us as soon as you have it your post office address. Until further orders, we'll address you at the college.

One mighty good thing you're learning now at some expense, however, is how to travel. Talk to travelers and learn all you can about traveling. It is an art in itself. Get people's points of view. Examine each specizer [sic] just like you would a new bird—objectively. Polonius will stock in his advice, won't he?

Well, well, hun, I feel mighty empty since you left, but I'd better take my own advice and get busy. Much love.

Dad

---

[1]E. E. Davis was dean at North Texas Agricultural College, later called University of Texas at Arlington.
[2]Lillian Bedichek's brother-in-law, married to her sister Louise.

❦

University Station
P.O. Box 1930
Austin, Texas
September 25, 1937

Dear Sarah:

Is it possible that I have reached that advanced stage of senility in which business seems more important to me than attention to my darlin dotter? For the last 11 days I have been bumping around over the southern part of West Texas, getting as far west as Van Horn, meandering in the Davis Mountains and reaching the foothills of the Guadalupe range. I have written several letters to you, in my mind. I gathered a few postcards which are enclosed to show you or rather remind you, of the country I have been in, and to indicate that I at least thought of you. There was little time for birds, even. I did get on intimate terms with the Cactus Wren, and in one of the draws this side of the Guadalupe Mountains I ran across several pileolated warblers, and sure enough, they are a richer yellow and a brighter green than the Wilson [warbler], whose color was fresh in my mind from our last excursion down on Walnut Creek. I enclose a carbon of my report to the President of the University on a "Wild Life" conference which I attended as a delegate from the University.

I got home hot and dusty on a bus Thursday afternoon, having relinquished my car to Roy[1] at Kerrville who came on home leaving me to fight it out with the conservationists. I found your mama in good spirits and entertaining with apparent relish Gay's sister, Elizabeth, who recently lost a leg in an auto accident. She is as sweet a little flower as was ever mangled by a drunken driver. If I could restore that creature's leg by sending every drunken driver in Texas straight to hell, the whole wretched crew would be stewing in their own alcoholic fumes long before this letter reaches you. But alas! that lovely dancing leg is gone forever, and Elizabeth will hobble through life. She is as sunny and sweet as Gay but in a distinctly feminine way. She is as uncomplaining as a crippled bird, but I can already see in her face the pathos of the cripple—or maybe I just imagine this. She sits by the radio for hours, and Oh, the pathos of it, she prefers *dance* music! Pop takes on terribly over her, and your mama, sentimental creature, declared that Pop mistakes her for you. My gross and animalistic mind prompted me to say that it was quite impossible, for each human being's odor is unique and readily discriminated by the canine nostril. This shocked Elizabeth so that she hasn't looked me straight in the eye since. I'm afraid that I was born for the cow camp and the cattle trail. The scent of the bean-pot will cling round me still.

I have been asked to contribute a 2000-word article on birds in and about the Capital to the *Dallas News*. The *News* is paying the Academy of Science for this series, and this money will be used to help defray the expense of the Oberholser book which is scheduled to appear in 1938. I wish I had you here for consultation in preparing this article.

Dear child, this is all the time I have now. I will write you again, perhaps tomorrow. Much love.

Dad

[1]Editor's Note: Roy Henderson was athletic director of the University Interscholastic League 1921–1938. He and Bedi had a long-running handball game.

❧

University Station
P.O. Box 1930
Austin, Texas
September 28, 1937
Dear Sarah:

Yesterday at lunch your mama and I counted the days necessary for a letter to be transmitted from you provided you mailed one on your arrival in England. I placed it at 8 days and expected a letter, therefore, today, calculating that you would arrive on the 20th. But when I returned to my office, the afternoon mail had just been delivered, and your letter of the 19th, mailed, I suppose, the 20th, was in the box. An hour or two later your mama rang up to tell me she had a letter from you. So we shall have to mark one up in favor of the good old U.S. mail. Even counting the gain in time coming eastward, it took barely 8 days. When the transatlantic air service gets going, we'll be closer yet, perhaps only four days. Then we shall have to redouble our epistolary efforts. We note that your two letters did not duplicate, one covering your New York period and one giving boat-experiences. You

*171*

may be sure that we found both of them interesting.

The still cool of fall mornings in Austin has apparently come to stay. A light coat is comfortable, and comfortably shed about ten o'clock; by four in the afternoon, a civilized man would be wearing nothing but shorts, but, in deference to the tabus of the semi-savage life in which I find myself, I retain shirt and trousers. Your grandchildren will look with the same tolerant disdain upon the clothes of this generation as we now look upon the bustles and corsets of the early nineties. When we free ourselves from mediaeval prejudices against nakedness and have exterminated bloodsucking insects such as flies and mosquitoes, the summer garb in Texas will be paper-shorts and Japanese sandals, and each bedroom will be equipped with a wastepaper basket to hold the discarded shorts of the day before. I here and now pronounce my blessing upon that emancipated generation. Instead of carrying around garments that absorb and accumulate the excrement of some millions of exuding body-pores, sun and air will convert this disgusting material into invisible and odorless dust which will pass off into the air, as it was intended to do, and leave the body free to develop and give off its own sweet and ravishing natural perfumes. Walt Whitman must have been sunning himself naked for days when he exclaimed: "The scent of these armpits, aroma finer than prayer!" But I shall have to close this nudistic sermon.

Bachman is settling down to work. He is undertaking an hundred-page-thesis for Redford[1] on one of our governmental agencies, perhaps regulation of truck traffic. This is a seminar course largely by conference, and it appeals to him. Redford must think well of him. Bachman was the only registrant for the course, and I think it was quite a concession, and perhaps a recognition of exceptional ability, for Redford to take on an undergraduate for what practically amounts to a thesis course. Anyway, it seems to inspire the lad, and I am hoping the inspiration will last. He looks like a bronze statue tinted with pink and gold. Really, his complexion is something that artists dream about, but rarely see.

Enclosed is a letter from Burdette which I de-enveloped to save postage.

Much love,
Dad.

---

[1]Emmette S. Redford was Professor of Government at the University of Texas.

[October 1937]

Dear Una

I am glad to know that you are taking up Christian Science in earnest. It is the most wholesome, liberalizing, superstition-killing study I know of. Not that you need it any more than anyone else does, but you need it. I know it chiefly through its effects upon other people. It marks them as I believe the faith of the early Christians set them aside and marked them as something better and higher than their pagan associates. The three gigantic frauds of the human race are medicine, the church, and the law. It actively opposes the two former, while it passively opposes the latter. They talk of the unreason of Christian Science—why, from the time that Galen prescribed an injection of putrid cow urine mixed with copper filings to cure sterility down to the present hideous custom of vaccination, medicine has been one vast, conglomerate of wretched humbug, gross, evil and nasty superstition. Do you know the reason medical remedies of ten years ago are considered out of date? Simply because that time is required for the people to discover they are no good, and the doctors are forced into perpetrating some new atrocity in the name of the latest discovery of science. Powdered mummies were a specific for ten different diseases in Queen Elizabeth's time; and these specifics have changed a hundred times since then. They change quicker now because the general diffusion of knowledge is greater and hence the quackery is sooner discovered.

If I read Mrs. Eddy until doomesday, I don't believe that I could make heads or tails of what she teaches. It is likely that she has no message for me at all. I can't seem to connect with her mentally at all. I judge C. S. by its effects upon the people who believe in it. It has produced the best newspaper in the United States, it has produced many of our clearest thinkers, it has relieved the hungry, cured the sick, and done everything except raise the dead. Therefore, I am for it. It has transformed wretched-tempered people into sweet-tempered people, which is greater than raising the dead. It is a leaven which is slowly transforming the sodden superstitions of the church into something beautiful and good. I am for it, but I don't know what it is, and probably never shall.

*173*

Affectionately,
Roy

🌱

University Station
P. O. Box 1930
Austin, Texas
October 31, 1937

Dear Sarah:

Too bad about the typhoid shots—never had one myself but from all accounts they're almost as bad as the disease. And then to have an attack of homesickness on top of that, it must weigh considerable upon your usually buoyant spirits. I feel by the way this thing is starting out that I am in no mood to write, and I shall put it off until morning. This is Sunday, and I've been slaving at this typewriter since seven o'clock and now it's 5:30. Just one word more: Felix is dead. Automobile.

November 1.

I've come out considerably since I abandoned this letter yesterday afternoon. Nothing like plenty of sleep. Be sure you take plenty—all, or as long, as you can stay asleep, and then lie there awhile and woo her again. If it takes nine hours, well and good. Don't again get obsessed with a sense of hurry. Life is long, if one will nurse it along. Long walks and bedroom exercises will help you sleep. Why take *three* math courses if three consume too much time? Maybe you're attempting too much—the one vice that my dear little daughter has. Otherwise, you're perfect. The best way to waste time is to attempt too much.

The Webbs[1] are coming over in February, and you'll have some real homefolks to associate with. They are fine as they make 'em. Webb has just gotten out a new book, *Divided We Stand*, the best thing he has published. If I thought you would have time to read it, I'd send you a copy.

Your mama is teaching today in Palm School.[2] Bachman cut wood yesterday afternoon for a while, went to a picture show with Ernest[3] the other night, briefed five cases yesterday, and is otherwise doing quite satisfactorily. We have heard nothing more from Mary or Gay.

*174*

Pop pops out of bed at every whiff he gets of another dog in the yard and whiffs are many judging from the way the little fool is acting these nights. He alarms us with his barks and I have been threatening to put him in the cellar. He is not himself at all. Goes around oppressed apparently with a sense of impending disaster.

I'm surprised to hear you talk of robins singing in England in October. That's better than they do for us. I lay awake sometime last night, however, listening to a mockingbird. And the screech owls have come back and send their eerie note a quivering across the night. One tried to compete with the mocker last night, but then gave it up as a bad job. But the robin's song is the first cheerful note I have heard out of England in many a day. How about Haldane's stepson[4] in Spain—is he still there?

Don't worry about puffiness under the eyes. That's often due merely to over-use of the eyes. Just let up a bit. Drink plenty of water. Chew each bite thirty-two times, and never feel hurried at meals. Loaf occasionally and invite your soul. That's what I'm going to do presently. I'm going to leave a lot of things undone here in the office and walk straight down East Avenue to the river and sit there a while in the sun.

I really enjoyed Muller's[5] *Out of the Night.* It's too long-range for the average reader. The next generation will consider it a greater book than this one does, in my opinion, which, by the way, isn't worth much, especially when it deals with prophecy. Whose does? Don't worry about the rotten deal the world gives the idealist. He has compensations. Many of them are happy, and Muller seems to be fairly so.

It must have been thrilling to stand at the foot of Darwin's tomb. I never much sympathized with Mark Twain's flippant attitude towards the sacred spots of the old world. The honoring of the truly great after they are dead inspires many of the living to greatness they would not otherwise attain. We really don't have enough reverence and gratitude to the great men and women who have made the world richer for us by their lives.

But I see I am drifting into homily, and very dull at that. Write to us. And don't begrudge the time it takes.

Much love,
Dad

[1]Editor's Note: Bedichek's good friend, Walter Prescott Webb, held the Harkness professorship at the University of London in 1938; he was a historian on the University of Texas faculty for forty-five years.
[2]Editor's Note: Palm School is the grade school nearest the Bedichek's home. Bach attended school there.
[3]Editor's Note: Ernest Villavaso, a good friend.
[4]Editor's Note: Haldane's stepson was involved in the Spanish Civil War. Haldane at one time was an admirer of communism.
[5]Hermann Joseph Muller, U.S. geneticist, awarded the 1946 Nobel Prize for his work showing that x-rays greatly accelerate mutation processes. Sarah studied under him at the University of Texas.

&

University Station
P.O. Box 1930
Austin, Texas
November 7, 1937

Dear Sarah:
Picking up Pop where I left him off in my last letter, I must report him a disastrous week.

Ill fares the night to hastening ills a prey
Where dogs accumulate 'round the female stray.[1]

Howls, snarls, snaps, moans, shrieks, growls from gutturals to the sharp, high piercing variety, thrashing in the shrubbery, registering every canine-motion from the deadly violence of the jungle to defiance, hysterics and on to the lost wail of a broken soul, murdered sleep and shook the autumn-turning leaves from the postoaks. Picture papa in pajamas out in the night hurling unavailing missiles hither and yon like some blind Cyclops raging against the taunts of the departing Greeks. Picture Pop, imagining that the Cyclops had come to his rescue, racing down this alley and that, up one street and down the other, uttering his staccato barks. Listen to mama from an upstairs window volunteering advice, and Bachman poking his head from another window with a pistol as long as your arm threatening to shoot the whole damn town up. Thus, night after night. Well, quiet reigns again. Pop has returned, skin and bone, throat swelled from frequent shaking, dirty, bedraggled but still belligerent, everything but his spirit broken:

In the fell clutch of circumstance
    I have not winced nor cried aloud—
Beneath the bludgeonings of Chance,
    My head is bloody but unbowed.[2]

And neither is his tail. It's stiff and pointing toward the zenith. I'll give him a bath.

The quotation of the above stanza from Ernest Henley has led me to discover the source of the title of Muller's book *Out of the Night*. Curious I had never thought of it before. Maybe you'd like the complete poem, and I give it to you from memory.

Out of the night that covers me
    Black as the pit from pole to pole,
I thank whatever gods may be
    For my unconquerable soul.

In the fell clutch of circumstance
    I have not winced nor cried aloud,
Beneath the bludgeonings of Chance
    My head is bloody but unbowed.

Beyond this place of wrath and tears
    Looms but the horror of the shade,
And yet the menace of the years
    Finds, and shall find me, unafraid.

It matters not how strait the gate,
    How charged with punishment the scroll:
I am the master of my fate,
    I am the Captain of my soul.

No greater or more defiant utterance in poetic form was ever hurled in the teeth of Life than is contained in these sixteen short lines. Sometimes when you want to know how ghastly poetry can be made, read Henley's series of sonnets entitled "In Hospital." It's really too horrible to be read and I wouldn't recommend it to a less valiant soul than yours. It's not well to put any except trained and hardened boxers barefisted into the ring for a genuine knock-down-and-drag-out with Life.

I noticed in the paper the other day that an eagle had attacked a negro girl near Jarrell about half way between Georgetown and Belton. I wrote to the superintendent of schools at Jarrell for a more detailed account of the incident, and I am copying his reply to enclose herewith. It will be a good note for you to use in your forthcoming work on Texas birds. I am now on trail of the taxidermist who mounted the bird, and I shall get a picture of the specimen for you. Some summer before I get too old to climb, I want us to spend in the Chisos mountains for a study of the birds out there. The Chisos are a chunk of the Rockies thrown off down there on the Mexican border. The Rio Grande runs hard by and you know the Rocky Mountain birds must follow down the river, and they're far enough South to catch the wanderers from the Mexican tableland. I can think of no more fertile field in Texas than this, and it's practically unexplored.

By the way, in one of your off-moments, if you ever have any, why don't you write an article on Texas birds for one of the English birds journals?

Your mama is getting pow'ful frisky these days. She "supernume–rates" frequently and then teaches in night school, marking up fourteen hours or so. She seems to absorb this punishment with gusto, and then takes on hours of coaching besides. She's apparently a pretty tough old bird. She sleeps like a rock when the dogs will let her, has no hay-fever, and seems generally in better health than in years. She and Bachman go over the football games with a fine-tooth comb, leaving nothing out, bawl out the referees for rotten decisions, keep up with injured players, and bandy gossip about recruiting and all the other fan-talk of the barber-shops and barrooms. Father gets an awful crop full, but he "ain't say nuthin."

Church bells are ringing, church choirs are singing, and soon the pastors will be haranging from the dozen or more pulpits of this be-nighted city. What a goshawful lot of bunk is being spilled! No wonder that a lot of weird and fantastic religions are cropping up: nazism, fascism, communism, and all the rest. Church religion has gotten away from life, and people insist on religion having some relation to life.

In a movie last night, Mrs. Chaing Kai-Shek made a talk. What a lovely creature she is! Her English is simply beautiful. The Japanese ambassador to this country read a little paragraph in horrible English just before they threw her on the screen. The audience tended to hiss him and cheer her. American sympathies are overwhelmingly with the Chinese. How do you find it in England?

Eat plenty of lettuce. It's got the vitamin in it of Texas sunshine, which you are missing in that foggy atmosphere.

Much love.

Dad

[1]Bedichek is parodying Oliver Goldsmith's, *The Deserted Village*:
   Ill fares the land, to hastening ills a prey,
   Where wealth accumulates, and men decay;
[2]William Ernest Henley, "Invictus."

January 28, 1938

Dearest Dad and Mother,

I've accepted a residency in Obstetrics, Gynecology, and Pediatrics at St. Joseph's Infirmary, Houston, for next year.

Gay has just one more final, thank goodness. I feel as if I were going through them myself. He was one of the high point men on the chemistry laboratory practical,[1] we have found out. We played a set of tennis this afternoon to celebrate the pretty weather.

I am learning lots and enjoying my work. The boys[2] are acting like angels now. I don't know what has come over them.

Lovingly,

Mary (over)

I did my third operation, to a woman—plastic work on an old vaginal tear due to childbirth (i.e. repair of cystocele) m.e.

[1]Editor's Note: Gay had majored in chemistry at the University of Texas, hearing that jobs in that field were plentiful. He and Mary were married in August 1936, when she was half-way through medical school. He soon decided he too wanted to be a physician and by 1938 was enrolled in the University of Texas Medical School at Galveston.
[2]Editor's Note: "The boys" were probably Mary's fellow medical students, who sometimes played tricks on the four girls who persisted to graduation.

University Station
Box H (*Please* note change of box number)
Austin, Texas
January 31, 1938

Dear Mary:

Although unanswered correspondence litters up two desks, one to the right of me and one to the left, and the telephone interrupts every two minutes, I must knock off a few lines to tell you that your note gives me and mama much satisfaction. We are very proud of you and Gay, and news of your accomplishments thrills and tends to defrost our aging emotional mechanisms.

How much will this residency you have accepted pay? Does St. Joseph's have a good reputation among the medical fraternity? Tell us all about it. How did the excised appendix turn out, or rather how did what was left of the patient turn out?

Bach and I started out afoot on a bird-hike yesterday morning at 7. About twelve o'clock we had identified thirty-five species, and I proposed that we go till we got 40, and he accepted. Well, the last five is always the hardest five, and we walked until about 2 o'clock before we got them, and just as we were at the furtherest point from home, a brisk and blue norther blew up, finding Bach in a thin shirt and dungarees. Fortunately, I had brought a sweater. We beat it for home and got here about four P.M., having covered in our meanderings about 25 miles, not bad, is it, for a sixty-year old? I left Bach in bed this morning at seven, having myself arisen at 5. So you see, I ain't dead yit.

Your mama is in fine shape. The sentimental creature has weakened, and let the animals back into the house: Keety, Felix III, and Pop. I think I'll give up. Man has his will but woman has her way.[1]

> Men, dying, make their wills. Their wifes
>     Escape a task so sad;
> Why should they *make* what all their lives
>     The gentle dames have had?

Bachman is B-ing it through the University.[2] Fall semester no A's, also no C's so far. Principally interested in motor truck regulation and building model ships. Has one of ambitious design now under construction. Much love.

Dad

[1]Oliver Wendell Holmes, *The Autocrat of the Breakfast Table,* Chapter 2.
[2]Editor's Note: Bach got his BA from the University of Texas in 1938 and his law degree from the University of Texas Law School in 1941.

❦

University Station
Box H
Austin, Texas
February 20, 1938

Dear Mary:

I am momently expecting your mama to honk for me—I mean honk the old Ford—nothing except autos and geese *honk*, and your mama doesn't fall in the latter category.

Your card came yesterday, and I'm awful thankful that you are on the giving rather than the receiving end of those ghastly operations. Four operations on one tiny postcard, *multum in parvo*, if I haven't forgotten my small Latin—There's your mama's honk. More later.

Next morning 7 A.M.

The engagement your mother and I had was with a function promoted by the Students' Committee on Interracial Relations at the University Presbyterian Church. One of those domino affairs such as you participated in as a student at Camp something-or-other in Arkansas or Missouri one summer. By domino I mean white and black affairs, although the coloration is not as definite as on a domino, there being plenty of shadings. We had Negro singing, most of which was uplifting and easy to listen to, but I was quite displeased with one selection "Drink to Me Only with Thine Eyes" sung acapello (can't be sure of spelling) with all the trimmings. It made this piece, which at core is artificial and the product of an artificial, dandified social set, really more artificial than it really is and hollow as all second-hand affecta-

*181*

tions are. But, boy, when that choir turned loose on Schubert's "Omnipotence" it lifted the roof, and, backed up with the pipe organ, stirred me deeply.

The psychology of these affairs is to accustom the two races to accommodate themselves together, a sort of effort at goodneighborliness in a difficult field. It is difficult from two standpoints: 1. economic exploitation, the whites generally being exploiters and the negroes exploited; 2. race, a problem that is now tearing Europe to pieces, and one which never in the history of man has been satisfactorily adjusted.

Thus it looks like an unsuperable difficulty. But Jesus turned water into wine, a trifling miracle compared with the sight I saw last night in the basement of the Presbyterian Church; blue-blooded whites, singing, eating and conversing on an apparently equal social plane. Authority for and inspiration of the entire affair came from the words of Jesus, and words, at that, filtered through generations of cold Presbyterians. How burning they must have been in their original heat to have retained sufficient warmth after such a process! No wonder Hitler hates Jesus.

A lovely University girl presided. Mrs. Banks, wife of the President of Prairie View Normal, Negress, read a paper on "The Negro in Literature," mostly a bibliography with short comments, and read much too rapidly, but quite intelligently prepared—I'd class it as a Number 1 Women's Club paper.

In the auditorium the color line was not tightly drawn, but approximately. I set your mother down by a good-sized Negro man. At the eating function, I called a lubberly embarrassed Negro boy[1] over to the chair beside me. So I tried my best to mix and mingle in true Christian fashion. A splendid Negro song leader lead the singing at this function with "Steal Away" and several others.

Well, well, Mary, don't cut any legs off until you have to.

Much love, Dad

[1]A note has been added here: "This boy had just sung Tschaikovsky's "None But the Lonely Heart" in French! L." (Lillian Bedichek)

University Station
Box H, Austin
Texas
June 9, 1938

Dear Sarah:

Yours of May 24, 1938, typed, but dated in pencil, was waiting for me at the office after a rather hectic tour in West Texas, bleak but beautiful—wind, dust, blazing suns and brilliant moons, icy (almost) in mountains camps, blistering on the plains—and all the rest that goes with that unconquerable region where you first saw the light (a candle light, I think). Ten days of it has browned my face, parched my lips, skinned my hands, corned my toes and greatly elevated my spirit. I don't have my notebook with me, having left it in the old knapsack. I'll write you the bird-lore I picked up when the notebook is available.

I find that I did not have to include the English Sparrow to make the fiftieth, for I overlooked six I listed on a page out of its order, as follows:

1. Kingbird
2. Shore lark
3. Least sandpiper
4. Wilson's Phalarope
5. Painted bunting
6. Red-backed Sandpiper

The Wilson Phalarope ought to be called the whirling dervish. He is called locally the "crazy sandpiper" on account of his eternal spinning around while feeding. I had a fine opportunity to see him at it. There was a long swamp broken into puddles from the size of your hat to considerable areas of shallow water. The sun was to my back as I looked up this long swamp of a thousand acres or more. Thousands of small sandpipers were feeding, sprinkled in with yellow legs/and red-backed sandpipers. Interspersed in this mass of shore-bird life were thousands of phalaropes, each one spinning around like a top and flitting to another puddle when he had worked out the one he was occupying for a moment. Each bird seemed to be making about forty revolutions per minute. So up this long stretch of water were solemn herons, busy least sandpipers, more dignified red-backs, interspersed at almost mathematical intervals with these crazy, whirling dervishes. It made quite a sight.

The bald eagle I saw was not bald, for he was young. They get the bald head (white head) in the third or fourth year. As soon as the young leave the nest, the old ones kite out for far parts, and the babies must shift for themselves which they seem well able to do. The specimen I saw was the noblest bird I have ever seen. Dark all over, nearly black, with his huge feet placed far apart on a limb, turning his head gradually from side to side, he had a certain kingly look about him as if he were granting an audience. When I edged up closer than court etiquette allowed, he sailed grandly away. I examined the nest from afar with my glasses, and I judged it to be about six feet in depth, and made of sticks, some of which were at least an inch in diameter.

Mary and Gay are here, happy as if they had good sense, Mary a little pale, and Gay far too fat—tips scales at 218. Mama Jenny is chipper and of good color—just saw her for a moment last night. No one was up this morning when I sneaked out. Bachman was out last night, so I can't give a report on him after my ten days absence. I notice, however, that the yard is still in the disgraceful condition in which I left it—only about ten days more ragged.

Well, duty calls—the office-force (much diminished) is assembling.

Much love,
Dad

University Station
Box H
Austin, Texas
June no July 1, 1938

Dear Sarah:

It's some satisfaction to get a letter from you that's carried through the mail with no foreign stamps on it. The North American continent, according to geologists, is older, and therefore, I think, safer than the European or any of its outlying islands. It's more satisfaction to know that you feel you have really gotten something from your year abroad. I'm really proud of your determination and courage in taking walking trips by yourself. I don't believe in incurring unnecessary risks, but at the same time, I do not believe in being deterred from doing something one really wants to do for fear of some vague thing that might happen, the probability of which is maybe one in a thousand or a million. Statistics show that probability of getting seriously hurt in a bathtub is high in proportion to risks that are so often dramatized in the movies, and still I think one should not forego his daily bath for fear of getting hurt.

Will you get any reprints of the *Annals of Eugenics* article? If so, I should appreciate getting one. And don't fail to send Davis one. Will the thesis be published anywhere, any time? I'll be looking for the record of the nightingale's song. Frankly and unpatriotically, how do you think it compares with the mocker by moonlight?

If Prof. Haldane said you "proved your point" I should think that would be high enough praise for any piece of scientific work.

Am mighty glad that you have had association with men like Muller and Haldane who are thinking about the social implications of their work, in addition to association with Painter[1] and Patterson who are both mentally incapable of entertaining a social idea. There is great danger of groups of specialists getting so technical and magnifying their own importance so much and inventing their own language to such an extent that they lose touch with the mass of humanity. Our roots are in the mass and we must get our nourishment from the mass. We must be human beings first.

As soon as you know when Haldane will come, wire me. If you know the name of the boat he is coming on and when it will reach New York, wire me that. I suppose he has many friends and acquaintances in New York, but if not, you might do well to write Dan Williams a note of introduction to him. Dan would like to meet him and they're both bolsheviks. Dan's address is 276 Riverside Drive, New York.

Mama has put up an unbelievable amount of tomato sauce and you know how good that is in potato soup. She is also making a preserve that is delicious from a little yellow pear tomato that I have grown a quantity of this year. Don't forget to send me the *Politics and Heredity*. I want to read it before I see Haldane, if I see him at all. I suppose I should go to the library and give other of his books the once over.

Have had a number of trips this summer, and occasionally I have had a round with the birds. I kept notes, and I'll write you a bird-letter soon. One thing that stands out in my memory more vividly than any other is the sight of a Texas Kingfisher on Devil's River. He displayed himself before me, and let me get within twenty feet of him. He is a dark, iridescent green with a brilliant white collar, and the same outline as the Belted. His flight, however, is more that of a sandpiper than you would expect. He doesn't pump like the Belted, but darts. I saw also on the coast the lovely bay-breasted warbler. There's no richer chestnut in the bird-world than this little fellow has on head and neck and breast. Black cheeks, grayish on back with white wing-bars, and lively as a cricket. But more about birds later.

Dad

[1]Theophilus S. Painter, professor of zoology at the University of Texas and president from 1946–52, was known for his investigations of the chromosomes in the salivary glands of fruit flies.

❦

University Station
P. O. Box H
Austin, Texas
October 6, 1938

Dear Mary:

Your very short note of October 2, written "on your knee" came duly and was consumed at once by all that remains of the family, viz., Lil, Bach & me. Although Gay is not afflicted with a diarrhea of words as is the above-named trio, we find that we miss him greatly. He is the best-humored and most prodigious worker I have ever known. Usually real workers are dour, or sour, or highly inflammatory (like Sally), but Gay's good humor seems as inexhaustible as his energy.

Did a Dr. Winship[1] call on you? I gave him your name, as he is likely to locate in Houston. A keen young fellow, he is, and his wife is a graduate nurse who has specialized in care of pregnant women—I can't think of the fool Greek name for this. You will find her quite an intelligent and efficient young mid-west yankee woman, from what I hear. I haven't met her. Winship's brother is now in our employ. That's how I came to get acquainted with the Dr.

Bachman is boning on his law. Doesn't waste a great deal of time and seems to be enjoying it. Your mama is going day and night with her maternal clinic[2] which has just been put out of the City Hospital by the City Commission. Sarah came last week-end. She's getting adjusted at Arlington and will like it, I think.

Of course, we are all wasting tons of energy in giving vent to our indignation over the rape of Czechoslovakia. Being a studious professional woman, you have perhaps not heard of it yet, and it's just as well. Medicine is such a serious business that there is time or thought for little else. But I give you the news in a nutshell: The English ruling class has just sold out a little country which twenty years ago it set up as a policeman to prevent the eastern expansion of Germany. When the policeman was attacked England & France repudiated him and turned him over bound and gagged to the robbers without even a verbal protest. That's all it amounts to; "further details will be found in your newspapers," as the radio announcers say.

I could go into a long tirade which you would not have time to read on what that means to our own national life; but instead, I shall say

Much love,
Dad

[1] Possibly the brother of Frank Loren Winship, a speech professor at the University of Texas.

[2] Editor's Note: Lillian, as a teacher of Spanish, had much contact with young Mexican women for whom over-large families were a crushing problem. She went on the board of the Planned Parenthood Clinic. There was much unpleasant opposition from angry Catholic spokesmen. She was called a "loose woman," as were others who supported it, and the clinic was forced out of the city hospital. (See letter October 9, 1938.)

❦

St. Joseph's Infirmary
Houston, Texas
October 8, 1938

Dearest Mother,

Tell me about this Maternal Health Clinic trouble. Today one of the head sisters here called me aside and asked me if I believed in birth control—that it had been stated by my Mother in Austin that I did.[1] I told her that I did believe in it when medically or socially indicated but that I didn't think such information should be indiscriminately given.

187

I said that since I was employed by a Catholic institution, I would not give out such information, if they so desired, as long as I am here. Then I went on to tell her that you have the greatest faith that you were doing the right thing in supporting birth control where indicated—especially in Tuberculous & Syphilitic poor families & in poverty stricken people burdened with too many children. (Was that OK?)

Looks like you're getting back into the schools by stages, doesn't it?

Lovingly,
Mary

[1]Lillian's note reads: "Father Duffy misquoted me. I said *no such thing*. L." And then added: "The Catholic Sisters did not dismiss Mary. They must have heard from the Sisters at the Galveston hospital, where Mary interned. They loved her!"

❦

University Station
Box H
Austin, Texas
October 9, 1938

Dear Sarah:

News budget:

1. Mama's birth control clinic was kicked out of the City Hospital by Mayor Miller and cohorts (mostly Catholic) and landed somewhere on East Avenue.

2. Mama chauffered Virginia Lee[1] and friend around yesterday afternoon. They were here on week-end visit.

3. Aunt Ina visited us for four days last week. But on second thought, it was before your last visit.

4. Merie spent yesterday with us sewing.

5. Mama's night classes begin this week.

6. Bachman is dour and inflammatory, by turns. Raised hell yesterday because Merie wanted to use sewing machine while he wanted to listen to radio. When he wants to shave with electric razor which also puts radio out of commission, he will break into one of mama's loved dramatizations without warning.

7. Your dad's humor is the worst in years.

8. Keety's three kittens occupy back doorstep.

9. Pop popped into the office just now and popped out again. I hope he popped home without getting popped by an automobile.

10. Mama Jenny writes that Bitsy is able to walk a little.

11. Bach cut yard yesterday. Consideration $.50.

Dad

[1]Lillian's niece, daughter of sister Louise and Frank Ramey.

❦

University Station
Box H
Austin, Texas
October 28, 1938

Dear Sarah:

Your good letter of the 24th was duly received and duly passed around. I meant to answer it yesterday, but flirted all day with the idea of coming to Dallas this week-end where I have some business which should be attended to, in which event I should have phoned you. However, I decided about 8 o'clock last night that I had best defer this trip and settle matter by correspondence, if possible. I am making the attempt today, and should I fail, I shall likely come to Dallas next weekend. If I find it necessary to come, I shall phone you about the middle of next week. In the meantime, if there is any of your junk you wish brought up there free of charge, send me a list of it.

Pearce's[1] death was a severe blow to me. He was one of my dearest friends, "faithful and just to me."[2] I was at Kingsville when the word reached me, and I returned to Austin immediately. Mrs. Pearce had an idea that she wanted me to speak at his funeral and I was so advised before starting home. Needless to say on the long trip (it took about five hours, in the night) I composed at least a dozen funeral orations. I believe I thought of all the kind things I ever knew of his doing and they are legion, and of all the wise and witty things he had said in my hearing, legion, also. But when I arrived that night, Mrs. Pearce had changed her plans and had the usual arrangements made

*189*

with a preacher who, by the way, proved to be an *un*usual preacher. He did the job so much better than I could have done it that I have not ceased admiring Mrs. Pearce's wisdom in changing her plan and her man. While he had nothing like the rich background of Pearce's life that I have, he had the ability to absorb in a few hours much of it from Pearce' friends, and he had the faculty of condensation and the gift of eloquent expression so far beyond my own, that as I listened to him, I felt that "my own tongue had become loosened" in him and that he was saying the very things that I would have striven ineffectively to say.

Glad you are getting a little social diversion. I was pleased to notice that your stay in England taught you a little of the art of "diplomatic disapproval" of others' opinions. I noticed this particularly in your discussion at the dinner table with Gay. You have learned that assertion is not argument, and that other people's prepossessions are flowers that must be delicately handled to avoid bruising. It's an art that I have never learned. Flat contradiction is the premier conversational vice of our own family. I think it is a good conversational rule never to flatly contradict anyone. Some phase of the other's point of view with which one can at least partially agree should be selected, emphasized, and taken as a point of departure. The best modern statement of the art of discussion that I have seen is that of J. L. Garvin, (by the way, a hard-bitten English conservative):

Good argument is a sharp process of investigation, leading by mutual criticism to some nearer ascertainment of truth.

Of course, if one wants to go to the classics, he could fill a book with quotations of similar import. One of the best occurs in Book V of *Plato's Republic*, which is too long to quote in a letter, but I'm going to quote it anyway:

Verily, Glaucon, I said, glorious is the power of the *art* of contradiction!

Why do you say so?

Because I think that many a man falls into the practice against his will. When he thinks that he is reasoning he is really disputing,[3] just because he cannot define and divide, and so know that of which he is speaking; and he will pursue a mere verbal opposition in the spirit of contention and not of fair discussion.

Yes, he replied, such is very often the case; but what has that to do with us and our argument?

A great deal; for there is certainly a danger of our getting unintentionally into a verbal opposition.

So dear old Plato observed this human failing 2,500 years ago and stated it more perfectly than it has ever been stated since.

Your abbreviation of "Assistant Librarian," Ass.Lib., is not according to Webster: do you mean it as suggestive?

Home affairs are about the same as usual. Bachman is really taking an interest in his law. Mama is working too hard. Two of the kittens are still with us. I'm afraid your mama is stringing us with an account of a good lady who wants these kittens; day follows day and night night, and still no kind lady shows up to take these kittens away. I hear her talking to them with notes of affection in her voice. I offered to "dispose" of them, but she made difficulties about it, the kind lady would be disappointed, and so on.

I mentioned above being at Kingsville. By reference to the map, you will see that Kingsville is near the coast. I spend the Sunday preceding my return on Riviera Beach on Baffin Bay, camping alone, living on potato soup, and, of course, looking around a bit at the bird life. I saw our usual coast birds, or many of them. Late in the evening and in the clear morning sky, many snow geese (lesser) went over, but I got no close up. I killed a harmless pine snake mistaking it for a rattler. I'll never make this error again. Coiled up, the pine snake looks much like the rattler, that is, to one who knows no more about snakes than I do. If I had time, I'd take up snakes seriously. I met an old German farmer who won't allow any snake on his place to be killed, except rattlers. His son came around my camp with a five-foot "prairie racer" in his hand which he allowed to lick his face repeatedly. The boy has a snake "farm" and pets and coddles all sorts of snakes.

The office force is assembling and I have to get to work.

Much love.

Dad

---

[1]James Edwin Pearce, chairman of the University of Texas Department of Anthropology, died October 22, 1938.

[2]Shakespeare, *Julius Caesar*, Act iii, sc. 2, l. 175.
[3]Bedichek's note reads: "Me, mama & Bach.

University Station
Box H
Austin, Texas
December 3, 1938

Dear Sarah:

All week I have been contemplating this epistolary essay, also I have been intending for a month to rake the leaves up in the yard, and for three months I have meant to straighten up my desk and find out what there is on it that I should have done six months ago, but at this moment (7 A.M.) I find my desk unstraightened, the yard unraked and this letter unwritten. If, indeed, the path to Hades is paved with good intentions, I have constructed one of those Hitlerian super-highways in that direction.

Last weekend I had my yearly nightmare lasting 3-1/2 days at the State Teachers Association. Crowds, overheated rooms, two of my own speeches almost as vacuous as those I had to listen to, endless kicks and complaints, violent disputes among impolite disputants, the trifling conversation of hotel lobbies, and all the rest that goes to make up the crowd-man, this bolt upright curiously forked animal that for some reason enjoys "swarming" like ants and bees. I was beset the whole time trying to recall a couple of quatrains that impressed me long ago, written by some minor poet. A line or a phrase would come to me in the middle of a conference, the chime of one of its rimes came into my head while I was making a speech, a picture of cold, wide spaces silent under the stars floated into my memory in the crowded elevator of the Adolphus Hotel. It simply dogged me until finally I got two lines:

> In the cold autumn dusk arise
> Orion and the Pleadies.

Then I remembered that Antares was in it somewhere. Then I knew that the poet somewhere spoke of the "mysterious summer night." I

mingled and jumbled phrases and pictures together like someone trying to work a jigsaw puzzle. I was almost tempted to go out and get a
pint of whiskey, retire to my room and get good and drunk, for I have
heard that that sometimes freshens the memory of things long past.
Maybe I repeated this thing sometime or other in my youth when I was
drunk and so [it] was buried in drunken memories which come to the
surface again only when one is again drunk. William James in his Psychology gives numerous instances of these freaks of memory, and compared them with the freaks of memory in hypnosis. But I didn't. Then
the rimes "light" and "night" suddenly appeared above the rim of consciousness, and I knew that rime was in it. Getting up one morning,
before I had really gotten my feet, stumbling around the little cubby-
hole which the hotel calls a room, I found myself murmuring.

The wonder of an ancient awe takes hold upon him.

Thus little chips and whetstones of the poem collected and arranged
themselves, and coming home on the back seat of the car by myself, I
actually brought the whole thing together in those five hours. Here it
is:

> The wonder of an ancient awe
> Takes hold upon him when he sees
> In the cold autumn dusk arise
> Orion and the Pleadies;
>
> Or when, along the southern rim
> Of the mysterious summer night,
> He marks, above the sleeping world,
> Antares and his scarlet light.

Now isn't that a pretty little poem? I think it was really worth salvag-
ing although the torment of recalling it was excruciating. Isn't that the
scene quiet and restful. It's almost as miraculous in conjuring up a
scene as a line from Whitman, say, for instance;

> The sundown shadows lengthen over lonesome and
> limitless prairies

I hear the bark of a coyote and the song of the little sparrow that rises in desert places around Deming, singing as he floats down fifty or a hundred feet. Mama used to call it the "little lonesome bird." I identified it once as either the Cassin or the Sage Sparrow, I don't remember which. The last time I saw one was when I was with Dr. Benedict[1] on his old home-place in Young County. I saw one also on the Laurelles Ranch near Corpus Christi about ten years ago.

I haven't remembered yet the author, but that will come in due time. Maybe I will send it to the *New York Times* for identifying on its page devoted to identifying scraps that people remember and can't complete. I know it was a minor poet; major poets don't turn off such lovely trifles.

Anyway, next summer, remember to look for Antares with his scarlet light along the rim of the mysterious summer night. So astronomy has its poetic as well as its scientific appeal.

This afternoon I'm going to take Lil to a football game, the first in about ten years. You know how she enjoys football. It's a shame she doesn't go oftener, but, honest to God, a game of football bores me as nothing else in the world. But your martyr will perform this afternoon if he has left any strength of character at all.

Would you be interested in reading a resolution I wrote for the Town & Gown Club on the death of J. E. Pearce? It will cost about three cents to send and the same to return, but if you would like to see it, I'll stand my share of the expense. By the way, Davis knew Pearce well, and if I do send it, show it to Davis.

We have the plans completed and approved for remodeling the house and it will probably be started within a week.

Bachman would surprise you. He is studying as hard as I ever saw you or Mary study. I offered to take him to the woods yesterday afternoon, but he turned me down—had to study. He full-dressed himself last night, however, and took in some sort of function, while your mama and Mrs. Kidd[2] attended the Ballet in the Gregory Gym. Father retired at 8 P.M. and read himself to sleep on *Pickwick Papers*, and left this morning before there was any stir in the house. I reckon they all got back safely, although I shall have to wait until noon to hear an account of their adventures. This thing is getting long enough, don't you think? I may put a special delivery stamp on it so you will get it tomorrow—

Sunday. Maybe I won't and you will have to be deprived of this classic until Monday morning. Maybe I will and maybe I won't. Since you will know my decision before you read these lines, I think it unnecessary to discuss it further.

Much love. Dad

[1] Editor's Note: Harry Yandell Benedict joined the University of Texas faculty in 1899, teaching math and astronomy. Roy Bedichek was a pupil of his in freshman math in 1900. He expected to find the young Harvard Ph.D. formal, crisp, business-like; instead he was easy-going, a relaxed conversationalist. He and Bedichek made many camping trips together to the coast. He collected birds' eggs and nests and kept a list of names and locations of birds he had seen. It may have been his example that started Bedichek's interest in and observation of birds. He made star charts for Bedichek. Their time together was mainly around the campfire, Roy Bedichek wrote in a memorial tribute printed in the *Alcalde* in June 1937. Dr. Benedict was president of the University of Texas from 1927–1937. Under his leadership an extensive building program was carried out. He chose the classical quotations inscribed on the main building.

[2] Mrs. Kidd, wife of Rodney Kidd, Bedichek's assistant in the Interscholastic League, who succeeded him when Bedichek retired.

❧

University Station
Box H
Austin, Texas
January 17, 1939

Dear Sarah:

Sunday morning I set out to write to you and Mary, but when I got a letter written to Mary it was dinner time, and then I had to go over to the Museum for a little speech (copy of which I will send you) and then I had to go over to Taylor and when mama and I returned it was my bedtime—so there's Sunday. Yesterday, accumulated mail kept me busy, and I am now stealing this time before Miss Thompson comes in and puts me to work.

The house is now at the nadir of Disorder or at the peak of Chaos,[1] from whichever viewpoint you care to look at it. I really don't see how your mama stands it. She wrangles with carpenters, contractor, architect, negro ditch diggers, cement men, and the other various hangers-on of a job of this sort; does her dishes on a chair (sink is out of commission); listens to the hideous slamming and banging; beats it to jr. high school for a class until about three; "does" a private pupil or two;

*195*

feeds the animals twice a day on a cardtable; and fares forth to night school for two hours three times a week. Bachman snarls, I grunt, the cats meow, and Pop whines an accompaniment to the general confusion. So please write a nice letter to the real victim of the family's ambition to better its living quarters.

Posted a batch of replies to Alan the other day. None particularly encouraging: "We have no vacancy now, but I shall be glad to file his application for reference in case any vacancy occurs"—that sort of stuff. One religious institution President pointedly inquired concerning the young man's religion, and is going to subject me to a personal interview on this point when I go to Abilene this week-end. I have a vague remembrance that he is a pious Presbyterian, sings in Choir, active in Sunday school, etc. but don't know whether I can make out a very good case against any sound fundamentalist cross-questioning. But I'll do my best.

Pop and Crimbo have renewed hostilities, and Fozzy[2] has joined forces with the latter. They had poor Pop strung out, (Crimbo had him by the throat, and Fozzy had him by the hindlegs) the other day, and they would literally have torn him in two if Bach had not rescued him in the nick of time. He couldn't walk for several hours after this encounter. He is up and coming now, however, and seems bent on revenge. I let him follow me to the office to keep him out of trouble. He is now sitting here wisely observing my progress with this letter.

No, I hadn't seen an account of Bridges' death. I'm afraid from what I have heard of him that he lived too fast to last long. I enjoyed your account of your autopsychoanalyzing with the conclusion that you are violent. Having observed you since you tried to kick the slats out of your cradle, I have had a suspicion of this, and now I am glad to receive scientific confirmation of my hunch. Are you not committing some sort of lese majesty in bringing the odor of cabbages and onions into the sacred precincts of a scientific laboratory?

Hordes of the hoi polloi are now assembling for the inauguration of "pappy" and he will shortly pass the biscuits in the Stadium.[3]

Much love.

Dad

---

[1] Editor's Note: The upstairs of 801 East 23rd Street was turned into a separate apartment. The old interior staircase, which ran up from a center hall, was removed and an

outside stair was constructed. The newly created apartment was then leased to students.

[2]Family dogs.

[3]Bedichek is referring to the inauguration of W. Lee O'Daniel, Texas governor, better known in Texas as W. Lee (Pappy) O'Daniel. As manager of Burrus Mill and Elevator Company of Fort Worth, he had hired musicians and named them the Light Crust Doughboys. They became popular on radio programs which O'Daniel directed.

❦

University Station
Box H
Austin, Texas
September 12, 1939

Dear Sarah:

Your card came yesterday, but I am sending this to Arlington, rather than to Grand Island, La., for I know it could not reach you before you leave there.

My trip to Panhandle took 11 days and I was on the go every minute, with thermometer part of the time ranging around 104 in the middle of the day. Nights, however, were cool. Had no chance to write.

Bach got home last night. Full of the war, and almost as full of prophesies and solutions. He has been hobnobbing with royalty, discussing world conditions with the president of Princeton University and others of equal rank. He shook his finger in the President's face in heated argument and reports that "the old boy got a little flustered."[1] He was out dating Mary Ireland last night. She leaves today for the *efate yeast*.[2]

Mama is well and in good spirits.

Didn't see any birds to speak of on Panhandle trip. A flock of about a thousand yellow-headed blackbirds, with sprinkling of magnificent mature males. Gorgeous sight! Also saw a fine hawk which I have not yet been able to identify.

Cool and rainy today—hope for early fall. Warblers are visiting the oak trees around the home place, and I am yearning for a chance to get out in the woods before the early migrations have passed on.

I am trying to ignore the war, for I can't do anything about it and there is so much idle, futile talk that one is drawn into if he thinks he knows anything that it gets to be a sort of dissipation. And everybody wants to talk about it.

Office force is assembling and I have to get to work. Much love, and write as you have the opportunity.

Dad

[1] Editor's Note: Bachman had been visiting his good friend Ernest Villavaso (who was later best man at our wedding) and his family at their summer home on Cape Cod where the President of Princeton University was a neighbor and frequent visitor. [2] Editor's Note: Mary Ireland Graves was a student at Vassar.

❧

University Station
Box H
Austin, Texas
October 30, 1939

Dear Mary:

Your telegram thrilled me and mama to the core.[1] I had been out all morning in the woods, and came in about 1 P.M. Mama met me at the door with the news. Her eyes were red as beets and I knew she had been weeping, although I pretended not to notice it and she said nothing about her secret tears. Why women want to weep about such things I can't say, because it is an utter mystery to me. I had no disposition to weep. Maybe you will weep twenty or thirty years from now when you get a similar telegram from Lillian Lee. Well, let them weep, if it does them any good, and I am quite sure that it does.

I wired Lillian Lee in behalf of Grandma and Grandad: "Welcome Stranger! If you want anything, just squall." I am quoting it to you for fear the young lady is secretive and does not show her mother her telegrams. The Western Union has a lot of made-to-order telegrams for such occasions, but none of them suited us. So we chose to tell her exactly what her mother did under similar circumstances.

Poor Gay is walking around as helpless and with the same feeling of utter inutility as I had on three occasions in my life. Tell him he will grow in importance as the young lady gets older and that he will be able to recapture some of that masculine aplomb with which the Lords of Creations are accustomed to bear themselves. Indeed, without it, they can hardly bear themselves at all.

A study of biology tends to reduce the male's estimation of himself. In lower forms of life he finds the male only a tenth or even a hundredth as large physically as the female. The male bee dies in fertilizing the female, and certain female insects ingest the males after the fertilizing performance is over. The dear creatures are hungry and the male is the only flesh in reach, so why not? Even as high up as the bird-world is in the biological scale, female hawks are uniformly larger and stronger than the males; and the poor male Phalarope is a worse hen-pecked husband than any human I have ever seen.

But the male human is always the dreamer, and he thus finds ways of preserving his self-respect, so don't get too sorry for him.

Well, much love, now to be divided in three, but each share as large as if it were not subdivided which is the miracle which occurs in the arithmetic of affection.

Dad

[1]Mary's and Gay's first child, Lillian Lee Carroll, had been born.

❦

Gay Vaughn Carroll, 1936, thirty years old, the year he married Mary Virginia Bedichek.
*Courtesy of Jane Derrick.*

Mary Virginia Bedichek (with striped scarf on front row), 1936, with other women students at the University of Texas Medical Branch.
*Courtesy of Jane Derrick.*

Sarah Bedichek, 1937, when she had been awarded a Rockefeller Foundation fellowship to study in England after receiving her Ph.D. in genetics at the University of Texas.
*Courtesy of Jane Derrick.*

Virginia Lee Greer, "Mama Jennie," Lillian Bedichek's mother c. 1930 at seventy years old. *Courtesy of Jane Derrick.*

Bachman holding Sarah's cat
Felix, in 1935, at the house at 801
23rd Street, Austin, Texas.
*Courtesy of Alan and Louise
Pipkin.*

Sarah (Sally) and Alan
Pipkin c. 1936.
*Courtesy of Jane
Derrick.*

Roy Bedichek, 1937, in the front yard of 801 E. 23rd Street. *Courtesy of Alan and Louise Pipkin.*

Lillian Bedichek cooking at 801 E. 23rd Street c. 1937. *Courtesy of Alan and Louise Pipkin.*

Roy Bedichek hiking on a Texas road, 1938.
*Courtesy of Alan and Louise Pipkin.*

Roy Bedichek and Sarah Bedichek Pipkin, 1938, with "The Beagle Hound Dog."
*Courtesy of Alan and Louise Pipkin.*

Alan Pipkin, Sr. and Roy Bedichek camping, 1938.
*Courtesy of Alan and Louise Pipkin.*

Sarah Bedichek Pipkin and Roy Bedichek on a bird
hike above Barton Springs, c. 1939.
*Courtesy of Jane Derrick.*

Roy Bedichek wrote on this photograph:
"'Candid Camera' far too candid, March 1939, on west side Congress
Avenue, Austin, between 8th and 9th St. R. B. in his declining,
verging on his reclining years." *Courtesy of Alan and Louise Pipkin.*

*August 2, 1940 to June 18, 1949*

University Station
Box H
Austin, Texas
August 2, 1940

Dear S&A:[1]

Your card received. Yes, I guess I'll have to hand it to you. If, with the slight equipment, you have stood 120 hrs rain and are still happy and looking for birds, you must have the real, he-man, camping stuff in you.

Of course, the pileated has the enormous crest and white on his wings and is the length of a crow, so it may have been the pileated and not the Ivory Bill you saw. If you do positively identify an Ivory Bill, I will be green with jealousy.

I am going to wander off into the woods about noon tomorrow and don't expect to return before Monday morning, in spite of my representations in last letter about futility of camping in August. Maybe I might find something. The rains have been so plentiful that I am in hopes of finding strange flowers.

The diabolical devices of the blitzkriegers have become positively humorous. I see in the morning paper that the parachutist comes armed as a burglar dropping on roof-tops and lowering himself by silken ropes through sky-lights and large chimneys. He carries some sort of concentrated soot which he can liberate and thus conceal himself in dense sooty smoke like an ink-fish. Can you imagine a more humorous scare-story to frighten English housewives with? I suppose they rush out of fireplaces into living-rooms shouting "Der Fuerher kommt." If England is defeated and goes down fighting to the last man, as present prospect is, they will furnish an example of heroism greater than Thermopylae. I hope they will not have to so immortalize themselves. Note in this week's *Time* the humor of English statistics on chances of getting killed by bombing; human .1; chicken .01; pig .001. I love the English, although they are the greatest exploiters and pirates that the world has ever known. But there is something downright lovable about them.

If they should collapse like the French, the world will not be for me quite as fine a place to live in: there will have passed a glory from the earth.

Much love,
Dad

P.S. Do you remember the monumental line of Simonides on the Spartans killed at Thermopylae? English rimed translation follows;

Go tell the Spartans, passerby,
That here, obedient to their laws, we lie.[2]

[1]Sarah and Alan.
[2]Simonides, *Fragment 92*. Epitaph for the Lacedaemonian [Spartan] king Leonidas and his small force at Thermopylae, who all died fighting to hold the pass against the invading Persian army [480 B.C.].

❦

University Station
Box H
Austin, Texas
August 29, 1940

Dear Sarah:

Well, I'm back, and it was one hell of a trip I had, all the time broken out with prickly heat and itching all over as if forty thousand needles were sticking into me. However, I'm better and am able to dig into some of the work that accumulated in my absence.

I found Mama alone, Bachman having deserted her for a trip to Beaumont. How he got the money I don't know. He got mama to advance him five dollars on his allowance, but $5 won't go far when one is traveling, as you know. He is visiting his friend, Everett Lord,[1] a boy who has never won my favor, although I have nothing against him. But I have ceased to worry about Bachman; he is either made or ruined now and nothing I can do will help or hinder him.

He has no sense of responsibility; he wants everything just as easy as possible; he would spend fifty dollars a month if I would let him have it with the same indolence and indifference that he spends

$5, never considering where it comes from, or that he has any responsibility whatever to economize or try to make any money by doing something useful. This is no indictment of him but of me and your mama who have certainly made a mess of raising him. But a man cannot raise more than one set of children, and hence cannot profit from experience.

In this month's *Reader's Digest* there is an article by Alexis Carrel[2] on raising brats that everyone who intends to raise any ought to read. His main contention is that American kids are too soft and I think he is right.

I wonder how many birds we got altogether on the Green ranch. Wish you would send me a copy of your lists so I may combine them with mine. I am trying to keep track of the birds in [the] local population [that] will be affected by the sudden introduction of so much water. We had a fine time up there, but it would have been much pleasanter camping in midwinter.

I saw my first crazy quail the other day. "Crazy" describes them. This bird fluttered around within a few feet of me for five minutes, and then flew away about twenty steps. I sat still and pretty soon from right under my nose came up a half grown bird the mother was trying to distract my attention from. But the little fool squawked and chattered to his mother who returned the salutations. I could have killed both of them with a stick.

Well, more later. I am not in a writing mood.

Yours, Dad.


P.S. I have your Schulz flower-book and will mail it to you as soon as you return to Arlington.

R.B.

P.P.S. You wrote a lovely letter to your mother.

[1] A law school friend of Bachman's from Beaumont, Texas.
[2] Alexis Carrel was a French surgeon who won the 1912 Nobel Prize for Medicine or Physiology for developing a technique for suturing blood vessels, opening up the possibility for organ transplants and blood transfusion.

University Station
Box H
Austin, Texas
September 9, 1940

Dear Sarah:

Yours of September 7th came on the second mail delivery this morning. It has been read by three people: 1. me; 2. Dan Williams; 3. mama. All of us enjoyed it, and Dan was so struck by some of your phrases that he was tempted to copy them out for future use. He was greatly pleased with "big business is baby food for the nazis."

If it be true that a whole culture may be wiped off the face of the earth by destroying a small exclusive set that has possession of it, how important it is that we broaden the bases of culture. That means extending welfare to more and more people so that culture may take root. But this is awful deep stuff. I once heard J. T. Patterson say that culture in his opinion was analogous to the blooming of a plant that blooms once, say, in a century. For some unaccountable reason, maybe due to the fortuitous concatenation of favorable circumstances, the plant puts forth a bloom and after a brief season of glory, dies down again to a drab, humdrum existence for another hundred years. Maybe man is that way—that normally he is very close to the earth, barely existing, actually vegetating, and then up comes the bloom which we call culture: Ancient Greece, the Renaissance; certain periods in China; the Mayas, and so on. But, as above intimated, this is far too deep, especially for one just after dinner. My belt at this moment encloses cauliflower, cabbage, potatoes, okra, tomatoes and a large slice of bread, together with a tall glass of buttermilk. Who could be philosophical with such an undigested burden?

Rather, I shall be objective. I saw yesterday morning down on Walnut Creek both the Philadelphia and the Red-eyed vireo. Hard to tell apart, but I got them within ten minutes of each other. The secret is that the red-eye has simply more decisive markings—he is marked just like the Philadelphia, but more so; and then he is fully an inch longer which is a great deal in so small a bird. I also had a boy kill a Cooper's Hawk so that I could study his markings closely. I think I shall never mistake this bird again. I saw, also, our friend the summer tanager gorging herself on the grubs out of a black wasp's nest. She sat just under it, and pulled one young wasp out after another devouring them leisurely and with apparent relish. She ate about a third of all in the nest. No adult wasp was about. Maybe she killed all of them to start with, the damned Nazi.

Thanks for your Green-ranch-list. You got several that I didn't see. Had a fine letter from Alan about bird-diseases which I have put in my bird-file.

My dear old friend, Norman Crozier, Superintendent of Schools at Dallas, died suddenly the other day, and I went to Dallas to attend the funeral. It was very sad for me. I had known him intimately since his first love-affair. Ah, me, how long a time is forty-two years! It's really long enough.

This prickly heat is still with me. I got up about 2 A.M. this morning, made ice-water, soaked towels and spread them upon my inflamed flesh for two hours before I got any relief. It is utterly hellish.

Please send back the bird articles I let you have. I have to refer to them, as the *Southwest[ern] Historical Quarterly* wants me to write an article about birds. Don't know whether I will or not, but maybe so I will.

I will bring your stinking bones when I come, but I can't say just yet when that will be.

Your fanciful trip to Yucatan by motorcycle had best be indefinitely postponed. Should you go, however, your mama says you had better return via Cuba, but I leave you to look that up.

Before you get this, maybe England will be completely knocked out. I don't see how London can stand such hammering as the Germans have been giving it. When London falls, the empire falls, in my opinion, in which I hope I'm wrong. When the empire falls, the world, as we have known it, falls. Then we either appease or fight. My guess is that we shall then elect Wilkie and appease. But let us not contemplate that nightmare until it comes.

I am quitting not because I have nothing else to say, as you are perhaps erroneously supposing, but because I have a little work which has to be done at this moment.

Much love
Dad

University Station
Box H
Austin, Texas
September 15, 1940

Dear Sarah:

Well, how does it feel to be back in the harness again? Galling, I
fancy. I should have been back in harness in dead earnest, but I can't
help just fooling around. I have done practically nothing that I should
have done by this time of the year. Carlyle, or some user of sesquipe-
dalian words, discovered the word "cunctation" and gave it currency,
and I find it describes me in my summer-ended mood. I hesitate, I
delay, I linger, I hanker, I hang back—not, of course, like the great
Fabius, the Cunctator, do I delay to any purpose, but simply delay to
no purpose.

This morning I got up with a genuine yen to get to work, but by
the time I had reached my office, the mood had worn thin, and I began
thinking it was Sunday, and how quiet and still it was and cool out on
the creeks, and that perhaps there were a few migrants coming through
and a few late flowers blooming, and before I knew it I was on my way
to Walnut Creek. Only too late did I discover that the dove season
opens here today. It sounded like the Nazis bombing London—pop-
pop-boom-boom—all over the woods and pastures, and occasionally
a swift dove flying far overhead who had also discovered that the dove-
season had opened. Very few birds were abroad, but I did find a young
painted bunting still lingering, cunctating, so to speak, and a female
summer tanager. By the way, I have seen many females lately, but no
males. I wonder if the males run on ahead as the orioles do.

So I turned my attention to plants—thank God, the gunners can't
scare them out of the country.

First was that evil-smelling Spider Flower which we identified
long ago, sometimes called Clammy Weed—do you remember it? The
long stamens look from a distance like daddy long-legs gathered on a
flower. Then I found blazing star lingering in bloom, cunctating; a
gaura and vervain, blue sage, and dilapidated sunflowers. Then I began fooling with shrubs and trees. I found burr oak and Schneck's oak,
Texas buckeye, Green Ash, Mexican Persimmon (possum plum). As I
was poring over a book to find a flower, I felt a gentle pressure on my

back and looked round to find that an old horse had nudged me. I scratched his ears, and then another, a younger horse came up for some scratching, which I gave; and then two young mules came out of the bushes and I said this is too much. I'll scratch horses but I won't scratch mules. And so I meandered on. Down the trail after me came the old horse, then the young horse, then several other horses and several mules, about twenty in all, solemnly following me. When I sat down, they gathered in a semi-circle about me. I scratched the old horse, then the young horse, then refused the mules. This little comedy was re-enacted every time I stopped. They followed me over a great pasture, under a railroad bridge into another pasture—all morning in fact. It was 12 PM before I got back to the office. Then I shaved and re-dressed myself and went home to dinner, and such a dinner! Three lovely vegetables, and a roast that simply melted in your mouth and oh so flavorsome. And then I lay on the bed awhile and read the *Living Age*, and dropped off for a short nap. Then I awake and say it's time to quit cunctating and get to work, so off to the office I come. Then I thought really, Sarah has just reached Arlington and is feeling so sad and lonely and it will be nice for her to have a letter from her dear, deah dad tomorrow, so I will write to her, and that takes me to this line and this moment 4:51 by my Westclox. The day is practically done and I have again done nothing. Tomorrow I shall set to work. I shall become stern and hard. I shall set my false teeth so hard they will crack and plunge into the gigantic tasks. But not now. I must dawdle a little longer. I have in the icebox at one of the ice-houses a large lucious watermelon cooled now for three days. It's the last rose of summer. I shall take it out and home in about an hour, and I wish you were here to help store it away.

This has been such a long paragraph, I believe I'll start another. Much love. Dad

❦

University Station
Box H
Austin, Texas
Oct. 21, 1940

Dear Sarah:

It doesn't seem to be so long since I saw you but the calendar says it's been eight days. I didn't get back home until last Wednesday, and I was out Saturday afternoon and Sunday, so I haven't been here much of the time. Certainly enjoyed my little visit with you. It is quite a pleasure to think of you so snuggly ensconced in your back room among the oaks.

It's now the tail-end of a hard spent day and no time to begin a letter—so this is deferred until in the morning.

It's morning now (Oct. 22) and about time for mail, so I am putting off further pecking on this typewriter in hope a letter will be in the mail from you and it will start me off on a more interesting line than I have yet been able to catch.

It's now 11 A.M. and the second mail brought your letter of October 19, and quite an interesting letter it is. Glad your head cold didn't develop in the next day or two after chow mein, or I should feel responsible. A week's intermission, however, frees me of all responsibility, and so I feel sympathetic but not guilty. Glad to have the star thistle identified. It is a striking flower, and I do love to get the striking flowers named.

A striking flower in East Texas, from Mineola to Marshall and from Gilmer to Thorndale, gave me almost a headache before I got back from my last trip. It was the most featurable plant in the country side. Clumps ten feet tall scattered over the cut-over pine lands and in deserted fields, and in ravines and waste-places throwing up huge heads of flowers, centered one's attention on them until you could see little else, especially after you had asked forty or fifty people, including heads of botany departments in half a dozen East Texas high schools in vain. I am sending you a pressed specimen under another cover. Finally I fell down on Tharp and he advised me that he had always called it "Sand Weed" because it grows chiefly in the sand, and that scientific name is *eupatorium compositifolium*. Look it up in your book. It has some interesting history.

I found also an anemic, hook-wormy species of blazing star growing in East Texas, and shall include a specimen of it with the sand weed—*liatris elegans*. I have found a curious thing about our blazing star. People clip off the heads, and in a week or two this sturdy plant has flowered again below the cut-off, making a stubby-looking, bob-tailed sort of thing. If you want some seeds of this I can send them. I have found a veritable storehouse on the Missouri Pacific right-of-way a few miles from Austin.

Give my regards to Jack Marquis[1]—He's a fine boy. Too bad he hasn't good health. Bad genes, I'm afraid.

As to distribution of reprints, Dean Davis might have an address to two to which he would like one sent.

*Women's Share in Primitive Culture* is one of my oldtime favorites. Did I give you it? Another eye-opener is somebody's (I can't think of name at the moment) *Folkways*: Sumner's[2] is the name.

Your mama talks of you often and is always threatening to write, but I doubt if she has so far. She is in her element. She's got a maid to boss around, some Spanish to teach day and night, a little girl to coach in the afternoon, rent to collect monthly, and the baby to tend to. She's happier than I have seen her in years. She's forgotten her ailments: game leg, smarting eyes, ankle-swelling, etc.

I am copying your note about birds onto card of the rusty blackbird in my file. That's what it is. Had it been a yellow-headed observer would have mentioned it, or red-winged. Grackles are not plentiful. The season is just right for the vast swarms of rusty blackbirds and I am sure that is the species. You've no idea how handy a card-file is for receiving notes of this kind, and references.

Much love.

Dad

---

[1]Possibly the son of J. L. Marquis, professor of biology at North Texas State Teachers College with whom RB corresponded.
[2]William Graham Sumner, 1840–1910, author of *Folkways*, the study of the sociological importance of usages, manners, customs, mores, and morals.

❧

University Station
Box H
Austin, Texas
December 4, 1940

Dear Sarah:

This is the last letter this week, for I am leaving tomorrow for a two-day trip in the Rio Grande Valley. I may drop you a note from down there, but it's doubtful, as I shall be very busy, or at least very busy making myself think I am busy. Of course, I am down there strictly on business, but you know me. I've a correspondent there, I discover (quite by accident) by the name of Mrs. D. C. Ring at San Juan, who, also quite by chance, is interested in birds, and who, I find sent me through the mail on June 19, 1938, a handsome list of birds she had observed around about her home. But I assure you that I have serious business in the Valley, and any ornithological excursions I take will be unpremeditated, accidental, adventitious, not to say, adscititious. I'm on a program down there for 3 short speeches, not about birds.

I should like to learn your Christmas whereabouts. Do you go to NO, or no? or to SA,[1] say? or to Austin? and when? I'm sending you in the next day or two a ten-pound box of large, luscious pecans, and please don't make yourself sick eating them; nor let Alan make himself sick on them. Five of them a day is enough for all practical purposes, especially during Christmas when one is surprising one's insides with all manner of rich and hefty offerings.

Mary is ill in the hospital with chicken-pox, and I guess the baby will have it, too, as she was with the baby while she was coming down with the ailment.

Mama has been having a perfect hell of a time. Her maid, Lola, lost her husband and vacationed a week, leaving mama with the bag to hold. Luckily, however, schools, both day and night, turned out for the second Thanksgiving, and stayed turned out until yesterday morning when Lola came back. So Jack has his Jill again, and all shall be well.

Bachman growls about our not declaring war, and getting in there while there's still time to do some good. If I oppose this view, even for the sake of argument, his growl rapidly becomes a very cacophonous bark, and the old philosophical turtle pulls his head quickly back into his shell. If we must have war, I'd rather it be foreign and not domestic.

Much love.
Dad

[1]New Orleans or San Antonio.

University Station
Box H
Austin, Texas
January 15, 1941

Dear Sarah:

Following the last shabby little letter I wrote you I said "Sally deserves better than that," but nothing better has come to me since. I did mean to tell you about a visit I made down in the Big Bend[1] to a frontier trading-post. There are few institutions of this sort left in the country. It is located on a mountainside which commands a fine view across the Rio Grande into Old Mexico. It is a big long affair, probably three hundred feet in length, and that's as long as an ordinary city block. It's narrow, comparatively, and contains divisions for this or that type of merchandise. Looks like the grandfather of a department store. A shrewd old merchant is in charge, and I happened along just in time to hear him chaffer with an old trapper who had come in with skunk, ring-tail, coyote, and bob cat hides for sale. They were likely smuggled over from Mexico, but neither of them raised this delicate question. Back and forth, offer and counter offer, wrapping up and unwrapping the hides, threatening to go away with them, lectures on the depressed condition of the market, criticisms and defense of the condition of the merchandise. About ten dollars was involved and it is indicative of how sedately time flows out on the borders that fully an hour was consumed in making this deal. Would that time flowed everywhere that way! This old trapper told me how he got his bait for trapping coyotes. It seems that it is the custom to take a live coyote, tie off his bladder and keep him until his bladder fills to bursting. Then they kill the animal and bottle the fluid, flavoring it with asafetida and cod liver oil. This is sprinkled in the vicinity of the trap, which, of course, is carefully concealed under ground. He told me that this is the most successful bait except the properly butchered female organs of the female coyote in certain seasons. The mind of man never conceived a crueller thing than this. As I looked at this man, I seemed to see him in connection with Nature, a part of it, a two-legged clever animal preying on other animals, and I compared his cruelty with that of the hawk, the wolf, and other predators. Except for the feline's disposition to play with the captured prey and keep it alive for practice, man is by all odds the cruelest of them all.

I found another character down there who is a sort of philosopher-hermit, living in an old bedraggled auto-tent, and a brush arbor for shade. Cooked in the sand and dirt living principally off wild animals and perhaps a stolen goat now and then. He lived fifty years in civilization as a commercial traveler, reared three boys, and at fifty was deserted by his wife who took a job as matron in the Home for Delinquent Girls at Gainesville. Then he did what he had wanted to do all his life. He had no ties, Thank God, and he crawled on the first freight-train that came through. Lived with Okies and other tramps in California, and finally wound up "as far away from civilization as one can get in the U.S.A." He has little education, but he has manufactured for himself a sort of Stoic philosophy—be free by doing without. Control your desires and you will be liberated—that sort of thing, and he is doing a pretty good job of Thoreau-ing it out there in the wilds. Webb and I camped with him and fed him up good. In the two or three days we were there I am sure we added not a cubit to his stature but certainly several inches to his girth. I shall never forget one breakfast he ate. We had made a big camp biscuit, one of those that you cut up like a pie. He took fully half of it, chipped it into small pieces in a large soup dish, then poured over it half a teacupful of melted butter, then emptied a can of log cabin syrup over that, and minced a large piece of Hormel's ham into it. This he quietly ate with great relish, feeding himself with one hand. I neglected to say that he is a cripple, having lost his right hand at the wrist. He can make a cigarette with this one hand—refuses ready-made cigarettes—preferring to roll his own.

Well, I wanted you to have these two items before I forgot them or the memory got blurred.

Much Love.

Dad

[1]Big Bend, located in a "big bend" of the Rio Grande, is largely wild, Texas's first national park, and approximately the size of Rhode Island.

❧

University Station
Box H
Austin, Texas
January 27, 1941

Dear Sarah:

Last Friday my friend Haley,[1] now manager of several of the largest ranches in Texas and New Mexico for an oil billionaire of Houston, invited me and Webb down to the Chupadero Ranch on the Rio Grande between Eagle Pass and Laredo. Friday afternoon we drove down there, two hundred miles, and reached the chuck-wagon about dark. For two days we followed the chuck-wagon about for meals, and ranged around between times looking the country over. Had a great time. I got time to look up a few birds and some desert plants.

Returned last night and found your letter. I see it was mailed on the 24th, and I am hoping that by this time you are fully recovered. Perhaps you did the right thing to go back to work well or not, but of course, that's contrary to the advice of the physicians. Anyhow, let me know how it works.

You have Lindbergh's psychology down about right. When a man begins to think he is an expert in half a dozen different fields, he is usually mistaken about at least five of them, sometimes, about all six. Of course, much of the opposition to helping England comes from interests that are so prejudiced against Roosevelt that they are against anything that he is for.

Yes, I should like to read the *Famous Letters* when you have finished with the book. I like letters. Fools are often wise in letters and the wise are often fools. There's really no telling what writing letters will do to a person. Did you ever read any of Swift's love letters written in what he called the "small" language? Walt Whitman and Mrs. Gilchrist carried on an extremely interesting correspondence—especially her letters are interesting, about the best of her writing, while Walt's are the worst of his. Robert Browning and Elizabeth Barrett write to each other in such a state of intense emotion that I have the feeling that each one is about to bust every minute. And literary people, I think, often write with an eye to posterity, feeling that their letters will be published, and hence are often not quite sincere. They have a tendency to pose for posterity. I think I am very sensitive to this and can spot it pretty definitely even in the greatest letters—even love letters. I notice that George Bernard Shaw threatens to sue the publisher if he publishes his (Shaw's) love letters to Mrs. Patrick Campbell. He stews around a good deal and declares that everybody wrote love letters to Mrs. Campbell and that he does not object to having them published after he dies, but that he does not want his gray hairs made ridiculous while he is still alive. I think his objections are legitimate.

We are getting along all right at home. Your mother has been "weller" than usual, Mary is completely recovered, I have only my red nose and a few bumps to complain of and only those when I fall from grace and eat a lot of meat. Haven't seen Bachman, (that is, since I returned from trip) and hence don't know just when he expects to come to Dallas.

I'll have to wait until another letter to retell some of the cowboy talk I heard down on the border, and something about birds and plants. I didn't learn much about the birds and plants, for I really didn't have an opportunity to get away by myself.

Much love.

Dad

---

[1] J. Evetts Haley served as executive secretary and general range manager for J. M. West.

❦

University Station
Box H
Austin, Texas
February 28, 1941

Dear Sarah:

The long finger of my left hand, one of my main typewriter fingers, has a deep slash in the end of it made yesterday when I was transferring a safety razor blade from whetstone to razor-frame. It's now sore, and typing is a trial.

You are making a mistake to pay the albinos anything.[1] It spoils 'em. Such cooperation as you need in such a matter should be obtained by smoosh. I know for I have worked with Lomax and Owens[2] in getting folklore. The moment a prospect gets the idea he has something of money value and begins to talk payment, Lomax and Owens quit him cold. Nine times out of ten he will come up later and offer cooperation free of charge. They are not giving you anything of money value. On the other hand you are giving them something, and you should not pay for it.

222

Martins (two pair) returned yesterday and began flying in and out of the box. I couldn't tell whether they carried in any nesting material. I believe I wrote you that they came about the 21st on scouting trip. I have tried to make them out patriotic, as the swallows of San [Juan] Capristano are said to be religious, coming back promptly on a Saints day, but my martins undershoot or overshoot March 2 frequently,[3] and I'm not as good a liar as the monks.

A letter came the other day from New York from a sentimental dog-loving lady who had heard the NBC broadcast about Hobo. She sent me a snapshot of her fox terrier. My two hobbies, dogs and birds, bring me into contact with all the sentimental gushers in the world. I must give up or shut up.

Did you send a copy of *PM* to Edgar Witt, as I asked you to some-time ago? You might call Davis' attention to this paper. I believe he will appreciate it, and your library ought to take it.

I am glad to hear that you are tinkering with the Professional Women's Club. It helps one's character, no matter how out of patience one may get sometimes with such organizations. A person with intel-lectual interests always runs the risk of retiring too much into himself and becoming a little moldy or sour. Human contacts keep up the cir-culation. In spite of my indisposition to do so, I forced myself to buy a couple of tickets to the Texas Ex[4] banquet here Saturday night and arrange for a table with a few friends. I'd much rather go to bed early and get up with the dawn to look for birds and flowers in the woods. But man is a social animal and when he neglects the social side he tends to become queer and screwy.

Much love.

Dad

---

[1]Sarah is conducting a genetic study using albinos.

[2]Editor's Note: In 1941 William A. Owens worked for the Interscholastic League under Roy Bedichek collecting folk songs. Bedichek later designated Owens as his literary executor. Owens in 1967 published *Three Friends: Bedichek, Dobie, Webb,* their correspondence, and in 1985 brought out *Letters of Roy Bedichek.*

[3]The Texas Declaration of Independence from Mexico was signed on March 2, 1836.

[4]The ex-student's association of the University of Texas.

❦

December 22, 1941
Regina Court
Monterrey, Mexico

Dear Sarah—

With your mama spitting & gesticulating Spanish & me seeing unfamiliar birds, we have decided to prolong our stay until Sunday or possibly Monday of next week, the 29th. We are both having a helluva good time & are too childish to turn it loose & get back to business as we ought to. If I had a typewriter, I'd describe our adventures, but this will have to serve now.

   Much love & Merry Christmas
   Dad

꽃

Box H
University Station
Austin, Texas
January 11, 1942

Dear Sarah:

Seems sometime since I heard anything from you or wrote to you, but not so long since I thought of you. Indeed, yesterday you constantly came before my mind's eye. I was out all day in woods and along water and among rocks and ledges. I got the best view I ever had of the Philadelphia vireo. He is certainly the least and the greenest vireo. The light was just right and the specimen I saw was gentle, so I don't think I shall ever mistake him again. It was cold early in the morning, so I built a little fire to warm by. Off a few yards and away from the sun was a dwarf sumac with great clusters of seed all over it. As I was sitting there half a dozen different species of birds came and ate the seeds. The ruby crowned kinglet, a blue bird, a phoebe, a myrtle warbler, and a couple of other species. Did you know these birds ate sumac seed? I didn't. The phoebe really surprised me. I have never seen him take a vegetable meal before.

   I am enjoying the book on diet very much—it is funny as can be. The man is a humorist and an excellent writer as well. I am taking Alan's word for it that he is a sound scientist. He quotes from one of

Edith Wharton's novels a description of a fat woman that I must copy out and send to you—I never read anything quite as adequate in describing a certain type of obesity.

I may give you a ring from Dallas sometime Tuesday afternoon, as it is quite likely that I shall have to go there. The phone numbers I have for you are: Office: 173; and Home: 144. However, I am not sure right this minute, as my coming depends somewhat on another individual from whom I shall not hear until about ten this morning. Maybe I'd better hold this letter from the mail until I can put definite information in P.S.

We hear nothing from Bach, except a word now and then indirectly.[1] Seems that the boys from here now in service in New Orleans all report very heavy work and very long hours. I try to write to him but find nothing to say. He can't (or at least he doesn't) tell us anything of his work, and it is very hard to write to someone who says nothing back. It takes two to make a quarrel, also a correspondence.

Miss Thompson had an auto wreck which cost plenty but fortunately she was not hurt. Mexican ran into her—knocking her car into another car—other car owner collected off her and left her to deal with Mexican. And she had such a nice new car!

Well, much love. You can read between the lines that I am rather down in spirit, but still kicking.

Dad

P.S. Yes, I have decided to come.

[1] Editor's Note: Bachman went on active duty November 1941 in New Orleans. He worked in Naval Intelligence handling reports from merchant ships in the Gulf of Mexico of German submarine sightings. After Pearl Harbor, he applied for sea duty. He was turned down because of his intelligence job. He reapplied and was finally assigned to Amphibious Forces with training at Solomon's, Maryland.

June 15, 1942

Dear Sarah:

Enclosed is tail of the "Pygmy Rattler," or "Ground Rattler." Killed specimen near Kountze in the "Big Thicket."[1] He's about 14 in. long, gray & spotted with golden-lined dark brown spots irregular shaped but about the area of a dime. Spots are scattered alternately on each side of yellowish strip down back. He will give no ground. Fights if attacked. You have to have a magnifying glass, almost, to see rattles. He buzzes with them, so I am told. This one did not.

    RB

[1]Region located in Southeast Texas and called a Biological Crossroads of North America because it contains both temperate and subtropical plants and animals, along with many from the dry, treeless west. One may find roadrunners alongside alligators, mesquite and yucca alongside cypress and orchids.

❦

University Station
Box H
Austin, Texas
June 21, 1942

Dear Sarah:

It was a lovely welcome to my office after two weeks gone to find your nice long letter tucked under the cover of my typewriter by the ever-thoughtful Miss Thompson. I came to the office last night very much tired out and looked avidly through my mail for a letter from you, but none showed up. I didn't uncover my typewriter, so the letter stayed in perfect cold-storage until this morning, and I'm glad it did. I'm fresher now and can enjoy it more than I could have last night with my much-jaded senses crying for sleep.

It is especially gratifying to find you preparing to fit into a new life and get the most out of it.

I have been in the deep woods, and "what I mean" they're deep and dark and noisome, especially the human beings in them. Would you be amazed (as I was) to find a school whose pupils tested out one per cent infected with hookworm? I heard one little human runt, three feet high, fifteen years old, with a big wad of tobacco in his jaw, spitting now and then out the window, say to his teacher about hookworm treatment;

"My dad says (spit) that I doan haveta tak that air treatment (spit) unless I wants ta—an' I doan wanta (spit)."

And that's all there was to it. This little runt stalked out, with the corner of a plug of chewing tobacco protruding from his hip pocket. The teacher threw up his hands—helpless: "They're many of them like that," he said.

And then I heard them slapping their thighs with delight around filling station radios as O'Daniel[1] poured out his Nazi poison: "Folks, the war'll soon be over—there aint agonna be no gas-rationing; and folks, a third item of good news I've saved for you good people deep in the heart of good old East Texas, there aint a-gonna be no run-off."

These good people are, like Othello, "perplexed in the extreme."[2] They don't know what to believe. Many of them think the war unnecessary. They have been permitted to lose sight of the fact that we were attacked after long and careful preparation by a powerful and crafty enemy. They either were never told this, or if they were told it, they have forgotten it in the warm slush of the gutter-mouthed traitors of the O'Daniel ilk.

You should have seen me preaching physical fitness and mental alertness in this region, and by the way, it looks as though our program is going over big. We really got a lot of encouragement.

I have just gotten the Jaques books[3] and am delighted with them. I want to work out with you some feasible projects in Nature Study for our Physical Fitness Clubs and for Boy and Girl Scout groups. It seems to me that this man Jaques has just the right idea.

Much love. Mama, the incorrigible, has become a member of a six-member committee to provide a course of study for the State Department of Education to promulgate in teaching Spanish in the Primary grades without Spanish teachers! She is putting in an 8-hour day on this and will be tied up with it until middle July. What-a-woman!

By the way, I persuaded her to let me chip in on Alan's hood, so we have ordered it.

Dad


P.S. You neglected to tell me about the condition of the female cat— were your suspicions confirmed?

I am trying an air-mail on this, feeling that there must be good airmail service to Corpus. I am mailing it at 10:30 A.M.—please tell me the day and hour you receive it. R.B.

Sarah's PA to Sarah's POP

Speak to me only with thine eyes
    The hunger only thou canst feel;

Speak to me only with those orbs
    O yearning and of mute appeal;
With them alone prefer thy suit,
    And I this ossicle of veal
Will yield to thee, thou charming brute:
    But bark, you wretch, and just for that,
I swear I'll toss it to the cat!
    R.B.

[1]W. Lee (Pappy) O'Daniel, after serving as governor of Texas 1938–1941, ran for a vacated United States Senate seat during his second term as governor and won in a special election. In 1942 he was elected to a full six-year term.
[2]Shakespeare, *Othello*, V, ii.
[3]H. E. (Harry Edwin) Jaques wrote several guides, including *How to Know the Insects; How to Know the Trees; Living Things, How to Know Them,* among other later writings.

🌿

University Station
Box H
Austin, Texas
July 10, 1942

Dear Sarah:

Mama Jenny is here, and we are enjoying her visit very much. However, the trip upset her and for the past twenty-four hours she has been ailing considerably. Indeed, we called Dr. Klotz last night. She slept well and I am hoping she will be ok today. By the way, she expressed last night some concern about the binoculars you have. They are, as you know, a remembrance of Frank,[1] and she does not want you to "contribute" them or loan them. I reassured her. The angle of vision is not what the navy wants, and indeed, the navy has just issued an appeal not to send binoculars except ones answering specific designation. They are now completely cluttered up with glasses they cannot use. There has been contradictory publicity put out on this matter, some from one Region and some from another. I am writing to the Naval Observatory for the right dope.

Mama Jenny is noticeably feebler, but she gets around well and seems to enjoy life. She can still talk Lillian down—the only human being I ever saw who could accomplish this feat and still live.

We hear practically nothing from Bachman. Mama Jenny heard indirectly from him through some Major who was acquainted with his work in New Orleans. This army man said Bachman was a whizz and that his work was extremely important. Bachman, however, writes quite deprecatingly, and seems dissatisfied with his contribution to the war effort. Has he written to you? We have had nothing from him in two weeks. He is back from Pensacola much improved in health.[2] Perhaps one of your delightfully descriptive letters of life in a naval station would amuse him as much as it does me.

I hope you are not drawn away from your scientific pursuits by some trivial so-called "war work." It is my belief that the best contribution anyone can make who has had thorough scientific training in any field is to work in that field, bearing, of course, towards goals which seem to promise most. It becomes more and more apparent that science is going to win this war, and I don't mean merely some one science. It is the whole scientific field—or more generally, the scientific attitude.

Tell me what you are doing. I am leaving today and will not return to Austin before Sunday.

Much love.

Dad

P.S. Mailed a considerable accumulation of *PM*'s today.

[1]Editor's Note: Virginia Lee Greer's son, James Francis, Jr., a pilot in the Army Air Force, was a flying instructor in France. He was aloft with a student at the controls when the plane crashed and he was killed in 1918. His name is emblazoned over an arch at the north end of the University of Texas's Memorial Stadium, dedicated to people who lost their lives in the service of the country.

[2]Editor's Note: Bachman was serving in the Navy in New Orleans as a Lt., jg, doing intelligence work. His station received reports from merchant ships who soon after leaving that port saw Nazi submarine periscopes surfacing; sometimes no Navy planes were available to go to the defense of the merchant ships. He was so tense and on the edge of an emotional blow-up that he was sent to Florida for a rest.

Austin, Texas
August 14, 1942

Dear Sarah:

You and Alan up a tree looking at birds reminds me of some fine experiences I have had down in that very place. The long beach, the sand dunes and the streamlined oaks looking in the distance like long-haired maidens with their tresses blown back toward the land by the strong salt sea-breeze, all comes up in my mind. Were you ever with me at Rockport[1] or along Copano Bay[2]? I know that Bach was, and we visited the ruins all over-grown with native vegetation of a pioneer settlement which was destroyed, I believe, in the great Indianola storm.[3] I remember Bach and I found (first time for him) a green-winged teal on a pond near the famous oak—largest in Texas down on the sandy peninsula. This is close to another favorite resort of mine—Aransas Federal Refuge—56,000 acres of native coast vegetation and worlds of birds and game including wild turkeys and thousands of deer. Here is where I found two bald eagle nests, and saw the thousands of Wilson Phalaropes twirling themselves, each in his own little puddle like so many miniature whirling dervishes.

I am sending three *PM*s which I want returned and am enclosing envelope for your convenience in returning them. Am marking each one "Return—no hurry, but eventually send them back."

Mama is going to see Mary next week—another promising little note from Bachman—I am in middle of a hard-pressing enterprise described in enclosed circulars.

Much love. Dad

[1]Rockport, Texas, is located in southwestern Aransas County on Aransas Bay.
[2]Copano Bay, an extension of Aransas Bay, a body of water in western Aransas County and southern Refugio County, Texas.
[3]Indianola, Texas, a ghost town on the west shore of Matagorda Bay, near Port Lavaca, which was destroyed by storms in 1875 and abandoned after another storm in 1886.

University Station
Box H
Austin, Texas
September 8, 1942

Dear Sarah:

I hope this gets to you before a package I mailed this morning. When you get it (if you get it before you receive this letter) you will think you are getting something, and be greatly disappointed when you open it and find only an assortment of old magazines, for the most part if not all, *Magazine Digests*. Maybe some of them are clipped, I know some are marked, but not for you. I thought if you don't want them, you can turn them over to some reading-room of an entertainment center for soldiers, whatever the initials of the thing is, I can't remember—or to the library of a soldiers camp. I like this little Canadian digest much better than *Readers Digest* which has become rich and respectable.

Lil keeps on talking about what a helluva a time she had visiting you, and murmurs under her breath, "Sarah is the sweetest child in the world." You must have had on your company manners while she was there. She says she borrowed five dollars from you and I am enclosing five dollars (currency) to discharge this obligation.

It is raining like the deluge here and has been for 24 hours. Ruining cotton. Depressing me beyond recognition. Messing up cellar. Driving Pop in house where he stinks. And so on. It never rains but it pours—bad news from everywhere. I'm looking to hear of Stalingrad's fall at any moment; and the damn Japs are driving towards Port Moresby. Somewhere either Lord or Lady Macbeth exclaims, "Hell is murky."[1] It's not a damned bit murkier than this afternoon is, I can tell you that.

And then, just as if in answer to what I had just written I get your nice cheery letter laid on my typewriter. Glad to have prospect of seeing you and Alan. Your mother had said something of your coming, but put it Oct. 1. Yes, I'll be here, waiting at the airport. The *PM*'s you returned arrived ok. I wanted them back on account of some articles on the vermin press. I had written some stuff along same line and someone challenged my facts. You're wrong about your mother not enjoying visit—she came back happier than I ever saw her come in off a trip before. I asked her if she nagged you and Mary like Mama Jenny does her and she swore she didn't. I leave that to you to answer.

You needn't send me the Haldane book. I read it, or as much of it as I could understand. It's nothing like as good as the book of his I read. I'll send you another volume of Voltaire whenever you holler. I am enjoying Tacitus—go to sleep on it every night.

You know how I used to swear by the *Living Age*, and at a cost of $6 subscribed to it for Mary. Well, the damn thing was a Jap propaganda sheet, and editors are now under arrest. What do you know about that, and me thinking I'm such a sleuth for propaganda. I don't know nuthin.

This is afternoon and I'm in no mental condition to write a letter—besides I've got a lot of business correspondence to attend to. More anon. And much love.

Dad

[1]Shakespeare, *Macbeth*, Act V, sc. 1, l. 40 [Lady Macbeth].

❦

University Station
Box H
Austin, Texas
October 20, 1942

Mrs. Alan Pipkin,
c/o Ens. Alan Pipkin, USN[1]
c/o Commandant, 12th Naval District
San Francisco, California

Dear Sarah:

Beagle[2] blitzed to New Braunfels, yelped to San Marcos, whined to Kyle, whimpered to Buda and slept to Austin. Bugs were delivered 5 P.M. in Genetics Laboratory to Mrs. Mainland, who said she would be glad to take care of them until you come back. I then went on home and deposited Beagle in baby-pen. Mama was glad to see him and he her. She immediately imagined Beagle was giving her special attention, but I, of course, saw through his shameless political trickery.

Enclosed are some bills and a letter from Muller.[3] I enclosed also (if I can find them) bird-lists made on California a few years ago.

Affectionately,
Dad

[1]Editor's Note: Alan Pipkin, commissioned ensign USNR, served as staff parasitologist, U.S. Naval Hospital, Corpus Christi, March to October 15, 1941. He was then sent to Malaria Control activities with the Third Fleet, based in San Francisco, and later with the Seventh Fleet operating in New Guinea area.
[2]Sarah's dog that Roy and Lillian took care of.
[3]Dr. Hermann Joseph Muller, (1890–1967), geneticist and University of Texas professor under whom Sarah worked. He produced artificial transmutations of the gene by X-rays (1927) for which he was awarded the American Association for Advancement of Science prize for 1927 and the Nobel Prize in 1946.

University Station
Box H
Austin, Texas
October 30, 1942

Dear Sarah:

If this attempt to communicate with you is successful, please give enclosed letter to Alan for his signature. If he has already gone, sign his name to it "by Mrs. Alan C. Pipkin" and state in P.S. below reason for your signature is that he has left the country. Mail this back to me by air mail, and maybe I will get it in time to secure ration-card. However, if I have no better luck with this letter than with others mailed you (so far as now reported) it will be too late to do any good. Rationing takes place here Nov. 12. It might be well for you and Alan to inquire there in San Francisco from rationing authorities to see if maybe you might not be able to get card there. If so, it will be better than for me to try to get it here.

Mama Jenny is here and she and your mother chatter continuously in the usual Greer style, neither paying any attention to the other, but both immensely enjoying the conversation, as much really, as if they understood each other. Each one is under the illusion that the other is understanding, and that makes for the success of the whole affair. And after all, practically all pleasures in this pail of beers is due to our capacity for accepting illusions as the real thing.

Your mama attempted to take Beagle out walking the other day, and he jerked her down and Duke, Pop and Beagle all had a furious fight over her prone (or prostrate) body. She escaped with only a slight contusion on the knee.

I would like to be able to feed your romantic illusions about Beagle by telling you that he is pining and refusing food and drooping like an undernourished flower, all for love of his absent master and mistress. However, frankness compels me to say that he is about as vigorous a specimen as I ever saw, fuller of pep, wilder with enthusiasm, than any dog I ever saw. He gobbles up everything that can by any stretch of terms be called food. He almost jumps over the fence, and I am afraid he will accomplish this feat with a little more practice. He has completely recovered from distemper, has no wheeze in his breathing, no moisture dripping from the eyes, and a cold nose. He whips Pop or Duke or both with no effort. He got Pop by the throat the other morning and I thought he would kill him. Really this Beagle is a problem. If I can find some territory where there are no goats, no sheep, no chickens, ducks or other domestic fowl, I'll take him out there and give him full rein.

Much love.

Dad

⁂

[No date]

To:  Alan C. Pipkin, Lt. (j.g.) H-V (S), USNR, 20th U.S.N.B.C.
     Fleet postoffice, San Francisco, Calif.

From: Roy Bedichek, Box H, University Station, Austin 12, Texas

Dear Alan:

The fall rains and a little cool weather are gradually bringing back to my old bones and tissues a little life. The summer has been unshirted hell and I mean unshirted literally, for a great part of the day & all the night I have gone shirtless: in fact, every moment except the time spent in my office. I have been going or rather doing-at two men's jobs all summer. My friend, Dean Shelby, has been ill in the hospital for months, and is only now beginning to come to the office for an hour or two a day. I have been helping him with his duties, and trying to attend also to my own. At home, as you have likely heard from Sarah, I have been gardening, and have produced not only vegetables, but eight shirts and three pairs of trousers. The shirts had been abandoned because I couldn't button them at the throat, and the trousers because I couldn't button them over my abdomen. Eight months of gardening have reduced both measurements to the figure they were when I purchased these dry goods, and hence they have become available for use again. So you see.

Sarah and Lillian make a great team. They are filling every forgotten nook about the house with canned vegetables and fruits. They take turns spoiling the baby,[1] and talk as a relay team in recounting the marvels of this little animal. To hear them tell it, the multiplying miracles of Nature do swarm upon him (pardon the paraphrasis). Of course, grandpa is overruled and must give grudging endorsement to some of their ecstasies. For really, this firm, rosy-fleshed, athletic little wiggler is about as charming a bit of human life as I have ever associated with. He has an unconquerable good humor. He's never sore or sulky. He never cries with pain or anger. He rarely shows fear of anything or anybody. He does have an apprehensive little pucker of his mouth when some stranger tries to become too familiar on short notice. His principal delight is dogs. He is entranced by them. Human beings lose interest for him entirely when a dog is around. He considers me a great joke. He wrinkles his little nose in laughter whenever I appear, and his eyes sparkle like diamonds. If he is lying on his back, he wiggles and bridges, that is, he lifts the middle of his body and rests his weight on his shoulders and feet. We confer secretly when the women are not around, and I assure him much to his apparent satisfaction that he will not always be dominated by women but that there will come a time when he will associate with men and will have a determining voice in decisions which affect his comfort or welfare.

I believe he is generally the healthiest baby I ever was around. He so radiates good humor and vitality that he could almost be taken as a symbol of the Joy of Life.

Of course he is not accidentally so. He has good heritage and Sarah is as conscientious in attending to him as she is about everything else. She leaves no stone unturned; she is utterly indefatigable in her service. She gets also much good advice from her mother.

And now as to Beagle: He is enjoying the liberty of a dog for the first time in his life, and you've no idea how much his health and self-respect have been improved. He no longer exhibits any of that disgusting abnormal sexuality; he is now a male dog among dogs, and when his rights are infringed, he fights like an infuriated tiger. All the dogs around the place have a healthy respect for him. He gets plenty of exercise, and has become sleek in appearance and quite muscular. He stays close around the place, and shows considerable judgment in attacking automobiles. I think he is in less danger of death than he was in when he was under confinement. You know he was developing so-called running fits, and they are often fatal. Being restored to normal life, he has completely overcome this ailment. I am quite sure he would not last a year if confined to his pen. I persuaded Sarah to let him run out, and if he were killed, she would be inclined to blame me, but I think of the two evils, we chose the less: "better fifty years of Europe than a cycle of Cathay."[2]

I notice in your letters an occasional remark concerning the labor situation which indicates you are blaming labor for not doing its duty. Really, it is a very small percentage of labor that is at fault—not more than one percent. The same may be said of big business, although the percentage is a little higher, say about three percent. Of course, each side makes the most of the deficiencies of the other, and so if one swallowed all the propaganda, he would soon come to believe that the people back home are generally falling down on the job. Not at all. They are doing the biggest job that any population of similar size ever did in the whole history of the world. American production of war materials has astounded the world. Of course, each front thinks it is being short-potted, but it is necessary in global strategy (such as is forced upon us) to withhold here and strengthen there for the very simple reason that there is not enough to go around. The men in the Southwest Pacific have been battling under terrific odds and have made an immortal story; and quite naturally many of them cannot understand why there is not more recognition in the way of increased men and equipment. The truth of the matter is that if you are assailed by a number of enemies, and one of them is at your throat, you want to get rid of him first so as to have more breath with which to fight the remainder. Germany is the heart of the Axis, and she must be put out first.

We certainly enjoy your letters. I often tell Sarah that you have a positive talent for writing popular science articles, and I shouldn't be surprised to see you cash in on that talent some time.

Well, that's all for the present. The office force is coming in.

R.B.

---

[1]Editor's Note: Alan Collins Pipkin, Jr., born February 25, 1943 in Austin, lived with his mother at his grandparents' home in Austin for the first two years of his life. His father saw him for the first time when he returned from sea duty to San Diego in early 1945.

[2]From Alfred, Lord Tennyson, *Locksley Hall.*

❧

801 East 23rd Street
Austin, Texas
January 9, 1945

Dear Josephine[1]:

I stole a look at your letter to Bachman as it passed through my hands on its way to him and Jane who are honeymooning in New Orleans. I was well rewarded for the theft. It was a delightful letter and one well-calculated to please the two discriminating individuals to whom it is directed. Enclosed is a clipping describing the wedding. Jane is a jewel. It is hard for a father to realize that his son has as much or more sense than he has, expecially in "Womanology." I fully expected Bachman to fall for the first little fluffy-haired fool who by some sort of animal instinct knew just how to flatter his vanity. But quite otherwise; by what seems to me a sort of divine guidance he wooed and won as intelligent and charming a creature as I ever saw— physically, mentally, emotionally. My only parental fear now is that he may not be able to live up to the high plane upon which this creature lives and moves and has her being. But, of course, I hide such fears out of fatherly loyalty.

It was fine to hear of you again luxuriating in the rural sights and scenes of your childhood: I have always dreamed of a peacock on the terrace but have never seen one except in English poetry.

Sincerely, your cousin,
Roy Bedichek

[1]Editor's Note: Roy Bedichek's cousin, Josephine Craven, first married Car Chandler; after his death she married Robert Horner. They lived in Illinois, near Roy's birthplace.

❦

July 27, 1945

Dear Mary & Gay:

Things at the nursery[1] are proceeding satisfactorily, in spite of a few minor ructions, and occasional disputes about what is whose. The big boss of the nursery talks about 300,000 words a day with the inmates, and is talked back to at the rate of about ten words to one. I haven't been able to see which gets the best of this talkfest, but one thing sure, it seems to be good practice for all concerned. Jane's bumps seem to be clearing up; Lillian's appetite is about what it should be; and, aside from a few little pleasantries like filling grandpa's plate with buttermilk just as he is squared off and ready to begin his dinner, Little Alan is lovely, just lovely.

We had quite an accession of toys, including a full grown pre-war hobby-horse when Alan and Sarah returned from San Antonio. This makes the back-yard look still more like somebody home. By the way, there has been a great shift in the Pipkin arrangements. Alan on reaching San Francisco found his orders changed and he was assigned to the Corpus Christi Naval Base, so back he comes, getting here 6 A.M. today. This shuttling back and forth across the continent hasn't done him up appreciably, and he is now preparing to go down to Corpus and try to find a domicile. If he is successful, Sarah and little Alan will be going right away.

I have gotten considerable notice from Lillian Lee lately. She, for one, seems to appreciate grandpa's activities and follows him around asking more or less intelligent questions. Jane still eyes me with suspicion and clings to the skirts of the women folks. I am gradually, I think, gaining her confidence. The damn dog came with the Pipkins, and at first he threw the little Carrolls into paroxysms of fright. He was bigger than they were used to, much friendlier and more familiar, had a longer tongue for licking one in the face, and so on. However, he quickly overcame their fear, and now all three kids play with him. He's the cleanest dog I ever saw, and one of the best for children.

We have regularly four or five vegetables at every noon meal, and the children, especially Jane, eat heartily. Our meat-points are scarce which I think is a good thing. We have, of course, plenty of eggs for breakfast, and an abundance of whole milk. Then grandma is opening up on the canned peaches and canned apples which rounds out their diet in good measure, I think, without much meat.

Mary, I hope you are getting the low down on anaesthesia, and Gay, I hope you are enjoying your freedom.

Much love to you both.

Dad

---

[1]Editor's Note: Lillian and Roy are caring for the Carroll children while Mary takes specialty training in anesthesiology; Alan, Jr. was also there for a visit.

Austin, Texas
August 3, 1945

Dear Mary:

We are having quite a lot of fun with the 3 little ones this summer—at least *I* am.

Lillian Lee is getting to be somewhat of a poet, and spoke a little poem this morning which resembles the Chinese free verse of a certain period. Alan, Jane and Lillian Lee has each a bowl which they eat cereal from. In Jane's bowl is pictured a spray of red roses; in Alan's a rabbit; in Lillian Lee's a cat playing a fiddle. So Lillian Lee quietly remarked as follows:

A rabbit is giving Alan some Easter Eggs.
A kitty is giving me a song.
A flower is making Jane smell good.

To me this seems quite imaginative and appropriate; don't you think?

We all enjoyed Gay's visit very much. He and I took Lillian Lee and Jane swimming, but I guess he has already told you. It looks as if poor Sarah is not going to get a house to live in at Corpus, and another period of separation is ensuing for her and Alan.

The presents came at noon and they are all highly delighted. Lillian Lee carries around the string picture-postcard and says, "This is Wisconsin, where my mamma is."

Much love,
Dad

Austin, Texas
August 13, 1945

Dear Mary:

Everything is ok. Chillun are thriving and brown as berries. Gay was here Sat. aft. and yesterday, and he and I took Lillian and Jane out to Deep Eddy. I haven't been able to arrange for them to go out there often enough to learn to swim. They are, however, overcoming their fear of the water. There was the darndest lot of talking over the place you ever heard of when the kids received the toy-telephones. They mainly gab, ride their tricycles, swing, play with blocks, read and look at the pictures of the books. Lillian knows a number of the Mother Goose and other rimes and stories almost by heart and she thinks she is reading. Glad to hear that you are starting back before long, and hope you have profited by and enjoyed your trip. Everybody is all agog about the atomic bomb and the end of the war. I think Sarah has decided definitely not to go to Corpus now even if Alan were to be successful in getting a place to live in, which is unlikely. She figures that if war ends, he will be out in six months and moving will not be worth the trouble for such a short stay. This is by far the hottest summer we have had in a long time, and it's about got me down. All kids show signs of heat-rash, but not much, except Lillian. She appears cool as a cucumber all the time. Bachman is again on the move, we know not when or where. I'm hoping Japs will throw up the sponge before he gets there this time.[1] Mama is healthy, but tires towards night.

Much love,
Dad

[1]Editor's Note: In October of 1943, Bachman was in the central Pacific with a Navy amphibious unit headed for Ellice Islands. After that the LST 240 made for Tarawa and Kwajalein.

❦

Cedar Valley (Travis County) Texas[1]
February 15, 1946

Dear Bachman & Jane:

This letter is to both of you, share and share alike.[2] I have not had much time to write to anyone, what with moving myself out here to this old rock ruin and establishing my "camp" in a 20' X 20' west room, second story. I have, however, finally gotten comfortable, and have come to have a feel of the place, but not a "feel" that makes it quite like home, as yet.

As you know, I began my leave February 1 on a grant from the Rockefeller Foundation and the Texas Historical Association. I am supposed to reduce some material I have been collecting to a book within a year, and it's a-going to take a lot of pecking on this old Oliver type-writer to do it. I came out here to be away from the telephone and to be difficult of access to people who are under the illusion that they have some business with me. I am sensitive to interruptions, and (Jane, psychologist, please note) a hot, go-to-the-bat dispute disturbs me so, emotionally, that I am unfit for any kind of writing for at least 24 hours. Then, too, there's hardly room in our little cramped apartment in town for me to spread out, as I like to.

I go in on week-ends (only 20 miles) and do my odd, neglected jobs about the place as best I can. I am very inhospitable, having been unresponsive to suggestions by friends who hope to relieve my loneliness a little by dropping in on me occasionally. Everyone seems to take it for granted that I *am* lonely. Truth is, I was never lonesome in my life, and I have been happier far away than close to people ever since I can remember. Besides, in this case I have the conscience of one employed. I have been hired and I want to put in my time, like any other good employee.

By the way, Bachman, here is a tax-problem[3] for you. Schofield, Collector of Internal Revenue here, seems to believe that my "grant," being for educational purposes, is not taxable as income. If so, I am getting nearly a thousand dollars per year more net income than I would have been getting in my regular employment with the University. How about it, expert?

My room is early pioneer, very early. First, the heart of it is a big stone fireplace where I do *all* my cooking. I am having a crane put in for handling pots. If I were still carnivorous, I would have an old-fashioned spit installed with mechanism for turning the roast slowly before the fire. But alas! my dead-animal-eating days are over. I have become *so* vegetarian in these latter years that I feel, or fancy that I feel a tendency now and then towards rumination.

And there are the andirons, sturdy relics, but I musn't get down to such details. I am not going to "tell all." I must be coaxed into being communicative.

I have a circular table of great amplitude. It was confiscated by a couple of Texas rangers years ago in a poker-hideout, accommodating a ten-hand game with no crowding. A poker-table of this size provides a location in the center for the "pot" so far from the rim that any suspicious fondling with that sacred area even by the longest-arm & light-est-fingered crook in the bunch is quite out of the question.

Then, (and I am quite proud of this feature) I have built out of appleboxes against the only *timbered* side of the room (east, opposite the fireplace) cases for books and files. North are two huge windows, and two in the south wall also. The three walls, south, west and north, are of natural limestone, rough hewn, with the excellent masonry of pioneer days exposed. The place was built in the 1850s. To harmonize with the yellowed limestone and also with the rough-and-ready look of everything, I had Sarah sew up some curtains for the four windows of 8-ounce duck, natural color. I persuaded her to make a couch-cover, also, of the same material.

Above the wide mantel piece, I have installed against the stone the family photograph-gallery. And that reminds me, Jane, I have left a space for you. I am going to substitute that last fine picture of Bachman for the one I now have, taken while he was a boy at the Academy. In the group are two pictures of the madam, one very large as she *is*, and a small one of her as she *was* during her first year in the University, 1903, 43 years ago. It was taken by Journey, the greatest photographer who ever had a shop in Austin. I have in one frame two views of Sarah, one front and one profile; also one of my mother taken in 1935, sitting beside her birthday cake, showing 86 candles. Mary's I don't like for she is smiling that photographer's "smile-please" smile. Well, if I had some Grant Woods for my other walls, the mural decorations would pass.

My two rugs are simply terrible—there's no other word for them. Oh for some good old rag-carpets. They would really set me up.

In one corner of the room I have rigged up (appleboxes, again) a cupboard-pantry combination for my food and kitchen utensils. I have a combination, also, in a typewriting and dining table—really, one must economize. You can't have a table for *every* activity. Scattered about are five rawhide-bottomed chairs, and I am looking earnestly every time I go to town in all the old furniture junk-shops for a rawhide-bottomed rocker. I have a student-lamp for looks, and an electric floor-lamp for light.

Exposed portions of the floor show 6-inch flooring boards, warped with age, and gaping cracks between them filled with the dirt of a century, packed, hardened, almost fossilized.

That was a lovely letter, Jane, you wrote the madam; and Bachman you did yourself proud in the one that followed shortly after Jane's. If you keep that up, you'll have her singing around, happy as a bird.

Much love

Dad

[1] Roy Bedichek is writing from Walter Prescott Webb's Friday Mountain Ranch, having taken a leave of absence to work on *Adventures with a Texas Naturalist*.

[2] Bachman and Jane married January 2, 1946.

[3] Editor's Note: Bachman was specializing in taxation in his study at Columbia Law School. Bach had graduated from the University of Texas Law School before the war, but when he came back to Austin, still in naval uniform, on terminal leave, he made visits to law firms where he had friends, hoping for a job offer. None came. All said they needed to wait for returnees who had been with them before the war. A Houston firm inquired about what business he could bring in. Mother said we should wait to get married until he had a job. No way would Bach consider that. I said New York firms were seeking brains more than business connections. (Bach was brilliant—top of the charts on exams and intelligence tests.) We decided on study at Columbia Law School for Masters of Law degree, paid for by GI Bill. We went to New York. He stood at the top of his class at Columbia, was offered a job teaching at Yale and Columbia, and practicing with a large New York law firm, Milbank, Tweed, Hope, and Hadley. He taught for a year at Columbia and then went with Milbank.

꽃

Cedar Valley, Travis County, Texas
April 3, 1946

Dear Bachman:

I can return a definite "yes" to your question about filing release of mortgage with county clerk. Brown Bros. saw to that and charged me for the recording. I phoned the liability insurance man and advised him of the auto accident, but don't believe I made any written report of it.

Of course, Winston Churchill has lost cast with me. I think he is a war-monger, an imperialist, interested only in keeping the British empire intact even if it requires the last dollar and the last man that America can produce. I think he must have been good and drunk at Fulton, Mo., for he injured his own cause very much by what he said. Even gentlemen wine-bibbers get so finally they can't drink like gentlemen.

The New England prejudice against Walt Whitman will never die. He had such a gravitational pull that he disturbed the literary astronomy of the country. New England had been the center of this literary solar system until the huge weight of this Betelgeuse of a Whitman began to make itself felt pulling things southward until it reached New York where it has been ever since. Of course New Englanders can never forgive this.

Then New England's literary men came from aristocratic families, and social snobbery reinforced literary snobbery. New England was prudish, Whitman and New York were not. New England had a church-religion; Whitman's religion was humanitarian. James Russell Lowell hated Whitman with a deadly hate. He was a literary snob, a poseur, a shallow, riming nincompoop, and a very striking justification of Ingersoll's crack that a university is a place where pebbles are polished and diamonds are dimmed. Lowell was certainly a pebble to start with and not a very large one at that.

Whitman was an evolutionist from the time Darwin's work appeared, and even before, for he was right in the current of the evolutionary thought which produced Darwin. Lowell, on the other hand, as late as 1884 "took God's side against evolution." He called Whitman narrow and unoriginal, couldn't understand why anyone would waste time reading a book like *Progress and Poverty*. Like the Republican Party he was wrong about everything, while he posed (and was so accepted by literary New England) as THE critic of his time.

One of his pets was Thomas Bailey Aldrich.[1] Who ever hears of this bird now except the delver into literary curiosities? But he was the darling of the New England School. Magazines which rejected Whitman's poetry vied with each other for some of the flat (not to say flatulent) verses of Aldrich. The crowning insult which New England never forgave Whitman was his contemptuous treatment of their idol, and Whitman did it quite unconsciously.

Whitman was invited to a great literary dinner and happened to be seated right across the table from Thomas Bailey Aldrich. Addressing him with all sincerity and in what he thought was a complimentary mood, he said,

"I like your little jingles, Tommy."

This to the man whom Lowell had lauded as the leading poet of his time! Of course, they had no business inviting this bull into their china-shop. They might have known some of the china would get broken.

Still, in a word, Whitman, off-hand and without meaning to be rude, pronounced posterity's judgment on the poetry of Thomas Bailey

Aldrich. Every one, even New Englanders, now concedes that he wrote only jingles which some people like.

But I forget you are studying law and not literature.

I knew Jane would be right about the gift from the Ayres's. Framing just the right phrases in that copper-plate hand of hers is not a mass-production enterprise and takes time, like any decent handicraft.

Well, much love and much law and hoping you are duly humble—accidents will happen—about having such a charming wife, I am

Yours truly,

Dad

[1] Thomas Bailey Aldrich, editor of the *Atlantic Monthly* from 1881–1890, and writer of poems, stories, novels and essays.

❦

Cedar Valley, Travis County, Texas
April 18, 1946

Dear Bachman:

Letter, clippings and copy of *New Yorker* all received. Also heard of you through Graves who gives a favorable report. Says you are looking well, studying hard, and full of discussion and ideas. He brought me a copy of a first edition, Hudson's *Birds of Town and Village*. He knows me pretty well since he never makes a mistake when he chooses to give me a book. That's a good test. Last book before this was a lovely copy of Gilbert White's *Natural History of Selborne*, excellently printed and illustrated with some of the liveliest steel engravings I have ever seen. I believe I have gotten more genuine satisfaction out of this little book than out of any gift-book I have received in years. If I am a species of onion, Graves knows his onions.

Your reactions to Churchill are interesting. You say you are reserving judgment on him and if so please consider following as a part of the record:

In 1927 he was an enthusiastic Mussolinite, praising his character and accomplishments in season and out.

In 1936 he supported Franco's side in the Civil war in Spain, because, in my opinion, Franco was supporting British vested interest in Spain and the liberals were threatening them.

In 1915 the disastrous Gallipoli campaign was almost wholly his baby.

Very good reports say that he held out against Roosevelt to the bitter end on invasion of Europe and delayed it to a time when German defenses were perfected. He never believed it could be done, in the opinion of some of those familiar with the controversy—I have, of course, no proof of this. I think, however, the remembrances of Gallipoli would naturally have made him extremely cautious.

Some say he wooed Mussolini in effort to detach him from Hitler.

He welcomed Stalin with open arms and a fervent kiss when Hitler attacked Russia. To his credit, but in all these cases he thinks first about the English Empire, and nothing else; right or wrong, the Empire is the first consideration. If we in any way threatened that sacred interest, he would turn on us like a bitin' sow.

Churchill is an artist rather than a statesman. He is often wrong about the right policy but never about the right word. He sings England's praises better than most of her professed patriotic poets. And how important this is to a nation's life! The ancient Greeks were not the most heroic but the most magnificently reported people who ever lived. Similiarly, the exploits of English airmen (for example) will live in three lines of Churchill's tribute, while generations of just as glorious achievement by other air corps and other arms of the military service will fade away, less memorable only because less laconically told.

There were doubtless many instances in Persian history of men dying nobly for the ashes of their fathers and the temples of their gods, but in the conflict between Greek & Persian we remember only Greek grandeur and Persian humiliation largely because, commemorative of Thermopylae some nameless poet carved a monumental line:

> Go tell the Spartans, passer-by,
> That here, obedient to their laws, we lie.

That is itself Churchillean. It is such Thermopylaen phrases as his that seed the memories of a whole people, pass into legend, grow into mythologies, survive and inspire long after the physical remains of the civilization that produced them have only museum-interest.

Churchill is an empire man and whenever any corner of that British-looted domain is threatened by so much as an inch, Churchill becomes all fire and fury. Our interests do not coincide with British empire interests at all, and we will be a lot of the damndest suckers ever born if we ever get it into our national head that they do.

England is naturally desperate. She is spread too thin, by far. The British lion has not only bit off more than he can chew, but more than he can hold in his mouth. Churchill is coming to realize the truth of what Hitler said that only continental countries have a broad enough base these days upon which to found a colonial empire. Mere seapower can't do it any more. Think of Holland's trying to exploit on the well-known colonial pattern the millions of Indonesia. Or Belgium's empire in Africa! It can't be done, and neither can England without our help. What a joke France's pitiful clinging to Indo-china!

If these countries were adopting the Russian technique which the Russians learned from us of granting full complete citizenship and status to every bit of territory acquired, there would be some hope. That is the social "atomic bomb" which Russia is using and will continue in her expansion to use. It's not so much England vs Russia as an outworn colonial technique vs. a modern one. You say it does no good to recall that others have sinned, but I submit that it does good to observe what is taking place right under one's nose here and now. Russia is doing no more than U.S. and England (actions of all three reprehensible) to bring on a war. What are our troops doing in Cuba, in Panama, England's in Greece, Syria, Iraq any more than what Russia's are (or were) doing in Iran. If we could just see ourselves as others see us it would make us a bit more tolerant. Enclosed cartoon is along this line.

I think, also, it is a mistake to identify the Russia of 1946 with the Germany of 1939. How many millions of Germans were there on how much land. Compare with present lebensraum of Russia. Compare the history of German aggression in 100 years previous to 1939 with history of Russian aggression during the same period. Compare German herrenfolk theory with Russian equalitarianism. If Trotsky had won out over Stalin there might be some grounds for comparison, for Trotsky was an internationalist advocating the communization of the world as the only means of maintaining communism in Russia, just as Hitler advocated nazification of the world to establish nazism in Germany; but Russia repudiated Trotsky whereas Germany embraced Hitler.

Well, I know you didn't want a treatise on internatonal relations but when the old typewriter gets to rattling it has to rattle on until it runs down.

I meant to write you about Whitman, a field in which I walk with more confidence, but I'll have to content myself with only a few lines.

Your point of Whitman's rudeness in making the remark I quoted is well taken. It was rude. But there is this to be said in extenuation. Whitman was reared in a different social atmosphere entirely from that of the Boston crowd. Whitman was a child of the pavements of New York. His pals and cronies were cab-men, ancestors of your present taxi-drivers. Outside western cowboys they were the most terrific "joshers" on earth. Everything was the subject of a jest—nothing was sacred if by any twist, turn, hook or crook it could be made into a guffaw. Practical jokes were accepted as part of the ordinary routine, just as in a cow camp and among cowboys. I remember two cowboy friends of mine who went off for two or three days fishing on the San Saba River. Most valued item of supplies was a quart of whiskey. First afternoon out, one went up river to kill a few squirrels for supper. The other one conceived this ghastly joke: He carefully emptied the sacred whiskey into another container and hid it in the bushes. Then he spread a pallet down, took just enough whiskey to taint his breath, left empty whiskey bottle by his side and 'possumed when he heard his companion returning. His pal took the whole situation in at a glance, or thought he did. During his absence his pal had consoled himself with a few drinks and then more until he had drunk the whole quart, their 3-day supply [and] had gotten dead-drunk. He began cussing. Hitched up the team and drove clear to Lampasas to get another quart of whiskey, returned past midnight to find the drunkard entirely recovered, sitting waiting by a low campfire. Question arose immediately about the etiquette of drinking up the whole supply of whiskey while one was absent. The accused maintained innocence, said he hadn't drunk a gill, and offered to bet that the other would find his damned quart of whiskey right where he had packed it away when the two had left town. Bet was taken, and stores were unpacked. Sure enough, there it was, apparently untouched. Accused stoutly maintained his innocence, declaring that he had simply fallen asleep, didn't hear other hitching up the team and driving away, was greatly surprised when he awoke about sundown and found himself alone.

He finally made his story stick, really made his friend believe that the empty-whiskey-bottle he saw by the pallet was an illusion, and

248

never confessed the truth until three years later when he got his friend in a crowd and told it on him.

Whitman would have roared and slapped his thighs at this story; Thomas Bailey Aldrich would have seen nothing funny in it and would have severely condemned the jokester for being so dishonest. The respective social climates of these two men varied so widely as to make their understanding one of the other quite impossible. To call a man's poetry "jingles" meant nothing to Whitman. He called his own poetry "barbaric yawp"[1] and named it that in one of his serious poems. I still think Whitman meant no offense.

I might offer some consolations for the privations you and Jane are at present enduring. By contrast, roomier quarters when you get them will be all the more enjoyable. There is always a compensation, for which see Emerson's essay on the same. Consider my meager self-cooked grub for a week and then my enjoyment on Sunday of one of your mama's gorgeous vegetable dinners. The *sum* of the week's pleasure is about the same, whether I spent week at home or in camp with one day at home. Change is of the essence of enjoyment. Privation alternating with luxury amounts to a multiplication, not of the disagreeable experiences but of the pleasures of plenty.

Well, this letter now really is of impossible length. I've a notion not to send it. I like the *New Yorker's* gentle Addisonian humor. Am not sophisticated enough to undertand all the jokes, however.

Please don't let this letter scare you into not writing any more. I pledge this is the last long one. I'll give you broken doses hereafter.

This time, damn it, I quit. Not another word. Not a line even to tell you and Jane you both have my love and fondest hopes. In short . . . but not another syllable.

Dad

P.S. I did mean to endorse Grafton editorial as quite sane & certainly well-said.

---

[1] Whitman, *Song of Myself.*

Cedar Valley, Travis County, Texas
May 2, 1946

Dear Bachman:

On last trip to town I left your long and much-enjoyed letter with your mother to read, so now that I am answering it I do not have it before me, always a risky thing to do, especially when the correspondence has grown disputatious.

In touching upon military history, I knew that I was getting out of my foxhole and exposing myself within range of an enemy armed with a sub-machine gun and plenty of ammunition. I got scared at one point and started to eliminate all reference to Churchill's military misadventures. As a matter of fact I didn't need it to prove my point anyway. Had I offered a dozen well-authenticated military blunders, Anzio and all the rest, it would have contributed nothing to the point I was trying to prove, because a mistake in military strategy is no proof of political unwisdom, and that was my charge against Churchill. Well, you make the most of the exposure and I withdraw my charge of military incompetence in re Gallipoli at least. However, since I wrote you, Ralph Ingersoll has published his book *Top Secret* devoted almost entirely to proving Churchill wrong in his "soft under-belly of the Axis" (my, what a phrase!) contention and that Roosevelt, Eisenhower and Stalin were right in their insistence on a frontal attack. Here, Ingersoll contends, Churchill was fending off Russia from the life line of the British Empire which is confirmatory of what I said in my letter about Churchill determining everything by one criterion and one only: the safety of the Empire. But I am granting that all this doesn't prove my point, and, as the lawyers say, the prosecution rests until you explain Churchill's political perspicacity in supporting Mussolini in 1927, Franco in his war on liberal Spain (a position he still maintains), his holding off an effective union or the proposal of one with France until France was prostrate, and his inveigling Truman into giving world-wide importance to his proposal of an alliance against Russia right when the UNO is in a most delicate state of negotiation with that power.

I now turn to a topic of greater interest and importance and one upon which I am better informed: the private life of the Mynah.

You told me an intriguing story of how the mynah holds a court of justice, with prosecution and defense, judge or judges, executioners, and other pomp, ceremony and functionaries of human courts. I am convinced that this is folklore. There's no doubt about their playlike brawls in which a tough fight is simulated and none of the combatants is hurt by so much as a permanently displaced feather. All the authorities are agreed on this. But the court of justice is another matter. Your book, *Birds of Hawaii* by George C. Munro, describes the mynah but doesn't mention any such remarkable habit. On this very page you have made several excellent marginal notes, but you do not call attention in margin to the omission in description of the mynah of the most spectacular thing about him, his habit of trying offending members, rendering judgment and executing the same. If this were true, it would be unique in the bird-world and a thing that every ornithologist would note in any description, however short, of this bird.

All the more would the scientist mention it, because it is a thing that has been disproved in the case of several other species to which sentimentalists at one time or another have assigned this practice. Under the title "Mr. Wise Guy—the Indian Mynah," *Nature Magazine*, January 1945, E. D. Neff describes the general brawls in which the birds engage, but says nothing about "court martials."

On the other hand, *The Mentor*, October 1926, describes court martials held by crows, and says "banishment is the punishment meted out by some birds." He says rooks do the same thing, and declares that the stork, having had chicken-eggs put under her in place of her own is accused by her mate when chickens are hatched out, and assemblies of storks try and kill the female who has thus presumably violated her marriage vows.

*Popular Science*, Vol. 33, 1888, article unsigned, quotes Reverend G. Gogerly in "The Pioneers" who quotes a missionary, Mr. Lacroix, to the effect that he saw flamingoes hold court and kill a criminal, and details all the usual points with great particularity: crime, assembly, prosecution, sentence, execution.

Here again we find the stork! Bishop Stanley quotes "a French surgeon" to the effect that hen's eggs were swapped for stork's and after chicks were hatched out, enraged husband goes off for a couple of days and returns with large numbers of storks who proceed to try and execute the faithless female.

Goldsmith quotes in his *Natural History* from Mrs. Starke's "Letter from Italy" an incident of a wild stork brought home by a farmer to be the companion of his tame stork. The tame stork, however, resented the intrusion and nearly tore the wild stork to pieces before he escaped. Four months later, according to Mrs. Starke, the wild stork return[ed] to the farmer's barnyard with three compadres and fell upon the tame stork and killed him on the spot.

The unfaithful female, however, is the favorite with the ministry. One of the brethren this time changes hen's eggs to goose-eggs and lays scene in Berlin. In this trial 500 storks participated, "one after another addressed the assembly." Finally the female is convicted on the evidence of cohabiting with a goose and is duly executed. In this same article the Rev. F. O. Morris reports a case of both husband and wife joining together and exterminating the chicks as soon as they were hatched out. It seems that here (although reported by the ministry) husband had greater faith in his wife.

Douglas De War in "Birds of the Plains," John Lane, New York, MOMIX, mentions street brawls of the mynah and calls them "mock fights," but says nothing of the court martial.

So I conclude that I shall have to file this story in the folklore collection.

To return to politics and our apparent determination to get up a war with Russia, I think Robert M. Hutchins, Chancellor of the University of Chicago, said a pretty good thing on the radio the other night:

> . . . when we are tempted to boast about our peaceful selfishness and the trust that other nations should repose in us, we might in fairness remind ourself that . . . the United States, in addition to engaging in five declared wars, has committed 144 instances of undeclared war, armed hostilities or armed occupation in 45 countries or islands. . . . When we criticize Russia for leaving troops in foreign countries, we might recall the list of foreign countries in which American soldiers now reside.

It strikes me that all this furor about Iceland's refusal to permit our constructing air-bases there and of Russia's reputed objection to it is nothing more than we might expect. What if Russia was demanding an immense war-base in Iceland. What would we say about it?

I notice with great satisfaction that your style in controversy is becoming more conciliatory. I can see the lawyer putting into practice Mr. Coleridge's great phrase "agreeing to differ."[1] When I think of all the useless heat I have expended in violent arguments during my long life, I come to appreciate the wisdom of Wm. Hazlitt's aphorisms:

> If you discuss a question amicably you may gain a
> clear insight into it; if you dispute about it, you only
> throw dust in one another's eyes. In all angry or vio-
> lent controversy, your object is not to learn wisdom,
> but to prove your adversary a fool; and in this respect,
> it must be admitted, both parties usually succeed.

I cannot but think with satisfaction of Jane's personality in this regard. She is just as tough intellectually as anyone, and has convictions just as dear to her heart, and yet in argument, what a velvet approach!

Well, you asked for it and you've got it—another long letter, so long I don't believe I have enough stamps to send it by airmail.

Much love to you and Jane and be assured it makes me happy to hear of your happiness.

Dad

[1]Perhaps referring to Robert Southey's *Life of Wesley*, "Agreed to differ."

※

Cedar Valley
Travis County, Texas
May 28, 1946

Dear Bachman:

Your letter of May 8, and your postcard postmarked "May 13" were both duly received. Your memory of the vermillion flycatcher has stimulated my memory. It was at Port Lavaca during our long walk in a gusty cold day on the beach of the bay and under a cliff about ten feet high fronting the Bay. This bird was cold and hungry. He ordinarily takes his insects on the wing, but that day it was too cold for insects to fly at all, and therefore this denizen of the upper air did not scorn to get down on the ground with the bird hoi-polloi and take his meal right off the dirty sandbar.

These birds are becoming common around Austin. I know of half a dozen nesting pair this spring. This was unknown twenty years ago. He is recorded as a "straggler from the South" in Simmons' book, and at time of publication in 1925 had been recorded only once, and that was on March 16, 1914. Finlay makes a sound prediction however, "Will probably appear more often and eventually become a rare summer resident." If he had left out the "rare" it would have been even better.

Simmons does not give any grounds for this prediction. I have been trying to be able to offer some explanation of the northward movement of the species. Best guess I can make is (1) more lakes; (2) more clearings in the cedar break.

In re "(1)," the vermillion flycatcher likes a desert country but must have bodies of still water. You remember we saw him in New Mexico. We saw him at Elephant Butte dam where he had desert hillsides coming right down to a large still body of water. Later, I saw him up on the Gila River in a similar environment. Sarah and I found him on the banks of the Medina Lake out from San Antonio. All of these cases were during the breeding season. You and I saw him in January at Port Lavaca as a winter resident. The dams on the Colorado backing water upon the desert hillsides of the Edwards Plateau creates this condition.

In re "(2)" the bird, (any flycatcher, in fact) has to have open spaces to work in. He is not a bird of the woods, that is the thick woods, for there he cannot sail out from his perch and nab off the incautious insect. Before the government began subsidizing the cutting of cedar around Austin, the cedar break was too thick for him. He didn't have enough operating room. Now, however, there are thousands of clearings in the cedar break making spaces for insects to fly in with no cover to dart into if pursued by an enemy. Hence, this bird finds a congenial habitat here.

He has some competition from other flycatchers. There is the phoebe, but he sticks down to water-level, almost, for his feeding-grounds. Then the scissor-tail breeds here, but he is a high-flyer and lives on high-flying insects, not as high, of course, as the martin's upper-air territory, but on the next lower level from the martin. Now the vermillion is inserting himself between the scissor-tail's level and the phoebe's level, where he has the competition only of the crested flycatcher. However, this is a hole-nesting bird and hence stays with the tall timbers, which in this section occurs only along creeks and ravines. He is more in competition with the phoebe anyway, for his food is largely beetles, moths and butterflies. He is not nearly so expert on the wing as either the vermillion or the scissor-tail.

I believe this most brilliant of all the flycatcher tribe is taking up with us permanently and will become more common still. I hope so, for he is a thrilling creature to watch. He hovers, you know, like a hawk, and so poised appears like a coal of fire in the blue of the sky, almost like a star shining in broad daylight.

Glad to be furnished with the "quote" from Henry George inscribed in the Columbia Law Library. In my opinion, he is one of the greatest, if not *the* greatest social philosopher this country has produced. His theory of taxation, while nowhere put into effect, has permeated and altered for the better taxation-systems all over the world.

I have been having something to do with Weaver Baker, whom I have found to be a most disgusting type of politician. Riding sentimentality, he has been trying to force us over our own Constitution and Rules to accept state schools for defectives into the Interscholastic League. In language as diplomatic as I can command, I told him to go straight to hell, and then he appealed to the Regents where, sad to say, he got some comfort. Then he charged into our State Meeting of Delegates and got sat down on very hard. He has some influence in making the budget, being Chairman of the State Board of Control, and will likely try to take his spite out on us by cutting down our appropriation. He's a cheapskate if there ever was one, and it will be disgraceful for him to be elected to a superior court.

It will not do to argue because some one or a dozen instances of animal behavior once thought to be folklore turned out to be valid, other popular beliefs will have a similar verification. As a matter of fact, it is the exception for a piece of putative folklore to turn out to be a fact of science. I agree that caution must be exercised and folklore should not be brushed aside because it seems unreasonable. I have been guilty several times, and one time I would have staked a good deal on a woman being a liar who recorded the catching and eating of a humming-bird by a praying mantis. It's quite likely true. I don't have time to tell you the whole story, but it's really a good one. Suffice it to say that I brushed it aside as bunk at first, but I am now not so sure. Maybe the praying mantis does catch and eat humming-birds.

But I think the court martial story fits in so perfectly with similar stories all over the world that have been proved folklore that it will turn out to be merely a local variation of the stork, crow, raven, rook, and flamingo stories.

Thanks for all the clippings. I read them with interest. Enclosed are two or three that I thought might interest you.

I am taking it for granted that mama has told you all the family news. Your last mention of Jane gave her a cold. Did she ever get over it? I enjoyed her letter to your mama, and certainly hope your forebodings concerning the examinations were ill-founded. Your mama was stirring up your tennis things when I left there yesterday. Likely they are mailed today. Don't embrace the fallacy that one can "make up for lost time" in the matter of exercise. Lost time is forever lost. One can mend his ways but he can't reach back into the past and grab up benefits he has neglected. The only way to take exercise is to take it in moderation and regularly.

Much love.
Dad

❦

Cedar Valley
Travis County, Texas
June 4, 1946

Dear Bach & Mary:

Well, I have gotten the publication matter settled. A pleasing gentleman from Doubleday & Company dropped in on me about a month ago and read the manuscript I had at that time completed for about two hours. Then he said quite matter of factly, "You've got something here. Doubleday wants this book, and I'll give you a contract with an advance of $1,000 as soon as I get back to New York."

I didn't expect such a prompt decision, and didn't respond at once. He mistook my hesitation for disappointment and offered to raise the advance, but I told him the thousand dollars was satisfactory.

I said nothing about this to anyone, not even to your mother, thinking that this man when he got out from under my spell might change his mind, and I didn't want to disappoint any of the family.

But sure enough yesterday, along comes a formal contract, drawn even more liberally than he had promised:

10% on first 2,500
12 1/2% 2nd 2,500
15% thereafter

Also, $500 on receipt of signed contact in Doubleday office, and $500 on delivery of manuscript.

This news for the present is to be kept in the family.

Yours,
Dad

Mary, your letter was the final thing that sent your mama away on her trip happy as a lark. Glad you got it to her on time.

R.B.

P.S. The man turned out to be a quite important official of the company. He warned me that this would not be a popular book but that his company wanted it for its "prestige" value. It is to be illustrated and sell for $3.50. At least that is what he said he planned, but these details are not in contract.

❧

Cedar Valley
Travis County, Texas
June 8, 1946

Dear Bachman:
Your card of June 4 give me very gratifying news: (1) the splen-

did grades, (2) the good time you and Jane are having. And number 2 carries the additional gratification that the enjoyment is far from the frivolous sort. No one was ever hurt by associating with Audubon or his pictures. I tried to persuade the Library Board at the University to purchase the Audubon prints (complete set) available at $3,500, and I believe the Board did recommend the purchase but the regents didn't act upon it.

I think I must give Jane credit for producing in you that happy frame of mind in which one can do his best work. There is a kind of duty to be joyful which I have not always been able to discharge. Theodore Roosevelt is quoted by Viscount Grey as saying, "He is not fit to live who is not fit to die, and he is not fit to die who shrinks from the joy of earth or from the duty of life." Viscount Grey is one of the most joyful men, or was while he was alive. I remember reading a delightful paragraph by him on the pleasure of reading in bed. I was seeking endorsement in high quarters for this vice which I have indulged all my life. What was my surprise when I found that this paragraph described Grey's pleasure, *since* [he] *had become blind*, of learning Braille and thus being able to turn off the lights, go to bed and, holding the book under cover, read himself to sleep with his fingers.

Your card about the vermillion flycatcher brings it all back to me, even to the one-strand barbed wire fence, and the crippled scaup duck. If I had a memory like yours, I'd throw all my notebooks away.

I have another problem in folklore upon which you may exercise your analytical mind and apply some of the principles of evidence. The wood duck nests in holes in trees sometimes as high as fifty feet above ground. Sometimes the nest is above water [and] sometimes it isn't. It has been assumed that when the young hatch, they are carried to the water in the beak or on the back of the parent duck. Many observers claim *to have seen this*.

However, Viscount Grey's gardener, Henderson, and a man for whom Grey vouches without reservation, saw the parent duck on hatching-day fly out of the hole and take her position in the grass and utter a peculiar call. Then one after another of the ducklings climbed from the nest up two feet to the entrance of the hole and tumble down into the grass, a distance of 31 feet. Then the mother duck led them through the grass to the water, 300 yards away.

What accomplished and sturdy ducklings, climbing a straight-up-

and-down wall to the mouth of the hole, two feet, taking a tumble of 31 feet, and then off through the grass after the mother for 300 yards and a swim at the finish.

Audubon *asserts* that the mother carries the ducklings, but records that he *saw* the tumbling method employed. Various correspondents of Mr. Bent[1] describe particularly the wood duck carrying the young, but they do not agree as to the manner of carrying, one saying in the bill, another, on the back. Those who say they ride the mother's back down to water usually notice that when the mother gets over the water she assumes a vertical position which spills the little fellow in the water.

It is possible, of course, that both methods are employed, but not likely. Instincts such as that run in a narrow groove with no choices.

The duckling is hatched out of the egg with long sharp toenails which would seem to indicate that nature knew he would immediately have some climbing to do. He is also supplied with an unusual lot of down and feathers. He is an unusually fluffy duckling which seems to indicate that he should be ready for a fall of some kind, but whether a tumble from the nest or from the mother's back or beak is not indicated. Practically all the authorities agree that when the nest is over the water, they *always* take the tumble into the water.

I am of the opinion that they *always* tumble, and that the other stories are nature-faking and folklore. What do you say?

It may be that observations later than the accounts I have have already settled this matter, but Mr. Bent does not take a stand on it. Bent's book giving a number of eye-witnesses to "carrying" was published in 1923.

If you can come through next term as successfully as you have this one, I don't see how you can escape landing a good job.

Much love.

Dad

---

[1] Arthur Cleveland Bent wrote a twenty-one-volume series of *Life Histories of North American Birds*. He records observations on bird behavior.

Cedar Valley, Texas
Travis County
June 29, 1946

Dear Bachman and Jane,

Especially Jane. As long as your mama received from Mrs. Gracy[1] Jane's letters, I was kept fairly well-informed about her, but since your mama and I have been divorced,[2] not a word. Bachman, your letters have been wonderful, but they have lacked Jane-items. Am I grown so old in your estimation that I am no longer interested in women or interesting to them? Jane's letters, by the way, were full of bachmanniana, but your letters, Bach, might come from bachelor's quarters. Now in the names of all the gods at once, let me have a line of or from Jane.

Well, one more day and the world is to be blown up so I fear I will not after all get any reply to the above pressing request. Sea water is said to be one of the trickiest substances known to chemistry and once started by atomic explosion may continue with increasing violence until the Pacific is consumed and then the world. I wish man were not so interested in killing other men; but we can expect nothing else from the present generation, educated solely in science, not *in what science is for*. Of all the bumptious egotists one can find anywhere, the scientific laboratories are producing by far the most bumptious—ignoramuses to the nth degree but dangerous ignoramuses because of the deadly skills they have been taught. I notice that these nincompoops, steeped in conceit and sublimed by ignorance, are now offering to teach the rest of mankind the social sciences. They propose to do this scientifically, establish a new science called "humanics," or some such beastly coinage, which will really organize the art of living, perfect human relations, and make everything just lovely. They are unaware that this new science they propose is the oldest one on earth, that religion, philosophy, law, sociology, anthropology, philosophic history and all the rest have been concerned with just this very thing, from the time man still labored with an anthropoid stoop. These "sciences" are the ones that have brought what little light there is into this beastly world; but they are all to be junked in favor of one proposed by scientists who are concerned chiefly with new and effective ways of killing people. It's as if in the closing years of the middle ages, we had not listened to the sages and prophets of the Renascence, but turned for guidance to an association of the King's armorers.

Much love, and remember that though I am dried up almost to the stage of the desiccated, cured and poisoned botanical specimens (many of which I have been examining lately), I have still an interest in women, especially in Jane.

Dad

[1]Jane Gracy Bedichek's mother, Bessie Wells Gracy.
[2]Bedichek is playfully referring to the fact that Lillian is in town and he is out at Cedar Valley.

Cedar Valley
Travis County, Texas
July 13, 1946

Dear Jane:

You should be a lawyer, too, for you always "cover the case." Now since reading your letter I know all I need to know about how you and Bachman are getting on, your decision to stay in New York, etc. Supplementing this, I have received from the Gracys a thick batch of family letters. They show the same nose for interesting items and the same clarity of expression as one finds in *Pepys' Diary*. Your letters, not mine, should be preserved. But no one should tell you that they *are* being preserved, for that might make you a bit skittish, and give you a psychological background of writing for posterity. One writes, I think, better for posterity if he doesn't know that posterity is to be the ultimate consumer. Posterity's interest is most often to know just what previous generations were interested in, and not what the writer thought posterity *might be* interested in.

Tell Bachman I got his good letter and applaud his decision. It will all be fine just so he doesn't get shunted into too narrow a specialty, as looking up points for some one else to use all within some little cubby-hole of the taxation field. With a hundred lawyers in the firm, there must be a high degree of specialization.

I wish you would do one more thing for him to be added to the hundred others you have already done: Make him take care of his eyes. One excellent way to do this is to encourage him to cultivate an outdoor hobby. He already has a long start on birds, and it just happens that the field study (not museum-study) of birds constantly exercises without straining the eyes, and it can be carried on only in good light and in the fresh air. I believe that fresh, clean air is as helpful a tonic for the eyes of a sedentary worker as it is for the lungs. He could soon become a bird-authority by giving even occasional attention to it merely as a hobby. Knowledge of Nature is a good introduction to a wide range of people, from the poor and ignorant to the most highly cultured. It's a kind of meeting-ground of common interest where all classes of people can associate together on even terms. Theodore Roosevelt and Lord Grey had one meeting (I believe only one) in their long lives and they devoted that to listening to the songs of birds and discussing them with the enthusiasm of boys and the knowledge of scientists. I have just read Lord Grey's Falloden papers,[1] and have been amazed at the penetration he shows in discussing disputed points with professional naturalists, and at the intimate knowledge he has some way found time to pick up, and he a man of large affairs—of the largest affairs.

Well, now, how do you like to have someone butt into your family affairs and tell you what you should do for your husband?

Class is dismissed.

R.B.

P.S. Have just received Bachman's letter asking low-down on the low-downs and higherups now seeking office. I am just as much in the dark as he is, or more so. I am going to town today and try to pick up some information to retail [sic] to him.

R.B.

P.P.S. I was sitting in my diggings last night reflecting deeply and listening for "authentic tidings of invisible things" when who should roll up but the whole damn family, Lillian, Sarah, Alan, Alan, Jr., and Roy B. We had a lot of chatter. They're all well, and stood trip well.

[1]Grey of Falloden, Edward Grey, Viscount (1862–1933), British foreign secretary from 1905–1916. He wrote *The Charm of Birds*.

August 3, 1946

Dear Jane:

Another day of filling boxes with books and getting them carted off to the freight depot. This afternoon Sally and Alan took an old steamer trunk of mine (vintage of 1907) down to Mullers to have some straps and maybe a lock repaired. It has crossed the Atlantic six times already—four on the *Normandie*—but they are desperate for usable luggage, athough they have some ten other trunks crated. This one must carry the precious microscope, binoculars, and lighting system. Science certainly complicates matrimony, but, in Alan's case at least, science has certainly smoothed his path. Alan taught Comparative Anatomy for the first time in Marquette, and Sally (who had taught it five or six years) helped him grade his papers. As he had two heavy quiz sections, her help was most welcome.

Thanks for the snapshots. I love them. But I wish I had the snap showing your face, altho' your back is eloquent and the waterfall is a lovely back-ground—and Bach is sweet.

In case Bedi hasn't answered your questions I. V. Duncan is Vance Duncan, Phi Delta Theta, football captain 1902–03, brother of Harris B. Duncan, Bedi's intimate friend, now dead, and husband of Annie Jo Gardner ("Precious" or "Presh" to the Grace Hall girls of my day). She was a Kappa, afterwards taught at San Angelo when Bedi did and thought a great deal of him. I am not sure but I think her son, Gardner Duncan, was in the University when Bach was. However, it might have been Donald Duncan, Harris' boy. Hal, Donald's older brother, was killed on D Day. Vance lives on a ranch near Eagle Lake. Eagle Lake, Texas, would get him, as he is well-known. I imagine Annie Jo sent the gift. It would be like her, altho' old Vance is a dear. The queer thing is that Bedi hasn't seen either Vance or Annie Jo in over 20 years, and didn't even send them an invitation.

The Van C. Kelly, Jrs. are Van and Elizabeth Tenney Kelly. They— the Tenneys—were our next door neighbors for eight years, and Leighton Tenney, her youngest brother, was Bach's playfellow and friend. Leighton was in the Bataan Death March and died two weeks later of dysentery in Camp Cabanatuan, the infamous Japanese pris-oner-of-war camp. Van and Elizabeth have a week-old son named for Leighton. Van's father is in the lumber business here in Austin.

The name John T. Jones doesn't waken a memory. Sorry.

Tell Bach that his friend Dorsey Hardeman was elected a senator from San Angelo in place of Senator Metcalf. Also, Herman Jones was magnificent at the Rainey[1] rally. Such vituperation of the Texas Regulars for "trying to steal the election" in 1944! Rainey's was the fighting speech. It reminded me of Jim Hogg denouncing Joe Bailey at a Democratic convention way back when I was a little girl. He went at R. R. Commissioner Jester hammer-and-tongs fashion and brought out some telling facts. He may not win but he is going to make the people of Texas conscious of their real masters, and the sleeping giant may turn, even wake up. At any rate, he has nothing to lose, so he will go down fighting. More power to him, I say.

Sally and Alan have gone over to the fly-lab to take some fresh bottles of food to the precious triploid flies, which are in a sad state. Due to lack of bananas, the flies have to be fed on all kinds of substitutes, corn-meal this time. They don't thrive on it as they did on the banana-agar-yeast formula. She has been studying this breed for over ten years. I believe they have three sets of chromosomes instead of the usual two. Only an expert can identify a triploid—tell him from a diploid. These flies (*drosophila melanogastit*)[2] show all sorts of queer mutations, especially in regard to sex. Some are half-male and half-female—intersexes, they call them. There are many shades of sex-mixture with many names descriptive of them.

It is terribly hot here, but the babies are thriving in spite of it all, and the rest of us manage to stay alive.

Alan and Sally and the babies leave Austin August 21 on the Missouri Pacific, just as you and Bach did. They sail Aug. 30, but have so much freight to round up and get aboard that they will need a week to get it all together. It will be eight or nine months before another boat leaves New York for Beirut.[3]

Well, good night, folks, and lots of love,

Mrs. B.


P.S. R.B. hasn't been in town in a week. I am looking for him Monday. A brief letter from him says that the hot weather almost got him down but the cool spell following it saved his life. We had a shower and 80 degree weather last Sunday following several days of intense heat (100°).

P.P.S. again—Sue Nabors Logan has never answered my letter, or, if she did, it got lost while I was in Milwaukee. Sue is far too busy on her Bucks County estate to bother with the likes of me. Of course, she adores Josh and is tremendously interested in what he is doing. Her daughter Mary[4] is a talented dancer, has appeared in Maxwell Anderson's plays, and with John Gielgud, the English actor. It was Susie's sister Irma who was my dearest friend and cousin. Sue is five years younger than Irma. You haven't missed much, honey. Now, Irma is different.

[1]Homer Price Rainey, president of the University of Texas from 1939–1944, when he was fired by the board of regents because he refused to fire two instructors, he then ran for governor.
[2]Lillian's footnote in the letter identifies these as "black bellied fruit fly."
[3]Editor's Note: Alan was on his way to the position of Professor of Zoology at the American University of Beirut. While there he would conduct research on schistosomiasis (liver flukes). Sally taught at the Catholic University of Beirut.
[4]Mary Logan Leatherbee was later travel editor for *Life* magazine.

꽃

Cedar Valley, Travis County Texas
September 5, 1946

Dear Bachman:

Your letter of the 25th was one of the pleasant surprises I found waiting when I returned to my diggings from a camping-trip at about the 6,000-foot level in the Davis Mts. Slept under two blankets every night, and two nights I had to pull up a tarp besides. It was glorious. I tramped every day climbing mountains, not with the gusto of twenty-five years ago, but enjoying it nevertheless, in spite of leg-tremors and short-windedness. I found two new birds: but of that later.

I am mighty glad to get the low-down on the APL, *PM*, the Communist Party and its devious ways, the compromising Republicans and the almost equally disgusting Democrats. I had already weakened a lot on *PM*, cut down to Sunday issue, and had decided to drop it entirely when my present subscription expires. *PM* centers too much in New York. It has the New York delusion that incidents on Manhattan Island are of more importance than events elsewhere. It's too much concerned with exploitation on a purely racial basis. One begins to feel that if Jews and Negroes got justice, all the rest could go hang, so far as *PM* cares. I don't like to draw race-lines even in exploitation. I would prefer to throw into one pot to be defended, every individual—man, woman, child of whatever race—who is defrauded of his just earnings. I would call "just" earnings sufficient to live in decency in return for an honest day of useful work. After such distribution of national income, I would be willing to let the predators play as fast and loose with the remainder as they chose, and put it down, or charge it up, to "experimental living."

Perhaps the more we defend Jews as Jews, and Negroes as Negroes, the more we stir up and develop the consciousness of race. We should never think of a man as anything but a human being. "The world is my country and mankind is my religion."

I am not as much disturbed as other liberals over the Rainey defeat, which, indeed, was no surprise to me at all.

In the first place, I have never seen in Rainey any political "it" at all. You know there are many handsome, beautiful and essentially lovable women who don't have and can't assume "that certain look," as the hill-billy Weaver Bros. used to call it—sex appeal. Just so there are men with right ideas, attractive programs, fine presence, and excellent education who haven't that certain element of personality which appeals to the people in their political activities. Many completely cold-blooded individuals have it (just as some icy women have SA)—it's not a matter of passion or warm-bloodedness, or even good-will—none knows what it is. I think it's a secret psychological current circulating mysteriously in the mob to which some men and women happen to be hooked up, while others are not. Rainey's connection in this circuit—if, indeed, he is connected at all—is defective.

In the next place, there are three disgusting accusations which the oil companies with their "locals" in every community in Texas, and using Grover Sellers as a cat's paw in the primary, were able to pin on Rainey. Each of these allegations is so surcharged with prejudice that it alone would have been sufficient to keep the majority of voters from considering the political issues at all:

1. "Nigger-lover." That itself alienates wide sections of the labor

266

vote, organized or not, the very place where Rainey's program should have made him strongest. There is nothing that arouses the po' white ire like the word "nigger-lover." Snobbery and economic interest fuse in the po' white to make this prejudice overwhelming.

The ruling classes of the South, descendants of slave-owners, have carefully nurtured this prejudice and kept it at a blazing heat for their own purposes of exploitation. If the exploited whites ever got together with Negroes and Mexican peons and came to feel a community of economic interest, it would be sad, mates, for the larger ranchers, plantation owners, big land-owners, industrialists and the employing classes generally.

The neo-carpet-baggers[1]—under which term I include the new industrialists, oil and utilities corporations with their attorneys, dependents, and hangers-on—see the point, also, and live in deadly fear of unions having finally enough sense to admit Mexicans and Negroes. They therefore join with the old aristocracy (native sons, in Texas) in keeping fomented to the highest pitch the hatred of the "nigger-lover."

They hold up their hands in holy horror at the suggestion of admitting Negroes to white schools, but send their own children to the much better private schools of the North and East, where their darling children sit in classrooms from day to day with Negroes, and return to their arms miraculously uncontaminated! And then the proud parents finish off the education of their beloved progeny in the "nigger-loving" colleges of the North and East without qualm or apology, while being ever ready to grab a machine-gun to defend the chillun of the po' whites from a contamination certain to follow if Negroes are admitted to our public schools.

A curious thing is that these people are sublimely unaware of any inconsistency in all this. They are sincerely for "white supremacy." So do people now, so have they, so will they always permit their own selfish interests to form a chemical mixture in their minds with their impulses towards the public good. Like cream in coffee the two motives cannot be analyzed apart. One and inseparable they ever remain.

As to the relative excellence of the better private schools, I had counted a year or so ago the number of individuals in *Who's Who in America* who had their secondary education in private schools and compared it with the number found to have had their training in the public secondary schools. If appearance in *Who's Who* is any criterion

267

of success in life, the individual educated in a private school has about 150 times the chance of attaining success in life as has the individual educated in the public schools. (I have forgotten the exact figure, but it's something enormous.) Of course, this figure is to be duly discounted by the fact that only the wealthy can send their children to private schools. Hence, chance of success is already statistically heightened by hereditary wealth; but even at that, there can be no doubt that instruction in private schools is vastly superior. The salary scale of teachers is higher by about one hundred per cent, or even greater in the more exclusive private schools. And it is just this superiority of training which makes the Southerner (even though a klukluxer) blink [at] the contamination his boy or girl will suffer from association in [a] classroom with Negroes.

Exploitation always begets fear in the heart of the exploiter for the exploited, especially if and when the exploited grow numerous. Consider the feeling of whites for Negroes in Ft. Bend County. You should read a letter from my friend, O. Sam McJohnson, just received, from North Africa. Frenchmen there are trembling in the presence of the exploited Arabs who outnumber them about ten to one. It is the same with the English in South Africa—it's the same everywhere.

I have a hilly-billy neighbor out here, starved, exploited, kicked around (but not by Negroes) whose solution of the race question is to kill all the Negroes. Have a regular St. Bartholomew's night, mass-murder, cut the throat of every son-of-a-bitch with color enough to identify! Of course, this man's landlord wouldn't go that far, although he claims to nurse in his heart a hatred just as intense. But his tenants really would destroy a lot of good cotton-pickers, and those that remained, like the children of his tenant, could demand and receive a higher price for this service.

Another item: Mrs. R. J. Kidd[2] was invited to a neighbor's house the other night and found assembled quite a neighborhood party. It's in the vicinity of the Country Club, a strictly middle-class part of town. Soon after her arrival, a big-bellied drummer began twitting Mrs. Kidd upon voting for a "nigger-lover." She attempted to justify her vote for Rainey, and the murmurs of "nigger-lover" grew so loud and scornful, and the bantering became so ill-natured, that she was driven home in tears. You know what a lovely woman Mrs. Kidd is, and the spectacle of her neighbors turning upon her thus brutally at a social gathering stinks strongly of genuine nazism. It's the identical thing that was happening in Germany while the Hitler movement was forming.

2 & 3. USA & Homosexuality.—I stopped for a moment at a hotel in Sonora the other day, and was greeted by a matronly old lady, proprietress of the hotel. At the same moment, a man was leaving the lobby, saying "I must get home to vote for Rainey." This led the old lady and my companion into an exchange of views. She began by saying that Rainey (and his wife, too) "ort to be put in jail and kept there." My companion remonstrated, and asked her to listen just a minute since he had known Rainey personally for many years. "It can't be discussed," she shouted with blazing eyes, "it can't be discussed," and she bolted out of the lobby, slamming the door to emphasize her indignation.

Here you see the homosexuality—and USA—lies working in this good old soul. And how diabolically they had been planted in her mind with the formula, "They're so terrible they *just can't be discussed!"* That not only puts the lie into your victim, but locks down the lid so it can't possibly escape. It sours and ferments.

So, I say, Texas may have become illiberal, but the Rainey defeat doesn't prove it, because his platform was never made an issue. The only issue that ever penetrated the strata of society where elections are settled, was "nigger-loving," homosexuality, USA.

The squirrels you feed peanuts are pleasanter company. I, too, have been having experiences with squirrels. You know pecans are just now getting big enough to be recognizable, but green with the husk tightly sealed to the nut. The squirrels become impatient for their favorite food, and begin tearing into them with a vengeance. They gnaw down to the shell of the nut where the bitter juice bites their thievish tongues, and then throw them down. Not only do they throw the gnawed nut down, but the two or three others on the same twig, the whole cluster, in fact, without testing them at all. About one in fifty of these nuts the squirrel finds a little palatable, and he eats about a third of it. I stood under a tree where one was feeding the other day, and counted the nuts he threw down in five minutes—46! Now your squirrel is very provident. As soon as he gets a sound, unblemished peanut he makes off to add it to his hoard. So, also, will my squirrel be when the nuts ripen. Then will they husband their resources, thrifty as a Maine farmer, and carefully bury a great supply of good sound nuts. But think of the vast crop the wastrels destroy before they ripen, just for a tiny taste of a nut almost-but-not-quite ripe—about one in fifty! I doubt if there is any connection in the squirrel's mind between a green nut and a ripe one. Once the ripe one arrives, however, he seems to associate it with a winter shortage. Or, say the scientists, they don't, and their hoarding is simply a blind instinct, as automatic as a slot-machine. It's funny that the blind instinct doesn't advise them that green nuts will ripen if left on a tree. To me it's more like Tommy finding the jam-jar, and wasting half of it and giving himself the belly-ache instead of waiting until dinner-time and having a bit of jam decently spread on a piece of bread.

I had a pleasing experience with a rock squirrel in the Davis Mountains last week. He chose to dig a burrow within ten feet of my cot. It took him a couple of days to finish it, and after his head got out of sight he would back out every now and then to look me over and see that I had not changed position. When he got his burrow completed, he then proceeded to improve each shining hour, storing the tiny acorns of the Gray and the Emory oaks. He came in with cheeks puffed out and left a moment later with cheeks sagging. He made exactly the same round many, many times: first a short gallop to a small tree, up in the topmost branches to feed awhile, then across to a larger one, sampling, sampling, sampling, and finally gathering proper acorns for storing; then down and by another route back to his burrow. At the entrance, he would pause for a moment, cheeks inflated, and take a good look at me.

His work may be all for nothing, as a skunk may oust him. You see, Mr. Skunk has delicate and tender paws, not at all suitable for handling this sharp granitic gravel, and he dislikes digging anyway. Perhaps he is wise enough to foment class hatred among the rock squirrels. At least they never join hands against him. So he prowls about until he finds a burrow just to suit, and quickly evicts the owner. Then the squirrel goes off and patiently hollows out another place to live in.

I don't know about Strickland's[3] effort to unload the University endowment—I'll investigate this—but I do know he was playing down in the Legislature, so as to be popular and more effective as an Interstate lobbyist, the University's need for more money. Rainey charged this, I think, in his sixteen original charges against the Board.

I, also, would be interested to see Communism out in the open. Maybe it would lose some of its terror if subjected to scrutiny in actual daylight.

Mighty glad to hear of your robust health. I can't, however, concede that unexercised flesh is ever sound. Keep up those belly-bending exercises, if nothing else, until you are able to resume your tennis.

Had two cards from Sarah while in New York, one to your mama and one to me. On one she crowded in this statement "Jane is a delight." On the other still more closely written postcard, she managed to margin, "Jane is the most friendly girl I know."

Give this same Jane my warmest regards.

I don't expect you to read all this stuff before examinations. It will be safe to skim through it even then, for when you and Jane come, I promise not to give you an examination on it, or even a ten-minute test. As a matter of fact, I have been writing principally to myself.

Yours,
Dad

P.S. I see that I forgot all about the two new birds mentioned in the beginning, but of them, another time.

R.B.

[1]Editor's Note: Roy's mistrust of the "new industrialists as neo-carpetbaggers" extracting Texas' natural resources took a personal twist when Bachman went to work in the legal department of Texas Gulf Sulphur which had its headquarters in New York City.

[2]Her husband, Rodney J. Kidd, was athletic director of the University Interscholastic League and became director of the league after Bedichek retired, 1948–1969.

[3]D. F. Strickland was a regent at the University of Texas.

October 2, 1946

Dear Bach:

You amaze me sometimes with what you have learned. Where, in God's name, did you learn how to write such an exquisite, such a convincing, post-guest note? Did you happen to read one in your high school days and simply reach down into your capacious memory and pull it out?

Seriously, this note will finish off the delight which your mother got from your visit, crown it and make it really perfect. I am not sending it in for I want to *see* her read it. Maybe she had a secret pinch of conscience over spending the money in an inflationary market for the bedroom set? Maybe she feels a little inadequacy in taking care of a guest like Jane who has experienced hospitality on a grand scale; maybe she has some self-accusings of not having done this or that. Well, if any of these things are harbored in her mind, this note of yours will scare and scurry them out and leave her memories of your visit an unalloyed pleasure. Besides this note makes me feel good, too;—a virtue in it not to be discounted.

I shall not see Jane again on this trip. The dear creature took your mama and me in her car and brought us out here the other afternoon. My car had stalled, by the way, and I had gone in home on a truck. She remembered (she has a memory, too) that I had spoken of my difficulty in buying powdered soap for my dishwashing, and of my fondness for Riley's milk. Well, she turns up with a large box of "DUZ," the very best dishwater soap, (really makes dishwashing a pleasure), and with a bottle of Riley milk and some bars of toilet soap for good measure.

She looked around over my baching quarters and exhibited just enough enthusiasm to get me started to talking about my baching experiences, my books, my methods, my this and my that until I had swelled myself up almost big enough to bust.

Well, if I don't write much from now on you can put it down to the fact that I am trying to catch up on my schedule. This cool weather puts me in fine spirits. I have a fire on the hearth this morning (first one of the season) and an old-fashioned tea-kettle is simmering over the fire suspended from my famous crane. It's quiet. Bright sunlight is falling on pastures of frost, and all except the very rugged wild flowers look a little sick. So, fall is here, and I have only four more months of writing to get done what I started out to do.

Much love,

Dad

P.S. I notice that I have not commented on your message to Jane about "protecting her interests." Even if I saw her I wouldn't deliver this message. I have found from long experience that women don't down in their hearts consider this a joking matter. Jealousy awakens of itself. It has always an uneasy sleep. A playful poke is just as apt to stir it up as a serious kick in the ribs. One may stimulate an immediate and quite satisfying response (i.e. either a man or a woman may) but it is distinctly a *stimulation*, and there follows the inevitable let-down that follows *any* stimulation. Taking the long view, there will be enough anyway to arouse jealous thoughts (coincidences, absorption with work, and a thousand other chances) without this joking about other women. Well, you may destroy this postscript for it in itself is provocative.

Dad

Austin
October 2, 1946

Dear Honey:

Jane phoned last night that she had a letter from Bachman written on September 26, the day after his arrival in New York. It had come by ordinary mail, arriving on Saturday, too late to be delivered until Monday. The precious child read it to me over the telephone so that I could tell you all about it.

It was a sweet, affectionate letter, such as you used to write to me when we were young and all, and full of good news. He missed her terribly, could hardly wait for her to return. He had received another A. Only one subject remains to be heard from, so far all A's and A pluses. He had been to see Dr. Dowling, in the hospital for a double hernia operation, but cheerful in spite of it. Dowling had entertained Bachman and Jane at a very enjoyable party last Spring. Only three students were present, all the others being faculty members. This happened last spring before Dowling's operation of course, but I mention it in order to show his connection with Bach, since he was not one of Bach's professors. In fact, he invited Bach when he first made his acquaintance. Now it seems that Bach is to occupy Dowling's big beautiful office.

Bach has been so very busy that he has not had time to go down town to have his new suit fitted, as requested. This is a mail-ordered, or tailored-to-order, suit, not a Brooks Brothers suit, but should fit him.

Now for the home front news. My car was ready late yesterday, so I am going down this morning to get it (in exchange for $35.05). I fear I must again cash some of my postal savings drafts. (I had to cash

$175.00 last month). So, darling, will you send me the usual check for household expenses? I promise to be as economical as possible with it. And I will be very careful with my glasses and the car, too. An ounce of prevention . . .

Good news. I was able to buy two quarts of salad oil, enough to make four batches of my famous mayonnaise, also a package of oleo. Good butter is now .80 a pound, but this very good oleo cost only .30 at Ritter's. Armin went under the counter for it. Our credit there is better since we bought the wine and beer. Should I purchase a few more bottles of Drewry's Ale in order to keep it intact?

Love must be contagious; perhaps there are emanations, impossible to register scientifically but subtly powerful, that reach into my long-neglected inner mind. It may be October (the first mild norther, the warm sun on my back as I walk to school, the wet leaves and red-berried vines) that send my thoughts swiftly back to the fall of 1910 and Deming. It wasn't so long ago, really. Darling, do you remember? The soft dry sand, the mesquite hummocks full of pack-rats' nests, the moonlight nights when the mockingbirds sang in the greasewoods and the moon came up over old Ben Franklin? Or the mornings when it was so hard for you to get me up? Wasn't the sleeping wonderful on the open prairie, under a horse blanket or big tarp, with Billy backing into our pallet almost swishing us with his tail? Or the summer days when it rained every afternoon and I had to run grab the dry diapers off of the mesquite bushes? Or the Sundays when we dug cedar and mesquite roots for our 'dobe fireplace or climbed the Floridas and saw Capitol Dome from close-at-hand? Or the coyotes and Hobo? "If I forget thee, Zion . . ."

I must go now. Worlds of love,
Lillian
I washed a lot of sheets, etc., yesterday. The sun was beautiful for drying. Will try to get some shirts ironed. God bless the man who invented the washing machine.

❦

Cedar Valley, Travis County, Texas
October 12, 1946

Dear Bachman:

Your two letters and nuthatch-postcard were duly received, also the clippings enclosed.

I was particularly glad to get the clipping on truck-regulations which confirms a suspicion I have had a long time that the railroad lobbies in State Legislatures have been at the bottom of the idiotic restrictions placed upon trucks, which have a tendency to Balkanize the United States. State governments, by the way, are rapidly becoming merely a "fence" for big corporate interests which find it easier to defeat the people in 48 installments rather than take them all on at once through the Federal Government. The sentimental slosh about states' rights we are now getting in Texas (and I suppose in other southern states) comes mainly from the neo-carpetbaggers, i.e., local representatives of the corporate interests of the North and East. And our slop-eared public brays back a chorus of appreciation for the "protection" from Federal encroachment which the wily boys are offering.

Quarantine regulations are abused in the same identical way. Frequently I want to bring a sack of oranges back from the Rio Grande Valley. All I have to do [to] get through a "port of entry" a hundred miles up the road towards home, is to go around to a friend (orange-raiser) and get a tag which I may attach to any sack I buy and she goes right on through with no inspection whatever to see if it contains any pink boll weevil or other noxious insect which threatens to devastate the country. It's a pure sham from start to finish. Without this magic tag I have had a sack of a dozen oranges or grapefruit confiscated at the "port of entry."

It is doubtless true that in some states the roads are not built to withstand as heavy trucks as can go without damage to the road of an adjoining state. But the remedy is not to let each state set up its own regulations. Since the Federal Government puts up much of the money and all of the specifications for the national highways, they should all be uniform, and made national arteries of commerce with identical *federal* regulations governing their use.

Now, of course, as the airplane business is becoming powerful, it will likely join hands with the railways in opposing any kind of control of highways which will serve the public interests insofar as trucking from state to state goes. The railways have succeeded in wrecking pipeline transportation of oil from Texas to the north and east, which is also an outrage.

I was stopped on the outskirts of Birmingham, Ala. once by a policeman who searched my car to see if I had an extra supply of gas in it. I found that the city had a 7-cent gasoline tax imposed by which to filch a little pin money off through traffic, an exact counterpart of feudal tribute on traffic in the Middle Ages in Europe and of what now exists in nomadic Arabia.

While the liberals are expending so much lung power on the One World idea, it might be well to save some for the One Nation idea, "one and inseparable, now and forever."[1]

The Werner clipping seems to me to be concerned principally not so much with the "*perfidious* Albion"[2] idea as with *exhausted* Albion. There is much in English history to justify the former, but it is a matter merely of resort to statistics to establish the latter. England is done for a generation, and England can never, even though completely recovered, stand an atomic war. Her military staff has already advised the Government so, and preparations are now under way for transfer of war activities to the colonies whenever she is seriously threatened. She can do nothing else. From a position of security in the old days of naval power she is now, in the airplane-atomic-rocket age, in the most exposed position of any country in the world. She can be wiped out in twenty minutes and she is canny enough and realistic enough to know it. So Werner says she can't risk a war, especially a war with Russia whose first step in such a conflict would be to occupy Europe. In such case, what would we do with no first beachhead for invasion such as England furnished us on D-day? In such case, shall we stand off and blow Rotterdam to bits and all the peaceful, pipe-smoking Dutchmen who wouldn't hurt a fly, along with their hefty housewives whose main concern is burnishing their kitchenware to knock your eyes out, along with their pink-cheeked children with their toy boats, along with their tulip-gardens—shall we blow all this to smithereens with atomic bombs, five thousand Dutch to get one Russian soldier? Thus with Belgium, France, and all of Europe. The thing reduces itself to absurdity. This is an implication of Werner's article. He points out also that Russia's friction with England is local not general, and he makes a good point of it.

England was awfully belligerent at the opening of the peace conference, Bevan bellowed louder than Byrnes[3] *until he got Byrnes started*, and then he softened his roar. England, in my opinion, wants to get a position she always manages to get: that is, she wants to mediate. She wants U.S. and USSR at each other's throats, *not fighting*, but nearly, while she mediates and makes her *trades*, not alliances.

War has come to mean a new and much more horrible thing, but "statesmen" like Byrnes strut around as if it meant the old, and, by comparison, chivalric contests, in which a few selected young men of each nation were laid upon the altar of glory in a superstitious, and, to many sentimentalists, a propitiatory as well as somewhat gratifying sacrifice, satisfying the old mystic urge to lay life down (somebody else's life) for something or other (almost anything will do) dressed up in idealistic trappings.

You will not find the pictures in the New York plates as flashy as in many other illustrations, or as diagrammatic as in Peterson, but you will learn to depend on them for they are very accurate. They are not overemphasized. Glad you have a nearby place to look for birds. There should be many birds come along the Hudson and stop awhile in the Park.

The red-breasted nuthatch used to be common here in migration, but I haven't seen one now in twenty years. I have seen the brown-headed nuthatch here once, several times in East Texas. At Grand Canyon, Arizona, I saw a white-breasted nuthatch whose hole was forty feet up a pinetree which was barely hanging on the edge of a precipice which looked like it was a sheer thousand feet to the bottom. That little bird feeding its young over that enormous chasm made me shiver every time she lit with a worm for her brood. I was afraid she would fall!

Tell Jane I am remembering her very tenderly every time I wash dishes.

Yours,
Dad

[1]From Daniel Webster's "Argument on the murder of Captain White," April 6, 1830.
[2]Attributed to Napoleon.
[3]Aneurin Bevan, British political leader 1945–1950, and James Francis Byrnes, U.S. Secretary of State, 1945–1947.

Cedar Valley, Travis County, Texas
October 19, 1946

Dear Bachman:

Enjoyed your "Russian" letter very much, although I don't go with you very far.

First, Russia can stand an atomic war better than England, or even than the United States. I am going on the assumption that the bomb will not be our exclusive possession very long. All the scientists agree on this, and it would be out of the question to immediately attack Russia, since the people are not ready for it and cannot be conditioned to the idea under five years or more. It is not as simple as a very religious old lady proposed to me, "Why don't we send an atom bomb over there and kill every one of 'em?" Even if we could, do we want to make a desert and call it peace?

As soon as this enemy was laid low, another would arise, if not a foreign power, then one inside the country. The atom bomb has so changed the character of warfare that a people who engages in it must be prepared to lose *all* their big cities and about forty per cent of their population. I look for private revenge to destroy a number of our large cities. A survivor of Hiroshima might do for New York and a survivor of Nagasaki might level out Chicago. Strictly a one-man war.

I can't get it that there is anything ahead for us if we can't quit talking and thinking war, nothing ahead except obliteration. With you and Jane in New York, you couldn't persuade me to accept the destruction of Moscow for the destruction of New York. I don't want to begin swapping out.

Dependence on some new weapon, some great war-secret has often betrayed a country into war, but has rarely won a war. Hitler and his minions were overconfident about the effectiveness of their secret weapons and that's largely what launched them into war.

At that, however, we are in no such danger as England is in. Her position in an atomic war is utterly untenable. Did you notice that she is establishing huge air bases in Africa? And did you notice that she is now withdrawing from the Middle East leaving Sarah and Alan at the mercy of any Mad Mullah who happens to gain a following. She is withdrawing because she knows she can't defend the Middle East from Russia, as much as she thinks of her oil fields there. If, as all the scientists say, atomic energy will become available, oil fields won't amount to much any longer anyway. Hard on Texas, or rather on the easterners who own Texas. In short, I think your argument is good but for the fact that you withhold the bomb from anyone else. That can't be done if we accept the highest technical authorities in the matter.

By the way, I haven't seen anything by Max *Lerner*, it's Max *Werner* I have been quoting.

Another thing you fail to give due weight to, in my opinion, is the treatment Russia got at the end of WWI, when five armies invaded her with no declaration of war at all, we among the others; and then how outraged we all became at the without-warning attack by the Japs. We participated in one *with* the Japs at the close of the last war. Do you blame Russia for being skittish? And then the high and mighty blustering way of Mr. Byrnes. Before he begins talking trade he spits in your face. England played him for a sucker by maneuvering him out of the position in which FDR had gotten us, (that is as a mediator between England and Russia,) and into a position in which England does the mediating, which she is now doing, trying to cool little boy Byrnes down a bit and then turning around and mollifying Molotov.[1]

Byrnes and Bevan pooh-pooh Russia's quite legitimate desire to control the Dardanelles but when Suez and Panama are mentioned, they throw up their hands in horror—it's all so different, but Russia can't see that it's so damned different. We take the position that we must preserve the neutrality of Turkey, but the Russians have in the back of their minds the Roosevelt rape of Panama—what's the difference, they ask?

This high-powered nationalism must cease if we are to survive at all—it's already worm-eaten with ideologies.

Like you, I can't see what Russia could have to lose by agreeing to the Baruch[2] plan for atomic control, and I think Russia will finally agree to it after due time and without permitting her people to feel that she was bragged, blustered and bludgeoned into it by the high and mighty and pin-headed Mr. Byrnes.

I note enclosure of striker's announcement. I don't see any prima facie evidence of violent intent, but I take your reading between the lines as valid. Our big business people have taught our workmen violence in trade disputes. Ford and General Motors have huge supplies of tear-gas and plenty of tommy guns for *their* goons. The Rockefellers shot up the tents of the strikers of the Colorado Fuel and Iron Company, killing men women and children not so many years ago that I can't remember it. In my opinion the outrageous distribution of wealth has got to be mitigated in some way or we'll have more and more violence until it blossoms out into a full-grown civil war.

Thanks for Ickes[3] column on Baruch.

Tell Jane that she has been ignored in the last three letters you have written. This is intolerable. The last thing you said about Jane was that she was now there and that you were ceasing *merely to exist* and were *coming to life*—but since then, nothing.

Dad

[1]Vyacheslav Mikhailovich Molotov, Soviet premier 1930–41 under Stalin and foreign minister 1939–49 and 1953–56.
[2]Bernard Mannes Baruch, influential adviser to U.S. presidents; under Truman he was U.S. delegate to the UN Atomic Energy Commission, where he proposed the "Baruch Plan" for the international control of atomic energy.
[3]Harold LeClair Ickes, Secretary of the Interior, 1933–1946, former head of the Public Works Administration 1933–1939.

❧

Cedar Valley, Travis County, Texas
December 13, 1946

Dear Bach:

Letter from Jane came duly home and was duly forwarded by your mother out here where it was duly read with great pleasure. It gives some sidelights I didn't have on your Christmas vacation. I approve of this trip to the wilds for you two city-raised chickens.[1] It will do you lots of good. I back the natural man against the artificial man and natural education against the artificial variety. City people generally miss the healing power of a natural environment and develop all sorts of neuroses as a consequence, ill-health, boredom with life and general cussedness. Therefore, let the moon shine on thee in thy solitary walks and let the misty mountain winds be free to blow against thee, as my favorite poet so eloquently advises.

There are birds in the snowy wastes and be sure to look for them. There's the cute snowy owl which sits by until the arctic fox has dug out a lemming. Then he dashes at the fox until Mr. Reynard is so infuriated that he tries to snap him out of the air, but what he does do is to release the lemming, and before he can turn and recover it, the snowy owl has beat him to it. There is also the great white gull—but I don't believe you will get that far north. But you should see the rock ptarmigan, a curious creature of the grouse family that makes a night of it wherever night overtakes him by burrowing in the snow, cuddling up, and going sound to sleep. They also in winter develop "snow shoes." Spreading flanges of growth appear all around their feet in cold weather, which keeps them from sinking too much in the snow. When warm weather comes again they shed these snow-shoes and grow another pair the next winter. Please tell me if you see one of these birds.

These two tales, one of owl robbing fox and of ptarmigan's snow-shoes sound like folklore, but I assure you they are verified scientific fact.

Much love for you both and a Merry Christmas.

Dad

[1]Editor's Note: Bachman and I went to the Laurentian Mountains, Canada, to ski on the first Christmas of our marriage.

*

December 15, 1946
(Copy of letter from Sarah, Beirut, Lebanon)[1]

Dearest Dad:

About a week ago we had a crop of letters from you and Mother, and I surely did enjoy them. I especially enjoyed the chapter from your book on the Golden Eagle. Alan thought it was most interesting too. I can't think of anything more horrible than slaughtering him by airplane. After the way we plant him on all our military and patriotic insignia it seems a complete betrayal to kill this noble bird, particularly by means of an airplane. It's as if the bird should say "Et tu, Brute."[2]

I have never seen a golden eagle outside of a zoo. . . .

Alan and I are slowly plugging along with our work. I have finished typing my lab manual and am working on a prospectus such as Mother suggested that I am going to send to various publishers. . . . I have spent probably 2500 to 3000 hours on this manual. . . .

Yesterday I was called to the Medical Dean's office and given the details of my new course in Medical Genetics. It seems it is going to be a real course after all. It runs for 21 lectures in the spring and I am getting paid $10 per lecture which is quite a bit better than the $3.50 per lecture I was offered by the academic school. The academic school wanted to give me 53 students who had to have quizzes every month and homework every day. The Medical Dean is allowing me $250 in his budget for library books and $40 for having a film strip of photographs for illustrating the lectures.

I never expected to get such a good offer and it will be a pleasure to teach this course. There will be only one exam. Students are fourth-year medical students and some of the staff. The Dean is very anxious to have the course a success; however, I can't promise that. Some doctors are so hardheaded and have their minds made up beforehand, I can only hope I won't offend any bigwigs who might disparage the course to the students. The course will run for two lectures a week so I won't neglect my family in that time.

My flies are getting along fine; triploids flourishing. So far I haven't caught any interesting new species although I have traps out. The reason is that we are having the rainy season and it is a bit cool (about 65 F).

I owe the Medical Genetics course in large part to Alan as he has talked to the Dean quite a bit about it.

I have been intending to write you about the different national costumes I have seen here. At first there were so many that I was confused and couldn't distinguish between or among them. Now I can make out quite a few. I know that a man who is wearing a white headscarf with black cord laced about it twice is a Druse; a gentleman in a red fez, European suit, and carrying a little amber string of beads much as an officer carries a cane, is a Turk; a filthy woman in flowing calico robes peculiarly hitched about the hips and with no shoes is a Bedouin; and, of course, all the Mohammedan women wear veils.

These latter intrigue me the most. First of all, the veils are usually black; rarely blue or brown. They are of varying degrees of opacity. The older the woman, the thicker the veil; the younger and most beautiful, the thinner the veil. It never fails. These veils usually fall only to the shoulders.

The women wear ordinary European street dresses, and usually wear a black coat the length of their dresses. I have seen young girls walking along, closely veiled, with their bare knees showing above their garters; so it seems that it is the face especially that has to be concealed.

Sometimes they drop their veils. When I talked arabic to a poor thin mother on the tram one night when Alan and I were going to the show, she replied concerning the age of her child and in answer to my compliments on the pathetic little creature, she dropped her veil although Alan was looking at her.

As Alan and I walk along the street we can sometimes see a matronly creature in black with her veil lifted. If she catches Alan's eye, she hastily veils herself, sometimes dropping the whole veil; sometimes catching it in her mouth, from either side.

The other day I observed the ultimate in dealing with veils. A woman closely veiled on the tram was eating peanuts. She would introduce the peanut under the veil, and carefully crack it with her teeth, and spit out the shells.

The children are in better health than they have been since we arrived. Alan is completely recovered. His playing equipment gets him out of doors, and it attracts friends for him. His cheeks are rosy and he is gaining weight. Little Roy is roly-poly. His lips have excellent color, but he is very pale. I recently had some trouble getting him to eat anything but milk, but he has snapped out of it completely. He especially enjoys the bread I make (toasted). He is so cute and says a number of words.

It is ten o'clock so I had better go to sleep. I'll have to get up several times to cover the children. Merry Christmas. We didn't try to send anything this year but are biding our time until things get a little cheaper. They say there are a lot more interesting things to be bought in the interior, particularly in Damascus.

Much love

Sally

[1]Editor's Note: Alan Pipkin was teaching parisitology at the American School in Beirut and Sally taught Medical Genetics. She also collected new varieties of fruit flies up in the Lebanon mountains and later wrote a genetics paper about them.

[2]A note on the letter reads: "Sarah is confusing the bald with the golden eagle here. But at that, the golden eagle is a much nobler bird than the bald eagle which lives mainly by robbing osprey of fish."—R.B.

October 10, 1947

Dear Mary:

I got home all right about 7 o'clock and found your mama very much refreshed, having been relieved of household cares for a few days. She was anxious to hear all about you and the children and I gave her as faithful an account as I could.

My office work is somewhat behind and I find many other demands on my time, such as going over to the bookstores and autographing books, answering letters about it, and so on. If I were thirty years younger, I know that I would get an awful case of big head about the way the book is being received. But, you know, pride goeth before a fall, and my pride has performed thus in advance of a collapse so often that I am very cautious. I don't think I can get very much puffed up at this late date over anything that I do, or seem to have done. As a matter of fact this book is in line with hundreds of others just as good, but in a different locale—that's about all.

I have been thinking a lot of the great patience you have with the children. You are about the kindest mother I ever saw, and by all the books your kindness must eventually be reflected in their characters. There is such a thing of course as over-indulgence, but I think where there is one case of that there is perhaps a hundred of harmful suppression and severity. Balzac's *Pere Goriot* presents an everlastingly classic case of over-indulgence and since I read that early in my life it has had an effect upon my thinking out of proportion, maybe, to its merits. Just how to handle two such characters as Lillian Lee and Jane together in the same small apartment is a problem that I could not undertake to solve. One seems unduly willful and the other unduly submissive, and both of them are incomparably sweet children. Then to have coming on such a character as Louise who is so different from either one must give you many anxious moments.

I certainly do appreciate the problems you have and your earnestness and intelligence and patience gives me confidence that you will come out all right with them.

Much love,
Dad

❦

October 31, 1947

Dear Mary:

Well, how's the budget getting along? Does it need any strengthening? If so let me know.

Your mama says you have some rugs that the moths will probably eat up in storage. If you and Gay want them used (for a price, of course) please let me know sizes, quality and condition. It might be that we could rent them, but I am not sure until I know more about them.

I have had a strenuous two days being photographed by a *Saturday Evening Post* photographer to illustrate an article which has been written about me and the book. This photographing is not as simple as it sounds and consists of a lot more than sitting up in a chair in a comfortable studio. All this stuff was done "on location," which means scrambling along cliffs, struggling through underbrush, talking to people along the road, etc. He also took a picture of your mama and me working over a manuscript, which I hope will be used, since it will give you and Sarah and Bachman a good photograph of your parents. This photographer is supposed to be tops. Book seems to be selling well here, but I have no way of knowing how it is getting on elsewhere.

Much love,
Dad

❦

Portsmouth, N.H.
134 Middle Street
October 31, 1947

Dear Roy:

I am sure you will have to look at the signature of this before you can even guess from whom a letter with this super-superscription, comes.

I have planned to write you for some weeks—months, even years, but I am a truly busy woman at this business of making a living.

The idea of writing years back came from a contact which I had in the Library of Congress, in 1941 (April) when I was in touch with the curator of Folksong, the younger Lomax. I was working on the folksong of New Hampshire then, and was in the library on research. He knew you very well, and the day of our interview—the first of several—he had returned from a broadcast in New York and strangely had told a story of you and your ranch when he visited you once over in New Mexico.

I intended then to write you immediately, but Mother whom I visited there just before she returned from Washington residence to Illinois (to live), was injured (later died from same) almost on arrival there, and that drove things out of mind. She heard Dr. Lomax tell the incident and gave a charming reminiscence of you when you visited our farm en route to Texas. Do you remember when you and I captured the hundred bumble bees from the thistles in full bloom in the front pasture, and carefully got them into a bunghole of a small wooden keg, alive?

The darned things made such a noise finally, that your mother who was sewing in our "front room" heard the roar and came out to investigate. Promptly a kettle of hot water was poured into the firkin—it was a firkin with tight lid but a bunghole for some reason, with a cork. I remember vividly how you and I got so bold we could catch the bees by the wings in our bare fingers and shoot him into the bung headfirst. What won't youngsters do! You and I made a pretty fine team doing things that summer. Josephine and Una were too little, we thought, to fool with. Dolls! And Ina and Ena were too big and absorbed in the new clothes Mother and Aunt Lu[1] were making for the Texas sojourns. I remember Una threatened to tell on us—the adventure lasted over two or three days—and you ran after her with a bee in your fingers and that shut her up, completely.

I can't think what we planned to do with the things! I think we did not think that far.

The more recent reasons for my urge to drop you a line have been contacts with old students of Texas U. who knew you. This past year I was at a Fine Arts College in Washington, D.C., and one of the directors of the Theater School was a young man and his wife who knew you—more from a distance than personally, (both grads) but they knew enough of your reputation to give me quite a nice thrill—if I needed more than I already knew from Aunt Lu and the girls at Roswell.

I now hear you have a book out—this has been filtering to me for a time, though I have never learned the subject it treats or is about. One person asked me if I had seen it and remarked that it was charming. I should like some first hand info about it, Roy, and if there is a sales possibility I want to get it. But I don't know where to begin, even to inquire. I am not hinting for a presentation copy, but I really want to get in touch.

At the present moment I am at more leisure for reading than in years—I mean reading for pleasure and not under pressure of research or study . . . the latter during the war when I was in W.W.; and recently driven by what I came up here to complete, ([unreadable] original writing) interrupted by the war and my going in, in January after Pearl Harbor.

I have had a recent setback by recurrence of the old trouble which requires some knifeless surgery and so am off my routine.

This is the first time, since [unreadable] I have attempted the machine, but my hand is not too legible at present. Even so, I must cease, for I find I am [unreadable] well I shall close [unreadable].

I hope you and yours are well and that the family of daughters and the son, together with their progeny, are well and thriving. I hear from Portia[2] when there has been something come up important. She is the truest of cousins to me; but she is very busy and has a large (and growing) family on whom to report. I used to get news of you, but not of late, from her. I adore those girls, as my own sisters.

Give me a line. I'll love all you can cram in of personal news besides the item about the book. You may have written many but I think they have had to do with your field; this seems to be something else from slight references.

Your coz,

Luna Craven Osburn[3]

[1] Roy's mother, Lucretia Ellen Craven, was called "Lu" by her family.
[2] Portia is Roy Bedichek's niece, the daughter of Ena.
[3] Luna and Josephine Craven were sisters. They, like Roy, were grandchildren of Samuel Craven and Harriet Trundle.

November 5, 1947

Dear Luna:

Your letter followed close upon the heels of one from Josephine, which I answered yesterday. It's very pleasant to get into touch with you two again, and to be reminded so vividly of the golden days of childhood. Someone persuaded me to begin an autobiography (which, of course, I shall never finish) and in the first 32 pages I took myself from my earliest recollections in Claremont, Iowa, down to my life as a boy on the open prairies of Texas. Along about the middle, I find Section II entitled "Illinois," and here I give my memories of the old Craven homestead, of playing "with my sisters and two cousins, Luna and Josephine Craven." I tell of getting lost in the blackberry patch and of telling God that I would never be a bad boy again if he would just let me find the way back to Aunt Sally's house.[1] And now since you remind me of it, I shall certainly insert a paragraph on the bumblebee episode. I find that I had a passion for bees. In an early paragraph of this autobiography I tell of trying to capture and incarcerate enough honeybees in a chalk-box covered with mosquito-netting to make up a "hive." This occurred in Iowa, ending in the bees getting loose in the house and getting under Ina's dress which was torn off her by our mother while she was screaming with pain. This doubtless accounts for the summary action of my mother when she found you and me with a horde of far more dangerous bees in a keg. And now I remember the thistles perfectly. I had forgotten them until I read your letter. In what obscure depths does memory hide things, and by what mysterious keys are they released from hiding, and how many other things do they drag along out into the open: often the most inconsequential things?

The book I wrote and which Doubleday published has gotten a number of very good reviews. *The Herald Tribune* (New York) sent me a number of copies of its book section contain[ing] Edwin Way Teale's review and I am sending you a copy under another cover. I think I sent one to Josephine, too. The *Chicago Tribune* gave me about a column, and I enclose one from the *New York Times*, which someone sent me. The *Saturday Review of Literature* of October 4 (or thereabouts) had a rather philosophical review of it by Louis Halle, Jr. Other reviewers over the country show evidence of having read these reviews, if not the book itself.

You have confused the younger with the elder Lomax, I think, since the younger never visited me in New Mexico. Or, it may be, Alan was simply dramatizing his father's visit. I know all the Lomaxes very well, and have for many years. Can't imagine who the young dramatics people are—maybe Jimmie Parks and his wife.

Josephine tells me in her letter that she is sending you a copy of the book. I hope you like it.

Awfully sorry to hear of your illness.

I have six grandchildren, one daughter three males, the other three females.[2] Mary, my eldest daughter, lives in Houston, Texas, and the other, Sarah, in Beirut, Lebanon. My son lives in New York, employed in the law firm of Milbank, Tweed and something or other.

Yes, this is the first book I have written out of "my field." It is in the field of my hobby. I have really written no other book at all— merely bulletins and scraps of this and that, and a monthly paper, and that mostly editing.

Well, it's fine at my age to hear from kith and kin, and to know that they're up and coming even with as many years as I have to weigh them down.

Your cousin,

Roy Bedichek

[1]Sally Craven Wilson, who lived in Chandlerville, Illinois, was Roy's, Luna's and Josephine's aunt.
[2]Lillian, Jane and Louise are daughters of Mary and Gay Carroll. Alan, Roy, and George are sons of Sally and Alan Pipkin.

March 1, 1948

Dear Dad

Mammon won.

Gulf Sulphur is willing to pay me $8600 (that's no typographical error) per annum for my legal services in their New York office. Plus, of course, retirement benefits, free insurance, etc.

I was prepared to ask $7000, and Mr. Fleming was prepared to offer $8000, but he offered first, and we quickly came to $8600. As a matter of fact, he offered $8000 on the assumption that this was double what I was getting at Milbank, but when I pointed out that I had recently received a $300 raise, he doubled that.

I am still a bit numb, thinking about all that money. Jane says that if I keep on at this rate that all my children will surely turn out to be Communists.

Apparently all that is required of me is my legal services, so that I feel that I am still in possession of my soul. It seems that legal services have a better market. At any rate, I don't have any influence to peddle, and I can't believe that I have really sold a bill of goods to these hardheaded businessmen, so I suppose that what they really want is legal services.

It seems that they wanted a Texan who had a knowledge of Texas mineral law. They have another attorney (I was wrong about my being the only one other than Mr. Fleming). He (this other lawyer is a Texan), but he went to Harvard Law School, so did not get Prof. Walker's famous course in mineral law. Of course, this gentleman also is a graduate engineer and an expert on patents, so I won't have anything on him.

The reason I am to get all that money is that my boss, Mr. Vernon, told the Gulf people that I was worth twice what Milbank was paying me. They took him absolutely literally somewhat to his surprise, I think. As I was telling Mr. Colgan (junior partner in Milbank tax dept.), "In six months I'll be thinking that I'm actually worth it."

My friends down at Milbank are all very happy for me. They all swear that they are going to cultivate Texas accents, since that seems to have been the principal requirement. Of course, the town is full of men from the south, southwest, and midwest who have done very well, so it is enough to discourage the local boys.

Honest to God, Dad, I don't know what it is. I haven't had time to demonstrate even to myself that I have any great ability. It must be my winning smile. Anyway, I have now had some experience in obtaining positions. I have never asked for one. Rule one: don't ever ask for a job. I always do a lot of listening, and wait to be sold. Rule two: Keep your damn mouth shut. Whenever the offer comes, I shift uneasily in my chair, frown slightly, and say that although the offer seems very generous to *me,* I shall have to consult my wife. Rule three: Pass the buck and preserve an appearance of modesty.

I now trust that I will be as successful in holding down jobs as I seem to be in obtaining them.

Yrs,
Bach

❧

Box H, Univ. Station
Austin, Texas
March 5, 1948

Dear Bachman:

I really don't know which gratifies me more, the sharp rise in your legal fortunes, or the ability you have recently developed to write a mildly humorous, gently self-deprecating, altogether charming letter about it. I think I am more gratified at the latter accomplishment, for no matter what your advancement in a professional way, if you couldn't express yourself by word of mouth or by letter as a genuine human being should, it would taste rather sour in my mouth. I like very much the idea of first being a man, and *then* a lawyer, doctor, plumber, or whatnot.

Your mother and I enjoyed this letter immensely; we are jubilant at the promotion, and completely stunned by the salary. With perquisites you mention, I guess it's not less than $9,000 per year is it? And by the way, should we treat this as a secret, or let it be known to our friends—I mean the actual amount?

It is true that your connection with this corporation is going to cramp my style somewhat when I am stimulated to go on one of my trust-busting rampages. Gulf Sulphur was one of my favorite examples of colonial exploitation. However, I can make substitutions—there are plenty sitting on the bench, so I do not blame the umpire for putting this one out of the game.

I talked to Dean McCormick[1] over the phone last night. He is pleased and, of course, I expressed my appreciation of his part in this, which was probably considerable, although he denied it, and graciously said that if anyone should thank him, it would be the company that had secured your services.

Mr. Gracy gave me the first news of this about an hour before I went to dinner and found your letter at home. He was as nearly excited as I have ever seen him over anything. You know he is rather Spartan and not given to any undue ebullience. But he told me and DeZavala[2] about it with considerable detail and arranged the details in proper dramatic order.

I wish you would give me your exact title, your new business address, the date upon which you assume your new duties, etc., so that I may (continuing as your publicity agent) furnish the item to the *Alcalde*, and maybe to the *Law Review* and the *State Bar Journal*, if that's its name.

This all finds me in the middle of our State Basketball Tournament and with the State Meet (now *two* State Meets) coming on pretty soon, and making my arrangements to get out, and repaying some of my promoters with certain services which require time, and other things.

Your mama has been really ill, but is now very nearly recovered. Much love, and tell Jane that, though this letter is addressed to you, it is as much to her, and surely it [is] as much credit to her as to you to win this fine promotion. The decision of you two to get out and away and trust somewhat to your own resources, win your own way, so to speak, has certainly proved to be a wise choice. Of course, I shall have, grudgingly, to give you the prime credit in having sense enough to select and nerve (and whatever else it takes) to persuade a young lady of Jane's accomplishments and native wisdom to make common cause with you.

　　Yours,
　　Dad.

[1]Charles Tilford McCormick served as dean of the University of Texas law school from 1940–1949.

[2]Editor's Note: Augustine de Zavala and my father, John Gracy, served on the Travis County draft board together and became good friends. His distinguished grandfather was Lorenzo de Zavala who had served in the Mexican Congress, represented Yucatan in the Spanish Courts in Madrid, and later brought families to settle Texas. He participated in the Texas Revolution and was one of the signers of the Texas Declaration of Independence. His aunt in San Antonio helped save the Alamo from destruction.

❧

801 East 23rd Street
Austin, Texas
March 23, 1948

Dear Bach:

I hope walking to the office through Central Park with binoculars becomes a habit. I can think of no better religious conditioning for the duties of the day than just such communion. It's better, I think, than the Catholic habit of an early morning devotion in the cathedral, which, of course, has its points.

The exercise itself is worth while—"I am the poet of the body, and I am the poet of the soul," says Whitman, and unless one brings both along together and keeps them healthy he is not a complete man. How terribly inferior and machine-like these specialists become! They not only become lopsided, but eventually they disintegrate.

But I can't hope for this to become a habit with you, for nightbirds can't be early morning birds. Man demands eight hours sleep. When one goes to bed at nine he can get up refreshed at five. But if he goes to bed at 11, a five-o'clock walk cannot be made enjoyable, but on the other hand saps the strength. So one has finally to choose between night-life and early-morning life. I have, as you know, for years chosen the latter. But at your age, alas! such a choice is practically impossible.

Glad to get the clipping about the birds in Central Park. I think Mr. Pearl[1] [sic] has the correct explanation of why the birds are plentiful there during migration periods.

I had a fine time in Dallas with the Texas Geographic Society. Had [a] fine audience and they made a great to-do over me. Enclosed is a clipping which please return, as I am keeping a file of mentions of my book.

I am warned by the daughter of the author[2] not to expect much of the *Saturday Evening Post* article which may appear now any time. This girl read the proof and gives it as her considered opinion that her dad didn't do the subject full justice—"lacks amplitude," she says.[3] How the younger generation puts the elder in its place. Can you imagine a journalism student in the University saying as much of the work of a man who was Editor of the *Herald-Tribune* for years? If the article is skimpy, I think it's likelier due to the subject than to the author. Anyway, I give you her judgment.

Yours,

Dad

P.S. Forty years ago Philip Cornick[4] was a promising young man, and fine company. What the years and his business have done to him I cannot say, but I have received a letter or two from him recently with the old flavor. The Cornick family simply took me in and made me a member of it when I was in Angelo 1905–1908, and what a family! Dr. Cornick, the bearded patriarch, was the finest conversationalist I have ever heard talk. Mrs. Cornick kept the best sweet milk and made the tastiest pies I have ever set my teeth in. Philip, George, Amie and Elsie were all charming young folks. Sweet milk and pies made up the refreshments after golden hours of talk. How much I loved the Cornicks, and how much they did for me!

[1]George Perl (correct spelling), a Scarsdale friend.

[2]Stanley Walker, a University of Texas journalism graduate, was the former city editor of the New York *Herald Tribune*, who was one of the best known city editors from 1928–1935. He wrote several books after his return to Lampasas, Texas, and numerous articles on Texas. The article "The Lively Hermit of Friday Mountain" appeared in the October 16, 1948 issue of *Saturday Evening Post*.

[3]Lillian adds a note here: "It is a wonderful article!"

[4]Editor's Note: Philip Cornick, a friend from Roy's teaching days in San Angelo, Texas, who at the time of the letter lived in Yonkers and was a consultant on municipal taxation. His father, Dr. Boyd Cornick, ran a tuberculosis sanitarium in San Angelo and was an enthusiastic supporter of Henry George's theories on land taxation.

❦

May 16, 1948
Austin, Texas
801 East 23rd Street

Dear Bachman:

The most satisfactory glasses for bird-study are 7 X 50, and, of course, the best make is Zeiss. Second best is Bausch & Lomb. A great convenience is to have glasses that are light-weight, with, of course, center focussing. But I do not have to have the ideal, I shall be satisfied with something practical if the difference in price is considerable.

Schoenig and Company, Inc., Dept. T, 9 Rockefeller Plaza advertise in *Science Illustrated*, brand new, coated, Bausch & Lomb, 7 X 50 Navy, for $140. With 20 per cent Federal Tax added, brings price up to $168.00. I don't know what "Navy" means in this description. It may mean that a more or less rush mass-production job was done for the Navy, and that the glasses are somewhat inferior. I wish you would take a look at these glasses.

Same firm advertises "Newly imported Zeiss, 8 X 30, coated, lightweight, for the same price." Please take a look at and *through* these glasses.

They also advertise an English glass I have never before heard of, the "Kershaw" 8 X 30, $119 plus 20% tax. I would certainly like to have a peep through these glasses.

Brownscope Company, Dept. 30, 24 West 45 Street, advertise Zeiss, coated, featherweight, 8 X 30 and 7 X 50, with center focussing, "now costs less than other leading makes." I should like to know how much less. I have sent for catalog of this outfit.

I don't want to burden you, but if you have time please look up these items. I don't want a used glass. One never knows what has been done to it. My friend Oakley[1] reports from Guadalajara that a Kershaw (The Portland) 6 X 30, which is smaller than I care for, at some less than $100 American dollars, $445 pesos, and quotes prices on a Swiss glass, "Kern AARAU, Alpin Stereo, at 575 pesos, with pesos at about 4.84." But I don't care to experiment with a glass I have never heard of, especially since my friend there is not an expert in judging glasses. But his quotations seem to show that glasses there are no cheaper than they are here in the U.S. I can get what seems to me an excellent glass of French make here for $90. I am taking it out in the field for a couple of days down on the coast to try it out.

I am completely lost without glasses. Didn't know how dependent I had become upon them.

Had two hectic days in Dallas, returning yesterday just in time to take in the Town & Gown picnic out at Ralph Goeth's[2] place. The old conservatism of the T&G[3] has broken down under the impact of whiskey-drinking propaganda, and a table of whiskey, cracked ice and other ingredients was set up out on the lawn with the result that there was an even greater amount of silly talk, spurious merriment, and synthetic goodwill than is usual even at such functions as this. One of our women guests got right tight and made much senseless chatter which seemed excruciating to her and to others whose critical faculties had been anaesthetized by similar doping. It hurt me like smoke to have to make the standard alcoholic deduction from the many flattering compliments I received about my book but I did it nevertheless. A physician out at the insane asylum tells me that some of the patients there are terribly gloomy until they are put with others afflicted with similar types of insanity, and then they become abnormally cheerful. Well, I was in the wrong ward last night. The effect was really depressing.

Vance Duncan and his wife (Annie Jo Gardner) invited Lillian and me down for the week-end of the 22nd to their ranch-place near Eagle Lake, and we are going. I visited the Duncans on the Matagorda County ranch just forty-five years ago. Vance, Harris and I took from there a train-load of cattle to the St. Louis market, and I bummed on from St. Louis to West Virginia, where I worked a bit in the coal mines, and from there to Pittsburgh Pa. picking up a little money from a reporting job on the *Pittsburgh Gazette*, and from there on to Boston, (by freight car) where I served a Boston clergyman as stenographer, thence with a trainload of garlic-eating Italians to pick berries down in New Jersey, thence to New York where I was employed as laboratory assistant by a fake-skin-doctor who had capitalized on the new discoveries of the effect of "rays" on sores of all kinds, and "cured" cancer by turning on red rays (colored by passing through a concealed red-glass). I treated some of the most horrible skin-affections [sic] I have ever seen at $2 a shot, which was really cheap, considering that the treatment was actually *harmless*, more than can be said of much of the present day medical fakery.

If I were not so much interested in natural history, I would write a book simply and solely of my own personal experiences with the medical profession, beginning when [I] was born (like you) without benefit of either midwife or physician, latter arriving just in time to collect a fee.

Your mama and I are gadding about too damned much for our age. Wednesday we are going down to San Marcos as guests of Mrs. J. R. Wilhelm who seems to be ramroding a picnic for some Club to which I am to make a speech about anything I want to talk about.

By the way, someone told me some lawyer, I believe it was F. L. (who knows everything) that probably your duties would eventually become more executive than legal. Is there anything to this gossip?

You needn't answer any of this letter except the part about the glasses unless you really want to. That's all I am really interested in at present.

Yours

Dad

[1]Cleatus Oakley was a visiting professor of mathematics at the University of Texas, from Haverford College, and a frequent visitor to philosopher's rock, Bedichek's perch at Barton Springs.

[2]Ralph Goeth, president of Tips Iron and Steel Co., a "Town" member of "Town and Gown."

[3]Town & Gown Club was an organization set up for discussion and an exchange of ideas between the faculty of the University of Texas and the business and professional men of Austin.

❧

June 18, 1948

Dear Bachman:

I enjoyed your description of the encounter with nesting colony of least terns. I remember well our experience with the "Little Striker" at Port O'Connor. He seems to me to be born of the sky and water, compounded of seafoam and the fleeciness of summer clouds. Another touch of innocence is added when he alights, for his legs are so weak that he stumbles along even on smooth sand like a baby learning to walk. I believe we agreed (you and me and Sarah) at Port O'Connor that against a blue sky his is by far the daintiest gray in nature.

Towards the end of the last century he was completely exterminated in the area in which you saw him. They were selling for ten cents apiece to the millinery trade, and in those days every Nellie had to have a tern on her top-piece. One hundred thousand least terns were killed in one season on Cobb's island off the Virginia coast. Their solicitude for their young and for each other made them an easy prey for the "plumers," as the hunters were called. The cupidity of man plus the vanity of woman all but did for [sic] the species. Finally, the ghastly business was stopped by law. I believe I like "sea swallow" the best of all his common names, and he has a lot, a number of them being attempted imitations of his several calls, like "kill-im-peter."

I am participating in the excitement about the house. I have read the descriptions, and noted the drawings which Jane furnishes indicating the locations, proposals for financing, etc. I judge from the fact that you have required your navy papers that you get some sort of concession on the purchase, or on the terms of the purchase, rather.

Someone of more caution than I have might advise you and Jane to wait for slump in prices, but after all life is going on, and the main thing is to live happily while it is going along. "Who knows but the world may end tonight?" And every golden hour you and Jane sacrifice at this period in your lives may be paid back in leaden ones later on. I think your mother and I would have been wise, and gotten more net enjoyment out of life, had we sacrificed a little more and gotten settled in a home of our own earlier. So I cast my vote for buying now, and also recommend very highly as a financial adviser, one John Gracy, in whose judgment I have great faith, and in whose integrity I believe you can place absolute confidence.

As to occupying guest-room, thanks very much. We hope to, but at present are detained, indefinitely.

    Yours,

    Dad

❧

801 East 23rd Street
June 30, 1948

Dear Jane[1]:

Thanks very much for the "happy birthday" card, and here's hoping that in about sixty-five years you will have just as happy a seventieth birthday as I have had.

I have one advantage over you, and that is that you won't have a sweet little grandchild as I have who remembers her grandmother's birthday and sends her a nice picture and message. But maybe you will have that, too, you never can tell.

Get ready to give granddaddy a good fat hug for he is coming to Houston and out to your "country place" on July 9 or 10 and [will] bring Lillian Lee with him. Be sure and tell your mother this for she will want to know.

Tell your mother, also, that her daddy received the nice scrap-book for a birthday present, and it saved him from buying one, for he wanted just such a book to paste his "retirement" clippings in. Quite a number of newspapers published accounts of him and notices which he wants to keep for you and the other grandchildren who may become interested in him.

Much love for you and Louise and for mama and papa.

Granddaddy

[1]The letter is to five-year-old Jane Carroll, daughter of Mary and Gay.

❦

Austin, Texas
801 East 23rd
August 18, 1948

Dear Bachman:

This account of "my day" in yours of the 18th satisfies paternal anxiety. I am glad you are getting a lot of really legal work to do, especially in harmonizing divergent views and drawing contracts to suit. I think this is, after all, the most valuable service which the legal profession renders to society. If we were all always in bodily good health, we could dispense with doctors; and if our minds were free from the disease of greed and its attendant evils, we could get along without lawyers. Each of these professions is set somewhat above the general level of the race, and the members of each of these professions should realize the responsibility, as any priestly caste should.

One of my bird-guides (Audubon's) says about water-thrushes:

The northern differs from the Louisiana in its strongly
yellow underparts and eye-line, its black instead of
brownish streaks, and its uniformly streaked throat.

The breeding-range of these two species overlap and it may be that intergrading has escaped the ornithologists, although New England birds have been studied more intensively than those of any other part of the country. The skin in the American Museum of Natural History ought to help.

Jane, your interlude in this letter is very welcome. Contrary to the assumption of your husband, I am considerably impressed by the names you introduce and the respective positions these dignitaries occupy. In re the flower-book about which you inquired sometime ago, I can give you no judgment. It is not available here in the Library or in the bookstores. Generally speaking, I have found "color-keys" difficult, because I think I am somewhat deficient in distinguishing colors, and flowers are of so many shades and so many colors, and they vary so with age of the flower and its position relative to sun and shade and with the soil in which it happens to grow that such a key must be difficult for anyone. I would prefer a good key based on external characters of which there must be many for New England flowers. After the flower has been identified, then the color-key would help a lot. Of course, I am writing only of the color-keys I have seen. There may be those which overcome the objections I have found to them.

Thank you so much for feeding the egotism of the author in me by repeating compliments on the book. I enclose herewith a copy I have had made of some of the first reviews of the English edition. Gollancz transmits them with following statement:

> It is getting excellent reviews. So far as space is concerned, our reviews can't compare with the United States, for, as you perhaps know, our morning papers still consist of four pages and the Sunday papers of six or eight—and you can imagine how much of that space it is possible to devote to reviewing. It is more often than not a case of "too little and too late," and we are all the more pleased, therefore, at the many enthusiastic reviews of your book which have already appeared.

It is too early to tell anything about the sale of the book there. Since writing you about sales in this country I received a statement from Doubleday up to May 1 showing royalties paid me amount to fourteen hundred dollars. I got thirty cents per copy and I leave the disagreeable mathematics to you to determine how many copies have been sold up to that date.

I wish I might have some sage and dependable advice to offer about buying a house. I am sure inflation is going to continue—but for how long? "Ay, there's the rub."[1] Tell me that and I'll tell you whether to buy or sell. The architect who helped me with the house I put up last summer tells me that it would cost twenty-five per cent more this summer.

So I check this matter to Mr. Gracy whose business it is to know about such things, and to some of your business acquaintances in New York who have a first-hand grasp of the local situation there.

I looked and looked at the copy of the *New Yorker* you sent me to determine why you took the trouble to send it, and at last found the invaluable article on how the English press is disturbed on the killing of rooks. Thanks very much.

We are anticipating a great time with Mrs. Gracy when she becomes available for a report of John.[2] Your success in rearing this boy to his present state of bodily health and apparent emotional stability is a triumph. Time is up for me to get to work.

Much love.

Dad.


P. S. Am sending copy of English edition.

RB

[1] *Hamlet*, Act iii, sc. i.
[2] Editor's Note: Grandson John Bedichek, born March 28, 1948, had allergy problems. Named John for John Gracy, Greer for Lillian Bedichek's family name. Bach protested that John Greer was a noted outlaw in New Mexico in 1910. I countered that our friends in New York would never have heard of him.

801 E. 23rd
Austin, Texas
August 20, 1948

Dear Jane:

About insects: This is a weird world I have never tackled, and hence I don't know how to advise you about a guide. There are some 750,000 species (estimated) of insects that have never been identified. Dr. Casteel, our authority here, has never been able to identify any specimen I have showed him closer than the genus, and often he refers hazily to a group when I have presented him with a "bug." I was wanting to make some comment in my book about a worm that simply eats up the Ohio buckeye here, binding clusters of leaves together into a ball half the size of your head by spinning a web about them. I took one of these balls to him and as near as he could say off-hand is that it is a "web-worm." Quite obviously it is! It's the webbiest worm I ever saw. I tell you this not to discourage but to brace you before you plunge into this unknown land from which travelers return with such scant tidings.

I carry around with me (and occasionally refer to it) a pamphlet entitled "How to Know the Insects, An Illustrated key to the more common families of insects, with suggestions for collecting, mounting and studying them," by H. E. Jaques, Professor of Biology, Iowa Weslayan College, Mt. Pleasant, Iowa, spiral binding $1 per copy, cloth $1.80.

You will note that the key professes to take you only to the "families" and that I think is quite enough for the beginner. Also, description of the technique for catching, preserving and mounting specimens for study is valuable, and one can't begin seriously to study insects without this. Even I, the most chicken-hearted of humans, don't mind capturing, chloroforming and impaling any insect. Thus one may have an outdoor and an indoor hobby, one for bright weather and one for the dull muggy days of winter. If I had several more lives to live, I think I would undertake this hobby. I should know a thousand times more than I do about insects seeing that they are so closely associated with birdlife.

I forgot to say that this is a *pictured* key.

The Swain book you mention may be a lot better than this one, but I think in any case you would want this key and it has the advantage of being cheap. Jaques is a teacher and he knows the pitfalls that beset the path of the beginner and how to avoid many of them.

Kinsey, of the Kinsey report, started out many years ago to study the gall wasp and became so absorbed in it that it took him all over North and South America, engaged and dominated the life of his family for years, and he wound up with something like 300,000 specimens! So beware—you may neglect John for an insect.

Affectionately,

R.B.

801 East 23rd
Austin, Texas
October 16, 1948

Dear Bachman:

Old Age—how the multiplying disharmonies of nature do swarm upon it!

I have just had an angry mole taken out from a part of my anatomy which I had always considered or taken as a matter of course—or rather, had not considered at all. If you will imagine the circle of flesh which sustains the torso in a sitting position, I shall try exactly to locate the annoyance. It sat not within the circle but barely outside of it at the tangent made by the right arm hanging down relaxed at the side. This is not the worst position, it is true, for a deep wound, but it 'twill serve. The neat little oval block of flesh which the surgeon removed was exactly three-eights of an inch thick according to my own measurement of it. It was an inch long and half inch wide at the greatest extent across. The offending growth was set like a dull, ruddy gem in the center of the pearly white flesh.

Had the thing been an inch to the left, it would have been so inconvenient that I should have [had] it cut out years ago and by this time would have forgotten all about it; had it been located by the gene which controls the destinies of moles a trifle to the right and thus relieved it of the pressures and occasional rubbings incident to the characteristic anthropoid posture, it would still be ensconced in its lily-white setting, an innocent chocolate-brown disc, rather ornamental than not. But its position was such that it could be tolerated just seventy years and nearly four months, and *no longer*.

So this morning I am sitting well to the right of center in my typewriter-chair, pillowed up, with my right leg straightened out to prevent flexing the muscles in the vicinity of the wound. I describe this particularly because it is my *only* operation and therefore has the interest which the unique always arouses. This operation comes as the climax of a series of physical discomforts I have suffered ever since my return from the Ozarks.

My sister Ina believes in feeding people and is an expert at it.[1]
Lillian dropped a hint on our first getting there that I didn't eat meat.
This perturbed my sister very much and she kept quizzing Lillian and
finally dragged from her the information that I did sometimes eat a
piece of chicken. That was enough. The deep freeze yielded the choicest chicken for me every meal while the others had beef, both roast
and steak, ham, boiled and fried, and so on. Strawberries as fresh as if
from the vine an hour ago, vegetables (salads & cooked), three or four
at every meal, and delicious pastries, including a rich peach cobbler
with richer cream—made up the daily menu. Well, I just had to eat the
chicken as a guest-obligation and I just had to eat the other things
because I liked them. In short I made a hog of myself. The usual result! Prickly heat which sealed up my eyes, & converted the loose skin
on my throat into wattles, red and rough as a turkey-gobbler's during
the mating season.

I was in the middle of a tree-country, unfamiliar flowers and quite
a lot of birds, so every morning about daylight, I fared forth through
the weeds and brush, tramping until about noon. Soon the seedticks
had pretty well buried themselves in the tenderer areas of my skin
where the digging was easiest. A scientist lately discovered the noses
of these little devils in their front legs. I hope they enjoyed my odor.
I'm told that for almost 100,000,000 years the trilobites, ancestors of
ticks, spiders and other arachnida, were the dominant form of life on
earth. I'm glad that my birth was delayed until 1878 when the species
to which I belong had come to have some say about the ordering of
this world's affairs.

But that wasn't all—the superimposition of seedticks upon prickly
heat! It had been raining all summer in the Ozarks, vegetation was
luxuriant, and redbugs swarmed upon every leaf. They were not so
particular as the seedticks in choosing location—they bit in just any
old place, but seemed to prefer my ankles and well up on my lean
shanks, around my waist, and wrists. I have since read up on this other
woodsy torment. I find that in a certain stage in his progress towards
adulthood, he is especially equipped for eating mammals. He has
mouth-parts sharp and powerful enough to penetrate the skin. He
doesn't burrow under as the seedtick does, but, having punctured the
skin, he pumps some of his digestive juice into the wound. This is an
acid which dissolves the flesh, and he then sucks up the emulsion into

his microscopic belly. Thus his victim is predigested. Having sucked up sufficient nourishment to promote him to the next stage of his earthly sojourn, the man-eating little monster drops off, but leaves a whale of an itching bump where he made his meal.

Now can you image *that* on top of seedticks after the seedticks had topped off the prickly heat? but I'm tough, and I had gotten all right, when one morning about a week ago I cracked down on a mouthful of good luscious apple and felt a tenderness in a bicuspid, upper left. This tenderness grew day by day until one morning I awoke to find a swelling on the gum which felt about the size of a basketball. When I looked at it in the glass, it was nearer the size of a liveoak acorn. Anyway, it was an unmistakable abscess. I found one excuse after another for not going to a dentist for several days, but finally I got out the phone directory and turned to the yellow pages to find about two columns of them. Then I began phoning, and after about the sixth try I located one who would "take a look" at the tooth. Well, he not only took a look but the tooth itself, which turned out to be a sound and healthy specimen. But, he said, there was no way of treating the abscess at the root without taking out the tooth, and my face was already swelling up with the poison of it, so I guess he was right. It certainly did away with the abscess. Now then, of course, I have to look forward to some bridgework as soon as the other end of me has healed up a bit.

This has all happened in less than a month. Meantime, nothing pleasant has happened. My old friend, Dr. Ellis,[2] died in his car down on Waller Creek at 26th Street with a bag of native grass seed in his hand which he had just gathered. Was discovered by a boy who notified police who in turn rang up Mrs. Ellis and delicately broke the news, by saying "That Mrs. Ellis? Yes? Well, I reckon it's your husband that's dead down on Waller Creek." I am at work on a sketch of his life for Mrs. E. He was born in 1871. As I look about, the tree of the 1870s has only a few leaves left on it and they look pitifully shrivelled as they waver in the wind.

The only really cheerful thing that has happened to me in a month or more was a bunch of Jane's letters Mr. Gracy brought over yesterday. What is this telescope-mirror business I hear of? Write me particulars. In these letters was one she started and you finished because the baby needed nursing. What a lovely little picture of domestic felicity this conjured up before my mind's eye! And the tea-set! must be a knock-out! and the co-operation in caring for babies, and all the rest. I find this minutiae extremely interesting.

Well, the fateful hour approaches when I promised the doctor I would meet him in his office so that he may "dress" my wound.

Much love,

Dad

[1]Ina Cowan had nine children and ran a cafeteria.

[2]Editor's Note: Alexander Caswell Ellis was a professor of education and psychology at the University of Texas. Roy studied under him in 1898 and became a student assistant in his laboratory of experimental psychology. He participated in a seminar Dr. Ellis held in his home one night a week throughout the school year for ten or twelve graduate students. A warm life-long friendship followed.

October 17, 1948

Dear Dad,

I am sorry to hear of your multiple ailments. However, having them all at once should be of some advantage—when you recover you should be completely refurbished and ready for another long period of good health. Your news about how the deadly little chigger works is very interesting. I can remember often trying to find the little devil in my hide. Now I see that I was merely scratching after he had done his dirty work and fled.

Have a monumental reading program on. Having just finished Breasted's *History of Egypt*, I engaged my divinity student friend, Vanderhoof, in argument. He maintained that Breasted and the other archeologists and Egyptologists of the "German" school did not give the Jews enough credit; that they were downright anti-semitic, in fact. So to give me the Jewish side, he lent me *The Book of Books*, by a gentleman named Goldman. The first chapter gives promise of a lively and scholarly effort; but I do not see how he is going to be able to refute the chiselings on the rocks of Egypt, if, indeed, he tries to do so. At the same time, I am reading Schliemann's account of his diggings at Hissarlik (ancient Troy).

Still, I have read only about 600 pages of *War and Peace*, of which I tired for some reason, and which I shall resume some of these days.

(I like to do my reading several books at a time.) Yesterday and today I read (just completed) a 400-page collection of Winston Churchill's reportorial efforts in the Boer War. His writing and outlook have both greatly improved, but it is quite readable, and he was a careful observer even then.

At the book auction Friday night I purchased, in addition to the Churchill volume, Lord Bryce's *American Commonwealth*, after spirited bidding, for one dollar. Further, some weeks ago I had subscribed (at a reduced price) to Douglas Southall Freeman's *George Washington*, the first two volumes of six arriving yesterday. The work should be completed by 1952. The Goldman work is intended, incidentally, to fill some thirteen volumes. I have not, by the way, been able to procure the last two volumes of Churchill's work on the first World War, and so am temporarily stymied after reading three volumes.

Law has not been entirely neglected either. I have just completed my third Practising Law Institute correspondence course, and am within one lesson of completing my fourth. Also, I have just finished a delightful book, *Gentlemen of the Jury*, by Francis L. Wellman, a famous New York trial lawyer.

We were, of course, delighted with the article in the *Post*. At present I am basking in reflected glory. The only slightly sour note was a rather slighting reference to the Interscholastic League, which is of course, your finest achievement. Stan Lambert[1] appreciates this one, apparently.

My course in telescope-making meets for three hours one night a week. During the next six months I plan to complete a six-inch mirror for a reflecting telescope. The telescope itself will require further work. The class is conducted by the Amateur Astronomers Association at the Hayden Planetarium.

Yesterday we dined with the greatest elegance with the Cheatham's.[2] I leave the details to Jane, who can do them much greater justice than I can. This afternoon we visited Prof. and Mrs. Hopper. John misbehaved for the first time at a party, and we did not get to see as much of those present as we would have liked. The trouble seems to have been that the little rascal wanted to stay in the room where all the people were, and where he was happily crawling around on the floor. However, so many people were walking around that I feared for his safety, and when I saw him nearly stepped on, I took him into the bedroom and bade him go to sleep. He was perfectly furious, and for the next half hour we endeavored in vain to quiet him. He was actually sleepy, but he was so angry at being taken from his element (a large group of admiring people) that he refused to go to sleep, indeed, refused to be comforted at all. He finally howled himself to sleep, and, of course, when we started home he was perfectly charming. Poor fellow, he dived out of his cradle this morning, and is now sporting a black eye.

We might get home within the next three weeks to a month. Mr. Fleming is talking of sending me on a "business" trip to Texas, and if so, Jane and John will come home and spend some time, perhaps a month. I will doubtless get a few days in Austin, too.

Yesterday afternoon my friend Nate Hall (colleague at Milbank) took Jane and myself to a football game, and an exciting one at that. The teams here do not have the professional polish that the Texas teams do, but they make that up by showing great enthusiasm. Somewhat like a good high school game.

Yrs,

Bach

[1]Editor's Note: Stan Lambert, Coach at Lamar College, Beaumont, wrote for the magazine *Southern Coach and Athlete*, September 1948 issue, a tribute to Roy.
[2]Editor's Note: Eliot Cheatham was a professor at Columbia Law School. Bachman was his teaching assistant.

❦

801 East 23rd
Austin, Texas
January 24, 1949

Dear Bachman:

Guess you are in the hurly-burly and I hope not bad temper of moving.[1] This is always a trying time. Maybe the way is smoothed by some commercial outfit, which takes the whole responsibility, for a consideration. In the old days of my moving it was not so, as you may remember. I think, though, we made but one move after you were old enough to remember anything. After you came we were practically stationary. Well, good luck to you and Jane in this trial, whatever it is.

Tell Jane I have a suggestion to make affecting the education of her son. (It can be remembered by making a brief note in his baby-book.)

When the lad is 9, 10, 11, or older—at whatever age he begins sneaking out the comic section of the newspaper and poring over the extravagant science-fiction of the superman genre (a barbarian literature at best) get for him a hefty volume entitled *Gods & Heroes* by Gustav Schwab. Here in pure, undefiled English are the cream of the Greek myths. Schwab reduced these classics to the best German for the past generation and now a Harvard professor has turned them into unbelievably good English. They must be "read" to a child—the language is just a little beyond the power of a 12-year old, and besides the difficulty with Greek proper names is more than a child of that age can handle. It is important, anyway, that at his first contact with them, they receive the right pronunciation. Much of the music of English poetry is lost without having these names roll off the tongue sonorously, as they are intended to.

The civilized part of our so-called civilization is practically all Greek, and it is utterly impossible for a child to be educated without an early grounding in the thought and fancy of the Greeks, as you well know. I had almost as soon see a grandchild of mine start taking some form of "dope" as become addicted to the comics as they are at present. But the soaring imagination of a child must be satisfied some way. Mr. Schwab has done the job for us, or rather he and his translator, have given us an antidote for the comics in these classic tales, beautifully done into the chastest [sic] English.

I haven't been writing any letters lately—not to anybody. Other writing has absorbed me completely, and will for some time to come. I fear I have bitten off more than I can chew.

The salary-raise is gratifying, but news of your colds is certainly not. I hope you early adopt the Gandhi cure for colds—worth more than all the cold remedies ever recorded in the supersititious medical books. The doctors generally are trying to make good health easy, but it is a rule of God that there is no royal road to good health. It is a discipline, and the very word "discipline" is hard for youth to swallow.

Much Love,
Dad

❦

May 30, 1949

Dear Mary:

We must have been thinking of each other at the same time for I see that our letters, mine of yesterday and yours of May 30 crossed in the mails.

Something (maybe the Carnegie course) is doing you a lot of good. I can see that by the greater confidence expressed in your handwriting and also in your expression. You seem loosened up a bit, for which I thank whatever influences are responsible—most likely your own will and natural development. I have often told your mother that the only thing I could ever see wanting in you (and I try not be critical—especially of my own flesh and blood) is a full self-confidence. Doubt is a devil and should be banished to attain that philosophic calm in which both mind and body function best. Anyway, and whatever the reason, congratulations!

Am glad, too, that you are getting some public speaking experience. I tried to get all my chillun to realize the importance of public speaking and have perhaps promoted more public speaking among other people's children than any other one person in Texas. But my own never seemed to take to it much. It was tremendously important for Bachman, but so far as I know, he never took a course or volunteered as an extra-curricular to engage in any such activity. In my opinion there is no other one thing that so expands the personality as public speaking. It's never too late to learn it, either. Geo. Bernard Shaw learned to be one of the best academic speakers in Great Britain, or in the world, for that matter, after he was forty. But he went at it with a vengeance, never fearing to make a fool of himself, and plunging into public discussions at every opportunity.

Enclosed are copies of some of the reviews of my book in the English papers. Under another cover, I am sending marked copy of *John O'London's Weekly*, one of the first literary journals in England. The review is by H. M. Tomlinson, a quite famous literary man and critic.

But the most surprising and gratifying item in your letter is about Gay's position in the Veterans' Hospital. Please spell out for me the amount of the salary. I know you are careless with zeros. Is it nine THOUSAND dollars—are you sure? Please give me confirmation of this figure by return mail if only a postcard. I'm afraid to tell anybody for fear you have made a mistake. I had thought such a position was out of the question until he had passed the Board's requirements, and very naturally, I am jubilant.

Thanks for snapshots. The kids look darling.

Much love,

Dad

Austin, Texas
801 East 23rd
June 4, 1949

Dear Lillian:

You did a great job of providing before you left. I have had an assortment of vegetables available with a little warming far beyond what any commercial eating place in Austin can furnish. Groceries to date: milk $.44, oranges $.64, total $1.08. I cannot lie except to amuse, hence confess that I have fudged a little on the milk-item. Really, I cashed in the accumulation of milk-bottles I found stuck around here and there.

Had my first splash of season solo yesterday in Barton's. Morrison, "old man of the pool," which he proudly told me they now call him, visited me on Caliban's rock[1] long enough to retail a bit of gossip: Fred Thompson and wife separated, and one sued other for divorce last winter, but Spring which brings a fuller crimson to the robin's breast seems to have effected a reconciliation and suit was dropped and they are sharing BED and board again.[2] Barton's is flowing twice or three times what it did last summer. Fills now in 2-1/2 hrs. whereas in peak of drouth last year it took 7 hours to fill. Nothing else of an objective nature sticks in my mind from Barton-adventure, and I shall not bore you with reflections.

So far I have failed to credit Mary's news of Gay: $9,000.00 per year in veteran's hospital there in Houston. Mary is so careless with her zeros and her estimates of time—maybe it's $90.00 per month. Anyway before telling anyone I am asking confirmation from her by return mail.

I judge from the fact that no advice has come to the contrary, that Braniff delivered you safely into the four arms of J&B. I watched with misgivings that ungainly mechanism taxi around the field before taking off. How like a parody it looks of some monster-insect, frozen or paralyzed, with arthritic joints! Airplaning has the identical relation to flying that aqua-planing has to swimming. Man doesn't fly, he planes, and a pilot is not a flier but a planer. In the first days of the airplane the pilot was referred to as a "birdman"—that is rarely heard now, but the just-as-illogical "flying" sticks. I grant that man can soar, but he can't fly; and he doesn't soar like a bird, but like an insect.

The Palestinians got in and I met 'em at the car with a key. Some palaver followed in which I fear the mutuality of hostility of landlord and tenant was established, although I was on my best behavior and madam was too. I granted in my grand way the use of the Summers garage for the month of June or until the Summerses return. Effusive thanks. She bragged on the trees. I admitted that they are desirable, especially in summer. The girl is in form and moving so express[ive] and admirable that I know the place will be swarming with beaus. So far only one very quiet party yesterday: supper.

Supper with T. N. Campbells was pleasant enough. She is pregnant and lonesome; he is faithful and solicitous. We talked mostly of food, anthropology, whooping cranes, the Karankawas, also of the "Aransas focus," which means the cultural remains left by the people who preceded the Karankawas in the Rockport and Aransas area. Every science quickly invents its own jargon so the hoi-polloi can't understand any more than is good for it. Under cover of adapting my conversation to the interests of my host (he is an anthropologist, you know) I secured some good notes for my forthcoming (I hope) book which, as Cervantes safely advised, should be seasoned with an *appearance* of learning.

I envy you baby-sitting with John[3] and the open-armed welcome you will be able to give the globe-trotters[4] to the grand old, damned old U.S.A., and such other and further excitements and satisfactions accruing from a break in the humdrum of 801 E. 23rd. Which remark is meant in no way as a bemoaning of my own fate: I am enjoying the one thing an old man can—solitude and routine. Wait till you come to seventy-years and see if it aint so.

Much love.

R.B.

[1] Editor's Note: Roy's spot at Barton Springs where the water was cold and deep.

[2] Note on the letter, written by Lillian, reads: "They stayed together until Fred died of cancer in 1959 just before Bedi passed on."

[3] Editor's Note: Lillian was visiting Bachman and Jane in New York and babysat for them occasionally.

[4] Editor's Note: The globe-trotters were Sally, Alan and sons coming back from Lebanon.

꽃

June 5, 1949

Dear Mary:

I see re-reading your letter that I didn't answer specifically all your questions about the book:

1. I have clippings of fifty-six reviews, some, of course, quite short, from American papers; and forty from British papers, including Australia, New Zealand, and South Africa. I know there were some Canadian reviews, but my clipper didn't supply them. Most important of American publications: *Saturday Review of Literature* (a kind of Bible for the literary), *New York Herald Tribune* which specializes in nature writings, *Atlantic Monthly*. In England and colonies, *John O'London's Weekly*, *London Illustrated News*, *Daily Record & Mail* (Glasgow), *The Birmingham Post*. I really don't know enough about English papers to give you any idea of relative importance of them, except the few I mention I know are quite important.

2. If any paper said it (the book) is "ranking non-fiction best-seller along with book by John Gunther," I have never heard of it. The first edition was sold out in three months after publication. Publisher is quite satisfied, says book is moving well for the nature-book class, and that it will be a *long*-seller—that is, publisher expects steady sales for years to come.[1]

3. If you have any personal friends who want autographed copies, have them send me list price ($3.50) and I will buy book here, auto-graph and mail. Of course, this is a lot of trouble and please don't

make any public announcement to that effect. Reserve for personal friends who want an autographed copy. First time I am in Houston I shall drop in at Foley's and autograph whatever books they have there.

Had enthusiastic letter from mama this morning. She is enjoying New York. Had fine trip on plane and is generally "Quite well tickled with herself" as your grandmother used to say.

Affectionately,

Dad

[1]Editor's Note: The book is still in print.

꙰

June 7, 1949[1]

Dear Honey:

Your lovely letter came duly. I am happy that you are happy and happily in good hands. Jane and Bachman will see that you don't get run over by a truck or the brewer's big horses as old ladies were in one [of] O'Henry's stories of the Four Million.

I should have qualified my statement concerning the pleasures of routine by saying that the routine must be of one's own making. I find the groove prepared by circumstances over which I have no control rather irksome on occasions. But most of the time I am guided and permitted to govern my actions according to my own sweet and way-ward will.

Tomatoes! three big, luscious, vine-ripened, now repose cooling in the refrigerator. I made up a big mess of mayonnaise and promise myself some superb salads with lettuce (fresh and crisp) the green sweet peppers, garlic and these wonderful tomatoes. My mouth waters as I write these lines.

There was only one refrigerator-casualty—the dish of mayonnaise you thoughtful[ly] made up for me went to the bad, developing huge freckles throughout and smelling awful. I am still eating the food you prepared. Last of the snap-beans last night, last of collards today noon, last of the black-eyed peas day before yesterday, corn and beets still to be sampled.

Received full confession from Fred Thompson yesterday at

Bartons. It was drinking that threw the wrench into the matrimonial machinery. I gave him one of my hot little lectures on the demon rum, and let it go at that. The thing is patched up for the present, but I note that he has become critical and unhappy. It's no fair test of a woman in matrimony to require that she put up once a week or so with a man out of his mind, nor conversely, of a hubby, either. I remember that frail little woman Harvey Case married who shot his head off with a monster load of buck-shot while he was drunk and drugged. And I think of Annie Doughty and her fifteen years of taking care of her pernicious anemia patient after he got too ill even to drink any more whiskey. And I think—but I better quit thinking or I will be messing around among some of your kinfolks, or with Homer Cowan or his doubly to be damned sire. Oh, hell what's the use of thinking about whiskey anyway? The human brute will have it and apparently nothing can be done about it. I am watching with great interest the Yale University approach. It studies only the 6,000,000 confirmed alcoholics in this country at present, but its studies may prove of some help as horrible examples. Wonder if Josephine has killed her captain yet. I've forgotten her last name, so I wouldn't identify her or him if I saw some such account in a California paper.[2]

There was a mysterious, granular substance in a green cup which I dumped suspiciously in the garbage can without tasting. I've read too many stories and seen too many movies to be tasting things left around indiscriminately. I'm a wised-up coyote such as Dobie writes about.

Man has his will but woman has her way: Mrs. Keenan insisted on paying me the balance due on apartment for June and I, weak soul that I am, received it and receipted her for Vera and receipted Vera for her. I didn't want to be bothered with this, but I've been henpecked all my life except, of course, by you, from whom I gladly receive wifely direction.

My dear little typist has escaped for ten days and I want some typing done. Guess I shall have to break-in another and "Lord how I due dred it."[3] I am eating dinner with the Leon Greens at Mrs. Ellis' tomorrow night, and I guess I shall accept enclosed invitation—quite a seductive affair, isn't it? Maybe I should refuse on ground that you are not here and am too modest to sponge on your reputation.

Lawns are prospering under my sprinkling, and ours needs mowing badly. I feel the gyves of an imposed routine.

Enclosed are a couple of clippings for Sarah.

Limas are reaching heavenward. Never saw such growth. Jack's bean stalk was no fable. They are loaded with blooms and little limas. The little plot planted to okra is now mantled completely with the most expansive okra leaves I have ever seen.

Talked with Mr. Gracy yesterday afternoon at Barton's. His fair skin was tinted with a touch of sun. Walter Fisher[4] invited me to New York with him when he takes car to Cape Cod soon. Said I am the only person in the world he knows whom he could possibly tolerate on such a trip—man, of course, he means. The old rascal only asks of a woman that she be beautiful. I told him you told me to stay put and put I shall have to stay until your return.

I love you, my dear, and will continue so to do.

Yours,

Bedi

---

[1]Dated apparently by Lillian: June 7, 1949, with the note: "I was visiting my son and his wife in Scarsdale, New York. *Kiss Me Kate*—Wed June 15 Century Theatre."

[2]Note on the letter, probably written by Lillian, reads: [Josephine] an alcoholic friend. No, the AA cured her after the captain divorced her. He wanted back but his new wife wouldn't let him.

[3]Note on the letter, probably written by Lillian, reads: Al Watkins said, "I've got to go down to El Paso and get drunk, and Lord, how I do dread it!" His wife replied, "Don't get cagey, Al."

[4]Walter W. Fisher, University of Texas football star from 1895 team; Austin resident; insurance legal representative.

June 12, 1949
Austin, Texas

Well, Beloved,

How goeth life in the wild, weird city? I can imagine you at late bedtime, released from the tailend of a tow-line from headend of which Jane has tugged you along all day—released at late bedtime sighing for the peace and tomatoes of 801 East 23rd, "as the hart panteth for the water-brooks."[1] Or am I wasting my sympathy and misjudging your hostess?

Tell Bachman I got the bird-clippings for which thanks.

Enclosed is deposit-slip.

Okra pods are forming and I shall have more than I can eat in a few days. I already am embarrassed with more tomatoes than I can eat. Greed struggles with neighborliness in my soul. Shall I supply the upstairs, for instance, people living right in my own house, under the same roof, and by all the tests of savage or barbarian culture entitled to any excess in my larder, or shall I hang on to these great red globules until they soften and are no good to anybody? The upstairs people live *distantly*, however. They seem to fear me, avoiding all conversational contacts as I avoid such with a certain neighbor we have occasionally. But then there is Mrs. Alsup and the Trenckmanns and the Dornbergers. I don't mention the Williamses as they are well supplied from Norma's vines.

A cat crouches in my okra often. The sweet soul is defending the moths and other insects from the voracious birds which otherwise would devour them. Thoughtful kitty, not a sparrow falls or a bug drops off a plant that he does not mark it. And people use him as a symbol of cruelty!

I noticed a jaybird with one of the rag strips I had torn off to tie up my tomato vines with. I had carefully put these strips down on a big stone and had gone into the house for a little bit to see after my dinner. Well, the devil had taken all but one of them and was toying with the last one. He needed nesting material and I grasped the situation in a moment. "You have met your match," said I, stopping still whereas I could possibly have scared him away and saved one strip. But I had a plan. I would merely watch him take this remaining strip to his nest, and then with my step-ladder I would climb the tree and retrieve every one of my strips. Off he flew with it trailing along like a banner. Above the house, across the road, over the Miller block, far and away I followed him with my eyes until he seemed to be above the stadium. The wretch was thus coming at least a half mile (I know not how much farther) for my few strips of calico.

This is showery weather—a quarter inch yesterday, a tenth of an inch today and still threatening. Delightfully cool.

Paul's saying, much-belabored by commentators, "I die daily," means just what it says. In these three words there is no esoteric meaning whatever. He means simply that he is so damned tired at bedtime, at end of the day, that he falls into a sleep so deep that it is like death. In the morning he experiences a resurrection, the glory of a new day. I do, too; I die daily and eight hours later undergo the miracle of resurrection. So when the day comes, the setting sun, the last weariness and I go to sleep, the resurrection will not surprise me for I shall have experienced it already a thousand times. This was Paul's way of quieting the uneasiness of his disciples about death.

I defrosted successfully yesterday. Cooked up another batch of blackeyed peas a portion of which I shall shortly consume along with sliced tomatoes, green peppers and onions. Also have nice mess of beets cooked up. Whatever pangs I may be suffering, there are no hunger-pangs.

Had my hair cut yesterday.

Cut yard.

Everything is watered, especially with these showers getting harder and harder.

My main fight with the lima beans is to keep them from joining hands overhead across the rows and thus making an arcade. They fling wild, beseeching arms to the sky during the night and next morning I tie them in place.

Tomorrow, and tomorrow, and tomorrow,
Creeps in this petty pace from day to day—[2]
By the way, does time *creep* in New York. It does here.

Much love and hoping you are having the time of your life and that shortly Sarah and her brood will land safely,

I am, as ever

Yours,

Bedi.

[1]Psalm 42:1.
[2]*Macbeth*, V, v

❧

June 18, 1949
Austin, Texas

Dear Lillian:

For a metropolitan wife you do a pretty good job of letter-writing

*318*

to a rural husband. I sent your letters over to the Gracys today, as Mrs. G. rang up last night and wanted to know how you were making out. I told her you were making "all-out" and passed on the letters as evidence. We had a quite pleasant chat over the phone and she was able to give me some recent and very vivid impressions of Haiti where Alan, I understand, is to do some of his research, for which reason I was particularly interested.

I am a professional diner-out having stuck Glen Evans,[1] or rather his wife, for a nice meal night before last. I was so pleasant that I may get bid again before you return. Mrs. Evans whom I had never met before is dark-eyed, plump, vivacious, East Texas and about forty. I like her very much. I told one rather risque joke which didn't set well, but I think I got it smoothed over before the evening was over. They have a smart little girl about eight who said to her mother the other day, "Mother, why don't you smoke. All the other women do. It makes you look so funny." I think the advertising agencies who handle tobacco publicity-contracts would smack their lips over that one.

Met Mrs. Joe Gilbert[2] at Checker Front Number 10 counter this morning. She told me she had moved over here. I expressed some surprise that she would leave West Austin and of her own will and accord come over here. I welcomed her to the ranks of the people. She then told me she was forbidding on her places in this neighborhood the cutting down of native shrubs and brush, inspired I think by my advocacy of the same—at least I gathered this. I commended her highly, and welcomed her into the ranks of the intelligentsia. She was pleased with her neighbor, Dr. Spruce,[3] the artist, because he cared for native shrubs rather than nursery importations. I immediately saw great merit in some of Spruce's pictures which I can't understand. All in all, we got along fine. I like her. She's an energetic little body with lots of business.

Evidence accumulates against the blue jay. This morning about sunup as I was coming over to my study I saw a jay deviling a young martin sitting on a telephone wire. A male martin (adult) simply gave him hell and presently routed him out. One killed a baby inca, I know; I suspect one of the death of one of my screech owls; one stole the rag-strips I had prepared with great pains to tie up my tomato-vines with; and this morning I found almost half of a large green tomato eaten away and can think of no other bird which would commit such an atrocity. And yet he is a proud, gay, gorgeously colored creature whose arrogance becomes him. But I have a temper: he'd better not let me catch him killing a baby inca.

Well, the grand Canadian, Professor Adair, is back on the banks of Barton's with Miss Williams. I had a word with them yesterday afternoon. They didn't, however, seem to want to prolong the conversation, so I governed myself accordingly. I certainly miss the Oakleys.[4]

Ena writes me that she and Beryl[5] went by to see Josephine in Illinois and got a photograph of the cabin in which I was born, and enjoyed the visit very much. Josephine would enjoy a letter from you. Her address is Mrs. Robert C. Horner, Whiteoaks, R. #1, Petersburg, Ill. You might tell her, quite incidentally (as all good lies are told) that I have been away from home a lot and seem to be absorbed in writing another book. This may ease the strain a little and then I'll write her one of my charming letters.

I thrill with triumph every time I beat the dishpan out of a dish. At lunch today, my victory came about as follows: I had just eaten a bowl of soup, leaving dish and spoon on table. I had also almost finished up that oleo you left for me in that bitterly dark brown dish, and it, with a little remnant of oleo was also on table. I had timed a beautiful head of cauliflower to be done just as I noisily lapped up the last bit of soup. I had a plate (clean) laid out to receive cauliflower, but just in the nick of time, the inspiration flashed through my brain. The cauliflower must be buttered, or oleoed, so instead of putting in on plate I plunged it head first into the oleo-dish and covered other over with waxed paper and put away in refrigerator for another time. Result: only one dish and one spoon to wash.

Yesterday I prepared and ate what I may call an "adulterated salad." It was like this: the soup-bowl with the cluster of grapes in it was chosen for the experiment. I first chipped up a medium sized bermuda onion. Then I gathered a big green pepper and chipped it on top of the onion. On top of this I diced two tomatoes, one big, one small, and salted and stirred this mess around. Meantime I had heating about four heaping tablespoonfuls of black-eyed peas with little chunks of bacon in it, and emptied same right on top of the salad. This I stirred around and ate with hot toast from Jane's toaster. It is a positively wonderful dish—a square meal in itself, and only one dish to wash and one spoon. For I ate it with a spoon.

Have you decided on about when you will be returning? I have a trip to make to Coleman County and man there wants me to come on or about July 5, and business there might require several days. Don't take this to mean that I am trying to suggest any time for your return. This trip could be made easily enough in your absence. As a matter of fact I may go out there in the next few days, anyway.

From what Sarah, Alan and the three little Pipkins?[6]

Much love.

[1]Glen Evans, assistant director, Texas Memorial Museum, Austin, and geologist with Louisiana Land and Exploration Company, Midland, Texas.
[2]A doctor's wife.
[3]Everett Spruce was an artist on the University of Texas art faculty who was known for his abstract and non-objective southwest landscapes, a neighbor of the Bedicheks.
[4]Cleatus Oakley and Louise his wife were a frequent visitors to Philosophers' Rock at Barton Springs.
[5]Beryl Yoder is Ena's daughter.
[6]The three Pipkins are Alan, Roy, George.

Bachman Greer Bedichek, c. 1941, near twenty-two years old, when he graduated from the University of Texas Law school. *Courtesy of Jane Bedichek.*

Grandmother Lillian Bedichek and fifteen-month-old grand-daughter, Lillian Lee Carroll, January 1941.
*Courtesy of Jane Derrick.*

Roy Bedichek with Bachman Bedichek, who is going off to war in 1942. *Courtesy of Alan and Louise Pipkin.*

Bachman writes: "The LCT here is coming by to take a hawser from LST 240 to assist me off a coral reef at Kwajalein, April '44. I finally got off in 1 hr. & 15 mins., assisted by a rising tide, and by shifting water ballast. It was a very uncomfortable affair altogether, but although I admitted bad judgment in getting aground, the big-shots generously refused this explanation and excused me entirely." *Courtesy of Jane Bedichek.*

Roy Bedichek with his Victory Garden at 801 E. 23rd. Written on the
side of the photograph are identifications of the vegetables.
*Courtesy of Alan and Louise Pipkin.*

Lillian Bedichek and grandson Alan Pipkin, Jr.,
1943. *Courtesy of Alan and Louise Pipkin.*

Alan C. Pipkin, Sr. and Jr.,
1945, in San Diego. Alan,
Sr. was back from the
Pacific and New Guinea.
*Courtesy of Alan and
Louise Pipkin.*

Lillian Bedichek holding grandson Roy, with Alan, Jr., sitting
nearby, 1945. *Courtesy of Alan and Louise Pipkin.*

From left to right: Gay Carroll, Lillian Lee Carroll, Mary
Bedichek Carroll, Jane Logan Carroll, c. 1945.
*Courtesy of Jane Derrick.*

Bachman Bedichek, left,
with his best man, Ernest
Villavaso.
*Courtesy of Jane Bedichek.*

Bachman Bedichek and Jane Gracy at their wedding reception at the
Austin Country Club, January 2, 1946. *Courtesy of Jane Bedichek.*

Bachman on his honeymoon in a garden near New
Orleans. He was birdwatching.
*Courtesy of Jane Bedichek.*

Jane and Bachman Bedichek, 1946, after lunch at a country inn in
Westchester. They were living in New York, near Columbia University.
*Courtesy of Jane Bedichek.*

Sarah and Alan Pipkin with their three boys, from left to right: George, Alan, Roy. Beirut Lebanon, 1949. *Courtesy of Jane Derrick.*

Mary and Sarah in the back yard at 801 E. 23rd, holding Jane and Alan. *Courtesy of Jane Derrick.*

The fireplace at Friday Mountain where Bedi cooked and the sturdy table given to Walter Prescott Webb by the Texas Rangers after they took it from a gambling establishment they had closed down. It was at this table that Bedi sat to write *Adventures with a Texas Naturalist.*
*Courtesy of Jane Bedichek.*

Roy Bedichek wrote on the back of this photograph he sent to his son Bachman: "Here's Silhouette of the 'philosopher' vacantly gazing out into vacancy evidently thinking thoughts of great pith and moment."
*Courtesy of Jane Bedichek.*

*June, 1950 to May 10, 1959*

June 1950

Dear Bachman:

We are missing Jane's letters to her folks, so are quite hungry for news of the N.Y. Bedicheks. We are delighted with the name of the new one. Louise Wells[1] couldn't be better. It's mellifluous and will do something towards sweetening the hardtack that follows.

Your mother is much improved. The doctors churned, mauled, stuffed, probed and photographed her until she was quite worn out. She has a feeling that they did their derndest to find something radically wrong, but could find nothing much more than normal aging. There's certainly no curing for aging, but the condition may be ameliorated. "I grow old," said Solon, "learning many things."[2] I do too, but also forgetting many things, so it seems rather an exchange of knowledge with little net gain—indeed, maybe a net loss. I am not in the condition of Somerset Maugham who says in his "notebook" that he has lost interest in everything because he must leave everything so soon. Compares himself to one waiting for a train which may come at any moment, hence doesn't care to pry into anything around the station—no interest. By the way, there are a couple of good articles on old age in the *New Yorker*, last two issues, by Dr. Martin Gumpert.

Your mama and I are of course alerted over the Korean affair, but I can't believe a major war is in the offing for the reason that neither Russia nor U.S. is ready. I think this is one of Russia's Asian incidents created to divert attention from what she wants to do somewhere else.

I manage to do a little garden and yard work every morning now, as morning is the only time cool enough for any kind of comfortable physical exercise. Heat begins about nine and gets worse all day. Nights, however, are still endurable.

Poor Sarah and Alan are disappointed in trip here this summer, and greatly concerned over tonsil operation on Roy. They wanted to bring him here for Dr. McCrummen to look after, but he got so bad that they were compelled to have the operation there; and the boy can't be moved all summer.

Write me and tell me about Louise Wells and Gulf Sulphur.

Yours,

Dad

[1]Louise Wells Bedichek was born June 16, 1950.
[2]*Fragment 22.*

801 East 23rd Street
Austin, Texas
November 14, 1950

Dear Josephine:

I'm terribly upset about your misfortunes.

How difficult it must be to preserve that "internal harmony" without which life is not worthwhile, suffering physical pain and mental anguish.

As to the latter, I think the mind has the power of fencing it off, encysting it, just as the body has the power of encasing some foreign object which it cannot expel. The way to help the mind to this is by *practicing* forgetting. I have several such mental cysts, acquired along the years. I practiced forgetting. Yours is one of those things which happen in our human affairs for which there is no solution. It just has to be, but it is not necessary that it be held in mind.

Physical pain is another matter. It can't be ignored. I haven't had much of it in my time, and so my experience is not worth sharing.

Anyway, you have my sympathy and Lillian's.

I enclose herewith a couple of clippings of reviews about my last book. It has been generally received very well. Texas papers have been really enthusiastic.

Sincerely yours,

Roy

March 5, 1951

Dear F. L.:[1]

Lillian and I enjoyed our little visit with you and Frances and Mrs. Nowlin and Mrs. McNeil. The two latter, however, had not much chance for self-expression in the voluble company of the Greers and the Bedicheks. I shall apologize next time I see them.

Lillian and I think that you and Frances are a great success, and we only regret that we missed seeing the most convincing evidence of the success, namely, Jim and Bob. We feel that you and Frances have created the environment in which the personalities of these two fine youngsters have had and are having an opportunity to develop along the lines Nature intended. And that's the best that can be said for any parents or for any school system or for any society in general.

Next time, we shall give ourselves a little more leeway by the clock. Thanks for the bottle. It will come in handy when we have some guest with a gust for such delicacies.

On my way back home I insisted on visiting the Eddy Cemetery in which repose the mortal remains of three generations of Bedicheks, earliest tombstone date: 1807. As I left the car, Lillian glanced at the desolate appearance of this remnant of sheep-pasture grass and observed that she would never be buried there, apropos of my announced intention of seeing if there were any room for me left on the family lot.[2]

And whom should I meet among the tombs but Bertha and Ola Connally. We at once engaged in a discussion of the relativity of graveyards. I argued that there is greater security for bones in a village graveyard than in a city cemetery, since the city often expands and ousts the dead for the sake of the living. In Europe this has been quite common and will be here in this country when we get a bit more crowded. Already metropolitan graveyards are imitating a practice prevalent in Rome two or three thousand years ago of making interment along the highways—witness the Waco "Memorial Park" out on the highway leading south to Austin, and approaching Austin you find the Austin dead moving up this highway to join hands with the Waco dead, if we may speak properly of fleshless members being "hands."

Now the Eddy Cemetery is already located on a highway, on two highways, in fact, since the Katy railway skirts on the north as does

Highway 81. So maybe, who knows, about the year 2551 Waco and Austin cemeteries will coalesce at Eddy, of course, allowing that Austin outgrows Waco as much in that period as it has in the last half century. No invidious comparison between our respective cities is here intended.

Another argument I voiced among the village Hampdens, Cromwells and "mute inglorious Miltons," (damn mute, if you ask me) is that a concentration of ancestral bones is a part of establishing a family tradition, and if the family tradition does not have too many ropes in it, it is a stabilizing influence upon the living generation of that family. If two hundred years of a strain has produced on the whole fairly honorable fruit, is not the accumulation of marble markers listing names and dates of those dead a reminder to the contemplative scion of the strain that he has a responsibility and an opportunity to continue in the same general direction; and doesn't it give him a sense of security which a self-conscious tree might get from the thought that its roots are after all pretty deep in the sub-soil?

I don't think the Connally girls enjoyed this disquisition very much, for each of them was anxious to cross the railroad and the highway for a visit with Lillian who was holding down the parked car in solitary grandeur.

But Bertha stayed with me long enough to help me determine the metes and bounds of the family lot, 30 x 30, and indicate an area 6 x 3 where my mortal remains might repose with whatever dignity they can at the moment command. We then rejoined Ola and Lillian at the car where a spirited, three-cornered competition ensued among the grandmas in the enumeration, description and glorification of about two dozen grandchildren. I think Lillian with genuine Greer prowess got the best of this contest, although she was quiet as a mouse until we got far past Temple, likely thinking of the things she might have said but didn't.

You are quite right in your assumption that I am fond of you.

Yours, truly,

Bedi

P.S. I think you are taking snap judgment on Jim Hart. He has been plunged into the legislative scramble without adequate preparation, and he is naturally confused. I have great confidence in the qualities of character I know he has: a sound mind in a sound body, excellent training, unimpeachable integrity, inexhaustible energy, and great determination.

R.B.


March 6, 1951

P.S. (again) We got home safe and sound with a fair minimum of back-seat driving at 8 P.M.

R.B.


[1]Editor's Note: F. L., Lillian's brother, and his wife Frances lived in Waco. Eddy is ten miles south on the highway to Austin.
[2]Roy Bedichek was buried in the family plot in that cemetery at Eddy.

801 E. 23rd
Austin 5, Texas
March 11, 1951


Dear Bachman:

You are certainly carrying out a pet theory of mine—unconsciously, of course, or likely the Bedichek perversity would hardly let you. I mean, reading the literary historians: Churchill and Gibbon. My contention is that only literary men should write history. Let the un-literary, factual, diggers, probers, detective mentalities and the genuine, old dry-as-dust antiquarians and documentarians excavate the facts for the literary men to use; and, then, after the literary men have written their histories, let these same wood-worms criticize, but do not let them kill the normal human interest in the past by feeding out their stuff to the public, and certainly quarantine all schools against them as we guard a population from the plague. Give me Xenophon, Thucydides, Livy, Plutarch, Winwood Reade, H. G. Wells, Gibbon and Churchill, et al. These give you the sweep of history without the sweepings. Science and the scientific spirit has invaded history as it has pedagogy and goddamnear killed all human interest in it.

By the way, if you want to get a genuine thrill, read Winwood Reade's *Martyrdom of Man*, if you haven't already. I've had a copy around the house for a long time, maybe as long ago as your boyhood.

It's a pity there's no law prescribing penalties for institutional guilt.

Maybe one way of getting at those institutions which make huge profits out of athletics would be to remove their tax immunity—both state and church schools, as well as endowed colleges—on the ground that their tax-immunity has been granted on the theory that they would engage in no activity for profit in competition with private business.

I question your first premise in your contention before the local Democratic Party meeting. You say "We" are at war with China. If your "we" included our allies working with us as members of the United Nations, well and good; but if the "we" includes only the U.S., then independent action on our part would at once alienate our allies and leave us vis-a-vis with both China and Russia. Militarily, of course, I would agree. Diplomatically, however, I wouldn't until at least our main allies can be brought to this same point of view.

I am glad to hear of your participation in the public discussion. One uneasiness I have concerning your present employment is that it required no public speaking. You can easily make up for this by attending meetings and expressing yourself on points which come up and upon which you are informed, and/or by joining out-and-out discussion clubs and debating societies, as Bernard Shaw did, making himself a good public speaker after forty; whereas before forty, he was always tongue-tied, or lost his temper every time he tried. Emotion and the restraint thereof are both necessary in effective public speaking, as they are in every art. Indeed, they make up 90% of everything that can be called art.

Another good thing about Gibbon is that if you are tired and yield properly to the long sea-swells of his sentences, he can rock you to sleep in short order. When I used to get perturbed over League disputes and was subject to telephone-calls any time of the night, I kept a volume of Gibbon by my bed for its somnolent virtue. It first interested me, took me away from the immediate annoyance, and then lulled me into repose.

I fear our trip to New York must be called off for this year. You are certainly filial in your insistence upon our coming and Jane is downright sweet, (as she knows so well how to be), but an accumulation of impediments has rather put it out of the question.

In the first place, I have at last gotten my teeth into the *History of the Interscholastic League*, at which I have been working only halfheartedly for so long. I can't now afford to break the spell. I must carry it on to a conclusion under the impetus I now have. If I were younger, things might be different. I'm not going to bring up the unpleasant subject always in the forefront of considerations influencing the actions of the commonsense aged person, but nevertheless it's there.

Another thing is that your mother's ailment last summer gave both of us the scare of our lives. It was really more serious than either of us betrayed in our letters to you and Sarah. Mary was taken in on it in her professional capacity; and, I think, gave your mother the only sound medical advice she got with her hundred or so dollars to diagnosticians whose information might be summarized thus: "You have nothing whatever the matter with you except that you can hardly walk; and we are sorry, but we can't find out why your ability to walk is failing every week."

Now I think, and your mother does too, that having established a regime that has restored to her the use of her legs, it would be foolhardy to break that routine as violently as a trip to New York would necessarily break it.

So, these two considerations have determined us not to undertake the trip this year, as much as we should enjoy it, if I were free and your mother was not under a constant threat.

By the way, does John have a toy lasso? If not, I want to send him one. Throwing a lasso is wonderful exercise for a child, and maybe will serve to remind him that after all his roots are in the soil.

Yours,
Dad

Epidemic Disease Control Unit #6
NAVY 3410, Fleet Post Office
San Francisco, Cal.
Sunday Morning
21 April, 1951[1]

Dear "R.B.":
Starting this off in true Pipkin form, I will apologize for all the letters I haven't written you for some time back—and my good intentions, notwithstanding. I trust that by now you are relaxing from your latest literary stint and are in a mood for this sort of dribble.

Writing finds me recovering from a recent field trip to neighboring islands of this area. The local Civil Adminstrative unit (Naval government organization) sends a small Navy cargo ship on a circuit of some 14 islands lying some 150–200 miles to the north and west of the Truk atoll to pick up copra and offer small trade goods and medical assistance to the natives of these low-lying coral reefs. The trip is made only three or four times a year, so I went although the weather was anything but promising. The ship was an AKL—Navy jargon for Auxiliary Cargo Light—about 125 ft. long and 25 ft. abeam. I had two men from the unit along and we had quite a trip. I knew the trip was hexed about 30 minutes after we left the dock, for we ran hard onto a submerged coral reef and after about 15 minutes of anxious waiting while the engines laboriously backed us off the shelf, we floated free and were fortunately none the worse except for a few more dents in the hull. TRUK atoll is a coral reef necklace strung with small islands making up a complete ring about 30 miles in diameter. Inside this circle are about a half dozen islands of volcanic origin which support a population of some 15,000 people in all. None are very large however, and Moen, where the administrative headquarters for the Trust Territory Islands are located, has a total area of about 7 miles square. The islands are all mountainous, the remains of the old volcanos rising to about 1200 ft. on Moen, while to the west and separated by about 5 miles of lagoon are several other cones of extinct volcanos, now forming islands. To reach the open sea, a ship steams out through one of four or five small passes in the coral reef. The water within the reef is fairly smooth, although on windy days there is a decidedly choppy surf. After reaching the open water, the relatively quiet gives way to the broad swells of the Pacific, and in stormy weather there is absolutely nothing peaceful about the Pacific.

We sailed about four o'clock in the afternoon and had time to eat supper and get our "gear" unpacked before we reached the southwest pass about dark. The night wasn't too bad and we had a movie on deck, and about 9:30 I turned in. All members of the field party (about 12 in all) were quartered in a canvass deck house built on the upper deck fan-tail. Bunks are arranged in three tiers deep, and reminded me of nothing so much as the tiered sarcophagi which I used to see in caves dug in the hillsides of the Syrian desert. By midnite we had hit rough weather, and by morning, I knew I was ready for sarcophagi—real or imagined. I had come prepared with some of the navy anti-motion sickness drug called dramamine, but like all navy men, I fancied myself a good sailor, and feigned indifference to a suggestion of nausea. When they called us for morning chow, I got up and dressed with the ship lurching and leaping through a mountainous sea, and stumbled out on the open deck in the driving rain to finally make it down a companionway to the officer's mess. There I was confronted with a breakfast where everything but the coffee was fried, and I don't drink coffee, so I tried some grits. After three mouthfuls, I knew that I wasn't a sailor and at four mouthfuls, I knew I was a sick man. My face, I fancy, was a close approximation of the color of this paper. To make matters complete, just about that time, we raised the first stopping place, an island called Pulusuk. We anchored about 500 yards out from shore and took a "pulling boat" in to the beach, passengers sitting atop of a pile of very dirty corrugated iron roofing and clutching to the gunwhales for support. I had recovered slightly from my retching by then and we made it ashore with no further mishap, though I was awfully rocky most of that morning. The water was so rough all that day that we stayed ashore and they sent sandwiches in to our group about two that afternoon. We spent the day trying to keep dry and looking for mosquito larvae in between showers. Our blood survey for filariasis could not begin until about ten that night since these tempermental little parasites do not appear in the blood stream except late at night and very early in the small hours of the morning. In the meantime, I had managed to lose my wrist watch—which I had put in my watch pocket to keep it dry—a new one I had just bought about a month ago, but fortunately a cheap one. What with the lingering nausea, weakness from lack of food, and the late working hours, I was feeling pretty low by the next morning. We had been forced to spend the night in the native dispensary since the ship had sought deep water before dark the night before, and didn't return for us until about 9:30 the next morning. By then I was so hungry that I ate some hot bread fruit which the native doctor had offered us for breakfast. It wasn't bad, but not too esculent unless taken as a last resort. Breadfruit looks like a ripened beaux'darc [sic] apple—you remember the green mammilated post apples which used to abound but somehow have escaped me since I was a child? Well, breadfruit looks a good deal like these, only somewhat elongated, and inside the meat is very starchy. In the middle are several nut-like acorn-shaped seeds which the natives roast separately. All has a distinctly smoky flavor which disguises the earthy taste.

In anticipation of the days to come, I had started taking dramamine and although it makes you feel sleepy, it does dispell the nausea and I felt much better for the remainder of the trip—which lasted 10 days in all. We got some 1500 blood smears and from an examination made on the spot of a goodly number of them, I found that the population was commonly infected—probably from 25 to 50 per cent, although there were few clinical cases of filariasis and I only saw two with elephantiasis while on the trip. The natives of these islands have been exposed to Christianity for several generations, and are somewhat Europeanized, wearing dresses and trousers on Sunday and while visitors are around. In Pulusuk, the weather was so bad, however, that they went around in their usual garb—the men wearing red cloth loin cloths, and the women colored pareaus covering from waist down. Some of the natives are fine physical specimens, the men in the group just mentioned standing six feet or more high, though many of the natives on other islands we visited were runts and showed some evidence of admixture with the Japanese.

I have been out here almost two months now and will probably be here through about 1 July. Sarah and children are comfortably housed in a suburb of Honolulu, as she has no doubt told you, and unless I find that I will be out here for 8 or 9 months more, I think it best for them to stay there. There is some possibility that the navy may want to continue with the survey which I have been working on in this atoll area, and make spot checks in representative islands of all districts of the Trust Territory. If so, I shall be in this area for some months, maybe a year, and in such case, I am going to try and bring the family out here.[2] It is relatively pleasant although it rains considerably more than in Hawaii, but the relative humidity isn't excessive and I have been more comfortable than while I was in New Orleans. I won't bring them out unless we are given suitable living quarters and we can be comfortable.

Moen Island offers little of interest in way of bird life—the rumor being that the Japanese killed off the birds during their occupation. I have seen some sea birds, and a few species of small wrens, but they are few and far between. The coral formations along the reef are interesting, but I have not had time to do any collecting as yet. We have been extraordinarily slow in receiving our supplies and it has taken us longer to get set up and started than was anticipated, so we have had little time for recreation. A few weeks ago I was out near an abandoned sea-plane base which the Japs had on the south side of the island, and I saw an interesting sight. A native fisherman was attempting to catch a young frigate bird. They train them to fish for them. He would hold aloft a small sardine, and when the frigate bird would dive down to take the sardine from his hand as he passed over his head, the native would attempt to grab the bird by the legs. When he would succeed in getting the fish, he would swoop down over the water as he swallowed the fish, and scoop up a bill full of water—apparently to wash his meal down with. He did this every time without fail, so it must be a habit. Needless to say, the fisherman never did succeed in making a catch, although it looked as if he was going to on several trials, but the bird always managed to get the fish and soar away just out of reach.

During the war the Japanese had airfields on Moen and kept a number of military personnel here to operate a large radio station atop one of the hills, but most of their some 40,000 men were stationed on Dublon island which is about an hour's ride across the lagoon by boat. I haven't been over there yet but will probably get over there soon. There is much evidence of the extensive military set up which the Japs had here, although it is of course all in ruins. The Americans never attempted to take Truk, but used it as a training run from Guam and other bases, and all bomber crews who were to be sent over Japan, first had a certain number of practice runs over Truk. For this reason, the buildings are pretty well bomb pocked and only one of the two air strips has been rebuilt here. There are a few old Jap planes still around, wrecked, of course, but you can see enough to make you realize what wonderful technicians the Japs were. I have heard it said that during the early days of the war, the Jap planes were better than ours, and even later, they continued to be better engineered. All rivets on the outside of the plane were countersunk to cut down air resistence, while American planes lacked these refinements, probably due to mass production. Well, sheer might predominated over persistent if ill advised fortitude.

How is Miss Lillian? I used to be able to kinda keep track of you while with Sally, but of course being separated, I don't get the benefit of hearing your letters. Maybe you can find enough time to squeeze out a few words to your wandering son-in-law. If Sally remains in Lanikai, it would be nice if you and Mrs. B could come out and see us. It is of course a very beautiful island—Oahu, I mean, although the island of Hawaii is much bigger. Lanikai is a strictly zoned residential district and there are no stores within a mile of our house, but it is very pretty. I am glad that Sally has the car and can get around. She does all her shopping at the naval commissary at Pearl Harbor, and that gives them a chance of getting out regularly. Of course she has nosed out all the museums, aquaria, etc. already and makes regular expeditions to these places, so she writes. I am so glad they are in Hawaii instead of the Bay Area of San Francisco. The latter, while colorful, has about as disagreeable a climate—in a cold damp way—as possible.

Well, guess I'd better close for now. Let me hear from you some-time.

Affectionately,
Alan

[1]Editor's Note: Alan Pipkin was called back into active duty by the U.S. Navy during the Korean War from 1951–53. He was posted to Truk in the South Pacific to survey and treat filariasis, a disease caused by a tiny worm that attacks the lumphatic system causing grotesque swelling of the limbs.
[2]Editor's Note: The family did come to Truk. Since there was no school, Sally gave lessons sent out by Calvert Home Study of Baltimore, Maryland.

Austin, Texas
June 6, 1951

*Private & Confidential*

Dear Honey:

After some forty years of our married life, I now feel constrained to make a confession, which I hope will not disturb you *too* much. From your standpoint, since there is a woman in the case, it may be hard for you to forgive me.

Going on for a year now, I have had only casual meetings with this woman. She has shown great interest in birds and in her pets, especially in cats and dogs. With only this slight basis of common interest, (she is certainly not the intellectual type), we got to have first a nodding acquaintance when we met on the street, and then, gradu-ally, as occasion offered, a few minute's conversation, but only when she had seen a new bird, or when she had a report to make on one of her pets. Her reports and interpretations of animal behavior I have thought to be unusually acute, although a little on the soft side and verging now and then on a bit of innocent nature-faking. She is partial to cats, which naturally drew me into a defense of dogs, and our talks began to be prolonger. She insisted several times on my stopping by her place to see her demonstrate her animals.

I know you will think all this very silly, especially when I tell you the disparity in our ages. I take her to be about thirty, and, allowing (in your opinion) for the ten years I accord every presentable woman, she is certainly not more than forty. Really, her husband looks younger— were I romancing this confession even the slightest bit, I would make him at least sixty, but I am trying to make every word of this literally true, and not trying to spare myself in the least item. I rarely see her husband. He is a busy man, hardly ever with her anywhere, and not often at home in the daytime.

Now I come to the part that is really difficult, as you will quite agree as you pursue this to the end. The other morning about nine o'clock I had a telephone call from this woman. She seemed to be in a state of great excitement, if not distress, and asked me to come to her home at once. I tried to get out of her what she wanted, but she wouldn't tell me. I told her that I was tied up and couldn't come just then, but that I would try to get around there in the afternoon. She was then even more urgent, saying that the afternoon would be too late. Finally, I consented to drop what I was doing and come. Little did I know!

When I got there the apartment was in great confusion. She was alone. Almost in tears. She told me that she and her husband were moving away and would perhaps never see Austin again. Her husband had been offered a position away off somewhere, a great improvement on the place he had here.

First, she wanted me to promise that I wouldn't refuse the request she had to make of me. Well, you know I can't resist a woman's tears, or a woman in distress, so, recklessly, with only the proviso that the request be a reasonable one, I promised. She was delighted, and led me into her bedroom and on up to the bed, where she extracted from me a reiteration of my promise. Then, and not until then, she snatched the coverlet off and there, neatly cuddled up, lay the cat that has been courting me for a year—the brindled tomcat which you remember has been following me about to my study, and to the garden or the front yard, wherever I happen to be working. He is the one that performs as

I tell him to, rubbing his face first on my elbow, and then on my knee, as I squat down to pet him. He lies down and rolls over, also, at my command—sometimes, indeed, *before* I give the command.

Taking the creature up and kissing him in the ear, she presented him to me to have and to hold, saying that they just couldn't take him with them, and that her husband and she had noticed the growing fondness of the cat for me and felt sure that his affection was reciprocated. I had enough force of character to resist these advances sternly; but she pled and the damned cat whines just at the psychological moment and looked at me so intently with his cold green eyes that I imagined for the moment that perhaps *this* cat did feel some affection for a human being.

To make a long story short, your lonesome hubby finally relented and accepted this feeble, feline consolation during your absence; and just then, her husband drove up with the car all packed—jam-packed, there wasn't room left in it for a cat even half the size of the one I held in my arms. So, the happy couple, released from the last tie that held them here, winged away for their new home, but only after the lady dug out of the refrigerator half a can of rather sour cat-food, presenting it to me with hasty instructions concerning how much and how often "Skeezicks" wants his food. Yes—"Skeezicks" is the name.

I feel confident in making this disclosure of my infidelity that you are "broad-minded" enough to receive this child of my second childhood's indiscretion, and make him feel at home, as "one of us" regardless of his origin.

Contritely yours,
Bedi

P.S. To make this confession complete, I feel that at least one of the children should know, and I have selected Sarah as the one who will have greater sympathy in the premises for "my fall," than either Bachman or Mary. Hence, I am sending a carbon of this to her in order that she may be fully informed.

R.B.

[The annotations in the following letter, recorded in the footnotes, were made by Roy Bedichek.]

#1110 South Bellaire
Amarillo, Texas
June 21, 1951

Dear Mr. Bedichek:

How is our cat doing?[1] If your wife doesn't[2] like him, or if he is being difficult to handle,[3] you can just let us know and we will send you the money[4] to ship him.

We took our dog to Texarkana with us. We had to leave her there[5] and Bill's mother has found a home for her with a lady from Mississippi.

We like Amarillo very much.[6] It isn't half so bad as the picture most people tried to paint to us. We don't miss the trees at all, because there are plenty of trees in the city. Of course, they are all planted, but lots of them are plenty aged.[7]

Bill likes his job very much. I suppose he told you he is with the Southwestern Public Service Co. Of course, we are afraid Uncle Sam is going to come calling before long.[8] But we will take it as it comes, I suppose. We hope Skeezix is getting fat. Love him for us, will you?[9]

Sincerely,[10]

Mrs. Bill O'Donald

Thus endeth my Roman Courtois with the tomcat Yclept Skeezix

[1]Note feminine instinct for indirection: (1) question is to suggest that letter is one of innocent interest in welfare of the cat; (2) use of "our" suggests that she still has property-interest in cat, although the gift was outright with no strings attached.—R.B.

[2]Note feminine instinct to throw blame, if any, on the "other woman."—R.B.

[3]Feminine insincerity. She knows the cat loves me better than he does her, and spent most of his time with me when she was here and available. "Difficult to handle!"—preposterous suggestion!—R.B.

[4]Feminine realism. The idea of introducing commercial considerations into an affair of the heart!—R.B.

[5]Feminine instinct for arousing sympathy, as much as to say "We have already lost our dear dog, and now, are you, you brute, going to deprive us of our cat also?" The perfidy of it!—R.B.

[6]Feminine instinct for changing subject at psychological moment, and by this indirection make it appear that this is just an innocent letter of inquiry, after all.—R.B.

[7]To what ends will a female go to make talk. "We don't miss the trees because there are plenty of trees," a sufficient reason, I should say for not missing the trees. "Of course they are all planted," you don't say! Was there ever a tree that wasn't planted in one way or another? She's just making talk, "and not much sense in it either, quoth honest I."—R.B.

[8]Astute appeal for sympathy. Widow's tears! Husband in the service, and you are going to deprive his widow of her only solace? Really, how could you?—R.B.

[9]Plaintative! I can see her wiping the tears away with the tip of her apron. The woman has been terribly mistreated.—R.B.

[10]The hell you are!—R.B.

June 25, 1951

Dear Mrs. O'Donald:

Your letter about Skeezix touches me very deeply. I know what it is to love cats and dogs. So I am sending Skeezix back by express and shall advise you by airmail just when to expect him.

He already imagines he is going. I can tell by the fact that he follows me around everywhere I go this morning, jumps in my lap every time I sit down, and [unreadable] my table when I shove him off my lap. I think I can see in his usually non-committal face a mixture of emotion—sadness at leaving the old place and a kind of joyous anticipation at the prospect of rejoining his beloved mistress. Maybe I am just reading these actions into his solemn countenance. I like to nature-fake a little sometimes.

I can tell you that his behavior since you left has been exemplary in every particular. He waits until I am out of bed to whine for his breakfast; after I have put him off my table the third time, he doesn't jump up there any more for the time being; he has caught only one lizard, so far as I know during the whole time. I like lizards you know, and scolded him for it, especially for his heartless torture of the thing. But that is cat-behavior and so can't expect anything else.

I shall send you a memorandum of the shipping expense.

Sincerely yours,

Roy Bedichek

May 2, 1951

Dear Alan:

I am delighted with your letter of 21 April. It gives me just the information I have been wanting, and in attractive form, so attractive that I immediately posted it on to the madam who is now disporting herself in New York and I hope having a hell of a good time. She is sufficiently juvenile to really enjoy the theater, and she will bubble with her experiences and with her impressions of this play and that for the next two or three years. She is practically well of her leg-ailment, and almost *skips* around, if you will use "skip" with a consciousness of the great principle of relativity. That is, she "skips" pretty well for a woman damn near seventy years old.

I have often told you that you have a real talent for humorous description which you should by all means cultivate, especially in periods such as this one so rich in unusual experiences. The life of those natives is an excellent field for such exercises. I wish you would investigate further the use of man-o'-war birds as fishers for the natives and their training. I would be greatly interested in the various steps by which this bird is taught to fish for its master, and just how it performs after it has been taught. This is one of the most interesting birds in the world, and every fact about him interests not only ornithologists but the general public. Why not write an account of this very matter for *Natural History*?

I greatly abominate drugs and it is disquieting to me to know that you have to resort to one for seasickness. Usually a drug which alleviates one weakness establishes another and a worser one. Nature tells one to puke and not eat when afflicted with seasickness, and that's what I did and got to be a fairly good sailor with this *natural* remedy. However, I was never churned about in any such fashion as you describe. Worst case I ever had was crossing the North Sea in a considerable storm on an immigrant ship of perhaps 10,000 tons.

I would like a little more detail on your filariasis study. Are you merely making a survey to determine number of people affected, or are you experimenting with cures and methods of prevention?

If Sarah and children went there, what would be chances of their contracting the disease? That causes me considerable uneasiness as well as uneasiness of your own account. Do you take drugs to prevent contracting the disease? or is there some immunizing technique?

The other day I sent Alan, Jr., *Kon-Tiki*, the best story of South Sea Island adventure I have read. It is "true" adventure and has really scientific merit as a study in how the South Sea Islands, that is those south of the equator, became populated. It is the author's contention that the Taumotu Archipelago as well as the Marquesas Islands were populated from the west coast of South America. He makes a mighty good case.

I am doddering around *trying* to write a book, *trying* to prepare about a half dozen talks I am scheduled for, *trying* to raise a garden, and *trying* to be decent in my old age—all very difficult.

I am much against MacArthur's idea of whipping China as a preparation (just getting warmed up, so to speak) for a war with Russia and eventual conquest of the world. I am definitely against fighting Russia when "our spurs are dull." I consider Europe an area of far greater strategic importance than Asia, and since it is impossible to guard both, I think MacArthur's position untenable if one believes in being governed by logic and common sense instead of by emotion.

But politics is dreary stuff.

Hope you'll have time to write me again soon.

I am sending a carbon of this to Sarah.

Sincerely yours,

R.B.

August 2, 1951

Dear Bachman,

I am full to overflowing with information about you and Jane, John & Louise. I leave you to exercise your detective powers in discovering the source of this private and confidential information.

To begin with the youngest and summarizing volumes in a word: Louise stands for sweetness and light; John for ingenuity and "imagination all compact"; Jane, civic activities and hospitality; you, creative craftsmanship & awesome omniscience.

Believe me your work with your hands[1] pleases me more than anything else which my source of information confided to me. If there is anything that is a cure-all for bodily ailments and mental ills it is this very creative work with one's two hands. People think with their bodies as well as with their brains, and their bodies are not so subject to aberrations. The stored up wisdom and experience of millions of years resides in the body. The brain is a new experimental contraption Nature supplied to accommodate the increasing backward-looking and prevision made necessary by the development of the hand. A few well disciplined brain-cells could direct the restricted activities of the fore-foot but when that forefoot became a hand, it was an opening of a Pandora's box of infinite possibilities for good and evil, for triumphs and disasters.

So, great is the mistake of overeducating this late comer, the brain, to the neglect of the old reliable body.

Fortunately for me, I grew up on a small farm and learned a lot of bodily skills unconsciously. I learned to milk, chop and pick cotton, take care of a garden, feed stock and handle them, yoke oxen, harness horses, plow, gather corn, shuck it, store it, and a thousand things it is necessary to do with one's body around a small place in the country.

This was the very education I realized you were not getting as you grew up. But thank the Lord you got a few mechanical skills in the vocational work in high school and maybe some extension of hand-work and training at Annapolis. But wherever you got your furniture-making and carpentering, my source of information says you are now a first class workman with your hands.

Nothing takes the place of this as a mental stabilizer. I would long since have been a "nut" and confined in a lunatic asylum but for the fact that I raised dogs,[2] and gardened, and camped out in very primi-tive conditions where one is dependent upon bodily activity. In the much more artificial situation in which your life is cast, bodily activ-ity, especially creative work with your hands, is all the more neces-sary.

I see that these pot-gutted, helpless grubs of civilization we still call men, becoming discontented in middle life, bored with bookkeep-ing, or selling, or lecturing, or whatnot, lean more and more to un-healthy dissipations to dissipate their boredom. They become depen-dent upon a cocktail for a "lift," or an illicit love-affair, or simple sheer eating, stuffing their fatty and distended insides with more and more, and richer and richer, and more and more highly seasoned, food. This only increases their mental depression, and it soon becomes a vicious circle from which there is no escape. It all comes from their original neglect of the body, which demands a life of its own.

I can attack my garden in a thoroughly dispirited humor and within half an hour be in a highly enthusiastic mood, enjoying every minute.

Tell Jane the magnificent start of Kentucky Wonder Beans which she saw while she was here, and which I bragged about in my letters for weeks, were finally a complete flop. Vines, tangles, luxuriant masses of vines—nothing else. Well, just the other morning I decided to make a "green manure" experiment with them, and dug a trench about 18 inches deep alongside the two rows and buried these enormous vines, wetting them down and covering with dirt, wetting and covering again, until they are now, I trust, disintegrating and enriching the soil for a fall row of something or other. I got a positive delight out of this simple procedure, and I am anxious to see how the "experiment" will turn out.

I am sure you have a similar enthusiasm concerning your furniture-making and carpentering, because it is also a bodily activity and is creative work.

You may think I am a little "touched" on this subject, but you just wait and see, observing yourself and others, with especial attention to bodily activity of a creative sort. The sanest people who ever lived on this earth developed the maxim "a sound mind in a sound body." If the really lunatic element in Congress (and it is no inconsiderable element either) had been disciplined with bodily activity of a creative sort, we wouldn't now as a nation be on the verge of disaster. Often it seems to me that the ship is even now among the rocks with a drunken pilot.

Well, I had no idea of homilizing to such an extent when I started out, but the great advantage of a letter over conversation is that one can't quit a conversation always when he gets bored, but a letter may be laid aside at any point without offense. So I feel free to run on to suit myself. As a matter of fact many of my letters are written more to myself than to anyone else. You happen to be the victim this morning. I left the water on my lima beans—now my only hope of August beans—and I must run turn it off. By the time I get back, the fever of communication will likely have evaporated, proving again my contention that bodily activity is a mental stabilizer.

I suppose your mother has advised you fully about Mary and Sarah, whose fortunes seemed to be changing rapidly. Certainly, Mary and Gay have reached a kind of plateau where traveling along with their three youngsters will not be so strenuous as their married life up to the present has been. Sarah is an unconquerable globe-trotter and pioneer and I think she is happy in her hardships. Surely, invading the wilds with the three boys should be hazardous enough to satisfy the most ravenous pioneering hunger. Then she gets some new species of fly and sees strange birds and plants. I really envy her everything except the family cares for which, I fear, I have little more appetite than a cowbird has.

Jane, thanks for the encouraging words and for calling my attention to Mr. Weeks' pleasant discourse on *Karankaway Country*. I have been getting almost enough encouragement here lately to move me to undertake another nature book as soon as I finish with my History, which, by the way, drags in places like an ill-constructed sled. I get sidetracked now and then, pursuing some collateral matter and find in the end that I can't use the material so collected. Also, I find myself disposed to run down some natural history item someone rings me up about or writes me. All this shows that my heart's in the highlands, and seeks every excuse unconsciously to desert the knitting I have undertaken. I resolve frequently (and as frequently break my resolution) to quit kidding myself.

Five pages is the limit a six-cent stamp will carry and certainly I am not going to spend any more on getting this to you.

Much love, and don't let John burn the house down to simplify the family's removal to Texas.

Dad

[1]Editor's Note: Bach made floor-to-ceiling book cases for the living room, soon filled them with books and made more book shelves for two bedrooms.
[2]Editor's Note: Roy Bedichek raised and sold airedales in the 1920s.

January 17, 1952

Dear Bachman:

Well, last word of you I have (via Van via Jane via your mother) is that your party landed safely in England.[1] By this [time] you may be dealing with royalty, for all I know.

But I write to tell you how I experimented with John the other day. You know my contention versus nearly all the pedagogs is that the competitive spirit is something so fundamental in the human being that it cannot be suppressed or even ignored without crippling the child. I claim it must be aroused and directed—that is, used to induce desirable activities, that is, those activities which develop desirable qualities and skills. The pedagogs reply that competition is the bane of man and a competitive society is the worst possible society, apparently (but *only apparently*) ignoring our own official and historic attitude towards competition, our own political theories, free enterprise, anti-trust laws, as well as the pedagogs' own practice in actual day-by-day conduct of the school. They claim that it is cooperation to the exclusion of competition that will train for the happy human society—etc., etc., too long to go into. My point is that both can be used effectively, naturally and to good purpose, depending upon circumstances.

Well, since I had a three-year-old, perfectly normal, and certainly an exceptionally bright boy in my exclusive charge for an hour or so the other day, I thought I would experiment with him. Mr. Gracy and I were on a wood-gathering expedition in the famous pick-up. As we began pitching the cedar stumps into little piles that could be collected later, we both noticed that John imitated us and was motivated by a desire to help (cooperation). Neither Gracy nor I tried to stimulate in him any competitive endeavor because he was working the hell out of himself anyway. He struggled with pieces too large, he showed a disposition to trot rather than walk, he didn't waste a moment. Cooperation was working perfectly and we instinctively encouraged him by thanking him and saying in a voice of commendation that he was doing us a great service.

But presently another desire struck him besides that of helping his maternal and paternal grandfathers, as laudable as that was. He caught a glimpse of the blue waters of Marshall Ford Lake gleaming in the sun only two or three hundred yards away. He left Grandpa Gracy to his task (un-cooperated with) and split off in a little toddling trot to the water. G. Gracy hollooed after him, whereupon G. Bedichek, some distance away, saw the situation and tried in a seductive halloo to entice him back. No response—continued progress towards the water. He had heard the primal call of water, the medium from which all life came. To dabble in it is instinctive and dabble in it he was determined to do. G. Gracy started lamely in pursuit, and they disappeared under the hill. I waited some time, and then went to a look-out where I could see if the race had been satisfactorily concluded. I then saw

John leading his grandfather by about a hundred yards up the road leading to the car. I soon found that G. Gracy had used the competitive motive to overcome John's instinctive desire to dabble in the water. He had first gathered him by the hand to lead him back. But the subject didn't lead; he balked, and it looked as if he would have to be dragged or carried away from the Great Mother towards which John's spirit was yearning, and the first home of land animals, the waterside. How did G. Gracy overcome this instinctive longing to dabble? Simply by inciting a still stronger instinct, viz., the competitive instinct. He told John that he was going to "beat him back to the car," and made a step or too in earnest of this announcement. Immediately John took the lead and by the time I had become uneasy and espied them from my lookout, John was far in the lead. We both, of course, congratulated John upon winning the race.

Then it came my turn. After satisfying his competitive instinct by beating his grandfather back to the car, he cooperated a little while in the gathering of wood, but soon the memory of that delicious water, and the little waves beating up on a sandy shore, and the damp soil, and the smell of the wet, overcame him and he bolted again towards the original home of man before he became man. This time I suggested he take his spade, which he grabbed up and made off, with me following as best I could. We reached the sandbar, and I became utterly passive, a person of no "don'ts," determined to see what the hell he would do of his own free will and accord. I was soon forgotten. He became busy shovelling sand rather aimlessly. Then he determined to cover up an old stump which protruded some 12 or 18 inches above the surface. He worked hard at this for a little while but gave it up in favor of edging nearer to the water—of course, alerting his overseer, since I didn't want him to get his clothes wet. I suggested that he cover the stump with wet soil from the water's edge. It was rather stiff mud and he made small progress even though striving manfully. He had to make some twenty of his little steps to carry the mud back to the stump. I thought I was smart, since I now had him occupied for at least an hour, and sought out a fresh plot of Bermuda to lie down upon. But I was mistaken. He discovered the task was hopeless and set off at a run down the beach to find more suitable material. I followed. On and on he went in search (I suppose) of a looser soil, but I think by the time he found it, he had forgotten just what he wanted with it and began simply digging right in the edge of the water. I didn't want to "don't" him, and still I feared he would fall in and wet his clothes. So G. Bedichek resorted to his wits.

"John," said I, "I see you are digging a canal."

"What is a canal?"

Then I took the spade and dug out a little trench at the edge so the water would follow my spading.

"That, John, is the way to dig a canal so the boats can come into the land and unload and load up again."

He caught the point immediately and demanded the spade back, which I unreluctantly yielded to his little hands. He began making a canal, delighted as the water followed his spade. He worked at this almost feverishly for half an hour until he had brought the water inland to a point where the soil was hard digging. When I saw that he was really working but not getting anywhere, I said,

"John, you have made a fine canal for little boats, row boats, but you can see that the really big boats can't get in with their loads."

He got the point. He wanted the great big boats to come in, too. So I told him that when a canal was too narrow for big boats the engineers widened it and I showed him with the spade the widening process. He grabbed his spade again and began energetically widening his canal, spading out the dirt on either side, which took him at least another half hour. I began to fear he would blister his hands and, as I was afraid G. Gracy would get uneasy about us, I suggested a return to the car. No. That didn't suit his plans. He wanted to dig another canal. We argued awhile. Then I used a little gentle force. I drew him away, but he pulled back like a perverse little mule wanting to go in any direction except toward the car. At first I thought he had lost his directions. The car was not in sight.

I happened to notice a good walking-stick and with no duplicity whatever, picked it up and began walking with it. John immediately wanted a stick. I soon found one suitable to his size, and he was delighted, using it almost exactly as I used mine. But he veered off in any direction except the one I wanted him to take. Then I (this time with duplicity) resorted to competition.

"John," said I, in challenging tone, "I have a big stick and you have a little one. My big stick is going to beat your little old stick back to the car."

The effect was magic. The little rascal has as good sense of direction as a wild goose. He immediately took a true course, and declared his little stick was going to beat my big stick back to the car. This competition brought us to the car in short order. G. Gracy had had his nap out and was busy with stumps, but was getting uneasy about us. John, on the least suggestion, began cooperating again in the gathering of sticks.

Now I suppose the "non-competing" pedagogs will argue that I have instilled an evil motive into this child's mind. That G. Gracy and G. Bedichek conspired to do this in the violation of sound pedagogical principles. But I don't think so at all. It's as natural and as wholesome for a child to want to compete as it is for him to want to cooperate. They are not mutually exclusive methods. They may be used together, as team-mates cooperating in a game against (competition) a team which is cooperating to defeat them. They may be used alternately to good purpose, as long as the activity which either one stimulates is a desirable one. So, that's my fuss with the damned pedagogs who knock the hell out of the Interscholastic League, and have really almost squelched our formal competitions on the grade school level. Come to think of it, I'll kill two birds with one stone and edit this letter into a chapter in my book.

Louise[2] is with us this morning, "fair as a star when only one is shining in the sky."[3]

Yours,

Dad

[1]Editor's Note: Bachman and his family were in Texas for Christmas when the president of Texas Gulf Sulphur decided on a trip to Bagdad that included Bachman and several others. Since Jane was seven months pregnant with two toddlers, the family decided that she should stay in Austin where there would be four grandparents to help. Bachman wrote Jane from London on the way to the Middle East. He and several others were going to try to get a contract to explore for minerals in Iraq. After six weeks of negotiations a contract was signed and the next day the governing party which had signed the contract fell. The Texas Gulf Sulphur people flew home knowing the time was wrong to pursue negotiations.
[2]Louise Wells, Bach and Jane's second child.
[3]William Wordsworth, "She Dwelt Among the Untrodden Ways."

March 9, 1952

Dear Bach:

Well, it's here, the n.b., and looks just like many other n.bs. I've seen him twice, asleep each time. The flower folded in the bud is hard to identify. The best that can be said of any bud is that it is perfect *as a bud*, and I can say this of Paul.[1]

The grandpas took John, no longer a bud, by the way, on third expedition for cedar-stumps, and found to our chagrin that rival entertainment had tempered his enthusiasm for association with this elderly brace of wood-haulers. He longed for home, was sorry he had come; but I must say for him, he endured it with equanimity. He ate heartily a lunch of steak, salad and milk; he dug up sand with his shovel and dumped it here and there from his wheelbarrow; he complained only when he was asked specifically if he were glad he came. He was yearning for Richard, his daily playmate while with the Gracys, and when we got back home, we gave up all hope of re-capturing his attention, for Richard was waiting for him with a lovely, long-eared, curly-haired spaniel-pup. Who can compete with that?

Grandpa Gracy came on over here about three hours later, and said John was off with Richard and the pup and that he had not sighted hair nor hide of him since we arrived with the wood.

Jane said yesterday she had a letter from you saying that Mr. Nelson had arrived, and so I suppose things are winding up there and you will be back in NY 'fo long. I am sending this to NY by slow mail and judge it will just about connect with your arrival.

You have certainly had a fine opportunity to get better acquainted with the Near East and especially with the archeological features. You will be returning, I hope, laden with lore.

I was greatly amused yesterday at lunch when Mr. Gracy pulled out a cigarette and immediately received a cautioning word from John about smoking, in identical language, I judge, with that used by Mrs. G. when he breaks over at home. John's tone was fatherly and tolerant, but firm, nevertheless.

If you get time (now that you're back in NYC, I suppose) I wish you would spy out for me a good second hand pair of binoculars, B&L or Z, 9X35 and advise me of the price.

Jane is looking well, and Louise, the darling little creature, has been with us now for about a week.

    Yours,

    Dad

[1]Editor's Note: The n.b. was new baby Paul Bedichek, born February 28, 1952. At the time Bach was staying at the Tigris Palace Hotel in Bagdad.

April 17, 1952

Dear Bachman,

    Had a fine time at Camp Tyler last week. Group gathered for Conference was a convenient size—about fifty people—all interested in the educational possibilities of outdoor living. There were no set talks, no papers, just orderly discussion under a master of moderators who could tactfully shut down on the garrulous and pull out of the reticent whatever of thought or experience on the subject he had. For some situations this is the best form of interchange between and among individuals all interested in the same subject. Of course, it is not best for miscellaneous groups of divergent interests. I guess it's the kind of thing you probably engage in every day with other lawyers trying to get as many sidelights and main lights as possible on a legal problem—but, of course, with not so many participating as we had at Tyler.

    I began each day with a group of five or ten people who wanted to get a line on the birds around the edges of Lake Tyler. We were out at daylight and returned for 8 o'clock breakfast. After breakfast we had a conference often running until noon. Afternoons we spent visiting various places around the Camp—especially the demonstration farm, and areas which were being reforested. After supper we had a summing-up period often quite fruitful. One windy, rainy night, rather cold, too, we semicircled around a huge fireplace which engulfed logs of cordwood length and told stories until 11 o'clock. I picked up several pretty juicy ones.

    I am busy and have been for two days settling up poor Nora Brady's estate so as to take care of her brother who is a 62-year-old moron, without having him committed to an institution. Leagued up with a middle-aged, ignorant, superstitious (but with sound sense and a heart of gold), Syrian woman who has neighbored with Nora for forty years—with this woman's help I think we have about saved old John from being confined for the rest of his life. This woman is a rich character and I'll tell you about her someday.

Had to put off a trip for firewood with Mr. Gracy today on account of what I hope is final conference of all concerned about Nora & John this morning at ten. We are trucking out for firewood tomorrow at ten. Tell John we wish we might have him with us. It will be rather lonesome without him.

Some reporter, whom I have completely forgotten, broke out with a page about me in the Magazine Section of the *Houston Chronicle* Sunday. I'll try to find a copy and send it. I can't remember any except two of the photographs, and they are quite intimate ones. My memory is evidently getting pretty flimsy. There's one of me in my okra, one at my old Oliver typewriter, and one is a terrible caricature so grotesque as to make me shiver. Your mama, however, says it looks just like me paddling around in Barton Springs. This assurance makes me shiver worse and almost determines me never to go into that damned swimming hole again. The information is about as accurate as usual, but that's not saying a great deal. I am a "world-famous" naturalist; I am "father" of the Interscholastic League, etc., etc. But, egotist that I am, I have pasted a copy in my scrapbook.

Speaking of scrapbooks, I promised some member of the family, possibly Jane, that I would give him or her such duplicate clippings as I have. Not a great many. If I promised you or her this and you still want them, I am ready to make good.

My friend—a good friend, by the way—Wilson Hudson, wrangled out of me a promise yesterday to deliver by Sept. 1 a 3,000-word article for the Texas Folklore [Society annual publication] of which he is now editor. It's to be folklore about animals of the Southwest. It makes quite a chore, and I've no business letting myself be diverted from my book, but I could hardly turn Wilson down, as he has gone to a great deal of trouble for me on several occasions. I haven't told your mother and shan't, for I don't want to get bawled out.

I promised St. Stephens School to take supper with it next Sunday night and talk after supper about some natural history subject—all, of course, free gratis fer nuthin'.

I am gradually accumulating camping stuff for next summer at the Outdoor Education Camp of the Sul Ross State College. I think I shall refuse to be accommodated in camp-barracks, and take myself off up some canyon with my truck and live out in the open while there. Or I may camp out near by, sleep in the open, and take my meals at the camp dining-hall. This would be time-saving, and that's the only reason it appeals to me. My services begin with bird-hikes at daylight, and end at 11 A.M.—rest of the time I have to myself.

By the way, one of Rodney Kidd's boys, Desmond, is near New York now and will be for some little time, taking his helicopter training. This is not the boy Kidd spoke to Jane about when she was here once. That was Byron, and he is still somewhere in New York State. This one is Desmond, and his address is: Ensign Rodney D. Kidd, USN, Helicopter Squadron II, Lakehurst Naval Air Station, Lakehurst, New Jersey. If you want to, and it is no inconvenience, you might show him some attention. No obligation, whatever. Just do it if you *rather than not.*

I forwarded a much-forwarded letter to Dick Fleming yesterday, and how it came ever to be sent here is more than I can figure out. Anyway it's on its way by air now.

Mrs. Gracy and Lillian had a long talk over the phone yesterday about letters the Gracys had received from you and Jane. I judged from coos and ohs and ahs at this end that there must have been a good deal in those letters about the children.

Yours,
Dad

❧

Camp Lobo
Ft. Davis, Tex
July 4, 1952

Dear Bachman—

When I was studying anthropology in my undergraduate days, there was a great argument on among the authorities about which came *first*: *clothes* or *modesty*. Did modesty demand the covering of man's nakedness, as suggested in the famous garden-of-Eden incident, or did our prognathous-jawed ancestors first adopt clothes, for one reason or another, & so become accustomed to keeping tenderer parts of the body covered, which *custom* gradually developed the feeling of modesty.

I don't know how the authorities finally settled the dispute (if it is, indeed, settled to the satisfaction of the scientific world) but this camp of thirty days has certainly settled it in my mind, leaving no vestige of doubt. Insects first drove man to artificial covering, as skimpy-haired individuals happened to be born. These "sports" were thus given greater range which favorably affected chances of survival. They could "go places" their furred brothers couldn't go which opened up to them vast opportunities denied those who were compelled to seek locations uninfested with insects and neither too hot nor too cold.

In my camp here, I am repeating this primitive experience. No human being could exist here without the protection of clothes. At this moment—just sunup—I am sitting encased in an overcoat, socks doubled, & with medium-sized bath-towel on my lap, which I am using as tailed animals use their rear-appendages to switch off biting insects from their tenderer & hairless parts. Just at present mosquitoes (very athletic species) are pestering me. Presently they will be relieved by biting gnats. As the sun grows warmer flies will succeed them, and so on around the clock. Of course, I have a bar which protects me while I sleep.

Now just think of a primitive human being in this situation, would he not grab up anything in way of clothing that his environment offered, maybe fig-leaves! Clothes-wearers would gradually come to think themselves superior to the poor naked savages, and develop a cult or religion of clothes-wearing with all the accompanying tabus which cults insist upon observing—*modesty* along with them. G.E.D.

My pace for this month has been a bit too rapid. I have lost ten pounds which I can hardly afford. Scales say I weigh now only 147 with clothes on. Highest [Lowest?] weight since I was a skinny boy of 18.

So I am going on up higher.

July 6
(and at this point something—I don't just remember what—stopped me.)

I have now gotten up higher—2000 feet higher—in the head of a canyon between Saw-Tooth Mt. & Mt. Livermore. Do you remember

Livermore? Highest peak in the Davis Mts.? It's high here, but not too high for gnats. Making camp yesterday 10 A.M. to 2 P.M. I was smothered with them—literally smothered—they swarmed into my mouth, nose & ears. I needed a bee-keeper's head-covering. It was exhausting work to stretch the fly, dig a fire-pit, lug up some cooking rocks, & do other necessary things on half breath—and half-breaths are all they allowed. At last, I got my cot under the fly & a mosquito-bar over it, & in there I lay until around 4 P.M. when the nuisance was abated by a fresh breeze springing up.

I am inside the Reynolds Co. Ranch, (or one of them)—gates double-locked behind me. I was mis-lead here with stories of rich animal life—it ain't so—it's a kind of death's valley, except for the gnats. Since arriving here yesterday, I have seen only a few woodhouse jays and a dozen or so turkey vultures sunning themselves on tops of dead trees their excrement has killed. Not a flower blooms—even the scrubby oak are nearly leafless from lack of moisture.

Am rather glad, however, for now I shall get a chance to write up my notes. You see I've been camping more than a month, with no time to write up my field-notes, & this is the place. Gnats not nearly so bad today & there are no mosquitoes. Nobody comes by. Only sound of another human in 24 hrs. was an airplane just now & there are no landing fields in fifty miles.

In other locations, have seen some quite worthwhile sights. Have detailed notes on a phainopepla's nest. Another set of notes on cowbird's parasital activities on the black-throated sparrow, also a few interesting beings with tales to tell. Also have some notes on "outdoor education" to write up. I was employed in an "outdoor education" camp for a month & got to see it from the inside. In short, I have enough to keep me busy for a week, even if no birds or "beasties" show up & demand to be studied. But oh, for a typewriter!

Camp Calendar says it is now Wednes (Drop of rain) day, July 9. Hour must be roughly guessed, since my shadow-markings are no good without the sun, & there is no sun. Say about 9 A.M. yesterday, much furor of the elements. Reverberating thunder tore up the canyons. Mt. Peaks around were swathed in the grayest mist I ever saw, which ventured down the arroyos, like timid tender-footed animals sounding out a virgin territory, & frightened back every now and then. Sound and fury signifying nothing,[1] at least no rain to speak of.

But last night with everything quiet—no wind, no thunder—in

the deep stillness, a gentle rain began to fall. It just drippled for ten minutes or so, stopped for a while, then again, & so on intermittently until the dull daylight came. The sound of it on the canvas fly was heavenly. I tried to stay awake to listen, but couldn't. Camp is soaked, but I was a canny camper. Nothing that counts is wet. Even had dry fire-making materials available & soon had a fire blazing in my fire-pit, a cup of hot coffee, & a good wine-sap apple for breakfast.

The canyons this morning are rivers of mist, & they threaten to overflow my camp. Up the mountain side a few hundred yards is so dense a bank of earth-loving cloud that I am sure one cannot see ten steps in it. Maybe it will come on down, maybe not. Drops detained in the trees from last shower hit the canopy of my truck, & the big fly, pleasant reminder that I am protected.

Animal & plant life here is still disappointing. When I first saw that immense concrete reservoir piping the water to two big circular, steel watering "tubs" for cattle, I thought surely animals & birds for many miles around would visit it—but they do not. The damned clever ras-cals who built this cattle-watering place have stopped every leak, & containers are sheer on every side so that only a bird which drinks on the wing could get a sip, and only venturesome animals like coons will hang with one foreleg & thus get his mouth down to the water. There's not seep enough in this whole place to water a wren. So this watering place doesn't attract much wild life.

Just now the manager of the ranch came by to see how I was getting on. Pleasant enough fellow, and a good public-spirited citizen; but he doesn't know beans about birds, or other wild life, for that mat-ter, except game. He is quite alert on game. Had a Mexican ranch-hand with him. I made them some coffee & we had quite a little visit. This is the Rockpile Ranch, & is the only one of several ranches oper-ated by the Reynolds Cattle Co., with headquarters at Kent. They all believe in God, high-priced beef, plenty of rain, & low taxes. The manager, however, is outraged at the way the cattleman-conspiracy (principally 4 men) refuse to permit taxes even for the public schools. Kokernut owns 400 sections in the Ft. Davis School district valued for taxation at $1.00 per acre. No one knows market price of this land because none is sold, & that is for the simple reason that none is for sale. It is shamefully overgrazed, & huge erosion gullies are being cut everywhere you look. In another generation or so, these friendly mountains will be as bleak as those once verdured mountains in Palestine, Greece & other areas of the Near East. Man will eventually starve himself off the planet and leave it to the turtles, scorpions, cockroaches & other forms of primitive life. Of course, some insects may make a go of it. I hope not gnats & mosquitoes.

Well, Mr. Miller was cordial, & told me if a flood cut off my retreat to the highway he would rescue me. The only danger of this of course is wash-outs along the wagon-trail, leading to the paved road, which is only a few *miles*.

Before leaving Ft. Davis I wrote your mother suggesting that we spend the little extra money I picked up at the Outdoor Education Camp on the Coast during August, as that is her favorite Texas summer resort. She always has hay fever out here, where it is really cool. Don't know how it will strike her. Reply hadn't come when I broke connection with the U.S. Mail.

This might go on and on, but doubt if a busy man has time to read it or the inclination, either, to give so much time to bucolic affairs. Anyway, I'll mail it when I get back to Ft. Davis. Hope your ailment is better if not over, & that Jane and three youngsters[2] are happy.

Dad

[1]William Shakespeare, *MacBeth*, V, v, 17.
[2]Editor's Note: John, four years old; Louise, two years old; Paul, five months.

December 1, 1952

Dear Bachman:

Rain! You who live in New York know not what it means. The Texas drouth is broken. Dallas, Ft. Worth, Corpus Christi, to say nothing of the arid country west of the 100th meridian, were getting desperate for water, even for drinking water. I covered some 1600 miles of that country on a camping trip in September, and you never saw anything like it for devastation. But now it has been raining slow rain for a couple of weeks. It is still raining. If nothing else happened during the past year pleasing or satisfying to Texas folk, this rain coming before and during Thanksgiving, should have made us all devoutly thankful.

Sarah, Alan and the three boys[1] were with us for four days at one time and three days at another. They make up an interesting and a quite happy family. Alan, Jr., is of an age to require new experiences. He happens at the moment to be fanatically interested in Indians and Indian relics. I took him out to an old Indian mound and fed his interest with actual contacts with the last Indians who occupied the mound. I knew from previous experience that the last Indians at this location made the little bird points, tiny arrow-heads not much bigger than my thumb-nail, and keen as a needle. Collectors prize them. They occur only in the top six inches of the mound, right under, sometimes *in,* the grass roots.

So instead of digging myself breathless, as I should have had to do in any deeper excavation, I got Alan and, to a less extent, Roy, interested in these small points that occur at a shallow depth. I gave Alan some experience in mapping by suggesting that he map the location so that he could find it again, and also map the surface we were to work on so that he would know from his map just where each specimen occurred. Then, with Sarah and the three boys, armed with rakes and brooms we attacked an area ten feet square (100 sq. feet) "scientifically" plotted first with the rakes to get off the accumulation of humus, and then with brooms, sweeping carefully among the exposed pieces of broken and burnt limestone of which the mound is for the most part made up. This sweeping operation is just about the physical exercise suited to my age and disposition. In your day, you remember, it was pick & shovel.

It turned out famously. Alan discovered all the points (four) which were discovered on this trip, and they were all exquisite little bird-points.

One tragedy occurred. Trying to show the boys how to make the campfire without paper I used my beautiful Sheffield pocket-knife making the usual fire-stick. It was windy and we all had to hover the fire to get it started. In this procedure I evidently dropped my pocket-knife and recovered it only the next day in the ashes, utterly ruined, of course. That was the knife the Campers last summer gave me on my birthday.

We all had several other camping experiences, building a fire, cooking our meal, etc. On one of these trips, your mother discovered a fine body of flint, enabling me to satisfy the longing of Mewhinney,[2] editorial writer on the *Houston Post*, whose hobby is making flint arrow-heads. I advised him of the find and up he came from Houston in his jeep and took away two or three hundred pounds. He declared this was the finest flint in Texas. I am quite sure it is the flint the Indians who camped so long at Barton Springs must have used. It is the blackest I ever saw and the slickest, the same qualities I noted long ago in the artifacts from the Barton Springs kitchen-middens. The material occurs in one of the ravines near Barton Springs.

I was sick in the soul over the election. Stevenson[3] is the greatest man offering himself for office in this generation, and one of the greatest in American History. I think he is as great as Thomas Jefferson—I mean as great in mind and heart. He naturally has the advantage of Jefferson in having before him two centuries of U.S. History which was not available to the elder statesman. He is conferring with Truman today about the future management of the party. It's my opinion that unless the party gets tough and kicks out the Texas traitors[4] as well as the Byrds and Byrneses, it will be blown up. And should the leaders of the party compromise (as now talked) on letting Dick Russell, or some such, speak for it, it had as well close up the shop.

TV is disturbing politics. That damned crook, Nixon, gave us a demonstration of what a soap-opera artist can do, especially with the women. It's the most effective weapon of Big Money since the advertisers put radio in every home.

I don't have clearly in mind your intentions, and Jane's, about the Christmas holidays. Are we to see you?

Yours,

Dad

[1] Sarah's three boys are Alan, Jr., Roy, George.
[2] Hubert Mewhinney wrote the Foreword to the 1961 edition of *Adventures with a Texas Naturalist*.
[3] Bedichek is referring to Adlai Stevenson.
[4] Bedichek is referring to the Democrats for Nixon.

January 19, 1953

Dear Bachman:

I am reminded by a letter from Jane to her mother and transmitted by phone to me that you are now entering the fifth period of your life according to the Solonian 7-year division. Since numerology attributed great importance to seven, and for other reasons, I am on this fifth seventh of your mortal career quoting Solon's account of the Ages of Man which, while not so picturesque as Shakespeare's in *As You Like It*, is certainly superior in conciseness and unity:

> A boy, before he cometh to man's estate, and while he is still a child, getteth and loseth his rampart of teeth within the first seven years. When god bringeth the second seven to a close, the signs of budding manhood begin to show. In the third period, a downy beard appeareth, though the limbs have not reached their full growth, and the boyish bloom of the complexion fadeth. In the fourth period of seven years, every man is at the prime of his physical strength. . . . The fifth period is the season for a man to bethink him of marriage and seek offspring against the future. In the sixth, experience of every sort carrieth his mind on to perfection, and he feeleth no longer the same inclination to the wild pranks of youth. In the seventh seven he is at his prime in mind and tongue, and also in the eighth, the two together making fourteen years. In the ninth period, though he still retaineth some force, he is feebler both in wisdom and in speech and faileth of great achievement. If a man attaineth to the full measure of the tenth period, the fate of death, if it come upon him cometh not untimely.

And, as for getting the most out of life's ten periods, he says that the riches of him who "hath much silver and gold, fields of nearing wheat-bearing lands, horses and mules, are no greater than his whose only possessions are these: stomach, lungs and feet that bear him joy not pain; the blooming charms, perhaps, of boy or maiden; and an existence ever harmonious with the changing seasons of life."

"In these things," he continues, "is the true wealth of mortal men; for no man, when he passeth to Hades' realm, carrieth with him all his vast horde. No ransom that he can give enableth him to escape death or dire disease or the creeping evil of old age."

From the perspective of my almost eleventh seven, I commend these words of the great sage.

Yours affectionaly,

R.B.

*

March 29, 1953

Dear John:

Our corn began coming up the day after you got on the train bound for Scarsdale. It comes up just as I told you it would by shoving up through the ground a very sharp point. If the sprout wasn't sharp-pointed it could never get up through the ground because you know we planted it about an inch or two down. So the grains you planted swelled up, burst open and sent sharp-pointed little sprouts right up into the air and sunlight. As soon as the sprout gets well out of the ground it spreads itself out to catch the sunlight, that is, it becomes a *blade* instead of a *point*. As it opens out from a point to form a blade it still has a little round hole in the center, like a piece of paper would have if you roll up and then let open at the top. Right in the center of this little hole another little pointed sprout comes out, and it spreads, leaving the same sort of a little hole at the center out of which another point comes out in a few days, and it spreads out into a blade and so on and so on, all the time forming a stalk to which these blades are attached. They keep feeding on the sunlight and making the whole plant green and healthy. You ought to be here and watch these corn-stalks growing day after day. But maybe you should plant one up there and watch it and see if it grows the same way in New York as it does in Texas.

Do you remember the flowers you gathered and left on the iron-seat by the tree near your sandpile? I told you they were sow-thistles, didn't I? Well, the flowers had turned to thistle-down, or maybe they had already turned when you gathered them. Thistle-down is fluffy, light grayish stuff, so light that the wind blows it sometimes for miles and miles when little tufts of it get loose from the flower-heads. I was working near the old iron seat yesterday afternoon when a little wren came and began hopping around under and on top of the old iron seat. I stood still, not moving hand or foot, so she would not be afraid of me. You know if you can stay perfectly still a bird will sometimes mistake you for a stump or something dead and so is not afraid.

This little wren kept looking for something. I knew that by the way she was acting, since she kept turning her head from one side to the other, looking first with her right eye and then with her left. A bird, you know, can't look at a thing with both eyes at the same time, as you can—or did you know that? Why can't a bird look at something with *both* eyes at once as you do?

She kept on for several minutes looking around and hopping here and there over the old iron seat, and I kept standing very still, not even turning my head. You know you and I can "wall" our eyes around and see at different angles, but a bird can't. First I thought when she began pecking at the flower heads that she was after seed, but then I knew better for wrens don't like seed. They like worms and insects. Then I saw what she wanted, for she tugged away and pulled loose some of the soft downy stuff, and hopped right away to the big kindling-pile. Into a hole she dived with her bill loaded with thistle-down, clear out of sight. What do you think she wanted with that thistle-down? It's not fit for a bird to eat, but she must have some use for it.

Well, when she gets her nest built, she likes some soft stuff to line it with so her babies will have a soft place to sit (bird-babies don't *lie*, by the way, they just sit). I think that's what she was after and so it is likely that she has built her nest down in the kindling pile, where it's nice and dark and where the cats can't get at her or her babies. Smart little rascal!

Hope you have some birds around home that you can watch building their nests.

Much love.

Granddaddy Bedichek

Austin, Texas
June 3, 1953

Dear Bachman:

Was it Nelson Glueck's *The Other Side of the Jordan* that you wanted back and which I told you I couldn't find? Well, I have found it and will send it to you if it's the book you want. It is published by the American Schools of Oriental Research, New Haven, Conn., and was issued in 1940.

I hope you have not forgotten to try to locate a second hand copy *cheap* of Rostovtzeff's[1] *History of Hellenic Civilization*, or some such title. We have here in the library his *A History of the Ancient World*, but you were telling me about this other work which continues his study for several centuries.

The days here are already purgatorial but not yet hellish. If I had the nerve and could overcome the palling inertia of old age, I would take you and Jane at your word—at your many, many kind words— and visit you in New York. But it will never be. I feel it, as my mother used to say of a final certainty, "I feel it in my bones." This doesn't keep me from affectionate remembrance of you and Jane and John and Louise, and moderately of Paul. Time presses hard upon me to finish up satisfactorily several tasks I have taken on, not the least of which is the League history, which is proving to be a genuinely Sisyphean labor. I am constantly diverted since I have no strength of character. I got dragged into "movement" lately which absorbed my time, and made two talks in which the mountain labored and brought forth a mouse.[2] And then my friends on the editorial staff of the *Folklore Magazine*[3] wrung from me a promise to do an article on Natural-history folklore, which promise made weeks ago, is only just now redeemed. Then a couple of weeks ago a perfect rash of social engagements broke out. Your mama and I, she 68 and me 75, actually were out every night for a solid week. This not only finished all my little store of energy but put a quietus on any ambition to do anything. "Oh for a lodge in some vast wilderness."[4]

I hear that you have been in Washington lately. I hope you called on and presented your respect to Senator McCarthy. By the way, that wretch recently polluted the soil of Texas with his feet. Newspapers say he visited a multimillionaire of Dallas and flew with him to the Dallas man's ranch in Mexico for a "sojourn."

I suppose you are glorying in the honors showered upon your hero, Sir Winston. He carries them off as he does everything else, superbly.

Just looked around this room. It's the damnedest, disordered, dirtiest place I was ever in. I shall remove the stove and clean up this very morning, if I never do anything else respectable in my whole life.

Tell John and Louise we are getting a nice mess of roasting ears every day now from *their* corn-patch. My Kentucky Wonder beans are twelve feet high and present the most perfect blanket of greenery I have ever seen. Its leaf is trifoliate, you know, and the individual leaflets are full six inches across—enormous! Tomatoes are coming singly, but prospects are good for quite a supply within a couple of weeks. My last compost poem is nearly perfect. Six feet high, 10 feet wide and about fifteen feet long. Vegetable waste, animal waste and good black dirt are layered in it in due proportion. I feel extremely virtuous in this time, when devastation is succeeding conservation as a national policy, to be engaged in my little conservation practices here on a half a block. I am justified by the greatest moral directive ever generated by a human mind, even Kant's categorical imperative: "Act only on that maxim whereby thou cast at the same time will that it become a universal law."

My old friend, Bill Owens, has just published a book. *Slave Mutiny—The Revolt on the Schooner Amistad*—a fictionalized account of an historical event in which no liberties are taken with the essential facts. The John Day Publishing Co. sent me a copy for my comment, and I complied with a letter. The president of the company, Mr. Walsh, says my account of the book is by far the best he has seen and that it will be circulated in promotion of sales. Bill Owens is an interesting guy—wish you would look him up sometime. He is professor of English in the "School of General Studies" Columbia. If you are interested in the book, I have a copy which I'll be glad to send you.

None of the kith and kin in Waco were hurt by the storm. It made kindling wood of residences, however, within a couple of blocks of your Aunt Ena's dwelling.

Kind regards to Dick and much love,
Dad

---

[1]Editor's Note: M. Rostovtzeff, *Social and Economic History of the Hellenistic World* in three volumes, which Bach had bought at auction and quoted in letters to his father.
[2]Horace, *Epistles*, Bk. III (*Ars Poetica*); Aesop, *The Mountain in Labor*.
[3]"Animal Tails: Function and Folklore" is the article which was included in *Mesquite and Willow*, Publications of the Texas Folklore Society XXVII.
[4]William Cowper, *The Task*, bk. II, *The Timepiece*, l I.

Feb. 28, 1954

Dear Sarah:

I had just finished a note to Bachman about a couple of huge tomes of early ornithological history, issued by the War Department back about 1860 giving account of Baird and Lawrence bird-observations. The books are second hand but in good condition. Guess he got it at an auction. I had just finished the note when it occurred to me that Dr. Whitney had called me over the telephone after I was abed last night to tell me that his flickers were back again doing all sorts of acrobatic stunts in his Chinese Tallow tree every morning about seven o'clock. The clock said it was now seven, but I had been working since 3 o'clock and felt entitled to a little let-up.

So I mounted my truck and took out. Whitney has been trying to show me these birds at their antics for two years, but every time I went there in the last two years—perhaps a dozen times—there would be no flickers. Sometimes I missed them by minutes and waited hours, but no flickers. Well, this morning virtue got its reward. Just about or maybe a little after sunup I was ensconced in a nice easy chair by the bedside of poor Mrs. Whitney who has been lying there for six months now with a broken back. The window out of which I watched the Chinese Tallow tree gave me a full view of it about twenty feet away. Soon four flickers came, but they fed on the ground and preened themselves in a hackberry and didn't go near the Tallow tree.

Whitney told me the birds—only flickers—had been eating the seed of the tree, and I could see that there was only a scattering of seed-pods left and they were hanging in little bunches on the ends of long threadlike twigs, the twigs nearly all hanging down. It was to see the birds get these seeds that I had come, but they didn't seem to be seed-hungry and kept hopping around in the grass.

Suddenly a flicker flew in from a distance, paid no attention to those on the ground, grabbed a long twig with a bunch of seed on its end—grabbed with both feet and slid down the swaying twig until his feet were stopped by the bunch of seed. A wind was blowing and the twig with the bird's weight was hanging straight down twelve or eighteen inches from the limb to which it was attached. The flicker was bottomside up clutching the bunch of seed in both feet right about the middle of his belly. Then he began husking and eating them with his bill. A flicker swaying in the wind, at the end of a long twig, bottomside up, husking and eating seed ravenously! Can you beat that?

Then another flicker came and repeated the stunt, and another and another until there were six of the rascals swaying in the wind and feeding, backs to earth and bellies to the blue sky.

Whitney told me he had seen as many as eighteen doing this at the same time.

Presently, one bird having eaten all his bunch up, simply held on and swayed and swung in the wind for ten minutes, apparently enjoying the swing. Then another took to swinging. When a bird turned loose, he righted himself quickly and managed to fly away in a normal position, although often only five feet above the ground.

You should have seen how these two old people, the poor old lady lying there with a broken back—how they enjoyed showing me this spectacle after two years of faithful trial. That was worth something.

When I got home, four martins were waiting for me. Just back from S.A.,[1] they were wondering why the hell I hadn't cleaned the sparrow-trash out of their house. I couldn't find anyone to help me lower the box, but I finally rigged up a contrivance and lowered it myself. Then those four martins sat on a limb of the sycamore tree nearby and watched me clean out the box. Your mama was watching from the kitchen-window. It took me an hour to clean it out, but the martins hardly left the tree. Occasionally one would sail off and take a round over the block, but would come right back, uttering his notes that you are so familiar with. At first they seemed to me a little quarrelsome, but it wasn't long before they were hallowing as cheerful as ever.

A nice old chap showed up just in time to help me raise the box again, and it was no sooner in position than all four birds darted into it. They ran around the platform, back and forth, fighting off the sparrows, but finding the warfare futile, quieted down and each pair took possession of a hole.

So you see that I have had quite some bird-experiences this Sunday before Lent, the last day of February, 1954, and I have been wishing for you to enjoy it with me.

Much love

Dad

[1] South America.

April 18, 1954

Dear Jane and Bachman:

It was generous to give us so much time. Visits are like stamping an impression in wax: unless there is the time to give a deliberate pressure the effect is not clear-cut and lasting. Especially is this true of old, stiff wax, the kind of which my memory is made. This visit was long enough to give me, I think, a lasting and very pleasant impression.

The "morning after" as I sneaked out the back door in morning twilight—sneaking to keep from waking Lillian—I saw a desolate sight. The spirit had all gone out of the sandpile. There lay the shovels: a big one for John, a little one for Louise, just where their eager hands had dropped them. The little toy wagon which had doubtless loomed in John's imagination as a sixteen-wheeled truck, lay disgracefully on its side, two wheels up in the air. An unfinished engineering project was quite obvious in one side of the sandpile. A square piece of board which was to have served as one of the locks in a vast canal stood leaning against the old iron stool ready for instant service. On the other side of the pile there was a simple heap of sand which Louise had patiently piled up for who knows what castle of beauty she was in process of modeling it to conform to what was in her mind. So without the spirit, the pile and the tools and the unfinished projects were desolate. It put me in mind to realize the poignancy of Eugene Field's "Little Boy Blue" which I read when I got to my study.

Hope you and Brood are now safe in 12 Fairview Road.
R.B.

October 13, 1954

Dear Bachman:

Enclosed is a clipping taking a conservative view of the present stock market which may interest you—a kind of summary from various sources.

Your mama will be here, she tells me, Monday at 8 A.M. Sarah is "getting stronger every day," "going out in a low-necked dress to cock-tail parties," (can you imagine such a prohi[unreadable] as Sarah enjoying a cocktail party?), "making reservations for the Midsummer Night's Dream ballet soon to be in San Francisco," and in other ways comporting herself as a normal human being in good health.

My concern is now transferring itself to your mother. She has had a rather strenuous summer for a woman of sixty-nine, which, according to the arithmetic I was taught in school, means that she lacks but one year of being 3 score and 10.

My book[1] is done except for a few loose ends that I am now busy gathering up. It turns out to be an exceedingly long book in a narrow field, so I do not expect many readers or any fame. But anyway, I have the satisfaction of getting myself on record in permanent form. Even a limited edition of a 400-page book, well-printed, substantially bound and on good paper, lasts a long time, especially in view of modern facilities for preserving books, good and bad. I cannot, of course, make the poetic immortality vaunt—still I know that a hundred years or so from now some high-nosed, bespectacled pedagog sniffing around a dusty alcove will run across this book.

Just why a mortal man should gain any satisfaction from this assurance, it is impossible for anyone except this author or a competent psychoanalyst to imagine, so I am not calling upon you to share the weak-tea stimulation of this thought with me.

Well, maybe the Gracys will soon be home. I see migrating birds from those parts every time I go out in the woods. And with their return I shall get a partnership in some of Jane's letters and thus learn how domestic affairs are going at 12 Fairview Road.

Tell John my garden is slow this fall. I haven't had time for it and besides the weather has been dry, hot and dreadful. However, I have some mustard fairly well along in the little plat which served as a model for his famous drawing, "Grandfather Watering his Tomatoes." Also have planted beets, carrots, and turnips. Am still furnishing my bachelor's table with okra from a July planting. More than that, I have put up about twenty quarts of nice, little, tender pods in the deep freeze.

Tell Dick I was mousing around yesterday in a forty-year-old file of the *Texan*, running down a date I needed, and Lo! out popped his name from a dim and dusty corner!

"Dick Fleming has got a two-mile parade up his sleeve."

I didn't have time to follow through and see whether or not he ever got it down from "up his sleeve." Maybe he will remember.

With much love for John, kisses for Louise, great respect for Paul, and affection generally for the whole household, I am

Yours,

Dad

[1]The book, *Educational Competition: The Story of the University Interscholastic League of Texas*, was published by the University of Texas Press in 1956.

November 26, 1954

Dear Bachman:

Yours of Nov. 15 contains four items of considerable interest to me, and just to indicate the width of my philosophic view, I enumerate them:

1. Reclamation of land after strip mining.
2. Nature-hike with John.
3. Jane's dancing.
4. Aeschylus' *Agamemnon* and *The Libation Bearers*.

Now for catholicity of interest, how's that? And I am not unaware of its bearing upon your interests also.

In south Texas there are great areas from which an overburden has been lifted in order to remove commercial gravel. The gravelmen have left the terrain in a terrible shape. Great mounds fifty feet high and hollows almost as deep that fill with water and breed mosquitoes. Even the river area here in the heart of Austin has been tossed and tumbled about by steam-shovels until we have a ghastly eye-sore all the way from Deep Eddy clear down below the Congress Avenue bridge.

I have been agitating in the papers and talks, public and private, the curbing of the river banks, deepening and straightening the channel from Deep Eddy to Montopolis, parking of the banks and instituting an herbarium of Texas vegetation. But the city administration is determined to build a dam down near Montopolis and have a lake. I claim a shallow lake will soon be nothing more than a swamp.[1]

The oxygen and information John gets on bird-hikes will have a mighty wholesome effect on his body and mind. You can't spend spare time to any better advantage than giving him instruction in Nature and awakening his interest therein. I notice that Westchester Co. is now the proud possessor of a Lewis Woodpecker. This bird is far, far, from home. I have seen the Lewis Woodpecker in New Mexico where he is common. I like to think of John's active mind wrestling with problems which Nature presents at every turn in the road. He is the age to wonder, and wonder is a kind of mental vitamin which stirs all the mental faculties. If grown people could wonder, they'd be much healthier mentally. The blasé are on the down road. And there are the morons who, Keats said, "giggle at a wonder." That was his phrase for the absolutely hopeless. Your mama and I got away from the rootin', tootin' Thanksgiving game yesterday by running out to the south bank of the Colorado in Zilker Park. We studied ducks, than which there is no other family of birds which presents such variety and tasteful arrangement of colors. We went on an aesthetic debauch absorbing the colors on the green-winged teel, the baldpate, the mallard, and the shoveller. We were entranced with the design and stylishness of the wonderful pintail, of which there were many. That crooked spear of white which rises along the side and follows the curvature of the graceful neck ending in a sharp point nearly opposite the bird's chin is really something so bold and still so delicate that it takes the breath away. Sometimes I feel genuinely intoxicated with color and design in the plumage of birds—genuinely, except that *this* intoxication leaves no headache or stomach ulcers.

The next thing to being beautiful is being useful. Keats (again) said a thing of beauty is a joy forever, but I say a thing of use is damned convenient. So amid all the praise that Jane may get for her dancing you should take some unction from the fact that scenery-moving has its place in the scheme of things. If one can't be *beautiful* he can at least serve beauty. And think what a *team* you two make.

In re Aeschylus and Euripides, I agree with Aristophanes in prefering A to E. In one of his take-offs on these two dramatists, the comic playwright sends Dionysus (figured as the Athenian audience) to hell to bring back Euripides to write another play. However, Dionysus returns with Aeschylus, reporting that he reached hell just at the conclusion of a great hell-wide competition in plays and Aeschylus had won out over Euripides.

*The Libation Bearers* was presented here a few weeks ago by the

University Drama Department. Your mother attended and thought it was a very creditable performance.

I am beginning to feel lost since finishing book, and having no set task to confront me every morning. I have never been in this situation since I was a boy. I don't know what to do with myself. That's one reason I am writing you such a hell of a long letter. I think I shall have to start another book whether I have time to finish it or not. It will keep me from the vice of writing long letters just to be doing. I think Edgar Allen Poe's argument proving that there can be no such a thing as a long poem applies equally to letters. When a letter begins to bore it's no longer a letter. I notice a disposition in myself to talk long, too— sign of old age. I bear in mind Hamlet's stricture on Polonious, "These tedious old fools."

I am going to send you and Jane a box of pecans, but the best I can find are not so good this year. The long drouth put a crimp in them.

If you have had the patience to read to this point you will see that I sign myself as ever with much affection,

Yours,

Dad

[1]Editor's Note: Roy Bedichek's prediction did not come true in this case. Town Lake in Austin is beautiful and much used.

November 26, 1954

Dear Jane:

I just wrote Bach that, having nothing else now to do, I have started in boring friends and relatives with letters. You seem to come next and I'll try hereafter not to take you out of turn. The burden should be distributed and maybe no one will kick much.

This is mainly to thank you for a clipping entitled "Age of Comfort Bad for Children." It goes into my file on that subject and being scientific it strengthens the case I have been making against this babying, physical and intellectual, that has been going on in this country for years. I sent you a couple of days ago a copy of the Interscholastic Leaguer with a good article by Dr. Rhea Williams on the present tendency to baby even football players. I think no mother or father or school teacher can do better than to read a chapter in Alexis Carrel's[1] *Man the Unknown* on adaptive mechanisms in the human body. Here this great anatomist gives sound basis for not babying the kids, or anyone else. Grown people shouldn't baby themselves, either. They should "welcome each rebuff that turns earth's smoothness rough."[2] We are built anatomically and physiologically for struggle, mental and physical, and we can't be healthy mentally or physically unless we constantly meet some challenge which puts us through our paces—strenuous paces, too. H. G. Wells' *Outline of World History* has a few chapters on how conquerors get soft and are then easy prey to peoples who stayed hard. Thousands of cases of this have happened, and are still happening and will continue to happen. Teddy Roosevelt was generally right in his *Strenuous Life* which had such vogue in my generation.

Henry George[3] tells a fable of a woodpecker that acquired absolute property in a big oak tree. No other woodpecker could come to that tree without paying this woodpecker-proprietor a nice fat grub for the privilege of hunting up and down the trunk and limbs of this big oak.

The proprietor was never hungry. It was a mighty soft life he lived there, sitting up on a limb and leaning against the trunk and eating nice fat grubs delivered punctually by his tenants. But a storm arose and the tree was blown down. No more fat grubs delivered. He got hungry and started pecking along the trunk of a tree, but found that the muscles in his neck wouldn't deliver a hard blow at all. And besides the point of his bill got tender and painful after a few pecks. And the poor fellow couldn't make a living and thereupon died.

I have a chapter in book on League entitled "Easyism" in which I criticize with whatever strength I have the damnable disposition of the public schools to baby the kids, everything must be made easy—plenty of electives, low grades passing grades—graduate if they stay in school long enough, etc. Absolutely nothing in some schools to challenge a vigorous child.

Well, enough is enough. I mustn't put your adaptive mechanisms [to] too severe a test in reading this letter.

We are quite well. We saw your mother and father a week or so ago and they were both in good fettle. Guess Lillian has told you about it, though. I always forget that I am not the sole dispenser of news of the Bedicheks.

Much love, and tell John, Louise and Paul that Grandma and Grandpa Gracy told Grandpa and Grandma Bedichek all about them and made us wish that we might associate with them, which, of course, we are looking forward to when they all come to Texas.

   yours,

   R.B.

[1] Alexis Carrel, French surgeon who won the 1912 Nobel Prize for medicine and physiology for developing a technique for suturing blood vessels, paving the way for organ transplants and blood transfusions.
[2] Robert Browning, "Rabbi Ben Ezra."
[3] Henry George, U.S. journalist whose *Progress and Poverty* saw the major cause of inequality as the possession of land.

December 21, 1954

Dear Bachman:

Your mother and I read your letter of the 16th together. At the conclusion, the fond mother sided with the son, but eliminated herself from the trip. I must go. She had been away a number of times and left me with the homebag to hold. Now this was an opportunity to let her pay her debt. (Of course, her stay of 4 months in California this last summer was by no means a pleasure-trip, but rather a terrible trial for her with lots of work and poor Sarah suffering right under her eyes the whole time.) But women don't reason: she slurred this over as if she had been lolling the whole time in one of California's most luxurious health and pleasure resorts.

However, if she is in earnest, and I have no doubt of it, it does eliminate or at least neutralizes one of my contentions against participating—i.e., that we both can't leave here at the same time. She had been arguing with me even before Jane's letter that I was due a visit with you and Jane in New York. Then I argued that her withdrawal broke up the party as proposed and would make the whole "dream" less attractive to the remainder, to which she replied that half a loaf was better than none, or something to that effect.

I then went over to the Press and talked with the manager about the book and he said of my services, a shift of my service of a couple or three weeks would make no difference in the date of the issue.

Your statement that the "camping" features should be eliminated greatly reduces the attractiveness to me, but I have been fooling with the idea that I might come by pickup and find a place in the environs of the respective motels in which you and Jane were housed. But that seems impracticable.

Your deadliest argument (no pun intended) is the one suggesting that this might be the last chance. That does hit me right in the core of my being, so to speak. In the large philosophic view, of course, farewells are futile, but in the intimate human sense, in what the philosophers call the "affective area," the appeal is overwhelming.

Your proposal to do something unreasonable is the very one with which my good friend W. P. Webb persuaded me about ten years ago to make a camping trip with him to the Chisos Mountains. And did we have a good time! Even Darwin set himself seriously once in a while to make a "fool experiment," a certain percentage of which proved to be fruitful. Coming back from the Chisos, Webb wanted me to promise him that we would do something utterly foolish at least once a year thereafter.

But I am minded also of another excursion of a similar nature which turned out disastrously, nearly costing the life of my good friend, Thomas Fletcher.[1] We planned a whole summer by correspondence a trip into the mountains of northern New Mexico. Every detail was laid out on the board and examined through the microscope; every possible fortuitous circumstance was rendered unfortuitous, as we thought; every contingency was sewed up in a good safe bag. We were off the middle of one September and such a joyous trip as we had to the mountains! But we had overlooked *one* thing: Tom's heart couldn't stand the altitude of our camp, 9,000 feet. The first night laid him out. We were completely isolated—not a human habitation in forty miles. Tom lay and groaned for two days and nights and got so weak he couldn't rise to a sitting position. He weighs 275 pounds, and you should have seen me in the third morning devising skids, and pulleys and ropes and whatnot to get him into the car. I was finally successful and got him to Santa Fe (itself 7,000 feet) and medical aid there said he must not be moved further until he got better. As soon as the medic said he could go and told me privately that unless he was promptly taken to a lower altitude he would die—just so soon, I loaded him in and in one day we drove to Plainview, Texas, (3,000 feet), and every mile I couldn't tell whether he was dozing or dying. Three weeks in a hospital at Plainview put him in condition for returning to Ft. Worth. As we were disembarking at his home he said, "Bedi, this has taught me how to enjoy a vacation." "How?" I asked. "Well, do just as we did this summer—take three months to plan the trip. Think up everything, every problem and solve it on paper. Dream about it. Enjoy the contemplation as well as the active, thoughtful preparation. Then, when the final moment comes, and you have your toe poised above the self-starter, change your mind and *don't go*."

So—shall we make this trip the Fletcher- or the Webb-way? It's worth considering. I am doing as you asked me to do, *re*-considering. In saying this, I do not have a secret conviction that it can't be done. I have opened my mind to the proposal.

One thing Jane was a little indefinite about was the time—how long can you two be gone? Another thing, what do you think of my coming in a pick-up? I could in a pick-up bring needed books and birding paraphernalia. Also, I could sleep better.

Really, I am *re*-considering, which only means what the dictionary says it means, "considering again."

Much love,
Dad

[1]Editor's Note: Thomas Fletcher was a fellow University of Texas student and fellow teacher in Houston.

March 23, 1955

Dear Bachman:
Since finishing the League book, I have become a divided and split-up man. The pieces don't fit and I can't find one that seems worth nursing along. I have permitted myself to become interested in a project assigned me by the newly born Heritage Society of Travis County, having as its purpose the preservation of things worthwhile from former generations—old houses, customs which have fallen into disuse, archives, and other things appealing to the generation that is passing out. Its active members are all rather old. By the way, at the last meet-

ing of the Board of Directors I found Dr. Duncalf,[1] looking much as usual.

I kept belaboring the Society about the destruction of natural beauty which I claimed is the greatest "heritage" yet. I deplored the sacrifice of 1000-year old liveoaks to filling stations, and the rooting out of native shrubs in favor of nursery exotics.

Well, I made myself so disagreeable that the Society created a committee for my chairmanship which I have called a "Land Policy Committee," purpose of which is to arouse a social consciousness of Austin's heritage of natural beauty and take some practical measures towards preserving it. My immediate purpose is to get the city dads to adopt a Land Policy in which I have included the following areas: (1) Streets and alleys; (2) Subdivisions proposed; (3) creek beds; (4) Colorado River bottom; (5) Parks and Prospective Parks; (6) Lake Travis; (7) Outdoor Advertising; and a final all-inclusive one (8). And any other area wherein the power of the municipal government may be exercised in behalf of preserving natural beauty.

Of course, each of these items may be indefinitely elaborated.

My procedure is to organize a federated committee to study and promote a proper "Land Policy," propagandize it, and finally after general agreement on plan is secured, present it to the city administration.

The more I get into it the more time it takes, and the more ramifications the thing has.

I am trying also to pursue my accustomed nature-studies, incorporating more fully certain conservation ideas I have picked up here and there. The Texas Director of the U. S. Department of Agriculture's Soil Conservation Service has taken me into his confidence and is giving me some memorable lessons which I hope to use later in some sort of a nature-book. He took me to the Brady Creek development last week, and this week to a remarkable conservation project including the area lying between the Little River and the San Gabriel. The part I visited the other day with one of the SCS men, a very competent young fellow, lay in the vicinity of Granger.

So you see I am turning to conservation, little and big, but there are many diversions. As a person retires, countless chores that no one else has time for are unloaded upon him since it is the general belief that when one is relieved of his job of making a living, he has time heavy on his hands. I find the fact just the reverse. I want to do more things right now than I ever did and have less time to do them in. You know how I like to get out among the spring flowers and migrating birds, and I pledge you my word I have not been out in a month. Just think! The golden-cheeked warbler should be coming in now and I haven't had a glimpse of one.

By the way, the martins returned in force. I have some six or eight pairs now building their nests. The screech owl hatched out her brood and is gone with them to taller timber. The golden-fronted woodpecker scorns the box I built especially for him; and the Bewick wrens have been scared away by a most ferocious cat belonging to one of our tenants (and therefore sacred). How I would like to deport this prowling predator.

News from you is getting scarcer and scarcer. How is the ancient coin business?[2] How are you standing the scorn of our present administration heaped upon Churchill? How about the new house? How is Dick's retirement affecting your status?[3] How is the fourth heir[4] progressing? These and dozens more questions arise as I think of the grand project you and Jane are engaged in: rearing a family. You two have made a most propitious beginning and your mother and I are mightily puffed up about it.

Love,
Dad

[1]Editor' Note: Frederick Duncalf, professor of medieval history at the University of Texas from 1914–1950. He was the uncle of Bach's best friend, Ernest Villavaso.
[2]Editor's Note: Bach was collecting late Roman coins, particularly Julian the Apostate, whose ideas on the oneness of all the gods is described with admiration in Gilbert Murray's *Five Stages of Greek Religion*, a book Roy Bedichek often quoted.
[3]Editor's Note: Richard Fleming, general counsel of Texas Gulf Sulphur, retired to Austin and Bachman succeeded him as general counsel.
[4]Editor's Note: Ellen Gracy Bedichek was born September 2, 1955.

December 22, 1955

Dear Josephine:

As the Roman poet observed about the Year 1, the years pass and are forgotten. My years certainly do. I am in my 78th year and so it must have been at least seventy years ago that we played around the old farm home of my "Uncle Joe Craven" in Illinois, but for only a brief period. How much of one remains after seventy years? Nothing, I suppose, except what my geneticist daughter would call a certain direction imparted by the genes in the chromosomes of which, of course nothing physical is left but the effect of the determinator (gene) still operating. What a piece of work is man!

I am glad to know that you are working at your hobby which must by this time have become a profession. The secret of staying young is mostly staying interested, and interested enough to make one active mentally and physically. Alas for those whose interests die before they do! I have three sisters, as you know; Ena, who must be 84, interested in painting, and she does pretty well at it; Ina who is eighty with a backyard garden and seven or eight "retarded" pupils who come to her everyday for instruction and inspiration; and Una, 76, just returning from a tour of the world, and hilarious over her adventures! Well, the Cravens or some strain that got mixed in with it certainly gave your family and mine genes that gave us lasting interests, a precious inheritance.

Mighty glad to hear from you, and hope you are having a merry Christmas.

Your "first"
Roy Bedichek

❦

April 1, (no foolin') 1956

John[1] is not interested in Nature, as such. He is interested in fish and how to get them out of the water. He is in the true phylogenic line, that is, he is now repeating the history of human culture about the beginning of the hunting-and-fishing period of our racial development. On our trip to Zilker Park yesterday morning I found that he couldn't handle my heavy binoculars at all. We forgot the light ones, and I think he will have to practice a good deal with Lillian's 3-power glasses before he can get any pleasure out of them. Then he may be able to control the tremor in the light Zeiss glasses—6X30. So our little stay with a bunch of ducks on the river yesterday morning, mixed in with coots was not productive. He was very polite but bored. There was little variety, however—all the ducks were gadwalls which have no color and coots (rather dull birds to look at) and a couple of grebes. Most of the bird-sounds during our walk came from the scolding, whistling, screaming long-tailed grackles. But they enlisted John's interest very little. He was interested in talking with fishermen along the banks of Barton's up to the pool and down the other side of the creek coming back to the bridge where we crossed over again and re-interviewed the fishermen from the bridge back to the point of beginning.

One boy about twelve years of age with a broken arm in a sling was still casting. He had been casting two hours before we saw him first and another hour between our two talks with him, and he hadn't had a single strike. Blessed boy, he was still as hopeful at every cast as he was with the first one. Such boys are born fishermen and business promoters and public relations men.

Going up towards the pool, we had talked with a little fellow across the creek who was completely absorbed with a drop-line. He told us he had caught several "nice ones," and continued his busy dropping of the line here and there, and climbing up this leaning tree and that over the water to capture fish that he declared had been jumping out of the water. We watched to see his efforts rewarded for a little while, but nothing came of it. As we came back on the other side, he was still at work. We asked to see the fish he had caught and he referred us to a can of water in which we found two perch, each about three inches long. Then we wanted to see the "nice" ones he had told us of. He became evasive and finally told us they were "staked out right up there." We searched bank "right up there" but couldn't locate the "string." I concluded (but not trustful John) that the boy was speaking from a rather "creative memory." We passed two canoes and hailed each one with the query "what luck?" The men rowing said they were out for the exercise and to make the kids (who had their lines out) think they were going to catch some fish.

John became interested in a line of leaf-carrying ants and we traced the line up the bank about twenty yards where the ants scattered. The ants which were carrying leaves over their backs met those going out empty-handed and now and then a little converse seemed to occur between the laden and unladen ones. Perhaps the ones going out were asking "where'd you get that nice one," quite as anxious for information as John and I were to find a good place to fish. I didn't speculate to John, however, because nature-faking and humanizing animals I think is a poor way to enlist interest in nature. They then begin to look for the wrong things. He noticed that a bed of our big Texas ants were a different breed. I told him something of the stinging ability of our big Texas ants and he became skittish at once and began avoiding them as if he thought they could jump a yard or two. Then he stopped a little over a hill of teeny-weeny little ants, noting that they were still different. He dismissed flowers, too, but very politely. His interest is fish and by golly he is going to get some fish right on his own line if there are any to be had within a reasonable distance of Austin. He has another interest—that is Indian relics, but the mounds are all monopolized by the Anthropology Department of the University to satisfy the field work of the students. Dr. Campbell told me of one location near Round Rock and I went over there the other day only to find three mounds utterly ransacked and sifted down to the last pebble the size of a pea. I know the location of one mound that has never been touched some twenty miles beyond Lampasas, and of another near Utopia south of San Antonio about fifty miles but they are far too far away.

John and I got back from our round among the fishermen about 11:30 and Lillian had a wonderful lunch under way. John consumed an apple with avidity. But that seemed to kill his appetite, for he ate only a helping of beets, three buttered biscuits and a glass of milk. Refused other vegetables and meat. His indoor interest is to learn a game of cards. His grandmother is undertaking to satisfy this yen. Yesterday about two P.M. Grandpa Gracy came for him to take him out to the farm and in order that he may become properly groomed for Easter services this morning. Mrs. G. insists on our coming over to lunch today and we are to bring the grandson back with us. Lillian and I are to go out for a day and a night starting Monday where there are real not imaginary fish.

    RB

[1]John was almost eight years old at this time.

[Replying to August 23, 1956, letter from Gay Carroll]

Dear Gay:

Even though there seems to be an undercurrent of a troubled mind in your letter, I must say that I enjoyed getting from you an account of your daily doings & thinkings. Irrespective of our in-law relationship, you are one of my heroes because of the courage, industry and perserverence you have shown in battling difficulties to a standstill. I often think of you patching up mangled humanity and of what a blessing your calling is to those upon whom those tragic accidents fall. I shall never forget your ward wherein I saw human beings in all kinds of weird positions, stretched, spread, hung up by the toes, bent, twisted and distorted in order that whatever was left of them might come back as nearly normal as possible. This is a grand, heroic work. I can think of no other vocation which so visibly, obviously, and immediately fulfills the direction Jesus gave to his disciples, "Go, heal the sick." Whatever minor troubles you think you have, this consolation (which so many lack) of having a lifework so unquestionably worthwhile should keep them pretty well anaesthetized. I have never been able to completely convince myself that my vocation (anyone of the many I have engaged in) was really beneficial to my fellow mortals. So, you have me there, and I have not been without the incidents that seem to be troubling you now.

I wonder if you have some vague, half subconscious feeling that you are not really entitled to a half day vacation each week in which you are perfectly free to do as you damn please? If so, banish the thought. You are not only entitled to it, but it is your bounden duty to take it. From the standpoint of mental health, I consider a hobby absolutely a necessity for every normal human being. I care not what it is so long as it is not criminal. A man with a genuine vocation, must have an avocation, that is a "calling away" from his vocation. He must forget for a while his vocation in a complete absorption in some other activity, else he goes stale. Expense is not to be considered in this matter. I have a hobby which is far more expensive than any banker-creditor could possibly approve of considering my age and income. I buy two hundred dollar binoculars; I have a $2,000 pick-up principally for camping out, and I never hesitate to buy on account of the price anything that I think will really minister to my hobby. And I have done it for years.

And don't fret about the worthwhileness of your hobby, for you do not have the option of choosing it—it chooses you. I am delighted with your boat-adventure. I'll bet the making of it brought you more mental and emotional rest than anything else you could have spent a like amount of time and money on.

I understand from Mary that I am to see you soon, and I look forward to it with great pleasure.

Nothing is better than a hobby that satisfies primordial, or what one may call, "racial memories." Hunting or fishing, or camping out takes one back not only to his own boyhood but to the boyhood of the race, when the animal man lived in the open or in a cave or under a rock-shelter and took his prey as other wild animals did and do. Millions of years of this have left an impress in some mysterious way upon his emotional mechanism. Indulging the hunting and fishing instinct is all but universal with civilized man. He doesn't always realize it but he is re-enacting experiences built into his heredity. It seems to be a kind of going-back-home of the human spirit.

All this may seem a little mystical, but it is a view science is coming to tolerate if not adopt.

Sincerely yours,

Roy Bedichek

October 15, 1956

Dear Mr. Bedichek:

Can you still get *Adventures* . . . and *Karankaway Country*? I had a few copies which I have let get away. We have only autographed copies in the house now. I am surprised at the number of people who are interested in these books. Some of them live in the section you wrote about in *Karankaway Country*. They seem to make excellent reading for the hospitalized patients.

Today I went to get a copy of *Adventures* . . . for a 55-year-old lady with a broken hip. The sales lady at Coblers looked at my copy shook her head and said "I'll see if it is still available." Then, "Yes, I can order it for you." At Foleys it was the same story. At Brown's two different girls looked for it on the shelves, and then looked it up in their catalog to see if it is available. Before leaving I showed it to the manager. He took only a quick glance at the book and said, "I wish I had a hundred copies—also a hundred of *Karankaway Country*. He said none of his orders had been filled lately.

Before putting in an order and waiting a few weeks on delivery I thought I would check with you. If you can have someone in Austin send me about 6 copies of each book C.O.D. to 10 Chelsea I will appreciate it very much. If you could possibly enscribe your name in them it would be better.

I appreciate your recent letter, and although it is not at hand now, I remember some of the contents. So far as personal satisfaction from my work goes, I believe that without the feeling you describe very few people would be in the practice of any branch of medicine. We are human beings though, and some of us think highly of the dollar bill. There is a little work involved but I think the one who limits his practice as we do has an easy life compared to the general practioner. He has to take the calls as they come from the patient at the office and home, at the emergency rooms, etc. He sees more patients for smaller fees and works long hours. About 90% of my patients come from other doctors. They usually talk with me first about them. I have two people to serve—the patient and the doctor. Some of it is straight charity but I know it in advance. On one day a doctor will call me to drive 50 miles or more to operate on an insurance case with a sure fee. The next day or so he may ask the same service for a charity patient. He gets the same service, too. Last Thursday I drove to Freeport 50 miles and did two operations. Friday I was back again for one and Saturday was back again for two more. Tomorrow I go to Conroe for one. Two weeks ago I drove to Conroe to operate on a patient's leg—straight charity. 2 months ago I operated on her shoulder—straight charity. In between have been two or three visits just to check her progress.

Still, people in general must be falling for the socialized medicine propaganda. I honestly believe those who need medical care—in any walk of life are getting it. I have never known of a case where a doctor refused treatment because of the fee. In fact the patients have usually had their service before the doctor knows whether they can pay or not. Still—medical care makes a good football for the politicians to kick around. Government medicine of course is no longer a thing of the future—it is here now. The recent bill providing care to the families of service men at government expense is the first victory. That bill provides for the wife or child of a military man to go to her private physician for treatment and the bill is paid directly by the government. Blue Cross gets a cut for handling the bookkeeping.

I also have certain organized charity work to do. For 3 months of the year I spend all of Tuesday morning in the Shrine Cast Clinic. For that I used to get one Coca Cola—now nothing. A second three months required that I give all of Thursday morning and all of Wednesday afternoon to the general Shrine Clinic and to the Adult Orthopedic Clinic. During this 3 months I also have to help the residents in the operating room on one other morning in the week. Also during this three month's service I have to help the residents on emergency orthopedic surgery—at night or whenever it occurs. We have a staff of 10 qualified orthopedists in charge of these clinics—the cream of the profession in Houston I believe—and any man, woman, boy or girl whether white, black or otherwise who has an orthopedic problem, and is unable to pay private fees can come and be cared for. The children are straight charity and the adults are required to pay a very small fee. Still, if you listen to the shouting, the poor people of Houston are not getting the medical care they need.

I have re-read down to here and know I should tear this letter up. I don't know why I am expounding in such a way. I suppose Adlai's TV speech the other night is the stimulus.

As an after thought, any needy *child* not only in Houston but in the entire *State of Texas* can come to the Shrine Clinic and Hospital for treatment at no charge. We usually get them after Hedgecroft Clinic, Gonzales Foundation and a few others have gotten all the polio insurance money at about $25.00 per day—or has wrecked the father's financial structure—whatever it is. This is bitterness—but truth, and a situation not known to many.

On the brighter side, our family is in good health and all are happy. School is in full swing. The summer holiday has dwindled to weekend fun. We have had several boat rides, and I have had two fishing trips to the bay.

I believe I can now greet Mrs. Bedichek, who, I understand, is back from New York. I hope you had a wonderful trip, that you are glad to be back in Texas, and that you will be checking up on Houston again some time soon.

Sincerely

Gay

January 22, 1957
801 East 23rd Street
Austin 5, Texas

Dear Bach:

Your powerfully succinct letter cannot be so succinctly answered, for I have not had your training in writing contracts. My training and indeed, my inclination, runs to the diffuse and the discursive.

Yes, I have decided not to brave the northern winter cold. I'm soft by living too long in this damnably debilitating climate. So I shall await the spring.[1]

Can't make up my mind about the means to use in making this transit. I have Greyhound Bus Co. working on a schedule which will give me stop off at nights to sleep. Then I long once again to see the open sea, and have actually considered a boat from Galveston. Then when I think how much fun it is to camp I look longingly upon my pick-up and imagine how I would pack it and how nice it would be to schedule myself for a night camp in national parks strung along the way. And then, of course, there is the airplane. If it weren't for fear of high-powered traffic in the big cities, I would surely make a camping trip out of it.

Bird list is very attractive. To give you an idea of what the drouth has done to us, your mother and I spent all afternoon along the lakes on the Widen place near Dripping Springs and were able to count only two birds, a bluebird and a mourning dove!

I deeply sympathize with your attitude towards the current administration.[2] It is stupidity thrice compounded with the most naive hyprocisy I have ever known with a substantial ingredient (I fear) of ordinary graft. What a holier-than-thou attitude the President assumed in cuddling up to that disgusting little whipper-snapper, Nasser, while humiliating England and France. The seizure of the Suez was an aggression he condoned, as he did the nightly raids on Israel and the shutting out of Israeli ships from the canal, as well as India's palpable aggressions. The secret of all this is oil—I think, perhaps, *our* oil interests welcome the displacement of English oil interests. Maybe all this with a parade of high thoughts and noble aspirations is founded deep down in a nasty mess of oil-rivalries. And of course, Texas oil interests own a good part of the Senate through Lyndon Johnson, and a smaller part of the House through Rayburn.[3] I'm hoping the newly formed democratic council will be able to evict the infiltrators from the democratic party.

I know your mother will greatly enjoy your letter when she returns, for you say so vigorously what she tries all the time to say about Eisenhower, but chokes up with pure indignation.

Your mother was to return yesterday, but I think she and Irma[4] are having such a hell of a good time that she will prolong her stay. Hope she does. I am making out fine on salads of my own, along with a vegetable stew now and then. Am doing some satisfactory writing, too, while my winter garden is the delight of the neighborhood since I share my triumphs with anyone who seems to appreciate them: the Van Cleaves, dear old Mrs. Alsup (nearly dead), the Dodges, the tenants upstairs, and the Davids across the street in the old Spruce place.

"And thus I keep this instrument in tune."

Jane, I love you; kids you're too precious for any words in my vocabulary. I'm looking forward to visit with fondest of fond anticipations.

Dad


P.S. I just don't know what to do with this check, returned and re-returned. I'm not used to getting a Christmas present of $100. Never got one for more than a tenth of that amount in my life. If I keep it I'll spend it foolishly and may sometime really need it. Wouldn't it be better for you to do as some fathers do their irresponsible sons—create a fund for them out of which to dole small amounts from time to time suited to the measure of their irresponsibility? Don't think I do not appreciate your intentions, but . . . but . . . but . . .

R.B.

[1]Editor's Note: Roy Bedichek is planning a trip to visit Bachman and family in New York.
[2]Present government under Dwight D. Eisenhower.
[3]Sam Rayburn, Speaker of the House of Representatives.
[4]Editor's Note: Irma Nabors Johnson, her cousin, part of the Lee clan in Louisiana. Irma's younger sister Sue was mother of Josh Logan, playwright. Irma, Sue and Lillian were all born on the Lee plantation, Keatchie, Louisiana. Sue Logan Noble, living in New York City, got theater tickets for her sons' hit shows for Bach and Jane, hosted Lillian when she came to visit them, and gave them all background on Broadway gossip.

[Written and mailed from Scarsdale, New York, sometime before February 14, 1957]

Dear Grandfather Bedichek:

The minite I herd that you were planing to stay only two weeks, I knew that was not ennuff time to do half the things we [plan]. So if you are going to come at all you shud stay about a moth if not mor.

[Here] are some of the things we will set up to do. Take severl caping trips. Take several walks along the Bronx River paths. Go Hayden plantarium. Help me, Louise and Paul with our gardens. Help Dady with the block house, Help me with my trains. Make long walks at Greenwich Audubon Center, take the boat up the Hodson River.

Much Love
John the Graet Greer Bedichek

❦

February 14, 1957

Dear Jane:

The "Dear B. Family" enjoyed that letter of yours immensely, and John's letter (did you see it?) was a complete knock-out. Enclosed is my paper on soil-water conservation in Texas.[1] You have in the Brandywine basin and watershed near Scarsdale exactly the program I contend for in this state, viz. impoundments upstream, land treatment practices to prevent erosion and therefore prevent silting up of reservoirs down stream. In short retain the water where it falls by every device possible and then let it pass on down from the watershed into the channels of streams clear of sediment and pollution in order to bless every human being living along the courses all the way to the respective mouths, and on to the sea.

The opposite view is that of the Army Engineers and generally of the Bureau of Reclamation, viz, great impoundments on middle and lower courses of streams. I am not against that either, if, (and it's a BIG IF) the watersheds and upper courses of the river are so treated as to prevent the erosion of soil and consequent siltation in a relatively short time of the down stream reservoirs.

When you finish with this copy of the paper, please return it.

Yours, as ever,
Roy Bedichek

<sup>1</sup>Editor's Note: Preparing to speak on water policy at a League of Women Voters meeting, I wrote asking his opinion on the issue. This letter was his response to my query.

March 12, 1957

Dear Bachman:

A sea-trip would be fine, and I thank you very much for your trouble in locating one for me passage-free. However, I can't tie myself to a date quite so definitely. I plan to arrive New York along with the warblers, say April 27, 28, 29, or 30—"Thirty days hath Sept., *April*," etc. So I am hoping to be with you, or "yawl," latter days of April and early days of May.

Transportation I found to be a simple matter and cheaper than I ever dreamed. I had the Greyhound bus make a schedule with a stopover every night in a good bed in a good hotel, and at that it takes only five days and costs, hotel-room included, only $125, round trip. Can you believe it. That will give me a chance to talk to the laity, such as ride the buses, and gather information as I proceed northeastward. This will keep me entertained, keep me fresh, keep me (most important of all) in a good humor. I had myself routed back via Chicago. I shall return a much-traveled man with oceans of lore. So I am anticipating a great time, going, staying and coming back. Mighty great treat, now that I've decided to do it. I am anticipating only one fly in the ointment, and that is fear of being "entertained," of being made trouble over, but I quiet myself by thinking of how much hard horse sense reposes in the two adult noggins at 4 Kingston Road. As a matter of fact I could hardly prepare a better prospectus than John delivered in 8 "musts," each duly numbered consecutively.

Now don't build me up to the kids for it would be a big green fly in the ointment if I left there feeling that they had been disappointed in me.

Affectionately,
Dad

*396*

[Written on Hotel St. James stationery, Knoxville, Tennessee]

April 18, 1957

Dear Honey:

The phone rang & rang right at my bedside this morning & could not break my sleep. Finally, I staggered around the room vaguely conscious of some racket which I must stop. I had left a call for 5 A.M. & this racket proved to be it. I tell you this to prove that the bus & a good conscience giveth sound slumber.

Yesterday was my longest bus-day of the whole trip—13 hours. I got into a hot argument with my seatmate leaving Chattanooga last night. He was fat and pompous in striking checkered coat, diagonally striped tie, ochre and red, & a big diamond on little finger of left hand. Physically, he crowded me into the wall of the coach, but argumentatively, I had him almost in the aisle. He had a big face and flashing brown eyes to match & a temper less under control than mine. He believed passionately in everything that I passionately disbelieved.

| He/Antinomies: | /Me |
|---|---|
| E.[1] the greatest Pres. of U.S. | The worst. |
| Attack Russia *now* | Never attack Russia |
| Summerfield right | S. wrong |
| Reduce Inc. Tax to 25% | Increase with steep gradation |
| Damn the Jews | Bless the Jews |
| Damn the niggers | Treat 'em right |
| T.V.A.[2] a failure | T.V.A. success |
| No danger in nuclear bomb | Great danger in it |
| etc. | |
| etc. | |
| etc. | |

So after a swerving, bouncing bus trip in mt. roads we ended at station 9 A.M. both heated up, but parting cordially. He accompanied me in friendliest way to the Hotel above named. I found out that he owned and operated a chain of movies here in Tenn. Fulton Lewis, in his opinion, is the "smartest" commentator in America.

Rain & clouds continue. Sun for half hr. or so yesterday. Dogwoods & redbud in glorious rivalry in among the dark pines all across Tenn.

Hope everything, including garden, is proceeding normally. Am expecting a word from you when I reach Rockville tomorrow.

Love
Bedi


P.S. Clothes still comfortable.

[1]Eisenhower.
[2]Tennessee Valley Authority, U.S. federal agency responsible for developing the water and other resources of the Tennessee River Valley.

April 27, 1957
1012 Paul Drive
Rockville Md.


Dear Lillian—

Thank God for the rains, but of course with a word of disapproval of the apparent violence of His goodwill. We could really (even my garden) do with a little less—and the 10 inches in some areas we must set down to godly carelessness. The washing out of the ground of 23 corpses duly and religiously buried at McGregor is of course carrying the thing a bit too far.

Sarah, the Indomitable, is maintaining the schedule, unperturbed by any circumstances that may arise. The best hours of the morning, viz. 5 to 10 or thereabouts are given over to the Seneca Canal where birds abide in the glory of mating plumage and the activity of "amorous conflict" as Balzac called this particular mammalian frenzy. Now our list stands at 57 species, & like an intense auctioneer, she is pleading and demanding, "make it 60."

It is now 5 A.M. & Sarah is sitting by pretending to read but inwardly impatient to be off. George goes with us, hanging on after all the rest have dropped away on one pretext or another. She has not felt a touch of asthma since last of December and looks healthy & vigorous. Her skin is clear & fresh & she is very active—I really am amazed at her tremendous vivacity.

I am o.k.—feel fine—had dinner along with Allen [sic] & Sarah with McTeers[1] yesterday.

Time's up & no foolin'. Am leaving 7 A.M. tomorrow for N.Y.

Much love

Bedi

P.S. George arrives and at mention of "Grandma" his eyes sparkled. I asked for a "message" & he said, "Tell her that yesterday near 'Old Angler's Inn' we found some pepper-plants which popped their seeds out & up when you touched them." RB

[1]John McTeer and his wife were friends from the Deming, New Mexico days of 1910.

May 11, 1957
Scarsdale, N.Y.

Dear Honey—

In spite of all the gracious efforts of Jane, & Bach and Johnny and Bill,[1] I begin to yearn for the fleshpots of freedom. I can't abide having my hours apportioned and provided for, designated for this and for that. I have always rejected pre-destination. I am entangled in a web of solicitude and find my noble spirits kicking like a caught fly. So I am adhering rigidly to my schedule. I am leaving all the allurements of these lovely people and of the great city at 9 A.M. May 20, &, God willing, should reach home as per schedule you have.

Too many impressions impinge upon consciousness in too brief a time. There's no chance for the digestive process to do its work. My memory, even, is overwhelmed. I can scarcely recall even in outline what I did day before yesterday. And the roaring of NY Central commuters' trains every few minutes as I take a morning walk along the Bronx River, & the lesser hum & swish of autos, & the enormous surging crowds in the city—all keep me in a subterranean stew. So away to the wide open spaces. Not to say that I am at all unhappy, but I am simply looking *forward*.

Bedi

[1]Editor' Note: Johnny (John Henry) Faulk had a radio program spinning Texas tales, quoting often Dobie and Bedichek. Bill (William) Owens, who taught at Columbia University, School of General Studies, and later wrote *Three Friends: Bedichek, Dobie, Webb* in 1967 and edited *Letters of Roy Bedichek* in 1985.

May 15, 1957

Dear Una:

In re your suggestion in a recent letter concerning the similarity of our respective "callings" as they have become more obvious with our advancing years, I quite agree.[1] The differences are of emphasis rather than of intent and belief. I think both of us are somewhat animated by a desire to do our fellow mortals good. We both believe in health, mental and physical. I think my emphasis has been on the physical side, but clearly connected with the spiritual side in that I believe the body is important only because it keeps the spirit in tune to hear and to act upon the promptings of the "still small voice" which Elijah heard after he heard the great wind, and the earthquakes, and other seemingly overpowering forces of nature, in each of which we are assured by the writer that God was not in it. But God was in the voice which said "what dost thou here?" that's the question everyone who lives above the purely animal level asks himself sooner or later.

We are spirit and flesh—they seem to me to be two worlds. Perhaps you sense them as one. Christian Science is a magical combination of words—it suggests the coalition of the two worlds, the seen and the unseen, the spiritual world and the world of sense experience. Your work and mine include both, but you approach from one side, and I from the other. Something of the sort, it seems to me.

Much love,

Roy Bedichek

[1]Roy's sister, Una, was a Christian Science practitioner.

[May or June 1957]

Dear Gay:

I have had the impulse several times to write you and Mary about your decision to move to Freeport, but the truth is I have been off my feed every since I got back from my six weeks in Washington and New York and aboard a bus. I am just now, this morning for the first time, feeling in a condition to hammer the typewriter for a little while.

One of my chief worries for the past several years has been the enormous mileage you have been compelled to travel in order to do your practice. It has seemed to me inordinate and an unnecessary drain on your vitality, as well as being heinously dangerous. I have pulled you mangled out of auto wrecks quite a number of times in my dreams. A man will slip sometimes when he gets too tired whether he is driving a car or walking against a fence-post, and I have been very fearful of the hazards you were taking in your weekly trips to Freeport. The move, as I understand it, will do away with this, and if for no other reason, I feel that the move is necessary.

There is a lot of fiction as I have lately learned about the advantages of life in the city. If one takes it seriously (and only confirmed philosophers as I am can refuse to take it seriously) it becomes a kind of rat race in which the more significant values in life are forgotten, or ignored. In your case, the time-element alone should be the deciding factor. Think what you can do and think of the time you have been spending in an automobile on the road! It is incalculable.

During the past thirty years many of my friends have chosen to move to the country and I have been constantly urged to do so. But when I have considered getting into a car every working day and driving ten or fifteen miles to the environs of Austin and then fighting the traffic for at least another half hour to get to my office, I have turned it down, and I'm damn glad I did. In the early days, of course, the problem of getting the children to school and home again made such an arrangement prohibitive.

The simple mathematics of it is convincing enough. Say it had taken me two hours a day to go and come, including, of course, extra trips to town. That is conservative. Two hundred working days in the years would have put me in the automobile for a straight 400 hours, or in thirty years, 12,000 hours. That means 1600 working days at 8 hrs per day. In other words four or five years of my working life would

*401*

have been consumed. One really does not have that much time to spare from his life. The offset, some of my friends claim, is that they *think* in an auto. Well, I don't, especially in traffic. My mind is generally idle except for watching the car and making fleeting observations of this or that. I think most people deceive themselves when they say they do constructive thinking anything like as effective in an auto as they do under office- or home-conditions. So I stuck near my work and took my outings voluntarily and not under any compulsion.

Then there is the expense of transportation. But enough. I approve of the decision, if that is any comfort. And I would choose a residence in Freeport as close to my work as possible.

I found poor Sarah and Bachman, too, in a kind of rat-race. Bachman is against the long transportation problem every day. He commutes and it takes a good two hours out of each working day. Of course, he has the advantage of a commuter's train, but must endure the slam-bang, starting, stopping, tunnels, crowds, etc. At that, he can think and read which is not possible in an auto. I suppose one could become conditioned to commuting, but in my short experience with it I could not. I can't think when I am jostled, when I have to watch for my station, when someone beside me sticks the corner of his newspaper under my nose, etc. But the seasoned commuters seem to like it. Bachman really has done a lot of good sound reading while on the morning train, and in the afternoon he keeps up with the news by reading a couple or more newspapers. But, reading or not reading, there is a tension of nerves which gives the commuter (in my imagination only, perhaps) a hunted look. I saw hardly a serene face in New York.

I'm one of those physicians who believes in the therapeutic values of absolute solitude. Here at home I can take a dose every day and I know it does me good.

While I can't get the religious comfort that many do out of solitude, I do get, it seems to me, a sort of stability, that is, firm ground to stand on while dealing mentally with the natural trials and tribulations which come to us all.

Sarah and Alan each has a worse transportation problem than Bachman has or than you have been having. It takes Sarah a good hour to get to her laboratory and another hour to get back. Alan is little better situated. They are now negotiating for another place to live which will partially cure the trouble, but not entirely.

Bachman has not only the transportation—two hours per day—but a large home place to take care of, including some actual construction work. Even under daylight-saving he has few daylight hours at home, except Saturdays and Sundays. Then four children! Sweet and lovely, but like all children, noisy and demanding. I verily believe I had a better chance to do something than my children have had, although they have had the opportunity of a better education, certainly a more orderly education, than I ever had. So it goes! But the rat-race element in the lives of the present generation seems to me the main defeating factor—I mean defeating insofar as a happy and serene life is concerned.

Well, well, I didn't mean to write you a book.

Much love for distribution among all six of you.

Roy Bedichek

PS—I haven't said a word about the scholarship and athletic honors won by your eldest, or of the pleasure Lillian had out of the visit from Mary and "kinder," as the Germans say. But that will have to wait a special letter. R.B.

August 30, 1957

Dear Jane:

It is a boon to this lonesome widower to be reminded so delightfully that he has kith and kin in the world. Your letter and Mrs. Gracy's note enclosed in the same envelope crossed in the mail a note which I wrote you back just yesterday, and the crossing occurred on my front doorstep, since the same postman on the same trip took my note to you and delivered yours to me.

I am pleased that you and Bach and the two older progeny have been out where you can get a good look at the firmament—birds, bees, animals and other living things sentimentally referred to as God's creatures. I recently was with a family from Dallas (Allen Maxwell,[1] wife and three lovely children, about 6, 8 and 11, respectively). I showed these kids the Milky Way for the first time in their lives, out there on the crest of the bluff overlooking Hamilton's Pool.[2] They were greatly

403

intrigued by the stars. They were surprised at the great number of them. Allen explained to me that they live in a well-lighted area in Dallas, where "God's illumination" plays a poor second to man's. They showed a profound ignorance of what I meant by the rise and set of the sun.

Of course, I suppose I'm a special pleader for Nature, but the ignorance of this generation of city children in the ordinary physical features of our own earth and our own galaxy, our own little island universe, is having a profoundly deleterious effect not only on their intelligence but on their moral characters. So I am naturally pleased that you and Bach are letting your progeny have an opportunity to wonder, for wonder is the parent of aspiration, and aspiration is the driving power responsible for man's being now on a level a little above that of other animals living on this planet—for details of which dictum see Browning's *Paracelsus*. Certainly Paracelsus would never have said "Festus, I plunge," had not his wonder and aspiration aroused him to that pitch. Does this all bore you? If so, take it on faith. And if you know it already, which you probably do, then take it as one other person's confirmation.

Tell your mother I appreciate her note and am glad, indeed, that she and Mr. Gracy have decided on the trip to Europe. I know they will have a gorgeous time, and I am expecting to hear of it *in extenso* when they return to Austin. Give my love to them and to the four darlings, and believe me

Always sincerely yours,

Roy Bedichek

P.S. I shall not forward your note to Lillian, for I think she will probably leave Washington before the letter could be delivered to her there. RB

---

[1] Allen Maxwell, editor, *Southwest Review* and Southern Methodist University Press.
[2] Editor's Note: Hamilton's Pool is a beautiful natural pool within a cave fed by a waterfall thirty miles from Austin.

December 20, 1957

Dear Dad,

I "sort of get the shivers" along with the W-T[1] editorial writer when I contemplate the implications of the testimony related in the editorial. It gives me the feeling that I have been through all this before in centuries, millennia past. The morning Sputnik I was announced, John, who has a perceptive mind and a great interest in that sort of thing, asked me "Daddy, are we going to be like the Roman Empire, *fall*, you know?"

I told him that I did not know, but that there was a deadly parallel—Honorius, Emperor of the West, 395–423 AD[2] lived shut up in his impregnable fortress of Ravenna, and was so stupid that he didn't even know the Empire had fallen! It seems we have had to wait 1500 years for comparable stupidity, but at last it has been achieved. (I think I may have written this before.)

We have had excellent luck with our backyard feeding station, until the squirrels discovered how to get at it. Up to that point, however, we had the following:

    1. English Sparrow
    2. White Throated sparrow
    3. Downey Woodpecker
    4. Hairy Woodpecker
    5. Slate colored Junco
    6. Robin
    7. Starling
    8. Black capped chickadee
    9. Tufted titmouse
    10. Cardinal

We do enjoy seeing the little creatures only a few feet away and the children are really learning to know them.

    Much love to you and Mother,
    Bach

[1]*World Telegram.*
[2]Editor's Note: Bach had selected for his coin collection a gold solidus of Honorius which showed the emperor with his foot on a captive.

February 23, 1958

Dear John:[1]

I was glad you remembered me with a valentine. I think of you very often. Sometimes when I am out camping, I think of you and wish that you were along. But I am not doing much camping any more. This winter has been very poor for camping, as it has rained almost continuously. A friend of mine and I went out about two weeks ago and it rained on us all the time. It was not a hard soaking rain but a drizzle and a sprinkle now and then, just enough to keep us at camp and hovering over a fire. It was hard to build a fire, as the wood was wet, but we managed to do it. We finally accumulated such a huge supply of hot ashes that we cooked all the vegetables in the hot ashes: cabbage, onions, potatoes, etc. We were camped by a huge cement or rock reservoir which was kept filled with water by a windmill pump. There was a two-inch iron pipe leading from the windmill to the reservoir under which we had to go to get from the campfire to our beds. It was just head-high and my friend bumped his head so hard against it that he nearly fell down. Each time we went under after that I told him to duck his head, and one time I forgot (although telling him) to duck my head and I hit it fair and square with my forehead and went down to the ground all sprawled out. Although it's bad manners to laugh at someone else getting hurt, still my friend laughed and still laughs when he tells it on me. Well, when we decided it was going to keep raining and raining, we gave up the camp and packed the truck for home. Then the truck wouldn't start. The engine had gotten wet. After scouting around for a couple of hours to find some help, we met a ranchman with a wife and a couple of children, girls they were and twins and very pretty. My friend decided to go on to Dripping Springs, about fifteen miles and get a garage man to come out and start the car. After he left I persuaded the ranchman to come and give me a boost over a down-hill road to see if I couldn't get the engine started. Well, he did. He worked about an hour pushing me around until he got me to the edge of the hill. Then I got a start downhill, rockety, rockety, bump, bump, bump, which nearly threw me out of the car. But I got the engine started, and I was off. However, I stopped until he overtook me and I gave each twin a dollar bill for I knew, being a ranchman, he wouldn't take a tip. I picked my friend up in Dripping Springs, and we came on home.

So, that's what camping in Texas is like when it's wet. Hoping we may have a camping trip together like we had in New York[2] and that it doesn't rain on us again, as it did when you and grandma and I were up

on the Marshal Ford Lake, I am
    with much love,
    Granddaddy

[1] Grandson John was at this time nine years old.
[2] Editor's Note: Roy and Bachman had taken John and Paul on an overnight camping trip to Ward Poundridge Reservation, Westchester County Park, New York.

July 9, 1958

Dear Bachman:

Your letter from Cape Cod made me feel that I had recaptured several years from that menacing eighty which the calendar handed me on June 27. The form, the fresh air in it and the solid content of it delighted me. I am especially glad to note from your bird-list that you are interested in behavior. That is really the intriguing thing about bird-watching. So many bird-watchers make a competition of mere listings. Identification comes first of course, and is of importance before anything else since faulty identification nullifies all other observations. But after the bird is identified the next big thing is "How does he act? What does he do?" Food, migration, mating, associations, plant and animal, and so on. And you can't get this point of view fixed too early in the children.

I am especially pleased also with the whole-family outing. Nothing is better for peace in the home than common experiences of outing together. If one stays here and another goes there this tie of common experiences is not tied. I am much gratified from reading a letter to her folks from Cape Cod that Jane is taking what many women would consider a calamity as an incident, a matter of course, a part of life.[1] It is fortunate that you have a satisfactory maid, which liberates the older children and you and Jane to make excursions together without the serious handicap of caring for a very small child.

We are expecting Mary this morning with her four daughters. She will take two of them, Jane and Lillian Lee, on over to San Antonio tomorrow to participate in a tennis tournament. She will leave Louise and Sarah with us until the tournament is over. I hope to let Louise demonstrate to me what a swimmer she is. Guess I'll be taking her out

407

to Barton. For her age they say she's tops.

From three and a half short rows of tomatoes, I have gathered already about 60 pounds of fruit and am still gathering. We have put up forty-odd quarts of juice and pulp in the deep freeze. We are deep freezing plenty of black-eyed peas and have a horde of corn on the cob from early May. I manage with my power mower to take care of the lawn at home and also the one at 800 Manor Road.

My book is going along.[2] Had a bite from a publisher the other day, but I fear it will be hard to sell. Of course, I'm not near done with it yet, and the subject becomes very unwieldy in spots.

Sarah writes that she is coming to Austin for three days early in November for a celebration in honor of her old instructor, J. T. Patterson. Meantime she is journeying to Minneapolis on some sort of mission with a consignment of flies.

Your reaction to Sherman Adams and Eisenhower is very much my own. Some of the cracks they are getting off about the case are very funny, but I can hardly laugh for I consider the whole mess a national disgrace.

Give Jane and the chillun my love, pat Paul on the head for me as one ornithologist to another, and tell John I think his robot with 106 electrical connections is marvelous, and believe me affectionately your

Eighty-year-old Dad

[1]Editor's Note: Bach and I were expecting our fifth child—Robert Caldwell Bedichek—born September 6, 1958. We had planned to have only three children. Bach consoled me saying, "Don't worry, Honey, he will probably be the joy of our old age." He has been, though Bach did not live to see the accuracy of his prediction.
[2]Editor's Note: RB was working on *Sense of Smell*.

[This letter was dated 1957, but because of the pregnancy mentioned, the date must be 1958. Robert Bedichek was born September 6, 1958.]

August 1, 1958

Dear Una:

Lillian and I were gratified with your report of satisfactory attendance at your association meeting.[1] It is a marvellous tribute to you that such an attendance is possible. And that from all over the country!

You are readily forgiven for not remembering by reminding me of my 80th. Really too much is made of birthdays after childhood is over. The count of years does not mean a great deal. There's another clock that I mind much more closely: inches of girth, for instance; acuity of vision, also; the clock of mood; and so on. My main ambition in life now, I told a friend the other day, is to avoid getting lumpy and grumpy.

I passed up an impulse to write you a letter July 26, and intentionally delayed for a few days.

My routine is about the same as ever. Early to bed and early to rise; writing for 3, 4, or 5 of the morning hours, depending on how I feel about it. Then I run errands, library, grocery store for something Lillian may have forgotten or for something I suddenly decide I want to eat. Yesterday a nice lady whom I met out swimming, gave me a kershaw which, she said, happened to be in her larder when she suddenly decided to join her husband in Mexico City for a vacation. Lillian baked it in the rind for lunch, and I swear I felt forty years younger while eating it, remembering how deliciously mama used to bake that curious member of the gourd family. It has pumpkin (the kind "frost is on") beat a mile and a half. Afternoons I begin with an hour's nap. Then I go out to a cold swimming pool, water for which gushes out of a crack in the limestone at the rate of 10,000,000 gallons a day. It is a great refresher. Then around sundown I do a little tail-end gardening, or lawn-mowing or whatever physical labor seems necessary about the place.

I make myself a tomato and avocado salad for supper which I eat with hard, dry toast made from bread Lillian makes out of whole wheat flour mixed with soy bean flour and a dash of "wheat-germ" whatever that is—it's a trade name. At this juncture I begin to get "tired eyelids" and soon close them upon tired eyes. Thus most days pass, with of course some friendly visits with friends, few but fit.

We are expecting our twelfth grandchild in September—Bachman and Jane responsible.

Much love.

Roy

[1] Probably a Christian Science meeting.

❧

409

September 19, 1958

Dear Bachman:

And how does it feel to be head of a family of seven? You must feel like a patriarch, all except the beard down the breast to the belly. And it should be gray, or at least, grizzled. That's the way they look in the religious art of the period of the prophets. I try to imagine you all gathered around the festal board, of grace being pronounced, the helpings, and the conversation which ensues. I try to imagine the bustle of getting 'em off to school, of their return in the afternoon.

I like the name given the latest arrival: Robert Caldwell Bedichek. Of course, it will be shortened to Bob Bedichek,[1] which alliterates nicely and is easily remembered.

Texas politics has fallen to its lowest ebb. Not much lower, however, than national politics. I think for the absolute ultimate of idiocy, Dulles' is it. He calls the Formosa "government" an "ally" or a "friendly power." He ignores a nation of 600,000 people and adding by propagation a population size of that of New York every year.[2] I suppose he believes in the Monroe Doctrine (everybody stay away from the shores of the Atlantic from the polar sea to Patagonia), and still insists that his "friendly power" must be protected in its claim to islands within eight miles of China mainland! Looks to me like his words would choke him and if he continues venting such poppycock I believe it will choke him.

But enough! My dietitian tells me that I should always sit down to a meal in a pleasant humor, and I am now enroute to lunch. Much love for you and for each and every of the other six.

Dad

[1]Editor's Note: His name was actually shortened to Rob.
[2]Editor's Note: He means China and 600 million population.

September 19, 1958

Dear Mary:

Gay's letter to Lillian arrived day before yesterday. Your mother immediately put in a call for her at the Kinsolving Dormitory.[1] She managed to establish telephonic communication with our sophomore yesterday morning about 8 A.M. and made an engagement for me with her at 11:30 in the lobby of the Dormitory. Promptly at that time I showed up in the vast and elegantly appointed lobby and there ensconced in a luxurious divan sat our girl. I delivered Gay's letter to her and learned by a little quizzing that she was proceeding well with her registration, having signed up for courses in biology, government, history and was considering a choice between English and a foreign language.

She looked not only well but distinguished with no allowance whatever for grandpappa's pride in the product. Her eyes were a little sleepy. I found that she had been to a cinema the night before with a young man of the name of Nowlin. She seemed in good spirits, and I told her to call us any time she felt the need of being out of the rush and rumble of dormitory life, and we would come and get her.

So, she is well-launched. It was mealtime so I talked with her only a few minutes.

Much love,
Dad

[1]Dormitory at the University of Texas.

October 22, 1958

Dear John:
Grandmother and I read your letter of September 23 together. Then each of us read it over several times. We didn't want to miss anything. Each of us enjoyed it greatly, especially the emphatic conclusion with the word "never," in capital letters, enlarged, in red and underscored four times, also in red. Really, you must mean it.

Since this letter came we have had bad and good news of you: the bad being your illness, and the good being the prospect of a visit from you.[1] That is tremendously (imagine tremendously emphasized in red, underlined, and spelled out in capitals)—tremendously good news for us. We are very lonesome for some intelligent company which your presence will furnish. Geese are coming south for the winter and why shouldn't you follow their example? They know how much more pleasant it is here in winter than way up north in Canada. In spite of the low opinion of most people concerning the goose's mind, they have more sense than a good many people. The ancient Romans thought well of the geese, and gave them special honors in state ceremony every year commemorating the cackling of the geese that saved Rome from the Gauls. Guess you know all about that, don't you?

I have been putting in a winter garden. So far I have planted beets, carrots, spinach, turnips, tender greens, collards and cabbage. I have put compost in each row and fresh soil so that you will find them of excellent flavor. We eat them this winter.

Hoping this letter finds you fully recovered, and looking forward with pleasure to seeing you, and with much love, I am

Your affectionate

Grandfather Bedichek

[1]Editor's Note: In mid-October of 1958, John, who often suffered from asthma, developed pneumonia. After examining him, the doctor said it was a bad way to begin winter. Jane asked if it would be a good idea to arrange for him to spend winter in warmer Texas with four grandparents who would give him excellent care. In Scarsdale there was a new baby—Robert—and three other children competing for mother's attention. Dr. Follette replied firmly, "I'd send him to Texas as soon as possible." The allergist concurred.

November 7, 1958

Dear Bachman:

John, so far, is doing just fine: physically and emotionally. He is a natural-born intellectual and the main problem, if any, touching him is that his physical and emotional nature be tuned-in to work consonantly with his mind. His naive wisdom delights me, also delights your mother, needless to say. His abundant energy makes the only problem with him: how to direct it. He has energy of the mind and also a tremendous physical energy, for which I was not prepared. From all I had heard and observed of him I expected a rather languid child. Far from it. He is intensely alert, never asks "fool" questions, catches on without any diagram.

Your mama and I are delighted with the association.

Are you sure you saw the water ouzel *dive*? I watched one for two or three days in the Costillo Canyon in Northern New Mexico and can't say I ever saw him *dive*—that is go under the water head first, like a duck. He either just sank like a grebe does sometimes, or walked under, usually that. If you have not read John Muir's essay on this bird, you should read it at once before the memory-image of him fades out. It is one of Muir's best essays, although the one on "stickeen," his little dog that trailed at his heels while he was exploring a glacier, is maybe a more thrilling piece of writing. You should have the Greater Yellow Legs on one of your Gulf Coast lists. I am sure we saw him there.

Much love and thanks to you and Jane for such a wonderful grand-child.

Dad

⁂

November 15, 1958

Dear Bachman:

The boy is getting on wonderfully well. To me he becomes more and more interesting as I have a little association with him. He is perceptive but naive. He has a sense of humor. He is something you never were nor I—diplomatic. He is full of energy. He wants to be up and doing every minute. The great job with him is to supply activities that have some outcome to them. He sat at the table the other night and told me and his grandmother one joke after another that he remembered from some newspaper cartoon feature. This I considered largely a waste of a good memory. However, he didn't tell a pointless one in the whole lot, but the humor was really far below him.

I have given him a section of one of my gardens for development. He planted a row of tender greens the other day and this morning he found the plants shooting up out of the ground. I showed him how to cultivate them to keep the moisture in the ground and he forthwith did a good job. But there is some fear that the infernal allergy may prevent garden work, especially handling compost, but nothing of the sort has showed up so far.

Like all boys he wants to learn to shoot. He is possessed of the idea, and apparently can think of nothing else for an hour at a time. I explained to him that my own personal opinion is that a boy his age should learn how to handle a gun and how to shoot with fair accuracy. All this can be taught, I told him, with a good air-rifle. I laid it down as fundamental that this weapon should not be used on any living thing, not even on a rat. The force of the bullet and the accuracy of the gun rarely permits a lethal shot and that to maim or cripple in any way any animal in casual purposeless manner is a sin against the holy ghost, although I did not refer specifically to that speculative entity. I promised him I would write you about it and if there were no objections, I would get him a gun of the sort above mentioned *for shooting at target only*. He wanted an exception made of rats, many of which he sees when he visits the Gracy farm, but I was obdurate. I told him it was legitimate to kill an obvious pest, but it was not to cripple one. So that's the way the gun-matter stands. Please advise.

I can't get any reaction from him about birds.

I am still writing on a book, but hope to complete it in a month or two. I have a fishing-location staked out which John and I shall visit as soon as he gets settled in his school work. Yesterday he entered the Robert E. Lee School. From all accounts, it is one of the best of the public schools in Austin.

Hope your business in Calgary turned out satisfactorily. By the way, if I were a young man I would move to Canada. In my opinion it is the most promising part of that which is left of the "free" world.

Yours,

Dad

Before December 30, 1958

Dear Bachman:

Yes, John is doing fine. He continues to embrace new experiences with enthusiasm. We were out all day Sunday on shore of Lake Travis some miles above the dam, and he greatly enjoyed the sapphire lake— never saw it a clearer color—but more especially he enjoyed a camp-meal—bacon, corn, fruit and a vegetable or two. He eats with relish. He doesn't show a great deal of interest in birds, but I am a poor teacher for I have not been out looking for birds in so long that I was very rusty Sunday morning and had to pass several up without identification. It's funny how they slip out of your mind unless you cultivate them. I felt like saying, "I know your face, but, forgive me, I cannot recall your name."

Your idea of a feeding-station so that you may make behavioral studies is excellent. Behavior is the big thing, I think, in the field of ornithology. What does the bird do? What does he like to eat? How does he get it? What of his association with his own species? With other species? etc., etc. It is endless and diverting. Your observation on the pugnacity of the dove is a good example. The dove of peace is very effective in war. I have seen domestic pigeons stand toe to toe and box like prize fighters. They carry an awful wallop in that wing.

John's pertinacity surprises me. The other day when we were out on the lake shore we waited to prepare dinner until we were good and hungry, about 2 P.M. I suggested that John build a fire, and he jumped into the assignment with his usual enthusiasm. Campers had been in the place that morning and from their breakfast fire there were a few feeble embers left. He appreciates a one-match campfire, but as usual in his desire to excel, he conceived the idea here of a "no-match camp-fire." He began nursing the few live sparks he could find in the ashes. I suggested that he could short-cut the preparations with a match. Although hungry as a bear, he kept gathering dry chaff from round about and blowing hard to coax a flame. It was a tedious process. Every time he got his face down to earth level and blew hard, the kick-back filled his eyes with ashes. I suggested several times that a match would do the trick, but he was hell bent and determined to do or die. It must have taken half an hour, but finally the flame leapt up and he was all pride in his achievement.

And that suggests something I have noted in him which I consider an excellent trait of character. He has a passionate desire to finish whatever he starts. There's no put-off in his mind, no alibi. He wants the job done, rounded out, finished. We started planting onion-sets in his part of the garden the other day about sundown. Soon, of course, it was nearly dark, the north wind was sharp, and we were up to our wrists in mud. I had at last almost to drag him away by the heels, he wanted to finish the row out.

It would be a mistake, in my opinion, to take him away before his school is out in the spring, which, I think, is about the last week in May. He would feel frustrated—started something but didn't finish it. I see so many of these futile people who are putters-off, never-finishers, self-excusers, alibiers, that when I see a passion in a youngster to finish the tasks he begins, I think it is a hopeful sign.

RB

❧

[undated]

Dear Bachman and Jane:

Having experienced the poignant anxiety of the parent over an absent child, I write you when there is no apparent reason for writing. But I always wanted to know there was nothing to report and perhaps even with your four present children you may want a similar reassurance. So I can say, everything is normal and John is getting on fine, with noticeable improvement in appetite, strength and energy. I wish I might devise a wrestling dummy for him—one that would stimulate his best exertions and still one careful not to hurt him. But I guess automation experts would give that one up. He wants to roughhouse me every time he gets a chance, and occasionally we have to protect our visitors from him. Bobby Greer[1] was over last night and it was all I could do to keep John off him. John's aggressiveness was doubtless stimulated by the fact that Bobby is rather small for his age. I have noted another thing about John's psychology: in the presence of a good-looking young female he has a tendency to show-off. Of course, he does not realize it—is not remotely conscious of why he feels that way, but I, having lately had occasions to examine what the psychologists say about secondary sexual characters and tendency on the part of males to display, I feel that John's unconscious impulses are a sign of strong sexing when he grows up, for which any parent should be thankful. His physical energy is tremendous and we have little opportunity to give it full vent. He should have every day some athletic game with limited personal contact to tire him out. That is the only outlet for the kind of excessive physical energy that boils up in him. We note that when we can [spend the] day out in the open with much walking and knocking about that his motor nerves quiet down. He returned the other day from a two-day visit with Gracy-kin in San Antonio[2] very much quieted. They evidently gave him plenty of work-out of one sort or another, as appears now and then in his account of his trip. Our weather has been so bad for weeks that we have had no real camping for him. As we get milder weather I am planning camp activities. I spied out a promising location yesterday on a large range much secluded about thirty miles from Austin. Ranchman will be delighted to have us.

Well, so much without any paragraphing. Suppose I make one. I note that Lillian has begun giving him Spanish lessons. Don't know whether that is to be a part of his regime or not, but you know what a pertinacious propagandizer for Spanish she is. She is wholly devoted to John. I think he is rarely out of her thoughts. And the other grandparents who take over on weekends are the same. Indeed, you are going to be given back a very spoiled urchin. But he can be unspoiled. A little spoiling is not so bad.

John's gardening activities don't give him nearly enough exercise. The only thing about the garden that he evinces tender and devoted interest in is a row of carrots, which, by the way, are coming along fairly well. He devils me to plant more and more carrots, altho I tell him repeatedly that carrot is not a vegetable you can store or keep. Overproduction simply means waste. He wants a chemical and a physical laboratory for making most complicated experiments, but of course we have no place for such adventures, and have to tell him so.

Much love,

Dad

Changing subject, I note on one of Kodak pictures that you, Bachman, are getting too hefty. Watch that waistline.

RB

[1]Editor's Note: A cousin.
[2]Editor's Note: Gracy kin in San Antonio: Mrs. Lutcher Brown (Bessie Gracy's sister), her daughters and grandchildren.

January 28, 1959

Dear Jane and Bachman:

Progeny prospers. I am losing out, however, for the competition is fierce and ruthless. A call for volunteers to report on some interesting scientific achievement took the boy away from garden and woodpile for two consecutive afternoons, while he was burying his nose in the Encyc. Brit., and scientific articles on (of all things) the laying of the Atlantic Cable. He produced a 4- or 5-page report that seems to have knocked the fifth grade of the Robert E. Lee School for a loop. Much praise. Ambition so fired he volunteered for a report on the early days of radio. His paternal grandmother, a natural born teacher, remembered an old radio you, Bachman, had many, many years ago, and exhumed it from some rubbish in the garage. This was a prize. The budding scientist began examining its innards at once. Grandma was stumped with questions. Then she had another pedagogical inspiration and took the boy, radio and all, down to our radio-repair man, and John proceeded to examine him. This lasted an hour or more. Again I missed him from the garden. So grandpa is losing out all around.

But I have a surprise in store for my rivals. Little do they, the grandmas, know what I am hatching up. I am preparing a fishing place in one of the canyons of Marshall Ford Lake, baiting it, that is, with alfalfa and cotton seed nutlets, so that the fish will learn to come there and feed, little suspecting that presently John and I will be carting small, sharp baited hooks into the "baited" waters. Shooo—don't say anything about it. But when the weather gets passable, I shall have an appeal ready for a basic male instinct—providing food by fishing and hunting for the poor female who must stay at home. This will be irresistible, I am sure. It will necessitate camping out over night, which has an appeal also.

Really, this has been the most discouraging gardening winter I have ever known here. Things freeze. John's row of tender greens, up and doing well, froze dead as a crisp one night. His flourishing row of carrots has been torn to pieces by loose cats and dogs which play over the garden at night. They haven't left half a stand of carrots. His row of beets the same. Having experienced no success he can't quite endure failure. I had fishing-trip with Kidd[1] planned, trolling for bass in the lake, last week and a norther blew up with a thermometer-reading the morning we were to start out of 16 above zero in a high wind which made trolling impossible.

So the grandmothers are outdistancing me due, as I alibi, to a concatenation of fortuitous circumstances. Anyhow, John is in fine fettle, full of talk, physical and mental energy and good humor.

Bach, I certainly enjoyed our early morning walks. Those were the first bird-walks I have had in a year. I had been having a hunger for something or other, but didn't know what it was until I got out in the early morning with binoculars and a partner interested in birds.

Affectionately,
RB

[1]Editor' Note: Rodney Kidd was Athletic Director of the Interscholastic League and successor to Bedichek as Director of the League. He ran a camp for boys at Friday Mountain Ranch, owned by Walter Prescott Webb, a project suggested and encouraged by Bedichek.

❦

February 4, 1959

Dear Jane & Bach:

I have just finished breakfast across the table from John, not the piper's but the lawyer's son, and beg to report his consumption of a heaping bowl of hot grits with butter and seven slices of fairly crisp bacon, along with an 8-ounce glass of orange juice along with a great deal of talk. Occasionally, he broke off talking and waltzed around the room making a noise and spreading out his hands in imitation of an American airplane downing a mig. He found occasion to caution his grandmother not to spend just $2.49 for groceries since by spending only one cent more she would be entitled to green stamps. His passion for green stamps almost equals that for correcting my physics which was cultivated before the atomic ages came upon us. Electrons, nuclei, protons, and anti-matter mean very little to me. He gave me a little logic-lesson, or rather example, which being a classical subject, is definitely in my field. Says he, referring to some of our gardening activities, "You know, Grandfather, some things look easy but are hard; and some things look hard but they are easy—" follows a pause in which he senses a logical hiatus—then, "some things look easy and are easy, and some things look hard and are hard." Thus he exhausted the logical possibilities of a positive statement.

The principal of the school called his grandmother aside the other day and told her what a fine boy John is, which she accepted without dispute. I left the party as John and this grandmother were having a warm dispute about how the pioneers used trees. As I closed the door behind me I heard the "Autocrat of the Breakfast Table" declaiming "fuel, furniture, mantlepieces, tools, wagon-wheels, . . . ."

John was picked up by Mr. Gracy at school Friday afternoon and returned to us Monday after having, of course, spent Monday in school.

He was radiant and bustin' to tell us of his experiences. He had been out to the farm Saturday. Sunday Grandmother Gracy had a friend of his to dinner (didn't get the name), and all afternoon which was a rainy one and cold, he had triumphed over his Grandfather Gracy in game after game of chess. He rang up his Grandmother Bedichek once during the time for professional medical advice concerning a pimple on his nose, whether or not to pick it. The "doctor" said no definitely no, just dab a little castor oil on it. "Picking," I heard her advise, eavesdropping the telephone conversation, "is absolutely the worst thing you can do for or to a pimple. Just opens it for infection." When he returned, I look closely for the pimple on his nose, but evidently the witch-doctor had charmed it away.

Yesterday afternoon our granddaughter, Lillian Lee Carroll, came over. John enjoys her company very much. She is the eldest of four children in the Carroll family and seems to have a way with the younger generation, and besides (something never lost on John) she's a darn good-looking girl.

I turned in my last chapter (No. 22) to the typist yesterday and feel like Christian in *Pilgrim's Progress* when he unloaded his Burden of Sin and dumped it into the slough of Despond, or like some imprisoned slave who manages at long last to slip the manacles off his wrists. I have two wire-baskets full of neglected correspondence which I am attacking this morning with fervor and hope of forgiveness.

Much love,
Dad

❦

February 12, 1959

Dear Jane & Bachman:

John is hilarious with a brand new bright chromium hot-spot. He tells me (upon polite inquiry) that it is to be incorporated into his chemical laboratory when he gets back to New York. In chemistry, he explains, it is often necessary to heat "substances." This acquisition came through his monopoly of the Gracy-Bedichek trading stamps. He gathers and pastes them into little books and when the reckoning time comes, he pre-sorts and chooses that which he thinks has the "best value." The only feminine trait I have observed in him is his delight in shopping and getting the best if possible of the mercantile gentry. He is avid for even small beats in his bartering.

I was trimming up the figs the other day and the party above named strolled in and observed that there was some good wood in the clippings. Of course, he doesn't know how utterly worthless fig-wood as firewood is, but I thanked him for the suggestion and suggested that it might be trimmed up for firewood—at least the larger stems. He dashed off and brought back an axe and began trimming with the expressed determination, "Before I leave here, Grandfather, I am going to have for you all the firewood you can use for the rest of your life." I don't know whether he felt he was making a safe guarantee of the supply after a lighting computation of my life expectancy, or was simply overestimating his ability as a good producer. Anyway he set to work with a will as if it were the latter.

I sometimes gasp at the maturity of his point of view, and then I excuse him on the score that he has spent most of his waking hours among grown people and naturally picks up the adult point of view. E.g., last night I said, "John, I'm writing to your father tomorrow. Shall I urge him to come by here on trip to or from San Francisco, and add your solicitations?" He replied very calmly: "That's hardly necessary, Grandfather. He will come by here anyway if he possibly can."

He tells me reprovingly that I should not make so much noise when I am eating dry toast, and cautions me also that I should not at the table chew with my mouth open. I tell him that I ate in a boardinghouse so many years of my life that I could not observe the niceties of eating since one had first to secure an amount sufficient to sustain life, and of course, nothing else matters.

The boy is staying in good health and spirits. Really, his spirits run high most of the time. Teacher brags on him. He reported to the proper authority the other day on a schoolmate, a girl, who, acting as "host," made a wry face at the meat. He declared that if she didn't like the meat herself she shouldn't try to make it unappetizing for the rest of the table. He didn't say, but I'll bet my last dollar that the "host" that day was a rather *homely* girl.

So it goes. Lillian and Mrs. Gracy are thoroughly enjoying the experience of having a "youngun" around. I think, however, that John enjoys Mr. Gracy more than he does any of the rest of the kin.

Much love for you both and for the four others at 4 Kingston Rd.
Dad

February 26, 1959

Dear Jane and Bachman:

Commercial considerations and a sudden passion for building something have broken my contact with John for several days so I have little to report. A $5 prize was offered in Robert E. Lee for the pupil who sold the most tickets to the great PANCAKE SUPPER of the Kiwanis Club and the School. A jail sentence should be given grown-ups who permitted such a prize to be offered; but, nevertheless, it was violating every pedagogical principal from Aristotle on down to John Dewey. John did the impossible of selling nineteen tickets by working every afternoon like a Trojan. And I regret to report that it was cupidity not patriotism that was the motivating power.

Then hardly was that spasm over before he became enamored of building from start to finish, lock stock and barrel, a radio—one that would function. Being an utter numbskull in such matters, I was able only to cart him around a bit but certainly unable to offer any constructive suggestions. With Lillian's valiant aid we have been able to moderate his ambitions in the interest of economy and now his romantic gaze is set on something far simpler and less costly than he originally contemplated.

Before any of this started, we had a fishing expedition with the "wonderful" Mr. Kidd. They (John and Kidd) simply captivated each other and again I was reduced to ranks. Kidd can think of more things to tell a boy to do that he *can* do than any other person I ever saw handling a boy. We trolled from about an hour by sun until dark—that is, John and Kidd did. No results except the exhilaration of momentary expectation of catching a whale at every ten-foot movement of the boat. I am far too much of a pessimist to derive any such illusory joy from fishing, but not so John and Kidd. They maintained themselves at the very peak of anticipation for the whole period.

Returning in the deepening dusk across a mile or so of fairly placid water John held the tiller with a pride and joy that I fear he will never know in adult life. Kidd sat beside him pointing out the lights to steer by, and I pledge you my word the little rascal guided that boat into the curved mouth of the right canyon and to within ten feet of the dock.

We were hungry. Kidd and I have a favorite camping dish of humble origin but of divine relish on a hungry palate: weinies [sic] and sauer kraut. We had bacon and eggs, toast, and our favorite dish. Kidd helped John's plate first thing to weinies and sauer kraut. John lapped it up and asked for a second helping. He managed some bacon and a hard-boiled egg, also, and slept like a top. I know for I was within a few feet of his cot. Once he kicked the cover off; but with that restored, he fell again into a deep slumber. Well, needless to say, a good time was had by all.

Jane, I'm afraid you think I was tattling on John when I told you of his reporting the gaucherie at the lunch-table. No, that is a part of the game. Each day a hostess presides, and the guests report errors, just as they would in class. It's a kind of game and I think it is an excellent way to teach what should and what should not be done in such situations. John was doing his part and I thought it showed some perspicacity to note that a hostess should not by hook or look belittle her viands. And so far as telling me that I made a noise with my toast and chewed with my mouth open, I simply considered that a part of the information he was passing on from advice that had been given him "for his own good." And anyway, let us have free speech, honest observations, and abandon that wretched old Victorian adage "children should be seen and not heard." There's no doubt that John's talk does require restraint. He tends to interpolate non sequiturs into the general conversation at times, but his ebullience is priceless. God deliver me from the silent and the subdued. From all which you will deduce properly that I am not one to teach manners, although I appreciate good manners above many other things the poets praise. John has an instinctive tact which is the very basis of good manners. He has the "makins" but I am not the one to employ as a tutor.

Weather is turning springy. Capitol elms are showing a tinge of green, wild onion is blooming all about, henbit is covering the place, and I am greasing and oiling my power mower for my annual battle with the lawn grass.

Faithfully yours,
R.B.

March 28, 1959

Dear Jane and Bachman:

Since my last (or rather late) communication I have been absorbed in sewing up the ragged, dangling ends of the book ms which was (I fear) prematurely submitted to a publisher about two weeks ago.[1] I doubt if this publisher makes me a satisfactory offer (or any offer at all) but I have another one on the string so I am not uneasy. The egotism of anyone who writes a book may be compared with justice only to very sizable objects, but the egotism of one who confidently expects a publisher and actual readers must be completely beyond the imagination of anyone not bitten himself by the tarantula of the writing ambition. Why should anyone write another book, when more books have been published and duly cataloged in the libraries on every conceivable subject than anyone in a lifetime could read even the titles of, working at it fourteen hours a day? And consider the millions pouring forth from the presses of the world every twenty-four hours! Why should any rational person insist at great pains and expense of tossing one more pebble into that ocean to form a microscopic part of the sedimentary rock forming through the ages at the bottom of it? You may answer "why" if you don't have to write a book to do it.

Well, the tag ends are about sewed up, references checked and corrected, letters to publishers for permissions to quote are in process of being typed, and little past-minute polishings-off made in my carbon copy which I hope to transfer ultimately to the original before it gets into the hands of the linotyper. Well, consolatory thought: there is a Malthusian jump in the world's population. The billions are breeding— maybe this geometrical progression will actually outrun the arithmetical production of books and eventually there will be a few straggling readers who will take up for a moment or two my book, "speaking of Moses—." Let us, or rather let *me* hope.

John continues my education. He is "of imagination all compact." And that is, I think, a danger. He came back from seeing a movie "Ivanhoe" with his grandmother the other night. His "impressions" as expounded at the supper-table were overwhelming. They completely submerged his supper. He forgot to eat. He, personally, stormed the castle with the Black Knight, wound the horn of Locksley ("Robin Hood" he hastily interpolated) calling forth 500 fully armed archers at each "blow" and so on. At one juncture a deficient pronunciation broke

*424*

the spell and utterly collapsed Lillian whose convulsions were gradually communicated (much reduced) to me and John. We all three joined in the hilarity of John's introduction of a firetruck into the assault on the castle by his curious mispronunciation of "Friar Tuck."

He tends to become abnormally excited with dramatic situations and with imposing personalities. He is a natural born hero-worshipper. Governor Rockefeller of New York formed the subject of an excited eulogium the other night, and the next night some other world character had captured his imagination, which, in my opinion, is too easily led captive. As long as his imagination is dominated by physical activity, devising some mechanism, making an experiment, playing a physical game, or even working in the garden, it is fine. But I do not believe too many exciting spectacles, especially TV and movies are really good for him.

He is the dream of the born teacher, for he has not only an inquiring but a critical mind. He quickly loses interest in explanations that do not explain.

The carrot-episode ended happily. By assiduous attention and much advice from the boss-gardener, he has now two of his carrots salvaged and thriving from two plantings of a 30-foot row. Of some hundreds of plants he has two—verily there is more joy in heaven over the one lost sheep recovered than over the ninety-and-nine others, only in this case the whole herd was lost and the blessed two recovered.

Lillian tells me the scales show that he gained 3 pounds in the last ten days. But do not fear that he will become a "fat" boy—that lean and hungry frame could absorb right now fifteen or twenty pounds and never know it.

Much love. By the way I meant to tell you how much I have enjoyed the little album of pictures Mr. Gracy brought over the other day. I was particularly impressed with Robert, robust and arrogant, and with the fine, benevolent face of Herta. But as I said above, "much love," for I have "spun out the thread of my verbosity longer than the staple of my argument."[2]

RB

P.S. Grandfather Gracy is taking us all out to the farm today for picnic lunch and a look among the animals and crops.

[1]Editor's Note: The book was *Sense of Smell*, published by Doubleday and Company in 1960. Bedichek had signed the contract for it with the publisher a few days before

he died May 21, 1959.
[2]William Shakespeare, *Love's Labour's Lost*, V, i, 18.

March 29, 1959

Dear, dear Mary:

Jane is a lovely girl. I guess you hadn't noticed it, so I thought I would tell you. She has come out like a flower in the spring. I think she is really beautiful, something I had not expected of her a few years ago. She's stately, robust with no hint of fat, and a smile to charm both age and youth—especially me. We enjoyed our glimpse of her and, of course, want her to come again.

We don't see half enough of Lillian. I think the child must be timid, for she rarely rings us up. I hear good reports of her from those who do see her. Tell Gay to keep up his golf whether or not he has time for it. He is getting to that age when a little fold (omnious sign)—a tiny fold of flesh begins to bulge a little above the belt. Bachman's fold is getting to be triple. Mama and I discussed without conclusion or decision coming to see you and Gay and the "chillun," and decided only that, *if and when*, it must be in installments.

Much love,
Dad

April 10, 1959

Dear Bachman:

I must have laid the enclosure away months ago with the intention of sending it to you.

I am remembering our walks and talks with great pleasure. John is so happy he retires to the bathroom to sing. There is music in the dear boy's heart but not in his voice. Mr. Gracy took him to Richard's pond fishing the other day. They caught a few perch.

We have just had a glorious 2-inch rain which is bringing smiles to every face still capable of a smile. It is really a life-saver, and as I potter about the place I smell that choicest of all smells: the good earth after the death of a long drouth coming alive again.

Give Jane my love and believe

Affectionately yours,

Dad

❦

Sunday—April 26, 1959

Dear Jane and Bachman:

John is today suffering from a head-cold with fever 102 and will probably have to miss school tomorrow. You will likely get a report from Mrs. Gracy and from Lillian, both more expert in reporting ailments than I am. Lillian went over to the Gracy's a while ago to see him, and came back feeling that he may miss two or three days from school. She says the Dr. prescribed the usual remedies for cold. John is very much alive intellectually, passing on the physician's approach to his patient and remarking that the M.D. was much more solicitous about Mrs. Gracy than he was about him (John). I shall see him tomorrow.

Friday afternoon he was in high fettle. The principal of the school, Mr Isabel, is taking a lot of pains with John, especially since he discovered John's interest in electronics. Isabel is a ham-radio enthusiast and twice now he has had John over to his home to try and get "home" by radio. Last Friday they got your phone but no one answered. Isabel is encouraging John and helping in construction of some electrical device (I don't even know its name or purpose) but it has John in its grip, except when he is absorbed in a book, or the TV. I have taken over his garden, and I can hardly be surprised at his loss of interest because it has been the worst gardening year I have even known in Austin. First drouth and cold, and then excessive rain and unseasonable cold—35 degrees some nights in middle April! And besides God, I mistreated the garden with some poisonous dirt which I thought prime gardening soil. The hillbilly was a good salesman. I am sending a sample over to the A&M for analysis for I want to know just what poison I paid my good money for.

Kidd has been busy with the approach of the state meet, so John and I have not had the trolling and trot-line fishing we had a while

427

back. Unseasonable cold has kept us out of Barton's, so all in all I am missing association with John.

He keeps reporting pleasure in the ball—and other games they play at school, so I feel that he is not entirely missing the physical exercise which, of course, every normal lad of his age requires. A short time ago, he lost a pound and a half, but regained it immediately.

Mary is insisting that Lillian and John come and visit them for a week-end. This is being arranged and John is enthusiastic at the prospect.

Hope everything and everybody is flourishing at 4 Kingston Road.
RB

May 1959

Dear Jane and Bachman:

Mrs. Gracy delivered John to us just a week ago today, bubbling and beaming with memories of the trip to New York. He was delighted with the trip, the seeing the family, and the place and especially the "block house."[1] He had interviewed the pilot in flight and reeled off to me a dozen terms I had never heard before with a ready description of the function of each as a part of the airplane anatomy. He has gotten a little behind with his school work, having missed altogether 7 days lately, but Coach Lillian says he is regaining some of the lost ground. I heard him confer this morning with great embarrassment to his coach that he had made "only" 72 on a test of some sort.

He is now tremendously absorbed in model-airplane flying. I took him down to the school playing field a couple of afternoons ago to test out a new machine he had acquired through trading stamps. He had devoted two hours to tuning the thing up, fueling and starting it. Finally, under his patient treatment, the thing let off a scream like a mating peacock, and he had conquered the problem of getting the engine up to flying speed. No Canaveral missile-man could have been prouder of a successful launching than John was as the engine continued its unearthly scream. Then we took it to the playground, and he held the reins while I gave the thing a boost. The first few trials went bad. The thing took a nosedive each time and I thought it would be broken up, but apparently it is ruggedly constructed. Presently it took off and John turned with it until he fell flat from the dizziness of turning round to guide the plane. Again and again he got the thing circling about until, apparently, he had mastered the technique of keeping it up and making it do a few stunts. So with the airplane the march of mechanization is going forward in the minds of the pre-adolescents. I don't think any other problem could have plunged the boy into such concentrated thought, care and action than this frivolous toy. Science (physical science) has taken over. Mechanization takes command. The humanities had as well close up shop.

The weather has gotten warm enough at last for Barton, and the mud has about cleared up from the last overflow.

We had John out in "society" until 11 last night. Mr. and Mrs. Dobie[2] and Lillian and I along with John went in the Dobie car. John made quite a hit with the host and family and with the Dobies. Coming home, I heard John carefully explaining to Mrs. Dobie the respective functions of several gadgets on the dashboard. I heard her say several times during the instruction-period, "Thank you, John, I never knew what that was for before." But the dissipation told on him. Just before I left the house this morning Lillian roused him from deep slumber, and groans ensued and continued all through the dressing-period. "Breakfast was served," but he had not yet made it to the table when I left the place. I am hoping John will recover lost ground in school before the session closes.

We are getting a lot of pleasure out of this boy. I was afraid when he went to New York you would keep him and I rather discouraged the trip, but all's well that ends well.

Yours,

RB

---

[1]Editor's Note: The blockhouse was a two-story structure he had helped his father build in the back yard, used as a play house by all the children in the neighborhood of 4 Kingston. See photo on page 434.

[2]J. Frank and Bertha Dobie.

# Epilogue

Wednesday, May 20, 1959, Bedi took John swimming at Barton Springs and reported they had such a good time in the water it was hard to persuade him to go home. Thursday, May 21, 1959, Bedi planned an afternoon hike with his old friend, Frank Dobie; fate intervened. He died while waiting for lunch. As Dobie said, Roy Bedichek left life in the way he had hoped to, without ever having been out of it.

He had faced the issue of death, and our short time on the stage of life, in many letters. Back in a March 5, 1951, letter to his wife's brother, F. L. Greer, he had written about the little cemetery in Eddy where he would be buried beside his parents and grandfather. Bachman and John Bedichek are also buried there. Bachman died January 24, 1964, while on a business trip to British Columbia. John died December 29, 1980, when the plane he was flying in a dense fog crashed during an attempted instrument landing at Tompkins County Airport in New York.

Bachman and John Bedichek at their home in New York.
*Courtesy of Jane Bedichek.*

John, Jane and Bachman Bedichek, Christmas, 1950.
*Courtesy of Jane Bedichek.*

Mary Virginia Carroll and Bachman at her home holding her
daughter Jane Carroll. John is in the tree behind Mary.
*Courtesy of Jane Bedichek.*

Bedi and John at the train
station in Austin, 1952,
seeing the Bachman
Bedicheks off. *Courtesy of
Jane Bedichek.*

Lillian Bedichek seeing the Bachman Bedicheks off at the Austin train station, 1952. *Courtesy of Jane Bedichek.*

Roy Bedichek with George and Roy Pipkin at a campout
at Friday Mountain Ranch, 1955.
*Courtesy of Alan & Louise Pipkin.*

Bedi showing John how to start a fire with a shaved stick,
March 6, 1953. *Courtesy of Jane Bedichek.*

Bachman and his children in front of the
blockhouse he built for them.
*Courtesy of Jane Bedichek.*

Bedi and John camping at
Poundridge in 1956.
*Courtesy of Jane Bedichek.*

John Gracy and John Bedichek at the Gracy
residence on Lorraine Street, Austin.
*Courtesy of Jane Bedichek.*

John Bedichek shows Louise Bedichek how Raggedy Ann pat-a-cakes. *Courtesy of Jane Bedichek.*

Written on the back of this photograph is the following notation: "Roy Bedichek in Central Texas, 1953. A framed copy of this photograph hung on J. Frank Dobie's bedroom wall for the last eleven years of his life." *Courtesy of Jane Bedichek.*

Roy Bedichek bird watching.
*Courtesy Austin History Center,*
*Austin Public Library. ID #: PICB 00416.*

# ❦ Appendix

## Chronology

| | |
|---|---|
| 1878 | Roy Bedichek, born June 27 in Cass County, Illinois, son of James Madison Bedichek and Lucretia Ellen Craven Bedichek |
| 1884 or 5? | Bedichek family moved to Texas |
| 1885 | Lillian Greer, born February 15 in Keachie, Louisiana, daughter of James Francis Greer and Virginia Lee |
| 1893 | Greer family moved to Waco, Texas, where James Francis Greer became vice president of Baylor University |
| 1896–98 | Roy Bedichek took dictation and read law in office of Boynton & Boynton, Waco |
| 1898 | Roy Bedichek went to Austin where he worked for Registrar John A. Lomax and entered the University of Texas |
| 1903 | Roy Bedichek received B.S. degree, University of Texas; Lillian Greer received B.A. degree, University of Texas, majoring in Greek and minoring in Latin |
| 1903–05 | Roy Bedichek taught high school in Houston; Lillian taught at Grayson College in Whiteright, Texas |
| 1905–08 | Roy Bedichek taught high school in San Angelo; Lillian taught in the public school system in Waco from 1905 to 1910 |
| 1907 | Roy Bedichek spent the summer in Europe with Harry Steger; returned to Montreal by tramp steamer and worked his way to Texas with odd jobs |
| 1909 | Roy Bedichek rode a bicycle from Eddy to El Paso and continued by freight car to Deming, Territory of New Mexico |
| 1909–11 | Roy Bedichek wrote for El Paso paper, wrote publicity for Deming, edited the *Deming Headlight* |
| 1910 | Lillian moved to Deming and taught; Roy and Lillian married |
| 1911 | Mary Virginia Bedichek born |
| 1909–13 | Roy was secretary, Deming Chamber of Commerce |
| 1913 | Sarah Bedichek born |
| 1913–14 | Family moved to Austin where Roy became secretary of Young Men's Business League |
| 1914–15 | Roy was Executive Secretary, Hogg Organization |
| 1916 | Roy was City Editor, *San Antonio Express* |

| | |
|---|---|
| 1917–20 | Roy was Director of Athletics, University Interscholastic League, Extension Division, University of Texas; Lillian taught at Austin High School and later became head of Department of Spanish |
| 1918 | Alston Lee Bedichek (name later changed to Bachman Greer Bedichek) born |
| 1920–47 | Roy Bedichek was Director of University Interscholastic League, Extension Division, University of Texas; editor for 30 years of the *Interscholastic Leaguer* and numerous bulletins |
| 1926 | Lillian Greer Bedichek received a master's degree from the University of Texas |
| 1932 | Mary Virginia Bedichek received B.A. in Chemistry from the University of Texas, Phi Beta Kappa; Alan Pipkin received B.S. in Zoology from the University of Texas |
| 1933 | Sarah Bedichek received B.A. in Zoology from the University of Texas, Phi Beta Kappa; Mary Virginia Bedichek entered the University of Texas Medical branch at Galveston |
| 1934 | Alan Pipkin received M.A. in Zoology from the University of Texas; Gay Carroll received B.A. in Chemical Engineering from the University of Texas |
| 1936 | Mary Virginia Bedichek married Gay Carroll |
| 1937 | Mary Bedichek Carroll received M.S. and interned at St. Mary's Infirmary, Galveston; Gay Carroll entered the University of Texas Medical School at Galveston; Sarah Bedichek received Ph.D. in Genetics from the University of Texas and won a post-doctoral fellowship, Kings College, University of London |
| 1938 | Sarah Bedichek married Alan Pipkin |
| 1938–42 | Sarah taught Zoology at what later became the University of Texas at Arlington; Alan entered Tulane Medical School and graduated with a Ph.D. in Entomology; Mary started a general practice in Galveston |
| 1939 | Lillian Lee Carroll born |
| 1941 | Gay Carroll received M.D. from medical school; Mary was a physician at Austin State School |
| 1942–45 | Alan served with the U.S. Navy as Fleet Malariologist |
| 1942 | Gay and Mary moved to Houston where Gay was accident surgeon for the Houston shipyards; Jane Logan Carroll born |
| 1943 | Alan Collins Pipkin, Jr., born |
| 1944 | Mary took postgraduate training in anesthesiology |

| 1945 | Macmillan published Lillian Bedichek's Spanish textbook, *Mastering Spanish;* Roy Bedichek Pipkin born |
|---|---|
| 1946 | Bachman Bedichek and Jane Gracy married; Roy Bedichek took leave of absence from the University of Texas to write his first book, *Adventures with a Texas Naturalist;* Louise Greer Carroll born; Alan Pipkin became Professor of Zoology at American University of Beirut; Sarah taught Biology and zoology at Catholic University of Beirut. |
| 1947 | Roy's manuscript accepted by Doubleday; Roy returned to Interscholastic League; George Pierce Pipkin born |
| 1948 | Roy retired; started research for *Karankaway Country;* John Greer Bedichek born |
| 1949–50 | Alan Pipkin became Professor of Parasitology at the University of Arkansas |
| 1950 | Doubleday published *Karankaway Country;* Louise Wells Bedichek born |
| 1951–53 | Alan Pipkin called on active duty during the Korean War, and posted to the South Pacific |
| 1954 | Gay passed board requirements to practice orthopedic surgery |
| 1951–55 | Roy worked on history of school contests and role of competition in learning; addressed seminars on public school camping, nature education; spoke at writers' conferences |
| 1952 | Sarah (Sally) Ann Carroll born; Paul Lee Bedichek born |
| 1955 | Ellen Gracy Bedichek born |
| 1956 | Roy's *Educational Competition, The Story of the University Interscholastic League of Texas* published and awarded the Carr Collins award as the best Texas book of that year by the Texas Institute of Letters |
| 1957 | Roy worked on "Memories, Chiefly of Animals" and a book on odors; Gay and Mary Carroll moved to Lake Jackson where Gay established a private orthopedic practice |
| 1958 | Robert Caldwell Bedichek born |
| 1959 | Early May, Roy's manuscript of "The Sense of Smell" turned over to publisher, published posthumously in 1960; May 21, after an early morning birdwalk, Roy Bedichek died |
| 1964 | Bachman Greer Bedichek died in British Columbia while on a business trip |

| | |
|---|---|
| 1971 | Lillian Greer Bedichek died |
| 1977 | Sarah Bedichek Pipkin died |
| 1980 | John Greer Bedichek died after crashing his Cessna 172 Skyhawk while attempting an instrument landing in fog |
| 1983 | Gay Carroll died |
| 1995 | Mary Bedichek Carroll died |

# ❧ Bedichek Genealogy

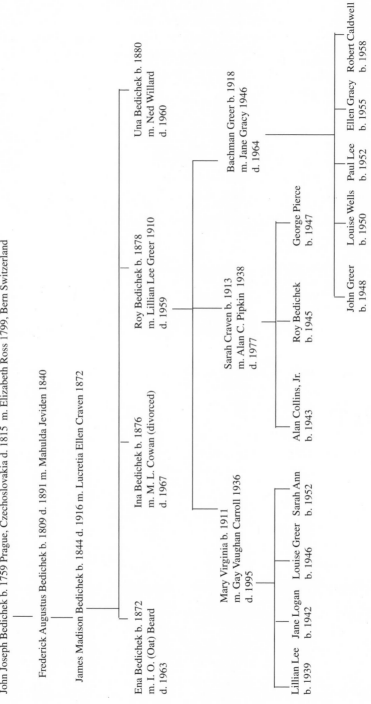

John Joseph Bedichek b. 1759 Prague, Czechoslovakia d. 1815  m. Elizabeth Ross 1799, Bern Switzerland

Frederick Augustus Bedichek b. 1809 d. 1891 m. Mahulda Jeviden 1840

James Madison Bedichek b. 1844 d. 1916 m. Lucretia Ellen Craven 1872

Ena Bedichek b. 1872
m. I. O. (Oat) Beard
d. 1963

Ina Bedichek b. 1876
m. M. L. Cowan (divorced)
d. 1967

Roy Bedichek b. 1878
m. Lillian Lee Greer 1910
d. 1959

Una Bedichek b. 1880
m. Ned Willard
d. 1960

Mary Virginia b. 1911
m. Gay Vaughan Carroll 1936
d. 1995

Sarah Craven b. 1913
m. Alan C. Pipkin  1938
d. 1977

Bachman Greer b. 1918
m. Jane Gracy 1946
d. 1964

Lillian Lee
b. 1939

Jane Logan
b. 1942

Louise Greer
b. 1946

Sarah Ann
b. 1952

Alan Collins, Jr.
b. 1943

Roy Bedichek
b. 1945

George Pierce
b. 1947

John Greer
b. 1948

Louise Wells
b. 1950

Paul Lee
b. 1952

Ellen Gracy
b. 1955

Robert Caldwell
b. 1958

Ena Bedichek m. Oatis (Oat) Beard

| Vivian Dangerfield b. 1893 | Maurine b. 1896 | Beryl b. 1897 | Portia b. 1899 | Pauline b. 1900 | Lowell Craven |
| m. Nannie Becker | d. 1897 | m. Kimball Artman Yoder | m. Amos Dee Jones | m. Jack Bernard Cooney | b. 1904 |
| d. 1968 | | | d. 1970 | | m. Cleo Webb |
| | | | | | d. 1977 |

Ina Bedichek m. Mark L. Cowan (divorced)

| Imogene b. 1895 | Hazel b. 1898 | Homer | Mabel b. 1900 | Carl Bedichek | Owen (Tincy) | Ruth b. 1909 | Casey | Kay Kipling |
| m. Sarge Holt | d. 1899 | b. 1899 | m. Elgin Chancey | b. 1903 | b. 1907 | m. Jack Shipe | b. 1911 | b. 1913 |

# ❧ Greer Genealogy

James Francis Greer b. 1858 d. 1907 m. Virginia Lee b. 1859 d. 1955

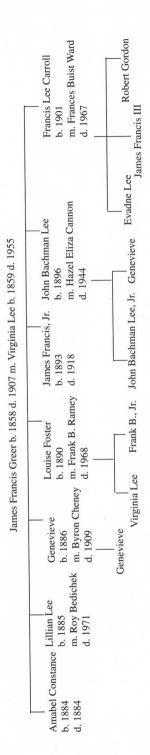

Amabel Constance
b. 1884
d. 1884

Lillian Lee
b. 1885
m. Roy Bedichek
d. 1971

Genevieve
b. 1886
m. Byron Cheney
d. 1909

Louise Foster
b. 1890
m. Frank B. Ramey
d. 1968

James Francis, Jr.
b. 1893
d. 1918

John Bachman Lee
b. 1896
m. Hazel Eliza Cannon
d. 1944

Francis Lee Carroll
b. 1901
m. Frances Buist Ward
d. 1967

Genevieve

Virginia Lee    Frank B., Jr.

John Bachman Lee, Jr.    Genevieve

Evadne Lee    Robert Gordon
James Francis III

# 🌿 Index

140; birdwatching, 152, 160–
61, 180, 403, 407; birth of, 83n;
coin collecting, 385n, 405n;
dating, 147; death of, 430;
health, 98, 140, 142n, 229;
honeymooning, 236; in
Germany (1936), 136–37; in
law school, 181, 191, 194; in
London (1936), 133–35; in
World War II, 240; letters to
father, 121–22, 132–37, 289–
91, 306–308, 404; on football,
308; personality, 104, 128, 138,
188, 210; physical description,
104, 172; playwriting, 121–22;
shooting, 149; trip to Bagdad
(1952), 357n; trip to New York
(1935), 124–32; work for law
firm, 261, 289; work for Texas
Gulf Sulphur, 271n, 289
Bedichek, Ellen Gracy, 385
Bedichek, Ena, 71, 72n, 81, 140,
148, 286, 320, 372, 386
Bedichek, Ina, 83–88, 188, 286,
288, 304, 306n, 386
Bedichek, James Madison, 88 *photo*
Bedichek, Jane Gracy, 237, 238,
239, 240, 242, 245, 249, 256,
258, 260, 261, 271, 272, 273,
280, 290, 292, 298, 300, 305,
308, 309, 314, 316, 327 *photo*,
328 *photo*, 338, 350, 358, 365,
371, 378, 407, 408, 409, 431
*photo*
Bedichek, John Greer, 301, 307,
312, 339, 350, 353–57, 358,
360, 365, 371, 372, 375, 376,
377–78, 381, 386–88, 403,
405–407, 408, 411–25, 428,
430, 431 *photo*, 432 *photo*, 434
*photo*, 435 *photo*, 436 *photo*;
letter to grandfather, 395
Bedichek, Lillian Greer, 86, 89
*photo*, 93 *photo*, 94 *photo*, 97,
105, 132, 139, 141, 164, 168,

176, 178, 180, 186, 191, 194,
195, 203 *photo*, 210, 218, 228,
230, 231, 239, 256, 261n, 262,
272, 284, 285, 296, 304, 322
*photo*, 324 *photo*, 325 *photo*,
335, 336, 343, 361, 408, 418,
419–20, 421, 422, 425, 427,
428, 433 *photo*; as head of
Spanish Department, Austin
High, 99n, 106; as history
teacher, 141; at University of
Texas, 2–3; birdwatching, 149,
152, 154–55, 160–61; birth of
children, 19; census-taking,
147, 149n; decision to marry
Roy, 4, 60; domestic chores,
16–18, 145, 157, 185, 234, 274,
388, 407; eating habits, 274;
encounter with Mexican outlaw,
19–21; fluency in Spanish, 21;
health, 58, 117, 197, 222, 238,
292, 333, 339, 376; helping
Mary at convalescent home,
119n; homesteading experience,
1, 4–25; in Mexico City, 99n; in
Waco, 3, 40, 53, 64–80, 87;
intelligence of, 31, 43; internship at St. Mary's, 140; leaving
Deming, 25; letters to Roy,
116–17, 273–74; loses teaching
job, 104–105; marriage to Roy,
10, 63; meets Roy, 2–3;
miscarriages, 78n; moves to
Austin, 63–64; moves to
Deming, 47; on love, 274; other
marriage prospects, 47–48;
personality, 43, 160, 227;
physical traits, 37, 41; publications, 18; southern ancestry of,
126; Spanish language exper-
tise, 224, 417; stamina, 195;
teaching in Austin, 174;
teaching in Deming, 8, 60–61;
teaching health classes, 178;
trip to California (1954), 376,

381; visit to New York (1949), 312, 314; visit to New York (1951), 349; trip to New York (1957), 394; work at Maternal Clinic, 186, 187n; work for Texas State Dept. of Education, 227; writing and publishing, 73, 99

Bedichek, Louise Wells, 333, 334, 350, 357, 358–59, 365, 371, 372, 375, 377, 381, 403, 436 *photo*

Bedichek, Lucretia Ellen Craven, 81, 82–87, 88 *photo*, 93 *photo*, 107, 117, 118, 140, 142, 148, 242

Bedichek, Mary Virginia, 64, 75, 78, 82–83, 86, 91 *photo*, 94 *photo*, 97, 99, 144, 145, 147, 155, 159, 169, 195, 200 *photo*, 230, 231, 242, 289, 311, 312, 324 *photo*, 326 *photo*, 339, 346, 352, 407, 428, 432 *photo*; appearance, 104, 147; as Phi Beta Kappa, 100; as tennis player, 100, 101, 108; at University of Texas Medical School, 105n, 106–107, 117, 118, 129; birth of, 19, 63; decision to marry, 137–38; educational achievements, 99, 101; health, 65–66, 156, 184, 218, 222; internship, 152, 153, 156, 161–62; letters to father, 105, 137–38, 179; letters to mother, 187; marriage of, 138n; move to Freeport, 401; personality, 102, 104, 112, 284; residency, 179; taking Carnegie course, 310; taking medical exams, 156; work for convalescent home, 119n

Bedichek, Paul Lee, 358, 359n, 365, 371, 377, 381, 408

Bedichek, Robert Caldwell, 408n, 410, 425

Bedichek, Roy, 90 *photo*, 91 *photo*, 92 *photo*, 202 *photo*, 203 *photo*, 204 *photo*, 205 *photo*, 323 *photo*, 330 *photo*, 432 *photo*, 433 *photo*, 434 *photo*, 435 *photo*, 436 *photo*, 437 *photo*; adopts Bo (dog), 12–13; ancestry, 142, 335; and unconventional lifestyle, 3–4, 45; as editor of *The Headlight*, 13, 19, 21; as publicity writer for University of Texas, 63; as reporter, 119–20; as secretary Deming Chamber of Commerce, 48n, 50–51, 54; as secretary Young Men's Business Club, 63–64, 70; as teacher at North Texas Normal School, 108–16; as teacher at Sul Ross State College, 361; as teacher in Alpine, 80–82; as teacher in San Angelo, 294; as writer for *El Paso Times and Herald*, 24; at conventions, 103, 127, 192; at Indian mounds, 366–67, 388; at University of Texas, 3, 57n; autobiography, 288; automobile accident, 120; birdwatching, 102, 108, 112, 113, 149, 150–51, 154–55, 157, 158, 160–61, 170–71, 178, 180, 183, 185–86, 191, 197, 209, 211, 212, 218, 221, 224, 253–54, 265, 280–81, 283n, 299, 304–305, 317, 319, 359, 369–70, 373, 378, 383, 393, 398, 407, 414–15, 418; camping, 191, 382–83, 405–407; childhood memories, 45, 288, 385–86; conservation practices, 372; courtship of Lillian, 3, 29–63; death of, 430; depression, 66; dreams, 65, 82; eating habits, 34, 98–99, 148, 212, 215, 238, 241, 249, 304,

birdwatching, 195, 261–62, 349; on birthdays, 408; on Bohemian lifestyle, 75–76; on businessmen, 59; on capitalism, 98; on cemeteries, 335–36; on childhood, 351; on children, 211; on Christian Science, 84, 85, 173, 400; on city life, 401–403, 404–405; on civilization, 309, 351; on commuting, 401–403; on competition, 353–57; on conventional living, 44, 47; on conventional medicine, 66; on cooperation, 353–57; on culture, 212; on dam-building, 158, 377, 397; on Democrats, 265; on dissipation, 116; on dog-catchers, 108; on drug-taking, 349; on exploitation, 266; on fate, 33; on father/son competition, 123; on fear, 106–107; on finance, 55–56, 57, 59, 67, 70, 104, 130, 136, 210; on fishing, 387; on flight, 312; on folklore, 255–56, 360; on football, 127, 129, 131, 139, 178, 194; on forgiveness, 85; on friendship, 34, 131, 143; on guns, 163, 413–14; on hazing, 125; on hobbies, 389–90; on history, 337; on homesickness, 168–69; on homesteading, 45, 54; on homosexuality, 269; on human condition, 76; on humanity, 219; on humor, 41, 248–49; on hunting, 214, 413–14; on imagination, 425; on Indians, 6–7; on insects, 301–302, 362; on international affairs, 98, 119, 187, 209; on intuition, 47–48; on justice and injustice, 97, 120; on Korean Conflict, 333, 350; on labor and big business, 236, 266–67, 279–80; on land use, 377, 384,

395; on learning, 131; on letter writing, 126, 153, 159, 221, 225, 261, 291, 352; on literary life, 126; on literature, 107, 109, 244, 248, 337; on loneliness, 241; on love, 52–53; on manners, 423; on marriage, 34–36, 38, 44–45, 47–48, 55–56, 58, 76–77, 81; on mediocrity at universities, 141; on memory, 192–93, 288; on mental health, 118; on movies and tv, 128; on nakedness, 172, 361–62; on native plants, 319; on nature, 29, 139, 262, 280, 377–78, 404–405; on nutrition, 66, 72, 73, 99, 131, 175, 179, 218; on overcoming adversity, 334; on overgrazing, 365; on overindulgence, 379–80; on overpopulation, 424; on overspecialization, 141, 185, 221; on parenting, 75, 335; on physical exercise, 79, 107n, 115–16, 125, 126, 139, 227, 256, 293, 350–51, 352, 400, 416, 428; on physicians, 118, 146, 173, 388–89; on politicians, 266–67, 367, 393, 410; on postwar international relations, 247, 252, 276, 278, 279, 338; on prejudice, 120, 266–67, 268; on private schooling, 267; on procrastination, 214; on prostitution, 44; on public speaking, 310, 338; on quarantine regulations, 275; on race, 120, 181–82, 266–67, 268; on racial memory, 386, 389–90; on relaxation, 148, 174, 389; on religion, 293; on remodeling, 195; on Republicans, 244, 265; on responsibility, 299; on retirement, 384–85; on revolutions, 97–98; on risk-taking, 184–85; on Romantic

Ideal, 32–36, 47–48; on science, 337; on scientists, 260; on segregation, 267; on self-confidence, 77, 310; on sentiment, 30–31, 32, 55, 59, 223, 255; on sense of smell, 114, 171, 172, 414; on separations, 168–69; on simplicity, 124; on sleep, 97, 157, 293, 317–18; on snakes, 191; on social activities, 87, 223, 260; on solitude, 402; on spirituality, 400; on states' rights, 275; on studying, 115; on teaching, 110, 111, 113, 119; on thinking, 42; on traveling, 130–31, 169; on usefulness, 378; on visiting, 375; on women, 37, 40, 47, 68, 116, 198, 237, 272–73; on World War I, 279; on World War II, 197, 209, 213, 227, 229, 231, 236, 250, 278; other marriage prospects, 46–47; plant identification, 165, 168, 209, 214, 216, 224, 300, 304–305; poetry of, 30, 39n, 41, 42, 45, 63, 227–28; praise of Lillian, 31, 37, 40, 41, 43, 56, 61, 62, 77; publication of *Adventures of a Texas Naturalist,* 256–57; raising and selling airedales, 353; reading habits, 306; rental property, 104; routine, 409; self-analysis, 30–31, 52, 66, 103; southern ancestry of, 126; trip to Camp Tyler (1952), 359; trip to Germany, 39n; trip to New Mexico (1908), 1–2; trip to New York (1954), 381; trip to New York (1957), 393, 396–400; trip to West Texas (1937), 170–71; trip to West Texas (1938), 183; trip to West Texas (1941), 219; work for Hogg Foundation, 63, 67; work for Interscholastic League, 80; work on Land Policy Committee, 384; work habits, 74–75, 234; writing methods, 29, 39n, 40, 81, 115, 123–24, 250, 371, 376, 424

Bedichek, Sarah Craven (Sally), 25, 64, 72, 75, 82–83, 91 *photo*, 92 *photo*, 93 *photo*, 97, 99, 105, 110, 112, 114, 118, 119, 121, 187, 201 *photo,* 202 *photo,* 203 *photo,* 204 *photo*, 231, 234, 235, 238, 239, 240, 242, 262, 263, 270, 297, 329 *photo*, 333, 346, 352–53, 366, 402; as teacher at Texas State College for Women, 140n, 141–42; birdwatching, 149, 229, 398; birth of, 63; education, 140n; fellowship in London, 150n, 152–72, 174–79; fly stocks, 162, 168n, 232, 282; health, 73, 174, 216, 221, 349, 375–76, 381, 398–99; in Beirut, 263, 264, 278, 282, 289; in Honolulu, 342; letters to father, 281–83; marriage of, 142n; personality, 86, 104; physical description, 104; return from Beirut, 313n; teaching in Arlington, 153

Bedichek Scientific and Literary Institute, 3

Bedichek, Una, 68, 71, 83, 85, 90 *photo*, 286, 386, 400

Bell-Jim Hotel (Jasper, Texas), 139

Benedict, Harry Yandell, 194, 195n

Benefield, Barry, 77–78

Bent, Arthur Cleveland, 259

Bevan, Aneurin, 276, 277n, 279

Big Bend (Texas), 219, 220n

Big Thicket, 225, 226n

*457*

wild onions, 423
Wilhelm, Mrs. J. R., 296
Willard, Ned, 104, 105n
Willard, Una. *See* Una Bedichek.
Williams, Dan, 124, 125n, 185, 212
Williams family, 317
Williams, Miss, 320
Williams, Rhea, 379
Wilson, Sally Craven, 288, 289n
Winship, Dr., 186, 187n
*Winter's Tale*, 168n
*Wisteria Trees*, 144n
Witt, Edgar E., 36, 49, 52n, 55, 223
Witt, Gwynne (Gwynn), 50, 52n, 71
*Women's Share in Primitive Culture*,
    217
Woodward, Dudley K., 63
Woods, Grant, 242
Wordsworth, William,168, 357n
*World-Telegram*, 124, 404, 405n
Wren, Christopher, 134
Wright, Sewall, 150n

Xenophon, 337

Yarrington, Mrs., 65
Yoder, Byrl, 320, 321n
Young, Stark, 122n, 124, 126, 129
yucca, 14, 25

Zilker Park, 378, 386
Zschokke, Johann Heinrich Daniel,
    35